Technology, Work and Globalization

Series Editors

Leslie P. Willcocks
Department of Management
London School of Economics and Political Science
London, UK

Mary C. Lacity
Sam M. Walton College of Business
University of Arkansas
Fayetteville, AR, USA

The Technology, Work and Globalization series was developed to provide policy makers, workers, managers, academics and students with a deeper understanding of the complex interlinks and influences between technological developments, including information and communication technologies, work organizations and patterns of globalization. The mission of the series is to disseminate rich knowledge based on deep research about relevant issues surrounding the globalization of work that is spawned by technology.

More information about this series at
http://www.palgrave.com/gp/series/14456

Nathalie Mitev • Jeremy Aroles
Kathleen A. Stephenson • Julien Malaurent
Editors

New Ways of Working

Organizations and Organizing in the Digital Age

palgrave
macmillan

Editors
Nathalie Mitev
Muenster University
Muenster, Germany

Paris Dauphine University
Paris, France

Kathleen A. Stephenson
Vrije Universiteit Amsterdam
Amsterdam, The Netherlands

Jeremy Aroles
Durham University
Durham, UK

Julien Malaurent
ESSEC Business School
Cergy, France

ISSN 2730-6623 ISSN 2730-6631 (electronic)
Technology, Work and Globalization
ISBN 978-3-030-61686-1 ISBN 978-3-030-61687-8 (eBook)
https://doi.org/10.1007/978-3-030-61687-8

This Palgrave Macmillan imprint is published by the registered company Springer Nature Switzerland AG.
The registered company address is: Gewerbestrasse 11, 6330 Cham, Switzerland

Foreword

A foreword is meant to be a section of introductory remarks that is written by someone who is not an author of the text itself. It is placed at the very front of the book by way of context, often analyzing the major streams of thought in which the book's project might be emplaced. This Foreword will concentrate upon providing some sense of location in space, and in time, for the many diverse ideas to follow. The contextualization we offer for New Ways of Working (NWW) is partly geographical and partly historical.

Much of what passes today for 'new' working practices has its origins in history, some of it many centuries old. It is simply that analysts have forgotten to look backward as well as forward. Conventional approaches that are 'run of the mill' (the unexamined output from early factories that was standardized and unexceptional in any way) to the central topic of organizations and organizing in the Digital Age assume that humanity is now, everywhere, facing something so new as to mark it off from all that has gone before. It is a form of assumed rupturism where the break with the past is clear, dramatic, and slightly painful. It is as if the mill went overnight from being water powered to steam powered with major consequences that were there for all to see and the event did not require questioning or examination. Of course, the 'Digital Age' (marked by initial capitals) does represent something new and transformative wherein information gathering becomes very extensive and work is increasingly expressed as high-speed procedures permitted by the use of microprocessor-based technology. Yet, the same attributes of work speed-up and a wider reach for gathering relevant corporate information have been associated much earlier with those previous revolutionary technologies of the telegraph and the telephone. These tele-technologies were claimed to have annihilated space in the same ways as the digital age was meant to usher in an era where the tyranny of distance was about to be overcome. One has to be circumspect about the assumption of, indeed desire for, organizational novelty. Indeed, it behooves us to turn to some lessons of history about how we should address strident claims for total newness. We need to constantly question just how 'new' some developments were, are, and will be.

Geographically, the role of the state is contingent. Encouragement of NWW might occur primarily via the state apparatus and a national emphasis, perhaps, upon the need for the state to modernize its surveillance technologies, its capacity to supply and analyze data, and its provision of a command structure for its internal security forces. Here 'organizing' is within a 'regime of regulation' which drives particular New Ways of Working in which centralized control figures large. In the neoliberal states of the world, NWW may well be encouraged more by market forces and the desire of organizations to be competitive in the face of new market entrants. This would represent a position wherein NWW would be linked much more closely to a 'regime of accumulation'. And if nation states cling to particular regimes of regulation and accumulation, it should not surprise us if there are differences: different 'business recipes', different industrial strategies, and different models of how the state and the economy interact. Given this disparate context, we might well expect different types of new working practices within different forms of teleworking, in open offices, in the gig economy, and within various types of crowdsourcing and co-working. For many organizations, the architecture of NWW is by no means fixed.

As this foreword loses its position at the beginning of the book, and other chapters move into the readers' eyeline, we are made all too aware of the spatio-temporal nature of all text. Writing, it has been said, is 'a machine for the suppression of time'. It passes knowledge down through the generations like the Dead Sea scrolls, allowing the reader to witness extraordinary interpretations of past events and emotions as if they happened today. But what this aphorism fails to grasp is that all writing is of and in its time. It cannot be anything else but contingent. Specific history and specific geography grasp us tightly. But within their grip, it is possible for committed writers to explore a little, to find the wriggle room necessary to learn about the past, the present, and the future and to ably communicate their research with us, the readers of this present volume.

Manchester, UK Gibson Burrell
Lancaster, UK Karen Dale

Contents

Notes on Contributors

Michel Ajzen PhD in Management, is Teaching and Research Assistant in Human Resource Management and Industrial Relations at the School of Work and Employment Sciences at the Université Catholique de Louvain, Belgium. He is invited lecturer at the Université Catholique de l'Ouest, France. His research focuses on New Ways of Working and managing, from a critical and interdisciplinary perspective. More precisely, he questions how the so-called new world of work as a set of practices (e.g. telework, flexwork, distributed workplaces, flexdesk, and flexitime) and discourses (e.g. freedom, empowerment, and entrepreneurship) produce and/or reflect a new social order within which power issues take place to define the 'newness'. He is also the Managing Editor of the *International Journal of Work Innovation*.

Marie Antoine holds a PhD in Business Management and Economics from the Université Catholique de Louvain, Belgium. Her research concentrates on New Ways of Working, organizational transformation, and human resource management. For her thesis, she studied the transition of an organization toward a 'new world/ways of work' environment and questioned how this led to a reconstruction of the organization's identity. Her research has largely been influenced by the thought of critical management studies. She is a guest professor at the Louvain School of Management, Faculty of Economic, Social and Political Sciences and

Communication at the Université Catholique de Louvain where she teaches organizational behavior, cross-cultural competences and management, contemporary issues in human resources management (HRM), and labor sciences. She supervises Masters dissertations on HRM and organization studies. She is also a senior researcher at Idea Consult in Brussels, Belgium, where she evaluates Belgian public socioeconomic and labor market policies.

Lise Arena is a tenured associate professor at the Centre National de Recherche Scientifique (CNRS; National Centre for Scientific Research), Groupe de Recherche en Droit, Economie, Gestion (GREDEG; Research Group in Law, Economics and Management) at the Université Côte d'Azur in France, where she also obtained her PhD in Management. She also holds a DPhil in Modern History from the University of Oxford, UK. Her major research interests are the history of management and the role of digital artifacts and practices in organizations. Her recent work in history of management has been published in *Entreprises et Histoires* and *History of Economic Ideas*.

Jeremy Aroles is Assistant Professor in Organization Studies at Durham University, UK. Prior to joining Durham, he worked as a lecturer in management and organization studies at The University of Manchester where he obtained his PhD in Organization Studies. His research gravitates around three different topics: the emergence of New Ways of Working (the future of work, digital nomadism, the disruptive potential of new working practices, the evolving relationship between 'formal' organizations and individuals in an increasingly digitized society, etc.), the management of culture, and the relation between fiction and organizational worlds. Conceptually, his work draws from the material semiotics of actor-network theory, the work of Gilles Deleuze, Félix Guattari and various phenomenologists. His latest research has explored the rise of digital nomadism and the organization of makerspaces.

Angela Bargenda is Professor of Marketing, Communication and Management at Ecole Supérieure du Commerce Extérieur (ESCE) (Higher Education College on Trade), International Business School in Paris, France. Her research areas include organizational aesthetics, architecture and art, organizational identity, cultural heritage, and semiotics. She regularly contributes on these topics to international conferences and publications such as *Journal of Brand Management*, *Journal of Marketing Communication*, *Studies in Communication Sciences*, *Qualitative Market Research*, and *International Journal of Retail & Distribution Management.*

Andrea Simone Barth is a research associate at the chair for Sustainable Organization and Work Design at Alanus University of Arts and Social Sciences, Germany, and a doctoral student at the Institute of Organization Studies at Vienna University of Economics and Business (WU Vienna), Austria. She holds an MSc in Management and a BSc in International Business from WU Vienna and the Graduate School of Management, St Petersburg State University, Russia. Her research interests center on issues of space, materiality, and aesthetics in new work environments.

Susanne Blazejewski is Professor of Sustainable Organization and Work Design at Alanus University of Arts and Social Sciences, Germany. She was previously Assistant Professor of Management and Organization at the European University Viadrina in Frankfurt/Oder, Germany. Blazejewski received her academic education at the University of Saarbrücken, Germany; University College Dublin, Ireland; and The University of Michigan, USA. She holds a double Master's degree in Business Administration and Comparative Literature from Saarbrücken University, Germany, and a PhD in Cultural Studies from the European University Viadrina, Frankfurt/Oder. Her research focuses on issues of identities, politics, and conflict in (multinational) organizations as well as on organizational design for sustainable development and innovation. Teaching organizational studies in the context of a School of Arts, she also works on and with aesthetics in organizational change processes and leadership development. Her work has been published in the *Journal of World Business*, *Journal of Cleaner Production*, and *Competition and Change*, among others. She serves on the editorial board of *Critical Perspectives on International Business* and the *Journal of Eastern European Management Studies*.

Claudine Bonneau is Associate Professor in the Department of Management and Technology at the Université du Québec à Montréal

(UQAM) School of Management in Canada. She is a member of Laboratoire sur la Communication et le Numérique (LabCMO) (Laboratory for Communication and the Digital) and teaches in graduate and undergraduate programs in information technology. She holds a PhD in Communication from UQAM. Her work focuses on new work practices, social media uses, and online collaboration. She is also interested in methodological issues related to qualitative research and online ethnography. Besides her contributions to edited books (such as *Experiencing the New World of Work*, 2020, and the *Handbook of Social Media Research Methods*, 2017), her work has been published in journals such as *Educational Technology Research and Development*; *Communication, Research and Practice*; and the *International Journal of Project Management.*

Gibson Burrell is Professor of Organization Theory at the Universities of Manchester and Leicester, UK, each on a fractional basis. Over the last 45 years he has been employed by the Universities of Lancaster, Warwick, and Leicester wherein he undertook a number of departmental and university roles. He was a founding editor of the journal *Organization* and is a section editor for the *Journal of Business Ethics*. He became a fellow of the Academy of Social Sciences in 2015 and obtained a research fellowship from the Leverhulme Trust 2014–2016. In 2014 he was awarded a 'trailblazer' prize from the American Academy of Management Organization Theory division for his contribution to the field. He has been responsible for a number of books and edited books as well as several articles in journals that are still cited.

Karen Dale is Professor of Organization Theory in the Department of Organization, Work and Technology at Lancaster University, UK, having previously worked at the Universities of Leicester, Essex, and Warwick and in the National Health Service and local government. She has published in the areas of gender and equality; on embodiment and organization; and on spatiality, materiality, and organization, including the books *Anatomising Embodiment and Organisation Theory* (2001) and *The Spaces of Organisation and the Organisation of Space* (2007) (with G. Burrell). Most recently she has edited books on Henri Lefebvre, with S. Kingma and V. Wasserman, and on New Ways of Working, with J. Aroles and F-X. De Vaujany. She has also produced expert reports for the European

Union Agency for Occupational Safety and Health on the use of enhancement drugs in the contemporary workplace.

Aurore Dandoy completed her PhD in Management Science at the PSL-Université Paris Dauphine under the direction of Professor de Vaujany. Her thesis was entitled 'Legitimization Practices and the Emergence of a Field: Ten Years of Parisian Coworking'. For four years, she studied coworking spaces and practices as a community manager in two coworking spaces where she observed and analyzed community management practices. She also worked as community manager in an international think tank (Research Group on Collaborative Spaces) for which she coordinated several international and local workshops. Prior to her PhD, she worked for eight years in human resources management as a project manager for a blended learning company and for a pharmaceutical company, as a consultant for IT projects in different companies, and as a regional manager in the automobile sector.

Hamid Ekbia is Professor of Informatics, International Studies, and Cognitive Science at Indiana University Bloomington in the US, where he also directs the Center for Research on Mediated Interaction. He is interested in the political economy of computing, in the future of work, and in how technologies mediate socioeconomic, cultural, and geopolitical relations of modern societies. His most recent coauthored book, *Heteromation and Other Stories of Computing and Capitalism* (2017), examines computer-mediated modes of value extraction in capitalist economies, and his earlier book *Artificial Dreams: The Quest for Non-biological Intelligence* (2008) is a critical-technical analysis of artificial intelligence. He is a coeditor of a volume titled *Big Data Is Not a Monolith* (2016) and the coauthor of a forthcoming book *Reconsidering Access: Individual Travails and Asymmetric Gains* (MIT Press). His research has been supported by the National Science Foundation, the National Institute of Health, the Clinical and Translational Sciences Institute, and the Fulbright Specialist Program in the US, as well as the Otto Mønsteds Fond in Copenhagen, Denmark, the Internationales Forschungszentrum Kulturwissenschaften in Vienna, Austria, and the 21st Century Japan Politics and Society Initiative.

Amany Elbanna is a reader (associate professor) at Royal Holloway, University of London, UK. Her research examines digital platforms, digital entrepreneurship, and crowdsourcing. She is an associate editor of *Information Systems Journal* and a member of the editorial board of *Information & Management*, *Journal of the Association of Information Systems*, *Information Technology & People*, *Scandinavian Journal of Information Systems*, and *Journal of Enterprise Information Management*. Her work is published in leading academic journals including *MIS Quarterly*, *European Journal of Information Systems*, *Journal of Strategic Information Systems*, *Journal of Information Technology*, *IEEE Software*, *Data Base*, and *Information Technology & People*. She is a regular speaker in industry and her research has been featured in *The Financial Times*, *Computer Weekly*, and *The Manufacturing Magazine*. She is the Director-elect of Professional Development for the UK Chapter of the Association of Change Management Professionals and the Vice Chair of International Federation for Information Processing (IFIP) WG8.6 on Diffusion and Adoption of Technology.

Nada Endrissat is Research Professor at the Business Department, Bern University of Applied Sciences in Switzerland. She holds a Master's degree in Organizational Psychology and a PhD in Management. Her research interest lies at the crossroads of digital technology and embodied encounters including the exploration of affective spaces such as hackathons, coworking spaces, and social media as well as (de-)humanizing practices in human-machine interactions and manual labor. She is also interested in new work practices such as branding and social media use and their consequences for workers' subjectivities. Her work has been published in journals such as *Human Relations*, *Organization Studies*, *Journal of Business Research*, *Leadership*, and *M@n@gement* as well as in edited collections including *The Organization of Craft Work: Identities, Meanings and Materiality* (2019); *Designing with Smell: Practices, Techniques and Challenges* (2018); *Leadership-as-Practice: A New Movement* (2016); and *How Matter Matters: Objects, Artifacts and Materiality in Organization Studies* (2013).

Philippe Eynaud is Full Professor at Sorbonne Business School and a researcher in Groupe de Recherche en Gestion des Organisations (GREGOR) (Research Group on Management of Organizations) at the

University of Paris 1 Pantheon-Sorbonne, France. He has experience in nonprofit management and information systems and received the award for the best thesis in information systems in France in 2008. His research focuses on social innovation, democratic governance, platform cooperativism, the solidarity economy, commons, and new forms of solidarity. He was a steering committee member of a European consortium on innovative platform for social services. He is a member of the French government-funded Laboratory of Excellence (LABEX), Sciences, Innovations et Techniques en Société (SITES) (Sciences, Innovations and Technology in Society), and a member of the Faculty Team of the Doctoral Education Network (EDEN) of the European Institute for Advanced Studies in Management (IASM). In 2011, he was a guest editor for a special issue on the governance of civil society organizations for the *Voluntas* journal, has contributed to several edited books, and has published two books, *Civil Society, the Third Sector, and Social Enterprise: Governance and Democracy* in 2016 and *Theory of Social Enterprise and Pluralism: Social Movements, Solidarity Economy, and Global South* in 2019.

Sophie Fauconneau-Dufresne is a PhD candidate and a research fellow at the Laboratoire d'Etudes sur les Nouvelles formes de Travail, l'Innovation et le Changement (LENTIC) (laboratory on New Ways of Working, Innovation and Change), a research center at the University of Liège, Belgium. Her fields of study include the transformation and modernization of workspaces, flexible work practices, and organizational change. Her work investigates the challenges of implementing workplace innovations such as New Ways of Working strategies, with an emphasis on the social construction of cultural norms and workers' identities. She holds an MSc in Business Management and an MSc in Risk Management and Well-Being in the Workplace from the Catholic University of Louvain.

Kutay Güneştepe lectures on entrepreneurship at Istanbul Medipol University. He holds a PhD in Management Engineering from Istanbul Technical University, a BS degree in Biomedical Engineering from Baskent University, and an MSc in Medical Informatics from Middle East Technical University in Turkey. His research interests span across disciplinary boundaries, and he focuses on how materiality is understood, conceptualized, or overlooked in social sciences, leaving it mostly to natural sciences and engineering. He is interested in researching materiality, technology, work, and organizations in healthcare and higher education. His research has previously appeared in *Research in the Sociology of Organizations*.

Anthony Hussenot is Professor in Organization Studies at the Université Côte d'Azur in France. He has researched the current evolutions of work, notably by studying how and why New Ways of Working emerge and how these new practices challenge the way we collaborate and organize. He focuses on theorizing the organizational dynamics emerging from these New Ways of Working. With others, he has developed the events-based approach as a way to understand organizational dynamics in a constantly evolving society. He has conducted studies in several sectors such as the maker movement, private banking, and education. He has published in academic journals such as *Organization Studies*, *International Journal of Organizational Analysis*, and *M@n@gement*. He has recently published a book about the maker movement in which he describes the events-based approach, *L'organisation à l'épreuve des makers. Propositions pour une approche par les événements* (2019), with Presses de l'Université Laval, Canada.

Ayomikun Idowu is Lecturer in Information Systems at the University of Sussex Business School in the UK. A doctoral researcher at Royal Holloway University of London, he graduated with an MSc in Business Information Systems from Middlesex University, London, and a Bachelor's degree with Honors in Business Studies. He has held several industry positions consulting for technology projects and managing digital transformation in organizations. His research interest centers around institutions, technology diffusion, adoption and use in emerging economies, understanding the practices emerging in the adoption of technology, and New Ways of Working in the global South. His research focuses on unraveling practices, work organization, identity, and institutional work engaged in by crowdworkers in the global South to ensure employment sustainability.

Grégory Jemine holds a PhD in Sociology and is working as a postdoctoral researcher on an Excellence of Science (EOS) project on sustainable careers and project-based workers in the Management School, University of Liège, Belgium. As part of his thesis, he conducted several case studies of New Ways of Working (NWW) projects and their underlying decision-making processes. He engaged in questioning the ways in which NWW projects emerge and take shape in organizations, and suggested to conceptualize NWW as projects of organizational change involving the making of strategic decisions and a translation process of this decision, shaped by the work of rational and political actors. His research on the power games and the legitimation processes behind NWW projects has recently been published in the *Journal of Change Management* and *Qualitative Research in Organizations and Management*. His research interests include NWW change processes and organizational change, project work, and career management.

Aurélie Leclercq-Vandelannoitte is a researcher at the Centre National de la Recherche Scientifique (CNRS), Institut d'Economie Scientifique Et de Gestion (IESEG) (Institute of Scientific Economy and Management) School of Management, at Lille Economie and Management University in France, and Professor of Management Sciences. She holds a PhD in Management from Paris Dauphine University, which received three national awards. She is interested in new work practices and new forms of organizing (remote work, telework, nomadism, coworking) enabled by the use of information technology. She relies particularly on the ideas developed by the French philosopher Michel Foucault to grasp the complex interplay between digital technology, people, and organizations. She frequently presents her work in major conferences on topics such as the digital transformation of work, technology-based organizational control, ethical aspects of the use of technologies at work, and critical perspectives on new forms of organizing. Her research has been published in leading journals such as *Organization Studies*, *Journal of Business Ethics*, *Journal of Management Inquiry*, *Journal of Business Strategy*, *Journal of Organizational Change Management*, *European Journal of Information Systems*, *Information Systems Journal*, *Information Technology & People*, *Database*, and *Systèmes d'Information et Management*. She serves as a member of the management committee of CNRS LEM (Lille, Economie & Management) University of Lille, and as the Head of the Individus, Organisations et Sociétés (IOS; Individuals, Organizations and Societies) research group.

Julien Malaurent has been Associate Professor of Information Systems at École Supérieure des Sciences Economiques et Commerciales (ESSEC) Business School Paris in France since 2013. His research is regularly published in top journals such as *Journal of Management of Information Systems*, *European Journal of Information Systems*, and *Journal of Information Technology*. He is also senior editor for the *Information Systems Journal*. His latest research analyzes digital transformation processes at the societal level from an ontological phenomenological viewpoint. He teaches initial training programs as well as executive education programs on the topic of digital transformation. He is also Academic Director of the Executive Master in Digital Transformation, which is the first degree of the new ESSEC augmented digital campus.

Attila Marton is an associate professor at the Department of Digitalization, Copenhagen Business School in Denmark. Marton holds a PhD and MSc in Information Systems research from The London School of Economics and Political Science (LSE), and a Magister in Sociology from the University of Vienna, Austria. He is a fellow of the Higher Education Academy in the UK and has been awarded with teaching awards from the LSE and the Danish Society for Education and Business as well as with the Early Career Award by the Association of Information Systems. His research is about propelling ecosystemic thinking to make digitalization serve humanity, exploring the co-evolutionary dynamics between platforms and their respective ecosystems in various domains, including the digital ecology of labor and artificial intelligence, social memory and forgetting, and the re-decentralization of the Internet. His research has been published in leading academic journals, such as *The Information Society* and *MIS Quarterly*.

Leo McCann is Professor of Management at the University of York, UK. His research and teaching focuses on globalization, organization, and work, with a particular emphasis on white-collar and uniformed professions. He is the author of *A Very Short, Fairly Interesting, and Reasonably*

Cheap Book About Globalisation (2018) and is writing a new book on the work of paramedics and ambulance services.

Nathalie Mitev was Associate Professor in the Department of Management, Information Systems and Innovation Group, The London School of Economics, and has held positions in several UK universities for 30 years. Her research focuses on the organizational aspects of information systems and how technology is used and implemented, drawing on science and technology studies. She has an international reputation for in-depth qualitative research, setting a critical agenda, and helping to bring this approach within mainstream information systems management research. She has applied actor-network theory and the sociology of translation to analyzing information systems failures. She has published critical work in management studies journals such *Personnel Review*, *Management Learning*, *Journal of Management Studies*, and *Culture and Organization*. She has also published in *European Journal of Information Systems*, *Journal of Information Technology*, *Information Technology & People*, *The Information Society*, *Information Technology for Development*, and *New Work, Technology and Employment*. She was track chair for the International Conference on Information Systems and co-chair for the IFIP Working Group 8.2 and is Associate Editor for the journal *Information Technology & People*. She is co-editor of *Materiality and Space: Organizations, Artefacts and Practices* (2013); *Materiality and Time: Historical Perspectives on Organizations, Artefacts and Practices* (2014); *Materiality, Rules and Regulation in Management and Organization Studies* (2015); and *Materiality and Managerial Techniques* (2018), all published by Palgrave Macmillan. She is a research associate at Paris Dauphine University, France, and Muenster University, Germany, and runs doctoral workshops on qualitative research methods, epistemology, and writing the thesis. She is also an academic coordinator for the digital Executive Doctorate in Business Administration at the Business Science Institute, Luxembourg.

Anouk Mukherjee initially trained as an electrical engineer and developed a career in information technology, eventually taking on software development as a project manager. After about a decade in industry, he decided to pursue a new career, this time in academia. Working on the topic of organizational space and its relationship to emerging technologies, notably mobile, he is keen to understand our daily experiences of space and the implications of technology on our work practices. Emergent work practices and new workspaces such as fablabs, coworking spaces, and other third spaces are very interesting objects of study for him since they put into sharp focus those innovative work practices benefitting from new technologies. These emergent work practices are disrupting organizations around the world, hence what is called digital disruption. He holds a PhD from Université Paris-Dauphine and is an assistant professor at the Institut d'Administration des Entreprises Gustave Eiffel, Université Paris-Est Créteil.

Natalie Paleothodoros is Lecturer in the Work, Management and Organisation Group at The York Management School, University of York. She holds a PhD in Organization, Work, and Technology from Lancaster University, UK. Her thesis, 'Intermediating Relationships: Technology, Spacing and Mobile Consulting', considers the role of technology and spacing in the organization of consulting and consultants at a distance. Her research interests are in taking ethnographic approaches to understand the constitutive role of materiality and workspace in the organization of work and mobile work in the digital era. Her research focuses on a range of socio-spatiotemporal arrangements, materiality, and consequences for New Ways of Working, organizing, and being.

François Pichault holds a PhD in Sociology and is Full Professor at Hautes Etudes Commerciales (HEC) at the University of Liège, Belgium. He is Scientific Director of Entreprise & Personnel, a French company focused on the future of human resource management. At the University of Liège he chairs the LENTIC (Laboratoire d'Etudes sur les Nouvelles formes de Travail, l'Innovation et le Changement) action-research center focused on the human and organizational aspects of change and innovation processes. He is involved in multiple international cooperation activities in Africa, Eastern Europe, and Asia. He has produced numerous publications in organization theory and human resource management (a dozen books, several dozen chapters, and several dozen papers published in peer-reviewed journals). He is studying the evolutions and roles of the HR function, the alignment between HRM policies and business strategies, new organizational forms and their impacts on social dialogue, new forms of job transitions on the labor market, the digital transformation of organizations, and change processes in public and private organizations.

Giseline Rondeaux holds a Master's degree in Sociology and in Social Anthropology and a PhD in Management. She is a senior researcher at Laboratoire d'Etudes sur les Nouvelles formes de Travail, l'Innovation et le Changement at the University of Liège, an action-research center focused on the human and organizational aspects of change and innovation processes. She is researching New Ways of Working and the impacts of artificial intelligence on jobs and competencies in several sectors (industry and education), as well as the digital transformation of organizational and change processes in public and private organizations. She is also the academic coordinator of an executive education program on NWW.

Viviane Sergi is Associate Professor in Management in the Department of Management and Technology at Université du Québec à Montréal (UQAM) School of Management in Montréal, Canada. Her research interests include process thinking, performativity, the transformation of work, leadership, and materiality. Her recent studies have explored how communication is, in various settings, constitutive of organizational phenomena, such as new work practices, strategy, and leadership. She also has a keen interest for methodological issues related to qualitative research and for the practice of academic writing. Her work has been published in journals such as *Academy of Management Annals*, *Human Relations*, *Scandinavian Journal of Management*, *Long Range Planning*, *M@n@gement*, and *Qualitative Research in Organizations and Management*.

Kathleen A. Stephenson is Assistant Professor of Organization Studies at Vrije Universiteit Amsterdam in the Netherlands and was Lecturer in Work, Organization, and Management at the University of Liverpool Management School in the UK. She holds a PhD from Vrije Universiteit Amsterdam, Netherlands, and her thesis was entitled 'Paperless Professors: Changing Academic Work and Workspaces'. Prior to her PhD research, she completed her Master's degree in Cultural Analysis from the University of Amsterdam and Bachelor's degree in English Literature and Cultural Studies from Drake University in the US. Her research interests include workspaces and organizing, ethnography, process research, identity, and organizational change.

Zehra Topal is a PhD candidate in Management at Istanbul Technical University. She has a BA degree from Adnan Menderes University and an MBA degree from Uludag University in Turkey. Her dissertation work is about how workplaces transform and novel organizational practices emerge as organizations explore New Ways of Working and organizing in the digital age. Her research interests include coworking spaces, digital workplace, new organizational forms, and humor in organizations.

Deniz Tunçalp is Associate Professor of Management at Istanbul Technical University. He holds a PhD in Management from Sabanci University, an MSc and a BSc degree in Industrial Engineering from Middle East Technical University (METU), an MSc degree in Information Systems from METU, and an MA degree in Law from Istanbul Bilgi University in Turkey. His research interests include how organizations emerge under, adapt to, and appropriate technological changes. He has held visiting research and teaching positions at Carnegie Mellon University and Politecnico di Milano. His research has appeared in *Organizational Research Methods*, *Management Decision*, *Research in the Sociology of Organizations*, *Operations Research*, *Journal of Global Information Technology Management*, *Computers in Human Behavior*, and *Journal of Organizational Ethnography*.

List of Figures

List of Tables

1

Introduction: New Ways of Working, Organizations and Organizing in the Digital Age

Nathalie Mitev, Jeremy Aroles, Kathleen A. Stephenson, and Julien Malaurent

Focus of This Edited Volume

This edited book revolves around the ways in which organizations and work itself have changed in the light of the digital age, with a particular focus on the role of materiality, body and technologies in these new organizational landscapes. This book therefore combines recent scholarly

N. Mitev (✉)
Muenster University, Muenster, Germany

Paris Dauphine University, Paris, France

J. Aroles
Durham University, Durham, UK
e-mail: Jeremy.aroles@durham.ac.uk

K. A. Stephenson
Vrije Universiteit Amsterdam, Amsterdam, The Netherlands
e-mail: k.a.stephenson@vu.nl

N. Mitev et al. (eds.), *New Ways of Working*, Technology, Work and Globalization,
https://doi.org/10.1007/978-3-030-61687-8_1

interest in organizational spaces and materiality with a focus on management and work practices.

This focus is aligned with the previous volumes on Materiality and Space, Materiality and Time, Materiality, Rules and Regulation, Materiality in Institutions, and Materiality and Managerial Techniques already published by Palgrave Macmillan respectively in 2013, 2014, 2015, 2018 and 2019, based on the Organizations, Artefacts and Practices (OAP) series of workshops that ran at Paris-Dauphine University, the London School of Economics, LUISS (Libera Università Internazionale degli Studi Sociali) in Rome, Nova School of Business and Economics in Lisbon and the University of Technology Sydney.

OAP was set up with the goal of facilitating discussions among scholars from a wide range of disciplines (e.g. management, anthropology, sociology, history, geography, philosophy, psychology, etc.) who share an interest in materiality in the context of organization and organizing. OAP relates to debates in the fields of Science and Technology Studies, (socio) materiality, organizational space, work sociology and organization studies, among others. Some of the recurrent OAP themes are: process, performativity, time, space, legitimacy, symbolism, iconography, discourse and materiality; artefacts as the constituents, results or outputs of organizations and organizing; materialization and performativity in organizations; the entanglements or imbrication between the material and social dimensions of organizational practices; new vocabularies to act or overcome the social-material dichotomy; power, discourses and materiality; the exploration of organizational space, artefacts and spatial practices; the affordance of materiality and space in organizations; managerial techniques and the evolution of work. It draws on various theoretical perspectives, such as phenomenology, pragmatism, institutionalism, critical theory, post-Marxism, critical realism, actor-network theory, among others.

This sixth volume is based on the 8th OAP workshop on *New Ways of Working: Rematerializing Organizations in the Digital Age* that took place at the Vrije Universiteit Amsterdam in June 2018. It was organized jointly

J. Malaurent
ESSEC Business School, Cergy, France
e-mail: malaurent@essec.edu

by VU Amsterdam, The Hague University of Applied Sciences, Paris-Dauphine University, LUISS and King's College London.

This book focuses on New Ways of Working (NWW) and sets up to explore the manifestations of these new practices with a particular emphasis on the place occupied by technology, materiality, space and bodies within contemporary working configurations. NWW can be regarded as part and parcel of the wider trend of workspace differentiation and flexibilization. This transformation encompasses the flexible use of home workspaces in terms of 'teleworking', the flexibilization of office spaces under the form of 'hot desking', 'coworking' or 'nomadic working', as well as 'mobile working' (i.e. 'third space') between all of these workspaces. Ever since the early 1990s, Information and Communication Technologies (ICTs) have played a pivotal role in the diversification and evolution of the workplace, thus fueling a fast-paced and changing world of work. The increased embeddedness of digital technologies within the core of our social, organizational and structural make-up, along with the heightened preponderance of digitalization, has raised a number of important and timely questions relating to materiality, embodiment, temporality and spatiality in organizational landscapes.

Topics covered at the Amsterdam workshop included flexible working, the evolution of workspaces, digital working, work practices and buildings, entrepreneurship and materiality in the digital age, the role of space and technology in the constitution of organizations, meaning and sensemaking in innovative workspaces, theories and methodologies of workplace studies, human-machine interaction and the working body, infrastructures of digital organizational technologies, the significance of time in relation to the change and management of workspaces, anthropology and ethnography of the workplace, the institutionalization and legitimation of New Ways of Working, Do It Yourself (DIY), hackers, makers, fab labs and the emergence of open knowledge and open innovation, boundary setting in new organizational forms, interfaces in combined virtual/material modes of working, creativity and commitment in digitalized modes of working, the materialization of labor relations in flexible work arrangements, leadership and organizational control in new work environments, identity in virtual and material workplaces, collaborative virtual spaces, the design and aesthetics of new work environments, sociomateriality and ontologies of New Ways of Working, digital modes of surveillance in the workplace, informal workspaces and social relations in organizations. The following chapters were selected from the 82 papers presented, and keynote speakers provide a preface and a postface to this volume.

Our intended readership consists of academics, researchers and graduate students in Management and Organization Studies. It has the potential of constituting a valuable resource for researchers and graduate students in organization studies and management, and scholars across disciplines who are interested to know more about the interrelations between New Ways of Working and material artefacts in organizations from a sociomaterial perspective. This book may also be of interest to researchers and postgraduate students in Sociology, Science and Technology Studies, Media and Communication Studies, Information Systems, Anthropology, Labor Studies, Architecture and Design and Cultural Studies.

New Ways of Working

The flows of globalization, together with the ever-increasing digitalization of our society, have fundamentally changed the nature of work by challenging 'formal' bureaucratic logics of organizing (Courpasson & Reed, 2004; Pulignano & Stewart, 2008) and positioning flexibility, adaptability and dynamicity as the core values of new working configurations (Kallinikos, 2003; Marsden, 2004; Pulakos, Dorsey, & White, 2006). This has been paralleled by the emergence of the post-bureaucratic rhetoric (Heckscher, 1994) through which various forms of organizations have flourished: the networked organization (Scott Morton, 1991; Sproull, Kiesler, & Kiesler, 1992), the virtual corporation (Davidow & Malone, 1992; Jackson & van der Wielen, 1998), the project-based organization (Hodgson, 2004), the modular organization (Garud, Kumaraswamy, & Langlois, 2002) to name but a few. Rather unsurprisingly, ICTs have played a pivotal role in the diversification and evolution of the workplace (Brocklehurst, 2001; Tietze & Musson, 2005; Wilson, O'Leary, Metiu, & Jett, 2008) by enabling an exponential acceleration of already-existing trends. Clearly, new technologies offer many opportunities when it comes to organizing and managing work; for instance, new forms of collaboration are facilitated by technologies (Faraj, Jarvenpaa, & Majchrzak, 2011); work is no longer bound to a particular place or time (Bosch-Sijtsema, Ruohomäki, & Vartiainen, 2010); there seems to be a greater sense of flexibility and autonomy (Baruch, 2000; Golden, 2009; Tremblay & Thomsin, 2012); new forms of entrepreneurship are facilitated through ICTs (Matlay & Westhead, 2005) and so on. Alongside these opportunities comes a series of concerns relating to issues of surveillance, control and power dynamics (Brivot & Gendron, 2011; Sewell, 1998, 2012; Zuboff, 2015), notably around the emergence of horizontal forms of control (Dale, 2005).

The ways in which the concept of work is evolving are riddled with paradoxes (Aroles, Mitev, & de Vaujany, 2019). On one side, it can be argued that we are effectively witnessing the 'dissolution of work' (as we know it), or perhaps the erosion of the specificities of the notion of work. In other words, work is becoming increasingly more integrated in other activities (Sundararajan, 2017) to the point that the boundary between private and work lives has become entirely spurious (Gregg, 2011; Tietze & Musson, 2002). Within that context, a wide range of places (such as trains, coffee shops, planes, etc.)—third places (Oldenburg, 1989) or third workspaces (Kingma, 2016)—have come to occupy a key position in the redefinition of working patterns and routines, thus arguably contributing to de-specialization of work. At odds with this stance is the view that work is not disappearing but reappearing under a completely different form (as if 'reinventing itself').[1]

Embracing the seemingly inexhaustible promises of the digital age, we engage in an ever-greater range of collaborative activities and in that context, work is seen to becoming increasingly more collaborative with regards to the rise of the so-called sharing economy (Bouncken & Reuschl, 2016; Hamari, Sjöklint, & Ukkonen, 2016; Sundararajan, 2017; Stephany, 2015; Widlok, 2016). This is noticeable through various trends, such as coworking (Spinuzzi, 2012), digital nomadism (Aroles, Granter, & de Vaujany, 2020), collaborative entrepreneurship, Do It

[1] See for instance mobile telework (Hislop & Axtell, 2009), 'hot-desking' or 'drop-in desks' (Brown & O'Hara, 2003; Felstead, Jewson, & Walters, 2005).

Yourself (DIY) movements (Wolf & McQuitty, 2011), prosumption[2] (Humphreys & Grayson, 2008; Ritzer & Jurgenson, 2010), crowdsourcing (Howe, 2008), new forms of freelancing and entrepreneurship (Taylor, 2015), but also through the emergence of a wide array of new spaces: makerspaces (Anderson, 2009), collaborative spaces (Gandini, 2015; Garrett, Spreitzer, & Bacevice, 2017), fablabs, hackerspaces and so on.

Therefore, while some formal structures of work are disappearing, work is becoming increasingly visible in the sense that it pervades all social spaces and is no longer confined to organizational spaces or dedicated spaces. The fragmentation of work, the multiplication and ramification of work practices, the emergence of new forms of collaboration, the rise of prosumption and so on fall under the umbrella of NWW. These various changes have considerable implications for organizations; the spatio-temporal reality of organizations has been shattered, as miscellaneous fragmented temporalities and spatialities have come to replace the once-dominant linearity of organizations and preponderance of bureaucratic logics. In that sense, the increased embeddedness of digital technologies within the core of our social, organizational and structural make-up, along with the heightened preponderance of digitalization, has raised a number of important and timely questions relating to the materiality, embodiment, temporality and spatiality of organizations and work practices.

Recent books have looked at the economic impact of changing work practices in the context of the sharing economy and the rise of online platforms (Munger, 2018; Scholz, 2017; Sundararajan, 2017). Others have approached the new world of work through the lenses of human resource management, focusing on the ways in which new work practices have altered 'traditional' terms of employment (Boudreau, Jesuthasan, & Creelman, 2015; Weil, 2014; Sweet & Meiksins, 2015; Ellison, 2004). Some have attended to specific aspects of the new world of work, including the development of makerspaces (e.g. Anderson, 2009); the

[2] It is however worth noting that prosumption (production by consumers) is not necessarily a new phenomenon (e.g. fast-food, automatic-teller machines, etc.), but rather that it has intensified and progressively encapsulated most sectors, services and activities.

consequences of automation (e.g. Ford, 2015); or the precarity encountered in the gig economy (e.g. Morgan & Nelligan, 2018). Advanced communication technologies, online platforms and automation are just a few technological advancements disrupting ways of working, organizing and consuming. Scholars are busy explaining the implications these technologies have on a range of topics such as organizational space (Alexander & Price, 2013; Dale, Kingma, & Wasserman, 2018; Flecker, 2016; De Vaujany & Mitev, 2013; Myerson & Bichard, 2016; Turner & Myerson, 1998; van Marrewijk & Yanow, 2010).

Our book complements these works and integrates their central themes by examining where and how contemporary work and organizing are enacted. Virtual, collaborative, open, flexible, coworking, maker and community spaces are becoming ubiquitous and are intimately entwined with ways of working, managing, organizing, collaborating and consuming.

Book Structure

By accessing these themes through work spaces, the studies that make up this book are woven into a comprehensive narrative of the new ways and worlds of work. It is divided into the following five parts.

- Part I: New Ways of Working and the Sharing Economy
- Part II: New Ways of Working and Collaborative Spaces
- Part III: New Ways of Working and Telework
- Part IV: New Ways of Working and Organizational Spaces
- Part V: Organizational Aspects of New Ways of Working

Part I: NWW and the Sharing Economy

In "Platforms and the New Division of Labor Between Humans and Machines" (Chap. 1), Hamid Ekbia and Attila Marton propose that historical perspectives deflect from a fundamental shift in the division of labor between humans and machines. Historically, machines were designed to augment and/or replace human labor by mechanizing and automating what humans are not capable of doing. In the current shift, humans are increasingly relegated to what machines cannot do—that is the creative, affective or organizing labor of human beings. Those aspects of human work that drive and enable the workings of current socio-technical systems are increasingly trivialized and made invisible, and consequently rendered uncompensated or undercompensated. They elaborate on theoretical avenues for explaining the sociotechnical mechanisms underlying this shift and the new ontology of work practices that comes with it. They contend that contemporary automation introduces novel mechanisms for converting humans into a standing reserve for machines.

In "Social Media as a New Workspace: How Working Out Loud (Re) Materializes Work" (Chap. 2) Claudine Bonneau, Nada Endrissat and Viviane Sergi argue that social media should be considered as a new workspace that needs to be inhabited and fed. Their study focuses on social media, defining them as distinct yet complementary workspaces. Based on a 'working out loud' approach, they provide an overview of the various visibilization practices of work on *Instagram*, and show that social media represent unfinished and 'behind-the-scene' aspects of work and new workspaces for showing work and performing new subjectivities that are being crafted through practices of posting. As such, investigating what is being done and performed on social media is key in understanding some of the current transformations of work.

In "Institutionalizing Crowdwork as a Mode of Employment: The case of Crowdworkers in Nigeria" (Chap. 3), Ayomikun Idowu and Amany Elbanna focus on crowdsourcing as a monetary profit-generating type of employment, particularly on micro-tasking as a method of income generation in Nigeria. Embracing micro-tasking on crowdsourcing platforms can be argued to provide opportunities as a source of income to the unemployed and low-income youth in Nigeria. They explore identities and social practices within crowdsourcing through a series of interviews with digital workers on online digital platforms to understand their experiences and crowdsourcing in the Nigerian context.

Part II: New Ways of Working and Collaborative Spaces

In "Materiality as Ingredients of Events: Comprehending Materiality as a Temporal Phenomenon in a Makerspace" (Chap. 4), Anthony Hussenot addresses the role of materiality in the formation of situated and social temporalities through an ethnographic study. He questions the definition and redefinition of temporalities that make activities possible by anchoring them into a history, present and anticipated future. Based on Whitehead's philosophy, he argues that materiality constitutes 'ingredients of events' that define temporality. The event is considered as a unit of analysis in which the social and the material occur as a unique phenomenon. His ethnography shows how materiality has participated in the definition and the redefinition of the past, present and future of a makerspace and its surrounding town. The main contribution is in the suggestion of a 'temporal relational ontology' in which the material and the social can be understood as occurring in the same event that defines shared temporalities, enabling makers to make their activity possible and anchoring it in a broader past, present and anticipated future.

"The Role of Digital Materiality in Organizing a Living Lab" (Chap. 5) by Philippe Eynaud and Julien Malaurent focuses on living labs which are clusters aiming to organize partnerships on a territory, support interaction among stakeholders and bring together academic and lay knowledge. Based on Leonardi's concept of 'digital materiality', which distinguishes between the physical and the digital material, the authors discuss the use of digital resources in the accomplishment of social practices and organizational routines in an organic agriculture living lab. They study how the digital artifacts are seen as collective and shared material for the group and how they are instantiated. Their research shows the importance of materiality in the organizing processes, how it takes both physical and digital forms and should be regarded as a hybrid object.

In "Do Coworking Spaces Promise a Revolution or Spark Revenge? A Foucauldian Spatio-Material Approach to the Re-Spatialization of Remote Work in Coworking Spaces" (Chap. 6), Aurelie Leclercq-Vandelannoitte investigates how managers of classic organizations deal with new workplaces. She develops a framework based on Foucault to conceptualize a spatial and material approach to the manager's role in these new work arrangements. It enables her to investigate coworking spaces along three dimensions: space as discursive construction, instrumental materialization and embodied experience. Through a qualitative case study with guided tours, observation and interviews, she identifies paradoxical tensions between autonomy and control and finds that these coworking spaces are materialized extensions of corporate settings at a distance, enabling work continuity, but in contradiction with the official discourse; they are based on the notions of collaboration and openness but are also associated with more conventional control. Paradoxically, where work can be everywhere, space and materiality are crucial to develop our understanding of organizational life and of the manager's role, whose identity, legitimacy and meaning are more than ever embedded in spatial and material issues.

In "More Than Perks and a Shared Office: How Coworking Spaces Participate in Entrepreneurs' Resource Acquisition" (Chap. 7), Kutay Güneştepe, Zehra Topal and Deniz Tunçalp investigate architects/designers/managers', entrepreneurs' and start-up employees' experiences and understandings of how place identity and coworking culture have emerged and intertwined with the physical space, artifacts and policy interventions over time. The study covers the unfolding of these dynamics from a process perspective with a longitudinal study of ITU Magnet, a coworking space located at a science park in a university campus, dedicated to selected start-ups at the post-seed stage trying to scale-up. They employ Bourdieu's forms of capital framework to understand the underlying mechanisms of resource acquisition enabled by coworking spaces.

Part III: NWW and Telework

"From De-Materialization to Re-Materialization. A Social Dynamic Approach to New Ways of Working" (Chap. 8), by Michel Ajzen, explores how teleworking is regulated through social dynamics, and how this social regulation process produces social norms. The author combines Reynaud's social regulation theory and the theory of conventions in order to question the potential for emancipation or alienation of teleworkers. Two in-depth case studies are presented, showing many re-regulations of work activities and with different rational conventions. He observed a process of de-humanization resulting in the 'invisibilization' and deskilling of work but, simultaneously, in strategies consisting in re-visibilizing people. Other results are a transformation of the meaning of the workspace; some shifts of responsibilities from top to middle management through local flexible work arrangements but also from middle managers to employees through the empowerment rhetoric; and some workers resisting the dominant order through the re-appropriation of spaces and times.

"Work/Non-Work? Laminated Boundary-Tensions and Affective Capabilities: A Case of Mobile Consulting" (Chap. 9), by Natalie Paleothodoros, concentrates on how boundaries are constructed and how they become meaningful in practice. Her aim is to understand the role, practice and meaning of the mobile phone in the organization of work/non-work boundaries from a sociomaterial perspective. Her research is based on ethnographic fieldwork in a firm of mobile consultants. She offers insights into the tensions of mobile organizing, how the material is implicated in boundary organizing and in (re)negotiating work and non-work boundaries.

Part IV: New Ways of Working and Organizational Spaces

In "Space for Tensions: A Lefebvrian Perspective on New Ways of Working" (Chap. 10) Andrea Simone Barth and Susanne Blazejewski propose a theoretical approach to study the tensions, paradoxes and boundaries associated with the introduction of new work concepts and offer a framework based on paradox theory to extend Lefebvre's theoretical concept of space. They argue that paradoxical relationships might emerge, be negotiated and be accepted through the act of producing, constructing or modifying space. They suggest that tensions in new work spaces arise and are addressed in the process of planning space; are negotiated through social practices of occupants that engage with the planned space; and are recognized and potentially accepted by occupants in the process of imagination. The process of imagining (lived space) from Lefebvre's concept may thus become a powerful instrument for handling inherent paradoxes for both designers and occupants of new work spaces.

In "Beyond Flexibility: Confronting Conceived and Lived Spaces of New Ways of Working" (Chap. 11), Grégory Jemine, Sophie Fauconneau-Dufresne, François Pichault and Giseline Rondeaux first characterize the NWW ideal discourse about space into four dimensions: fluidity, activity-based, deterritorialization and horizontalization. Their chapter questions how this discursive ideal type is translated into concrete devices and practices in organizations. They perform a comparative study of two contrasting cases, by employing Weick's concepts of sensemaking and sense giving to understand how the ideal type of space advocated by NWW promoters is embodied into concrete spatial devices and patterns. In both cases, the ideal type of space ultimately became an object of contestation. Four forms of contestation related to the four aforementioned dimensions are analyzed: sedentarization, activity-based constraints, colonization and stratification. What seems to matter, beyond sense giving and sensemaking activities, is also the users' political relationships with space as well as their individual and collective strategies of appropriation.

In "Transmateriality of Architectural Representation and Perception" (Chap. 12) Angela Bargenda critically examines architecture as an expressive system of organizational values and symbols, and as a social space that generates workplace identities. A longitudinal analysis of the architecture of bank buildings is presented, and their spatial, temporal and social dimensions related to cultural and societal phenomena. She conceptualizes architecture both as a material artifact and a mediator of organizational identity, and sees architectural expression as offering symbolic resources for identification. Stylishly redesigned flagship bank branches and innovative aesthetics provide experiential value to stakeholders. The study presents architectural semiotics as an interpretive framework to uncover the deeper meanings of architectural text. It shows that the materiality of built forms interconnects with social, historical and cultural systems, thus producing persuasive regimes of meaning.

In "Technology and the Simultaneous Collapsing and Expanding of Organizational Space: A Covid-19 Experience" (Chap. 13) Anouk

Mukherjee first reflects on his experiences with videoconferencing during the Covid-19 pandemic, which leads him to theorize that organizational space is both simultaneously collapsed and expanded through Information and Communication Technologies. He explores our experience of space by drawing on neurosciences and how they provide support for the Merleau-Ponty's phenomenology of perception. Using key concepts of Merleau-Ponty he shows how the concept of the Bayesian brain helps explain the experience of organizational space, both proximate and remote.

Part V: Organizational Aspects of New Ways of Working

In "From Innovations at Work to Innovative Ways of Conceptualizing Organization: A Brief History of Organization Studies" (Chap. 14) Lise Arena and Anthony Hussenot discuss how organization studies have accounted for innovations at work and their influence on the way organization has been conceptualized over time. Based on the time period from the 1950s to the 2010s, this historical analysis puts the emphasis on the interrelated evolution of the technological context (from industrial to digital innovations), the organizational phenomena (from centralized bureaucratic hierarchies to fluid organizations) and the ways of working (from the rise of professional management to the projectification of work). It is argued that organization theories have evolved along with evolutions of work practices and technologies. Industrial innovations led to a rather monolithic way of conceptualizing organization while entrepreneurship, nomadic ways of working and digital innovations favored increasing processual ways of conceptualizing organization.

In "Community Management Practices in Coworking Spaces: Being the 'Catalyst'" (Chap. 15), Aurore Dandoy studies the community dimension of collaborative spaces through a participative ethnographic design in which she acted as a community manager, conducted interviews and visited coworking spaces. She explores how field actors describe their feeling of community in which the community manager appears to have a key role. The community manager can be seen as an incarnation of the space and is significantly involved in the community and the sharing of emotions between coworkers. She analyzes community feeling through a phenomenology of activity as an outcome of the coworking space and the community manager's daily work. Embodied phenomenology helps include the community dimension and explain the impact of the community manager on community feeling in these new workspaces.

In "The Rise and Fall of a New Way of Working: A Testament of an Organizational Identity Mimicry" (Chap. 16), Marie Antoine addresses the failure of the implementation of an NWW project in a private company by focusing on the spatial component and the changes it introduced for workers and organizational identity. She envisages organizational identity as organizational members' shared interpretations about the characteristics which compose their organization and distinguish it in its social context. Data were collected through observations, document analysis and semi-structured interviews on the official purpose of the project, the new work environment, workers' perceptions and the concrete changes it brought in their daily routines and their reflections about the company. The failure embodies an identity mimicry, that is a desire and attempt to target a different organizational identity by adopting new rules and ways of working which prove difficult to implement. The original organizational identity is related to its technical core business which relies on employees' practices and experiences and cannot be successfully supported in an NWW activity-based workspace.

"Deconstructing New Ways of Working: A Five-Dimensional Conceptualization Proposal" (Chap. 17) by Grégory Jemine aims to understand the progressive normalization and the mechanisms through which NWW have become a legitimate reference in its organizational field. This chapter provides support for five ways of conceptualizing NWW: (1) as a management fashion disseminated across organizational fields; (2) as a set of discourses and narratives; (3) as an organizational change project; (4) as a material workspace; and (5) as a set of work practices and behaviors.

Gibson Burrell and Karen Dale offer a foreword and Leo McCann an afterword to this volume on *New Ways of Working: Organizations and Organizing in the Digital Age*. Most of these chapters were completed before the Covid-19 pandemic; Leo McCann and Anouk Mukherjee both made a start in addressing its implications which have been immense in terms of New Ways of Working in the digital age. We hope this volume will inspire further research on these recent developments and their long-term repercussions.

References

Alexander, K., & Price, I. (Eds.). (2013). *Managing organizational ecologies: Space, management, and organizations*. Abingdon, UK: Routledge.

Anderson, C. (2009). *Makers: The new industrial revolution*. New York: Crown Business.

Aroles, J., Granter, E., & de Vaujany, F. X. (2020). 'Becoming mainstream': The professionalisation and corporatisation of digital nomadism. *New Technology, Work and Employment, 35*(1), 114–129.

Aroles, J., Mitev, N., & de Vaujany, F. X. (2019). Mapping themes in the study of new work practices. *New Technology, Work and Employment, 34*(3), 285–299.

Baruch, Y. (2000). Teleworking: Benefits and pitfalls as perceived by professionals and managers. *New Technology, Work and Employment, 15*, 34–49.

Bosch-Sijtsema, P. M., Ruohomäki, V., & Vartiainen, M. (2010). Multi-locational knowledge workers in the office: Navigation, disturbances and effectiveness. *New Technology, Work and Employment, 25*(3), 183–195.

Boudreau, J. W., Jesuthasan, R., & Creelman, D. (2015). *Lead the work: Navigating a world beyond employment*. Hoboken, NJ: John Wiley & Sons.

Bouncken, R. B., & Reuschl, A. J. (2016). Coworking-spaces: How a phenomenon of the sharing economy builds a novel trend for the workplace and for entrepreneurship. *Review of Managerial Science, 12*, 1–18.

Brivot, M., & Gendron, Y. (2011). Beyond panopticism: On the ramifications of surveillance in a contemporary professional setting. *Accounting, Organizations and Society, 36*(3), 135–155.

Brocklehurst, M. (2001). Power identity and new technology homework: Implications for 'new forms' of organizing. *Organization Studies, 22*, 445–466.

Brown, B., & O'Hara, K. (2003). Place as a practical concern of mobile workers. *Environment and Planning A, 35*, 1565–1587.

Courpasson, D., & Reed, M. (2004). Introduction: Bureaucracy in the age of enterprise. *Organization, 11*(1), 5–12.

Dale, K. (2005). Building a social materiality: Spatial and embodied politics in organizational control. *Organization, 12*(5), 649–678.

Dale, K., Kingma, S. F., & Wasserman, V. (Eds.). (2018). *Organisational space and beyond: The significance of Henri Lefebvre for organisation studies*. Abingdon, UK: Routledge.

Davidow, P., & Malone, M. (1992). *The Virtual Corporation*. New York: Harper Collins.

De Vaujany, F. X., & Mitev, N. (Eds.). (2013). *Materiality and space: Organizations, artefacts and practices*. Basingstoke: Palgrave Macmillan.

Ellison, N. B. (2004). *Telework and social change: How technology is reshaping the boundaries between home and work*. Westport, CT: Greenwood Publishing Group.

Faraj, S., Jarvenpaa, S. L., & Majchrzak, A. (2011). Knowledge collaboration in online communities. *Organization Science, 22*(5), 1224–1239.

Felstead, A., Jewson, N., & Walters, S. (2005). *Changing places of work*. New York: Palgrave Macmillan.

Flecker, J. (Ed.). (2016). *Space, place and global digital work*. London: Palgrave Macmillan.

Ford, M. (2015). *The rise of the robots: Technology and the threat of mass unemployment*. London: Oneworld Publications.

Gandini, A. (2015). The rise of coworking spaces: A literature review. *Ephemera, 15*(1), 193–205.

Garrett, L. E., Spreitzer, G. M., & Bacevice, P. A. (2017). Co-constructing a sense of community at work: The emergence of community in coworking spaces. *Organization Studies, 38*(6), 821–842.

Garud, R., Kumaraswamy, A., & Langlois, R. (Eds.). (2002). *Managing in the modular age: Architectures, networks, and organizations*. Oxford, UK: Blackwell Publishers.

Golden, T. D. (2009). Applying technology to work: Toward a better understanding of telework. *Organization Management Journal, 6*, 241–250.

Gregg, M. (2011). *Work's intimacy*. Cambridge, UK: Polity Press.

Hamari, J., Sjöklint, M., & Ukkonen, A. (2016). The sharing economy: Why people participate in collaborative consumption. *Journal of the Association for Information Science and Technology, 67*(9), 2047–2059.

Heckscher, C. (1994). Defining the post-bureaucratic type. In C. Heckscher & A. Donnellon (Eds.), *The Post-bureaucratic organization* (pp. 14–62). Thousand Oaks, CA: Sage.

Hislop, D., & Axtell, C. (2009). To Infinity and beyond? Workspace and the multi-location worker. *New Technology, Work and Employment, 24*(1), 60–75.

Hodgson, D. E. (2004). Project work: The legacy of bureaucratic control in the post-bureaucratic organization. *Organization, 11*(1), 81–100.

Howe, J. (2008). *Crowdsourcing: How the power of the crowd is driving the future of business*. New York: Random House.

Humphreys, A., & Grayson, K. (2008). The intersecting roles of consumer and producer: A critical perspective on co-production, co-creation and prosumption. *Sociology Compass, 2*(3), 963–980.

Jackson, P. J., & van der Wielen, J. (Eds.). (1998). *Teleworking: International perspectives: From telecommuting to the virtual organisation*. Hover, UK: Psychology Press.

Kallinikos, J. (2003). Work, human agency and organizational forms: An anatomy of fragmentation. *Organization Studies, 24*(4), 595–618.

Kingma, S. F. (2016). The constitution of 'third workspaces' in between the home and the corporate office. *New Technology, Work and Employment, 31*(2), 177–193.

Marsden, D. (2004). The 'Network Economy' and models of the employment contract. *British Journal of Industrial Relations, 42*(4), 659–684.

Matlay, H., & Westhead, P. (2005). Virtual teams and the rise of e-entrepreneurship in Europe. *International Small Business Journal, 23*(3), 279–302.

Morgan, G., & Nelligan, P. (2018). *The creativity Hoax: Precarious work in the gig economy*. London, UK: Anthem Press.

Munger, M. C. (2018). *Tomorrow 3.0: Transaction costs and the sharing economy*. Cambridge, UK: Cambridge University Press.

Myerson, J., & Bichard, J. A. (2016). *New demographics, new workspace: Office design for the changing workforce*. Abingdon, UK: Routledge.

Oldenburg, R. (1989). *The great good place: Café, coffee shops, community centers, beauty parlors, general stores, bars, hangouts, and how they get you through the day*. New York: Paragon House Publishers.

Pulakos, E. D., Dorsey, D. W., & White, S. S. (2006). Adaptability in the workplace: Selecting an adaptive workforce. *Advances in Human Performance and Cognitive Engineering Research, 6*, 41–71.

Pulignano, V., & Stewart, P. (2008). Bureaucracy transcended? New patterns of employment regulation and labour control in the international automotive industry. In V. Pulignano, P. Stewart, A. Danford, & M. Richardson (Eds.), *Flexibility at work* (pp. 17–44). Basingstoke, UK: Palgrave Macmillan.

Ritzer, G., & Jurgenson, N. (2010). Production, consumption, prosumption. The nature of capitalism in the age of the digital 'prosumer'. *Journal of Consumer Culture, 10*(1), 13–36.

Scholz, T. (2017). *Uberworked and underpaid: How workers are disrupting the digital economy*. New York: John Wiley & Sons.

Scott Morton, M. S. (1991). *The Corporation of the 1990s: Information technology and organizational transformation*. Oxford, UK: Oxford University Press.

Sewell, G. (1998). The discipline of teams: The control of team-based industrial work through electronic and peer surveillance. *Administrative Science Quarterly, 43*, 397–428.

Sewell, G. (2012). Employees, organizations and surveillance. In K. Ball, K. D. Haggerty, & D. Lyon (Eds.), *The handbook of surveillance studies* (pp. 303–312). London, UK: Routledge.

Spinuzzi, C. (2012). Working alone together: Coworking as emergent collaborative activity. *Journal of Business and Technical Communication, 26*(4), 399–441.

Sproull, L., Kiesler, S., & Kiesler, S. B. (1992). *Connections: New ways of working in the networked organization*. Cambridge, MA: MIT Press.

Stephany, A. (2015). *The business of sharing: Making it in the new sharing economy*. Basingstoke, UK: Palgrave Macmillan.

Sundararajan, A. (2017). *The sharing economy: The end of employment and the rise of crowd-based capitalism*. Cambridge, MA: MIT Press.

Sweet, S., & Meiksins, P. (2015). *Changing contours of work: Jobs and opportunities in the new economy* (3rd ed.). Thousand Oaks, CA: Sage Publications.

Taylor, S. (2015). A new mystique? Working for yourself in the neoliberal economy. *The Sociological Review, 63*(1), 174–187.

Tietze, S., & Musson, G. (2002). When 'work' meets 'home': Temporal flexibility as lived experience. *Time and Society, 11*, 315–334.

Tietze, S., & Musson, G. (2005). Recasting the home–work relationship: A case of mutual adjustment? *Organization Studies, 26*, 1331–1352.

Tremblay, D. G., & Thomsin, L. (2012). Telework and mobile working: Analysis of its benefits and drawbacks. *International Journal of Work Innovation, 1*, 100–113.

Turner, G., & Myerson, J. (1998). *New workspace, new culture: Office design as a catalyst for change*. Farnham, UK: Gower Publishing.

Van Marrewijk, A., & Yanow, D. (Eds.). (2010). *Organizational spaces: Rematerializing the workaday world*. Cheltenham, UK: Edward Elgar Publishing.

Weil, D. (2014). *The fissured workplace*. Cambridge, MA: Harvard University Press.

Widlok, T. (2016). *Anthropology and the economy of sharing*. Abingdon, UK: Routledge.

Wilson, J., O'Leary, M. B., Metiu, A., & Jett, Q. (2008). Perceived proximity in virtual work: Explaining the paradox of far-but-close. *Organization Studies, 29*, 979–1002.

Wolf, M., & McQuitty, S. (2011). Understanding the do-it-yourself consumer: DIY motivations and outcomes. *AMS Review, 1*(3-4), 154–170.

Zuboff, S. (2015). Big other: Surveillance capitalism and the prospects of an information civilization. *Journal of Information Technology, 30*(1), 75–89.

Part I

New Ways of Working and the Sharing Economy

2

Platforms and the New Division of Labor Between Humans and Machines

Attila Marton and Hamid Ekbia

Introduction

Current debates about automation and the future of work have generated varying perspectives and prognoses about the implications of this trend for human jobs (Abbatiello, Boehm, Schwartz, & Chand, 2018; Frey & Osborne, 2017; Manyika et al., 2017; WEF, 2016). However, the debates are dominated by the question of whether automation will destroy or create jobs (and which kinds of jobs) and whether it will displace workers (and which kind of workers). While the importance of this discourse is understandable, it deflects from a more fundamental shift in the division

A. Marton (✉)
Digitilization Department, Copenhagen Business School,
Copenhagen, Denmark
e-mail: a.marton@cbs.dk

H. Ekbia
Center for Research on Mediated Interaction, Indiana University
Bloomington, Bloomington, IN, USA
e-mail: hekbia@indiana.edu

N. Mitev et al. (eds.), *New Ways of Working*, Technology, Work and Globalization,
https://doi.org/10.1007/978-3-030-61687-8_2

of labor between humans and machines. Historically, machines were designed to augment and/or replace human labor by mechanizing and automating what humans are not capable or willing to do. Typical examples of such systems are the automation of mass production of cognitive tasks (Gleick, 2011; Zuboff, 1988). The current narrative and ideology of automation, however, reverse this relationship as humans are increasingly relegated to what machines cannot do—for example, the creative, affective, or organizing labor of human beings (Ekbia & Nardi, 2017). In other words, machines used to do what humans could not do. Now, humans do what machines cannot. The upshot of this development is that those aspects of human work that drive and enable the workings of current socio-technical systems is increasingly trivialized and made invisible, and consequently rendered uncompensated or undercompensated.

This shift in work practices and the pragmatics of labor, and the resulting changes in its division between humans and machines, has short-term and long-term implications that we have examined elsewhere (Ekbia & Nardi, 2017). In this chapter, we elaborate on theoretical avenues for explaining the sociotechnical mechanisms underlying this shift and the new ontology of work practices that comes with it. We contend that contemporary automation introduces novel mechanisms for converting humans and their *vita activa* (Arendt, 1958) into a standing reserve for machines (Heidegger, 1977). In particular, contemporary computing has vastly expanded the labor of humans into what can broadly be understood as "system-sustaining labor". These activities are based on a whole new division of labor, which Ekbia and Nardi (2017) refer to as "heteromation". In certain scenarios, machines heteromate to people who work, for instance, on *Amazon Mechanical Turk* and are paid on a per-task basis. In most scenarios, however, heteromated labor remains uncompensated and unrewarded, as is the case with self-service of customers in a grocery shop or of passengers in an airport, the leisurely activities of gamers and *YouTubers*, or even the so-called voluntary work of citizen scientists.

With these distinctions in mind, we note that the varieties of heteromated labor introduce a new ontology of work practices, which differs from waged labor (be it employed or contractual freelancing) as well as traditional unwaged labor (be it domestic or industrial). For instance, computerized automation does not replace or displace the bank teller with the ATM. Rather, it is the ATM that allows the bank customer to re/displace the bank teller, because technology allows bank customers, without any training or skills in banking, to do the work themselves (Zwick, 2015). Likewise, heteromation is a core aspect of the platform economy and the new organizational forms it gives rise to (Constantiou, Marton, & Tuunainen, 2017). For instance, *Uber* is capable of involving casual participants in the work process, who would not participate otherwise. In particular, riders act as middle-managers, when they rate drivers (Rosenblat & Stark, 2016), a role that is indispensable for algorithmically managing millions of drivers worldwide.

Heteromation, thus conceived, constitutes a new division of labor, which is typically low-cost or free (for those who benefit from the labor) or even naturalized (such as user-generated content for social media platforms) (Ekbia & Nardi, 2017). We examine these developments within the context of the current burst of the so-called gig economy and the new political economy of computerized automation, which we all grapple to understand. Hence, given its foundational nature, this chapter addresses a variety of themes and issues. As heteromation is a new mode of organizing work, it changes the material basis of labor, work, tasks, and actions. Such changes require new regimes of legitimacy in order to be institutionalized, new approaches dealing with the increasing fluidity of organizational boundaries and new machine-human interactions to be digitally organized and algorithmically managed, to name but a few. Underneath these developments, we suspect, lies a more fundamental shift in the division of labor between humans and machines.

Complementation, Substitution, and the Decomposition of Jobs

The history of the division of labor between humans and machines is typically viewed as the history of complementation and substitution. At a first glance, contemporary developments in digital automation and AI (Artificial Intelligence) seem to be no exception (Zysman & Kenney, 2018). On the one hand, digital automation has the potential to relieve humans, particularly high-skilled workers, from repetitive work (Langlois, 2002), improving their overall performance (Marton & Mariátegui, 2015). On the other hand, digital automation also substitutes humans, replacing, displacing, or even removing labor (Kristal, 2013). Software agents, for instance, are increasingly involved in organizational coordination of tasks and transactions on digital platforms (Constantiou et al., 2017; Nissen & Sengupta, 2006).

Put into such a historical context, digital automation is the current outcome of long-standing developments going back to the early days of industrialization (Greenbaum, 1996). The industrial division of labor led to a comprehensive re-design of tasks through machines as well as to the structuring of everyday life to better fit the clock-time of factory production (Braverman, 1974). Craft production was broken down for the purpose of increasing the efficiencies of mass-production and automation (Wallace & Kalleberg, 1982). Likewise, the post-industrial division of labor introduced IT systems, which led to, for instance, IT-enabled outsourcing and Computer Supported Collaborative Work (CSCW), re-engineering of entire industries, and business models (Boynton, Victor, & Eaker, 1992). Labor became more flexible while being detached from physical locations and existing employment forms, giving rise to alternative work arrangements, such as outsourced workers and freelancers (Katz & Krueger, 2016).

The explanation for these developments typically builds on the economic notion of "comparative advantage", namely that machines are comparatively better at performing routine tasks (Kalleberg, 2011). In the same vein, digital technology is therefore understood to be good at complementing humans in their non-routine tasks (such as complex communication activities and problem-solving) and substituting humans when it comes to routine, programmable tasks (Autor, Levy, & Murnane, 2003). Big data analytics is a telling example, as it is, for instance, employed in customer service to automate rule-based services and tailored content-delivery based on the customer's online behavior while, at the same time, it supports customer service personnel to proactively provide individualized services to customers (Lehrer, Wieneke, Brocke, Jung, & Seidel, 2018).

On closer examination, however, digital automation not only substitutes or complements humans, but also enables a new political economy, giving unprecedented rise to digital platforms and data-based services and products (Constantiou et al., 2017; Kallinikos & Tempini, 2014), algorithmic management practices (Rosenblat & Stark, 2016), and new forms of labor and its exploitation (Greenhill & Fletcher, 2013). As new loci of value creation and production, digital platforms, in particular, blur the conventional boundaries of formal organizations, industries, and markets as well as of private and public, lifeworld and commerce. This blurring marks a fundamental shift in labor institutions (Braverman, 1974; Ekbia & Nardi, 2017), as private life (often unwittingly) is mined for personal data for corporate value creation (Kallinikos, 2006; Zuboff, 2019), disrupting the traditional notion of value being created by labor (Nicolescu, Huth, Radanliev, & De Roure, 2018). As a consequence, labor is newly divided between humans and machines.

Rather than history simply repeating itself, these technological developments propel deeper, structural changes in labor markets and institutions. For instance, as it is not (yet) feasible, either economically or technically, to automate high- and low-skilled jobs, automation increases employment for both (Autor, 2015). By contrast, routinized mid-skilled jobs, such as clerical work, can be automated relatively easily (Frey & Osborne, 2013), displacing mid-skilled workers primarily into low-income service occupations, expanding the polarization of employment into "lovely" and "lousy" jobs (Goos & Manning, 2007). Adding to this structural change, the current, so-called second wave of AI (i.e. neural networks, machine learning) seems to be increasingly capable of performing tasks, which were once believed to be out of reach for machines (Smith, 2019), such as driving cars or winning at *Go* (Autor et al., 2003). Indeed, it appears that the domains of tasks, which humans are good at, are rapidly shrinking.

A Brief Excursion into the Gig Economy

The expansion of machines into domains once believed to be the exclusive purview of humans affects jobs and jobholders in more than just the two ways typically discussed in public discourse. That is, in addition to complementation, which changes the task composition of jobs (i.e. people will keep their jobs as only some tasks will be automated), and substitution, which changes the distribution of jobs (i.e. people will learn new skills to fill new jobs) (Brynjolfsson & Mcafee, 2014), there is a third way, which has received not nearly enough attention. As digital platforms have given rise to the so-called gig economy, the bundling of tasks into stable jobs and employment is not necessary anymore. Rather, platforms such as *Amazon Mechanical Turk*, *Uber*, and *Taskrabbit* demonstrate that automation can also be used for the decomposition of jobs into tasks or gigs for the benefit of the task provider and the platform owner (Hill, 2015). The polarization of employment into lovely and lousy jobs is intensified by the growing gulf between those who have and those who do not have a job (Standing, 2016).

Proponents of these developments see digital platforms lowering the barriers for participating in economic activities, enabling previously unfeasible forms of micro-entrepreneurship, production, and consumption as well as non-proprietary regimes of common ownership as viable alternatives to firms and markets (Benkler, 2006; Botsman & Rogers, 2011). As a case in point, *Wikipedia* benefits from pooling large numbers of crowd-sourced tasks, ranging from writing entire articles to micro-tasks, such as correcting only a single typo (Aaltonen & Kallinikos, 2013). Critical voices, by contrast, take issue that, aside from a few flagship examples such as *Open Source Software* and *Wikipedia*, the gig economy displays the same "winner-takes-most" dynamics characteristic of the digital platform economy in general, leading to monopolistic and, more importantly, monopsonistic labor markets dominated by big tech (Schmidt, 2017). Against such a backdrop, the narrative of empowerment, participation, and sharing is the ideological superstructure driven by Silicon Valley, covering their exploitative and unethical business practices—be it *Uber* exploiting its drivers or *Facebook* profiteering from user-generated content (John, 2012; Rosenblat & Stark, 2016). Indeed, platform capitalism captures much of the value created by labor by disguising it as participation. This is a reversal of earlier forms of automation. Rather than being closed off from human intervention, digital platforms require human participation to provide labor and data for the sustenance of their automated, algorithmic operations (Ekbia & Nardi, 2017).

More empirical research is required to understand the scope and societal impact of the decomposition of labor by digital platforms and the gig economy. Existing studies about so-called alternative work arrangements provide some points of reference. In their US survey about temporary help agency workers, on-call workers, contract workers, independent contractors, and freelancers, Katz and Krueger (2016) found that their share in the entire worker-force rose from 10.7% in 2005 to 15.8% in 2015—a 50% increase in ten years. Ten years before, there was hardly any change in this share. More telling, 95% of the net employment growth in the US economy (2005–2015) occurred in alternative work arrangements, while for standard employment arrangements the growth amounted to only 0.4%. Finally, only 0.5% of all workers provided services through online intermediaries such as *Uber* or *TaskRabbit*. Such shift toward alternative work arrangements is not contained to the USA. For instance, in Denmark, despite its highly developed welfare state and social partnership between employers and employees, of the 150,000 new jobs created in 2012–2017, 44% were part-time jobs with 20 working hours per week or less (Damm, 2018).

Consultancy reports about the digital economy found similar numbers. JPMorgan-Chase (Farrell & Greig, 2016) reported that 0.9% of all adults (not just workers) in the USA participate in the online platform economy—0.5% offering their labor on platforms such as *Uber* or *Taskrabbit* and 0.4% renting or selling assets on platforms such as *Airbnb* or *eBay*. The study also reports that the growth rate has slowed down to 102% in mid-2016, following an all-time high of 400% during 2013 and 2014. Such growth is accompanied by high turnover rates, as every one in six participants is new to these platforms, while around 50% exit the respective platform within 12 months. In their study about the gig economy in the USA and EU-15, McKinsey Global Institute (Manyika et al., 2016) found that 20–30% of the working-age population engages in independent work. Among these 30% are "free agents" (independent work is their main income by choice), 40% are "casual earners" (independent work is a supplemental income by choice), 14% are "reluctants" (independent work is their main income by necessity), and 16% are "financially strapped" (independent work is a supplemental income by necessity). Corroborating the above numbers, the study reports that only 4% of the working-age population has used digital platforms to generate income. By comparison, 15% of independent workers use digital platforms—6% of them provide labor (e.g. on *Uber*, *TaskRabbit*), 63% sell goods (e.g. on *Etsy*, *eBay*), and 36% lease their assets (e.g. on *Airbnb*, *Getaround*).

While its share in the workforce is relatively small, the gig economy is growing rapidly, normalizing the decomposition of jobs into tasks. This normalization is indicative of a larger shift in the institutions of labor, leading to a new political economy and a new division of labor between humans and machines, which is organized around the digital platform as the dominant locus of value creation and the exploitation of labor (Ekbia & Nardi, 2019; Katz & Margo, 2014). It is to this new political economy of platforms that we turn next.

Of Workshops, Factories, and Platforms

With the rise of the digital platform economy and the big-tech superstar firms that came with it, platforms have emerged as fundamental structuring devices of contemporary society. In this section, we will delve deeper into this issue by comparing the ideal type of the digital platform to those of two other important loci of labor and value creation—the workshop and the factory (Stabell & Fjeldstad, 1998). We construct these ideal types, as we focus on the differences between them in terms of what product architecture they are set up to produce and how labor is divided as a consequence of that setup.

The Workshop

The workshop is the locus for crafting products based on a so-called integral product architecture. Such products are characterized by a complex mapping between the functions a product is designed to perform and its components crafted to perform those functions (Ulrich, 1995). A case in point, an F1 racing car is specially designed and built to deliver high performance for a specific task. Its parts and the interfaces connecting them are purpose built, resulting in a highly integrated product consisting of tightly coupled components. At the same time, however, these kinds of products are not capable of absorbing changes in functionality or in individual components without having to change other components or even the entire product.

In terms of the division of labor, this setup of crafts production is referred to as the vertical division of labor between artisans, contributing their specializations and expert skills during all stages of the production (Ames & Rosenberg, 1965). Because of their varied skills, artisans can easily adapt to changing circumstances, which grants them greater autonomy and power over the production process. As a result, the division of labor between human and machine favors the artisan, as they are utilizing technology as a tool, complementing their skills. The machine, in other words, is adapted to the needs of the artisan to provide non-standard, tailor-made quality products and services. This setup can still be found in today's world in small batch manufacturing, the arts, and the skilled professions but also in housework, where a stay-home spouse (typically the wife) has a broad set of skills, operating specialized tools to wash dishes, dry laundry, reheat food, and so forth (Sennett, 2008).

In her critique of Marxist political economy, Hannah Arendt (1958) describes crafts production as a distinctly human activity. As *homo faber*, humans use tools to make "things" by forcing raw material to conform to their skills and vision. The collaboration of artisans in the workshop, therefore, is organized in such ways that artisans with different specializations and skill sets come together to craft a work (such as an F1 racing car). Arendt calls this arrangement the specialization of work, which pools the differences between the artisans' expertise, making them difficult to replace. As we will discuss next, a factory, by contrast, pools the sameness of labor power, making factory workers substitutable by other workers and, ultimately, by machines.

The Factory

In contrast to the integral product architecture of the workshop, the setup of the factory is geared toward producing according to a so-called modular product architecture. In this case, there is a one-to-one mapping between the functions a product is designed to perform and the components produced to perform those functions (Ulrich, 1995). To again use an example from the world of automobiles, the typical example would be Henry Ford's *Model T*. Importantly, the component parts are loosely coupled through standardized interfaces rather than tightly coupled through special-made interfaces, as is the case with integral product architectures. Hence, a modular product architecture leads to more flexibility, because a change in one module does not necessarily require for other modules or for the entire product to be changed as long as the standards of the interface are adhered to. It is because of such architecture that the various components of a product can be mass produced and the incremental innovation of those components can be fostered.

The division of labor that complements the mass production of modular product architectures is traditionally referred to as the horizontal division of labor. As the skilled artisan is replaced by unskilled laborers, who only know how to use specialized tools designed to accomplish only one particular step of the production process, the production process itself becomes more routinized, mechanized, and ultimately automated in the factory. Already observed by Adam Smith, factories emerged as the new loci for labor and value creation in response to growing markets and technological developments (Langlois, 2002). Sufficiently large markets demand high production volume and, consequently, artisans have to specialize in fewer and fewer steps of the production process in order to scale production to meet market demands. At the same time, technological developments lead to better machines and the mechanization of the production process, enabling unskilled laborers to do the work of an artisan in a piecemeal fashion. The deskilling of work that follows such a transition was the hallmark of Fordism (Katz & Margo, 2014), making laborers replaceable and vulnerable to changing circumstances as they, lacking the wider skillset of the artisan, are less able to adapt.

The factory setup of arranging laborers for mass production does not only change the division of labor between humans but also between humans and machines. As production is geared toward machines, delivering volumes beyond what humans can do by themselves, the production process is designed to fit the logic of automation rather than human capacities and talents. Such design marks an important qualitative difference to crafts production, in which the relationship between humans and machines is such that the latter is a tool adapted to the needs of the former. As Karl Marx anticipated in the early days of industrial production:

> [O]nce adopted into the production process of capital, the means of labour passes through different metamorphoses, whose culmination is the machine, or rather, an automatic system of machinery...set in motion by an automaton, a moving power that moves itself; this automaton consisting of numerous mechanical and intellectual organs, so that the workers themselves are cast merely as its conscious linkages... it is the machine which possesses skill and strength in place of the worker...The worker's activity, reduced to a mere abstraction of activity, is determined and regulated on all sides by the movement of the machinery, and not the opposite. (Marx, 1857–1858, pp. 692–693)

With automation, therefore, machines produce and laborers have to adapt to the needs of the machine, which requires to be tended and its environment sufficiently simplified in order for it to work. In other words, the machine is not a tool anymore that serves the artisan, but an automaton with its own rhythms and motions of mass production. It is against this backdrop that Arendt (1958) laments that humans have become subservient to machines. In contrast to the workshop, the factory pools labor power and, thus, treats laborers as replaceable cogs; executing routinized tasks, they become replaceable—first by other laborers, then by machines.

Economic historians, however, point out that the kind of deskilled labor that is associated with early industrialization may only have been a transitional period toward full automation enabled by electrification, introducing a different kind of division of labor (Ames & Rosenberg, 1965). Beginning with late-nineteenth century, labor was increasingly reskilled to be able to operate and oversee the complicated machinery used to automate entire production lines (Frey & Osborne, 2013). Automation resulted in continuous producing and processing as one, large-scale machine integrated the mechanized tools, which were previously used by laborers. In other words, a new division of labor emerged between humans and machines, as machines displaced humans on the production floor and humans found new employment, such as designing and tending machines (Langlois, 2002). This complementary relationship between capital, skill, and labor marked a good part of twentieth-century manufacturing; it is now assumed to be the rule and the deskilled, Fordist approach being the exception. However, researchers observe that there "are substantial similarities between […] technical change and labor demand shifts by skill in nineteenth-century manufacturing with those embedded in the application of recent 'task-based' models of computerization and skill-biased technical change" (Katz & Margo, 2014, p. 20). That is, the gig economy raises the question whether twentieth-century manufacturing may have been in fact the historical exception. This brings us to the platform as the dominant locus of labor and value creation of the digital economy.

The Platform

As digitalization has introduced new, digitally born products and services, it has also given rise to new forms of production and organization of labor. In contrast to purely physical artifacts, digital artifacts are editable (i.e. components can be edited, deleted, and added ex-post), interactive (i.e. they allow for an increased spectrum of choices contingent upon user choice), open (i.e. they can be modified in ways unintended by the producer), and distributed (i.e. components are networked, defying clear-cut product boundaries) (Kallinikos, Aaltonen, & Marton, 2013). The corresponding product architecture is layered, separating a device layer (e.g. hardware, operating system) and network layer (e.g. cables, network protocols) from a service layer (e.g. WWW, e-mail) and content layer (e.g. websites, blogs), which combined make up the internet (Benkler, 2006). The architecture is layered because the logic of operation of each layer stays within that layer, making them only loosely coupled and relatively agnostic toward each other. Innovation can occur on one of the layers, without concern or the need to even completely understand how the other layers work (e.g. creating a new feature for an e-mail client does not affect the underlying transmission protocols). More importantly, however, the digitalization of physical products, such as phones and cars, merges the modular architecture of mass production and the layered architecture of digital production into a hybrid, layered-modular form (Yoo, Boland, Lyytinen, & Majchrzak, 2012).

A layered-modular architecture enables products to become product platforms; that is, they can be expanded by complementary modules even after they left the factory. A case in point, the value proposition of a smart phone does not only derive from the product itself but even more from it being a platform for complementary apps created and offered by peripheral app developers (Eaton, Elaluf-Calderwood, Sorensen, & Yoo, 2015). Research into product platforms typically studies them in terms of innovation and business models (de Reuver, Sorensen, & Basole, 2018; Tiwana, 2014). There is, however, hardly any consideration given to the political economy of platforms, especially with regards to how labor is divided among humans as well as between humans and machines on digital platforms. Similar to how integral architecture and workshop, on the one hand, and modular architecture and factory, on the other, complement each other, there is a new division of labor for the new layered-modular architecture and the digital platform to complement each other.

The question concerning the division of labor on digital platforms has been approached in various ways. In open source software (OSS), for instance, Garzarelli and Fontanella (2011) observe that labor is divided in very different ways from planned production. Any contributor to an OSS production self-selects the task s/he wants to do, regardless of whether the task matches the skill-set of the contributor. A highly qualified programmer, for instance, may choose to do user-testing, which would be considered a waste of time in a workshop or factory environment. Second, producing OSS runs in parallel, overlapping tasks, and is mostly decentralized. Any number of contributors may be working on the same task at any given time. This mode of production is referred to as the "bazaar" division of labor, combining vertical and horizontal arrangements

(Garzarelli, Limam, & Thomassen, 2008). Contributors can self-select whether they want to partake in the vertical or horizontal division of labor; that is whether they want to pool their particular expert skills (in this case, they pool their specialization as in a workshop) or do something that does not require their particular skillset or no special skillset at all, such as testing and bug-spotting (in this case, they pool the same labor power, as in a factory). This setup results in redundant economies, which are beneficial in OSS production, as they drive experimentation and innovation based on the particularities of digital artifacts, the ethos of openness (e.g. everybody has something to contribute), and the intrinsic motivation of the volunteers (e.g. learning is reward enough).

A bazaar-like division of labor, similar to OSS production, can be found in a variety of other domains as well, ranging from open science projects and open bibliographic databases to *Wikipedia* and open innovation initiatives launched by for-profit companies (Chesbrough & Appleyard, 2007; Garzarelli et al., 2008). In the same vein, the corporate platforms of the gig economy draw inspiration from the success of such open projects, such as OSS and *Wikipedia*, and commodify it. Based on an ethos of entrepreneurship and libertarian ideology, which is but only a particular variety of the ethos of OSS production (Benkler, 2006), the gig economy constructs a similar narrative of participation and inclusivity. However, instead of donating time and skills for the love of creating software and gaining new knowledge, a tasker is expected to labor for the love of being an entrepreneur and of making profits, by not letting one's idle resources go waste—be it time, attention, or a spare room (Hill, 2015). In this sense, the gig economy extends the mechanisms, by which it taps into the idle resources of private individuals, beyond the amateur love of OSS volunteers to a much broader range of individuals and their physical assets and resources. Such is the political economy of platforms, as the logic of profit-making and commodification colonizes the life-world of the everyday, of personal friendships, of hospitality, and so forth (Alaimo & Kallinikos, 2017).

While the OSS literature addresses new forms of dividing labor between humans, Ekbia and Nardi (2017) introduce the concept of "heteromation" to address the new division of labor between humans and machines. The term brings into relief how recent developments of digitalization put humans at the margins of machines, as now machines hetero-mate tasks to humans, so that they can do the tasks machines would not do. A case in point, if an AI is not able to fulfil a task, such as filtering offensive content on a social media platform, it is crowdsourced to *Amazon*'s *Mechanical Turkers*. This is a fundamental shift in the relationship between humans and machines, as heteromation is extended into all domains of social life, extracting value from human engagement and labor through mechanisms other than employment. A large number of people are creating economic value for corporations as users, searchers, and gamers, when, for instance, they communicate by e-mail, text, or phone with their family and friends, or simply in the name of customer review or self-service at banks, airports, grocery stores, and elsewhere. These are significant sources for value creation, from which particularly big-tech corporations are profiteering immensely; however, these activities are not considered to work in the traditional sense of the term and, therefore, are unaccounted for, as they are purposefully made invisible or disguised as voluntary participation, gaming, or sharing.

As a consequence of heteromation and the ways it extracts value from our everyday interactions with digital machines, capitalist class structures are reinforced. While class structures are reproduced, class formations are changing, that is, the way collectives organize themselves on the basis of their interests at any given historical moment (Wright, 1997). In early nineteenth-century American capitalism, classes formed between family-owned enterprises and their employees, before it shifted to large corporations controlled by non-owner managers. In contemporary platform capitalism, by contrast, class formations have acquired a fluid character, largely embodied in computer-mediated network relationships with a global span and the so-called walled gardens of corporate platforms. In contrast to previous forms of capitalism, the current form is inclusionary, as it secures value by bringing and keeping large segments of the population into its fold in the form of unwaged, unpaid, or minimally compensated labor disguised as participation, self-expression, use, fun, and empowerment (Ekbia & Nardi, 2017). Digitally born corporations, such as *Google* or *Facebook*, want the whole world to be on their platforms, as exclusion only eliminates new means of value extraction. Instead, digital inclusion—in the sense of being connected to a network rather than being a member of the privileged class—has become the modus operandi of current capitalism (Ekbia, 2016).

Discussion

Despite contemporary developments of automation and AI, labor remains to be the source of value created in capitalist economies. What is new are certain types of labor, which are very different from what we usually mean when we observe an activity as "work" or a task as part of a "job". Those categories refer to industrial capitalism, which developed industrial labor as a new type of labor organized in assembly lines, followed by post-industrial capitalism, which adopted the shape of flexible labor organized in new working arrangements such as project teams. In both these cases, employed labor was the dominant type of relationship between the producer and extractor of value—that is, between the laborer and the employer. In the current digital platform economy, however, value is increasingly created outside employment. This can take the form of the "alternative work arrangements" of the gig-economy (Katz & Krueger, 2016) or the heteromated arrangements of computerized systems, where "users" create value in the form of user generated content, "modding", design competitions, reviews, self-service, and so on through their activities on social media, search engines, and gaming platforms, or simply as customers (Ekbia & Nardi, 2017).

In contrast to workshops and factories, platforms introduce novel mechanisms for the conversion of the *vita activa* (Arendt, 1958) of human beings into a standing reserve for digital machines, dividing the labor between humans and machines in new ways as a result (see Table 2.1). Historically, machines were designed to augment and/or exploit labor by mechanizing and automating what humans are not capable of doing—be it the automation of mass production or the computerized automation of cognitive tasks. The current narrative and ideology of automation, however, reverse this relationship: the primary focus is now on what machines are capable of doing and leaves what they are not capable of doing, such as being creative or emotional, to humans (Ekbia & Nardi, 2017). By the same token, human labor, as it still drives and

Table 2.1 Comparison between the workshop, factory, and platform as loci for the division of labor (authors' own)

	Workshop	Factory	Platform
Human individual	Artisan	Laborer	User/gig worker
Pooling of	Expertise	Labor power	Participation
Division of labor	Vertical	Horizontal	Vertical and horizontal (e.g. Bazaar-Like)
Relation between humans and machines	Tool	Automation	Heteromation

enables the workings of digital platforms, is increasingly trivialized and made invisible, because we are being told that all the work on digital platforms is now done by digital automation and by supposedly autonomous AI (Lanier, 2013). Consequently, the human labor that goes into making digital automation work remains uncompensated or undercompensated, relegating it to a standing reserve or resource for digital platforms (Heidegger, 1977). In other words, digital platforms are not mere tools or automatons, but rather a new locus for the extraction of value. Disguised as casual or even pleasurable participation, users generate content for social media platforms and "share" personal data to be sold to advertisers, while customers essentially work for corporations as "self-servicing" machines. These and many other examples represent a new kind of labor that stands in stark contrast to traditional notions of labor as a life-sustaining activity (Arendt, 1958; Marx, 1961). They rather seem to predominantly serve the purpose of tending to the platforms—not life-sustaining but "system-sustaining" labor. Let us explain.

Waged labor is certainly the most well-understood form of life-sustaining labor ever since Marx identified and explained surplus value as the key mechanism of value extraction from waged labor (Marx, 1961). Be it employment or contractual work, waged labor still remains a fundamental form of relationship between labor and capital to present day. Regardless of the rise of big-tech, there are still plenty of sweatshops and factories around the globe. Certainly, this will not change with digitalization, as technological development maintains a class-based structure, unevenly distributing the benefits of digitalization (Kristal, 2013). Staying within the purview of waged labor, digital automation appears then to be no different from mechanized automation, as it puts laborers out of employment, moving them into precarious labor conditions, such as having to drive for *Uber*. In doing so, labor turns into "labor-as-a-service" as part of an on-demand workforce of the gig economy without sufficient level of job security, legal protection, and welfare support (Vallas & Prener, 2012). Such a workforce is then a contemporary variety of the reserve army of labor already observed by Marx (1961).

System-sustaining labor, by contrast, refers to all the gigs and micro-tasks by which users and gig workers provide labor to digital platforms without even noticing it. Thus conceived, the term resonates with notions of uncompensated labor, which has been exploited by capitalist economies from early days on. A case in point is domestic labor, such as housework and childcare, typically provided by women. In the wake of digitalization, the scope of such uncompensated labor has expanded tremendously, from the self-service labor of customers in a grocery shop or of passengers in an airport to leisurely activities of gamers and *YouTubers* all the way to the personal communication of people on social media that has turned into the main source of advertisement income for companies such as *Facebook*. What these all have in common is that they are relegated to the domain of the everyday, as they are considered and institutionalized as non-work activities, such as playing, sharing, childcaring, self-servicing, and so on (Alaimo & Kallinikos, 2016).

The *vita activa* of the everyday, as it were, has become the resource for the sustenance of sociotechnical systems we call platforms, and replaces labor not by machines but by a different kind of labor purposefully kept invisible (Fisher, 2015). For instance, computerized automation does not replace or displace the bank teller with the ATM. Rather, it is the ATM (and, more recently, online banking) that allows the bank customer to re/displace the bank teller, because technology enables bank customers, without any training or skills in banking, to carry on their own transactions (Zwick, 2015). Indeed, the digital platforms of the so-called sharing economy and gig economy have emerged as digitally enabled modes of extracting value not only from overt, waged labor but also from system-sustaining labor, as they tap into the value hidden in informal economies and social life worlds. For instance, *Uber X* is built on the restructuring of labor relations, as it shifts risks to the platform participants. In this setup, the drivers perform overt labor, as they receive payment for their services (Schor & Attwood-Charles, 2017). The digital platform, in turn, increases labor control with software code and algorithmic management techniques. As a result, the platform is capable to also involve the casual participation of the *Uber* riders as labor that contributes to the sustenance of the system, nudging them to rate the performance of the driver and, thus, to control the quality of the service (Rosenblat & Stark, 2016). In other words, the riders, by being users of an easy-to-use, mobile app, replace what used to be the purview of paid middle managers. This and other kinds of hidden, system-sustaining labor, such as generating data for AI applications, including for future self-driving *Uber* cars, are indispensable for the digital platform economy, especially the gig economy, which relies on the labor provided by users "casually participating" on digital platforms to scale their operations and to algorithmically manage millions of transactions.

The new division of labor between humans and machines is based on heteromation—a new logic of capital accumulation, where digital platforms extract value from labor, which is free for the platform owners and naturalized as part of being a platform participant. Viewed in this context, our contribution to this book raises critical questions about current developments under the rubric of digital automation. Some concerns can be traced back to historical developments of converting the *vita activa* of human beings into a standing reserve. In this sense, history repeats itself, as the owners of digital platforms benefit disproportionally more from extracting value from labor. However, we argue that there is also an unprecedented structural shift in the semantics and pragmatics of labor and its social institutions, leading to a new political economy. As we argued in this contribution, the contours of this new political economy are yet to be clearly outlined, and the ways it brings forth digital platforms as the new loci for the exploitation of labor clearly understood.

References

Aaltonen, A., & Kallinikos, J. (2013). Coordination and learning in Wikipedia: Revisiting the dynamics of exploitation and exploration. In M. Holmqvist & A. Spicer (Eds.), *Research in the sociology of organizations* (Vol. 37, pp. 161–192). Bingley, UK: Emerald.

Abbatiello, A., Boehm, T., Schwartz, J., & Chand, S. (2018). No-collar workforce: Humans and machines in one loop—Collaborating in roles and new talent models. In *Tech Trends 2018: The symphonic enterprise* (pp. 24–38). Cambridge, UK: Deloitte Insights.

Alaimo, C., & Kallinikos, J. (2016). Encoding the everyday: The infrastructural apparatus of social data. C. In R. Sugimoto, H. R. Ekbia, & M. Mattioli (Eds.), *Big data is not a monolith* (pp. 77–90). Cambridge, MA: MIT Press.

Alaimo, C., & Kallinikos, J. (2017). Computing the everyday: Social media as data platforms. *The Information Society, 33*(4), 175–191.

Ames, E., & Rosenberg, N. (1965). The progressive division and specialization of industries. *Journal of Development Studies, 1*(4), 363–383.

Arendt, H. (1958). *The human condition*. Chicago, IL: The University of Chicago Press.

Autor, D. H. (2015). Why are there still so many jobs? The history and future of workplace automation. *Journal of Economic Perspectives, 29*(3), 3–30.

Autor, D. H., Levy, F., & Murnane, R. J. (2003). The skill content of recent technological change: An empirical exploration. *The Quarterly Journal of Economics, 118*(4), 1279–1333.

Benkler, Y. (2006). *The wealth of networks. How social production transforms markets and freedom*. New Haven, CT: Yale University Press.

Botsman, R., & Rogers, R. (2011). *What's mine is yours. How collaborative consumption is changing the way we live*. London, UK: Harper Collins.

Boynton, A. C., Victor, B., & Eaker, M. (1992). The post-Fordist transformation: Information technology and organizational change. In *12th international conference on Information Systems*, December 13–16, Dallas, Texas. Atlanta, GA: Association for Information Systems.

Braverman, H. (1974). *Labor and monopoly capital: The degradation of work in the twentieth century*. New York, NY: Monthly Review Press.

Brynjolfsson, E., & Mcafee, A. P. (2014). *The second machine age: Work, progress, and prosperity in a time of brilliant technologies*. New York, NY: W.W. Norton.

Chesbrough, H. W., & Appleyard, M. M. (2007). Open innovation and strategy. *California Management Review, 50*(1), 57–76.

Constantiou, I., Marton, A., & Tuunainen, V. K. (2017). Four models of sharing economy platforms. *MIS Quarterly Executive, 16*(4), 231–251.

Damm, E. A. (2018). *Stor Stigning Stillinger på Mindre end 20 timer om ugen.* Copenhagen, DK: The Economic Council of the Labour Movement.

de Reuver, M., Sorensen, C., & Basole, R. C. (2018). The digital platform: A research agenda. *Journal of Information Technology, 33*(2), 124–135.

Eaton, B., Elaluf-Calderwood, S., Sorensen, C., & Yoo, Y. (2015). Distributed tuning of boundary resources: The case of Apple's iOS service system. *MIS Quarterly, 39*(1), 217–243.

Ekbia, H. R. (2016). Digital inclusion and social exclusion: The political economy of value in a networked world. *The Information Society, 32*(3), 165–175.

Ekbia, H. R., & Nardi, B. A. (2017). *Heteromation, and other stories of computing and capitalism.* Cambridge, MA: MIT Press.

Ekbia, H. R., & Nardi, B. A. (2019). Keynes' grandchildren and Marx's gig workers Why human labor *still* matters. *International Labor Review, 158*(4), 653–676.

Farrell, D., & Greig, F. (2016). *The online platform economy. Has growth peaked?* Washington, DC: JP Morgan Chase & Co Institute.

Fisher, E. (2015). Class struggles in the digital frontier: Audience labour theory and social media users. *Information, Communication & Society, 18*(9), 1108–1122.

Frey, C. B., & Osborne, M. A. (2013). *The future of employment: How susceptible are jobs to computerisation?* Oxford, UK: Oxford Martin Programme on Technology and Employment.

Frey, C. B., & Osborne, M. A. (2017). The future of employment: How susceptible are jobs to computerisation? *Technological Forecasting and Social Change, 114*(1), 254–280.

Garzarelli, G., & Fontanella, F. (2011). Open source software production, spontaneous input, and organizational learning. *American Journal of Economics and Sociology, 70*(4), 928–950.

Garzarelli, G., Limam, Y., & Thomassen, B. (2008). Open source software and economic growth: A classical division of labor perspective. *Information Technology for Development, 14*(2), 116–135.

Gleick, J. (2011). *The information: A history, a theory, a flood.* London, UK: Harper Collins.

Goos, M., & Manning, A. (2007). Lousy and lovely jobs: The rising polarization of work in Britain. *The Review of Economics and Statistics, 89*(1), 118–133.

Greenbaum, J. (1996). Labor is more than work: Using labor analysis to study use situations and jobs. *Scandinavian Journal of Information Systems, 8*(2), 49–62.

Greenhill, A., & Fletcher, G. (2013). Laboring online: Are there 'new' labor processes in virtual game worlds? *Journal of the Association for Information Systems, 14*(11), 672–693.

Heidegger, M. (1977). *The question concerning technology and other essays.* New York, NY: Harper & Row.

Hill, S. (2015). *Raw deal: How the 'Uber Economy' and runaway capitalism are screwing American workers.* New York, NY: St. Martin's Press.

John, N. A. (2012). Sharing and web 2.0: The emergence of a keyword. *New Media & Society, 15*(2), 167–182.

Kalleberg, A. L. (2011). *Good jobs, bad jobs.* New York, NY: Russell Sage Foundation.

Kallinikos, J. (2006). *The consequences of information: Institutional implications of technological change.* Northampton, MA: Edward Elgar.

Kallinikos, J., Aaltonen, A., & Marton, A. (2013). The ambivalent ontology of digital artifacts. *MIS Quarterly, 37*(2), 357–370.

Kallinikos, J., & Tempini, N. (2014). Patient data as medical facts: Social media practices as a foundation for medical knowledge creation. *Information Systems Research, 25*(4), 817–833.

Katz, L. F., & Krueger, A. B. (2016). The rise and nature of alternative work arrangements in the United States, 1995–2015. *Industrial and Labor Relations Review, 72*(2), 382–416.

Katz, L. F., & Margo, R. A. (2014). Technical change and the relative demand for skilled labor: The United States in historical perspective. In L. P. Boustan, C. Frydman, & R. A. Margo (Eds.), *Human capital in history: The American record* (pp. 15–57). Chicago, IL: University of Chicago Press.

Kristal, T. (2013). The capitalist machine: Computerization, workers' power, and the decline in labor's share within U.S. industries. *American Sociological Review, 78*(3), 361–389.

Langlois, R. N. (2002). Cognitive comparative advantage and the organization of work: Lessons from Herbert Simon's vision of the future, *Economics working papers*, 2002-20. Storrs, CT: University of Connecticut. Retrieved from http://digitalcommons.uconn.edu/econ_wpapers/200220

Lanier, J. (2013). *Who owns the future?* New York, NY: Simon & Schuster.

Lehrer, C., Wieneke, A., Brocke, J. V., Jung, R., & Seidel, S. (2018). How big data analytics enables service innovation: Materiality, affordance, and the individualization of service. *Journal of Management Information Systems, 35*(2), 424–460.

Manyika, J., Chui, M., Miremadi, M., Bughin, J., George, K., Willmott, P., et al. (2017). *A future that works: Automation, employment, and productivity*. New York, NY: McKinsey Global Institute.

Manyika, J., Lund, S., Bughin, J., Robinson, K., Mischke, J., & Mahajan, D. (2016). *Independent work: Choice, necessity, and the gig economy*. New York, NY: McKinsey Global Institute.

Marton, A., & Mariátegui, J. C. (2015). De/Contextualizing information: The digitization of video editing practices at the BBC. *The Information Society, 31*(2), 106–120.

Marx, K. (1857–1858). *Grundrisse der Kritik der politischen Ökonomie* [English Translation: Foundations of the critique of political economy]. London: Penguin Books.

Marx, K. (1961). *Karl Marx. Selected writings in sociology and social philosophy*. Harmondsworth, UK: Penguin Books.

Nicolescu, R., Huth, M., Radanliev, P., & De Roure, D. (2018). Mapping the values of IoT. *Journal of Information Technology, 33*(4), 345–360.

Nissen, M. E., & Sengupta, K. (2006). Incorporating software agents into supply chains: Experimental investigation with a procurement task. *MIS Quarterly, 30*(1), 145–166.

Rosenblat, A., & Stark, L. (2016). Algorithmic labor and information asymmetries: A case study of Uber's drivers. *International Journal of Communication, 10*, 3758–3784.

Schmidt, F. A. (2017). *Digital labour markets in the platform economy*. Bonn, Germany: Friedrich-Ebert-Stiftung.

Schor, J. B., & Attwood-Charles, W. (2017). The 'sharing' economy: Labor, inequality, and social connection on for-profit platforms. *Sociology Compass, 11*(8), e12493.

Sennett, R. (2008). *The craftsman*. London, UK: Penguin Books.

Smith, B. C. (2019). *The promise of artificial intelligence: Reckoning and judgement*. Cambridge, MA: MIT Press.

Stabell, C. B., & Fjeldstad, Ø. D. (1998). Configuring value for competitive advantage: On chains, shops, and networks. *Strategic Management Journal, 19*(5), 413–437.

Standing, G. (2016). *The Precariat. The new dangerous class*. London, UK: Bloomsbury.

Tiwana, A. (2014). *Platform ecosystems: Aligning architecture, governance, and strategy*. Waltham, MA: Morgan Kaufmann.
Ulrich, K. (1995). The role of product architecture in the manufacturing firm. *Research Policy, 24*(3), 419–440.
Vallas, S., & Prener, C. (2012). Dualism, job polarization, and the social construction of precarious work. *Work and Occupation, 39*(4), 331–353.
Wallace, M., & Kalleberg, A. (1982). Industrial transformation and the decline of craft: The decomposition of skill in the printing industry, 1931–1978. *American Sociological Review, 47*(3), 307–324.
WEF. (2016). *The future of jobs. Employment, skills and workforce strategy for the fourth industrial revolution* (Global Challenge Insight Report). Geneva: World Economic Forum.
Wright, O. (1997). *Class counts: Comparative studies in class analysis*. Cambridge, UK: Cambridge University Press.
Yoo, Y., Boland, R. J., Lyytinen, K., & Majchrzak, A. (2012). Organizing for innovation in the digitized world. *Organization Science, 23*(5), 1398–1408.
Zuboff, S. (1988). *In the age of the smart machine: The future of work and power*. Oxford, UK: Heinemann Professional.
Zuboff, S. (2019). *The age of surveillance capitalism: The fight for the future at the new frontier of power*. New York, NY: Public Affairs.
Zwick, D. (2015). Defending the right lines of division: Ritzer's prosumer capitalism in the age of commercial customer surveillance and big data. *The Sociological Quarterly, 56*(3), 484–498.
Zysman, J., & Kenney, M. (2018). The next phase in the digital revolution. *Communications of the ACM, 61*(2), 54–63.

3

Social Media as a New Workspace: How Working Out Loud (Re)Materializes Work

Claudine Bonneau, Nada Endrissat, and Viviane Sergi

Introduction

New ways of working exemplify how network technologies have rendered work more virtual and mobile (e.g. Aroles, Mitev, & de Vaujany, 2019). While work can now basically be done anytime, anywhere, it continues to be linked to specific spaces to be carried out, such as the home office or so-called new spaces of work including coworking spaces, fab labs or maker spaces (e.g. de Vaujany, Dandoy, Grandazzi, & Faure, 2018; Salovaara, 2015). However, as we suggest, work is also currently performed in another space that has, up to now, rarely been conceived as a 'workspace', namely social media. Given the relative newness of social

C. Bonneau (✉) • V. Sergi
Université du Québec à Montréal (UQAM), Montreal, QC, Canada
e-mail: bonneau.claudine@uqam.ca; sergi.viviane@uqam.ca

N. Endrissat
Bern University of Applied Sciences, Bern, Switzerland
e-mail: nada.endrissat@bfh.ch

N. Mitev et al. (eds.), *New Ways of Working*, Technology, Work and Globalization,
https://doi.org/10.1007/978-3-030-61687-8_3

media, proposing that these platforms might present similarities with traditional and physical workspaces is a timely project. Despite the fact that many workers spend a lot of time on social media during work and non-work time, social media tends to be seen mostly as a simple communication channel or as a stage for self-presentation, but seldom as a workspace *per se*. Yet, recent studies of online activities suggest that work is not only shown but is actually 'taking place' on social media under different forms. For example, critical studies of digital capitalism have shown that the activities performed by social media end-users—which generate data and content that are monetized by the platforms' owners—constitute new forms of unpaid digital labor (Fuchs, 2014; Scholz, 2012). Management scholars and sociologists of work have also looked into the online labor platform workforce in the context of the 'gig economy' (Casilli & Posada, 2019; Kuhn & Maleki, 2017). Meanwhile, a wide spectrum of new roles has flourished under the label 'social media professionals', which encompass various responsibilities, such as creating and distributing content across platforms, acting as community managers and monitoring content, to name only a few (Duffy & Schwartz, 2018).

Social media has also become a workspace outside the media and marketing industries, for entrepreneurs, freelancers, consultants and artists, who now include online content creation in their daily work practices in addition to their primary work. For instance, they write articles on *LinkedIn*, share stories on *Facebook* and *Twitter*, upload videos on *YouTube* and post images to *Instagram* to maximize their exposure and to present themselves as "hirable" (Gershon, 2016). These changes suggest that social media is more than a communication channel but rather constitutes a new workspace that is voluntarily inhabited by different types of workers, not only in settings where digital interactions are important (such as software developers or marketing professionals) but also by people who are performing more conventional work (e.g. farmers or bakers) that does not necessarily require the use of online tools (Sergi & Bonneau, 2016).

In a context where work and organizations are undergoing significant changes, and where boundaries between work and non-work activities are becoming blurrier (Fleming, 2014; Ollier-Malaterre, Rothbard, & Berg, 2013), social media offer valid and rich entry points into a variety of organizational phenomena (Leonardi & Vaast, 2017). Our study focuses on social media platforms as distinct yet complementary workspaces where people do things related to their work: they develop and test their skills, craft ideas and devise solutions, express and present themselves, share knowledge, think reflexively and experience a full specter of emotions (Sergi & Bonneau, 2016). We hence suggest to explore the idea that these platforms are more than virtual spaces for banal interactions or personal content sharing, but that they fully constitute workspaces where what is done and what is happening can have significant implications for both workers and organizations. But in which ways are social media platforms akin to workspaces? This is the central question that we will explore in this chapter.

To do so, we build on our previous work; this allows us to examine a variety of sociomaterial practices on social media, gathered under the broad label of 'working out loud' (WOL), where individuals voluntarily turn to public social media platforms (such as *Instagram* and *Twitter*) to share what is part of their daily work (Bonneau & Sergi, 2017; Endrissat & Sergi, 2017; Sergi & Bonneau, 2016). These previous studies have led us to uncover a variety of forms the WOL practices can take. At the heart of our inquiry lies the observation that individuals use these sites to share material (thoughts, impressions, experiences, moods, etc.) linked to their personal life, but that they also invest social media to perform activities that are related to their working life. While our previous work has led us to also discuss the performativity of WOL tweets, in this chapter, we move from individual posts to consider in a broader view how we can conceive social media sites in themselves as workspaces.

This chapter is structured in the following way: we begin by describing empirical examples that were collected on *Instagram* and *Twitter* outlining what we can see when we look at workers' working out loud posts. Our inquiry is hence empirically led, as we elaborate our reflection on social media as workspace based on our ongoing analysis of the data collected. We will highlight five dimensions that render visible elements of work and rematerialize, so to speak, elements of workspaces as we know them including (1) the work, (2) the worker, (3) the work process, (4) the experience of work and (5) the work context. This allows us to describe various ways in which social media is integrated in the work of different types of professionals, artists and creative workers, and to examine New Ways of Working featured in that workspace. This presentation is followed by a discussion in which we propose that these work dimensions—including those that are intangible or usually invisible such as the experience of work—are rematerialized through these WOL practices, and that it is by combining them that we can see that social media are more than simple tools used by workers: they constitute workspaces. These observations echo ideas found in the literature on workplace studies, organization studies as well as space design, which have each developed different aspects that characterize workspaces (i.e. their location, properties and constitutive nature). We conclude by presenting a brief research agenda that indicates how these streams could open interesting lines of research and could inform future studies on work practices on social media.

Elements of Method

Since the emergence of sites like *Facebook* and *LinkedIn* in 2003 and 2004, social media have become increasingly integrated into many individuals' everyday habits, and now also span personal and work domains (Boyd & Ellison, 2008; Ollier-Malaterre et al., 2013; Pigg, 2014). These technologies comprise 'Internet-based applications that build on the ideological and technological foundations of Web 2.0, and that allow the creation and exchange of User-generated content' (Kaplan & Haenlein, 2010, p. 62). The term 'social media' thus refers to different types of online platforms, such as social networking sites (SNS), wikis and blogging platforms. Before going further, it is important to distinguish 'enterprise social media platforms' (ESM), which are corporate versions of social media platforms, designed only for internal audiences (Oostervink, Agterberg, & Huysman, 2016) from extra-organizational tools such as public social media (e.g. *Facebook*, *Twitter* and *Instagram*). In our study, we are focusing on the latter in order to see how workers are using the same social media tools that are already integrated in their personal life to perform work activities. Considering these public social media is also relevant as their use is mostly voluntary and not made mandatory by the organization that employs the workers.

Researchers studying social media at work have mostly looked at the interactions and articulation practices these tools afford in the workplace and in virtual teams. Yet, these studies mostly focus on formal aspects of work and how they are supported by social media, such as online collaboration and knowledge creation (Leonardi & Meyer, 2015; Leonardi & Vaast, 2017; Majchrzak, Faraj, Kane, & Azad, 2013). Here, we rather consider public social media as a workspace located 'outside' of the organization, but alongside to it, and open to anyone who chooses to join it, on a voluntary basis.

The reflection we propose in this chapter builds on an inquiry into work-related sharing practices on social media by workers, professionals and artists we have started in 2015. This inquiry has led us to document a new practice, labeled 'working out loud' (hereafter WOL) that we define as a communicative and sociomaterial practice where individuals voluntarily turn to social media platforms to narrate and broadcast what is part of their daily process of work (Sergi & Bonneau, 2016). In this chapter, we are focusing on *Instagram* and *Twitter*, which are social networking sites where users publish short posts combining both visual and textual elements. Our methods rest on a qualitative approach, inspired by digital ethnography (Hine, 2015) and is based on the manual collection of three small corpus of posts between 2014 and 2017: 200 *Twitter* posts from workers and professionals in several domains; 20 social media profiles of artists, mainly mobilizing entries on *Instagram*, but also posts on *Twitter*; and 150 *Instagram* posts from workers and professionals in several domains. Such a 'small/thick data' approach allowed us to capture the specificities of the phenomenon under study, since we explored the "traces in their 'native' format, as they are envisioned by social media users" (Latzko-Toth, Bonneau, & Millette, 2017, p. 204).

On an operational level, we connected to *Instagram* and *Twitter* platforms with our own accounts and manually extracted data from the user interface. We began the data collection with the general aim of documenting the kind of work practices taking place on social media. We began this general data collection process by using the site search engine to find posts using work-related hashtags (e.g. *#work*, *#working*, *#showyourwork*, *#shareyourwork*). Using a snowball sampling approach on the posts we already collected, we were able to find new users through their comments and to find other hashtags describing work contexts (e.g. *#workingforaliving*, *#behindthework*). In order to collect posts in various professional areas, we also performed queries on *Instagram*'s and *Twitter*'s internal search engine after asking ourselves, 'Who would share his or her work and what would he or she say about it?' For example, we searched for domain-related hashtags such as 'nurse', 'firefighter', 'accountant' and so on. All posts collected were captured using a screen capture tool and were documented in a log, along with their date of publication, URL and details about how we found them and field notes. Qualitative textual analysis was used to proceed to a manual thematic coding of each post in an open and inductive manner (Miles, Huberman, & Saldana, 2013). We considered posts as "holistic units, in which images/videos, text, emoji, and hashtags should be interpreted together" (Laestadius, 2017, p. 588). Therefore, our analysis considered the visual and textual elements of posts together, using the descriptions, hashtags and comments to contextualize the pictures. For example, the hashtag *#deadline* adds a temporal context that would not be considered if only images content were analyzed.

Delving into WOL

Having assembled this repertoire of illustrations of the broad WOL practice, we have been able to consider different facets of working out loud. Building on a performative understanding of language, we have first identified the various forms the WOL practice can take on *Twitter*, revealing how these tweets produce actions (such as creating ambient awareness or a cathartic space) that are useful for the continuation of work (Sergi & Bonneau, 2016). Then, our analysis of WOL practices on *Instagram* revealed that the visual, photographic aspect of work-related posts made visible elements linked to the daily accomplishment of work and the mundane side of organizational life (Sergi & Bonneau, 2017). Finally, we focused our attention on artists and creative workers, and found out that their WOL practices revealed specific aspects of the artistic work that are now conducted on social media, such as providing access to the progression of the making, documenting the creation process and sharing incomplete pieces of work (Bonneau, Endrissat, & Sergi, 2018). All this material also lends itself to the inquiry we pursue here, and considering the posts collected allowed us to see how workers actually constitute social media as a workspace.

Figure 3.1 illustrates the type of publications we collected as part of our research.[1] In this example of an *Instagram* post, we see a photo taken during an educational activity taking place in the classroom, which involves the manipulation of LEGO blocks and the use of a videoconferencing platform. The textual description and the hashtags inform us about the objective of this activity ("experimenting distributed collaboration") and the location where it takes place ("UQAM", a university in Montreal). This instance of working out loud on *Instagram* makes the work of a professor visible to people outside her class, and gives access to the context and material aspects of her work activity.

Fig. 3.1 A teacher shows an educational activity taking place in her classroom

[1] As the material we have collected could not be included in this chapter for copyright reasons, we provide this example which was published on *Instagram* by the first author.

When working out loud on social media, we noted that users are presenting their work, revealing themselves as the worker they are, documenting their work processes, sharing their experience of work and describing their work context. Building on our empirical observations, we provide an overview of these five dimensions of work that are made visible through WOL practices on social media (see Table 3.1 for an overview). In the next sub-section, we go through each dimension and illustrate them with examples.[2]

1. Work

Social media offer opportunities in terms of space to present one's work. Workers expose, present or exhibit their results and share their finished work output. For example, a designer of wall banners shows her products ready to be shipped to customers. A farmer shares a picture of his orchard to illustrate the result of his planting efforts. Knowledge professionals and service workers—whose work does not necessarily generate tangible manifestations or material output that can be captured and

Table 3.1 Dimensions of work on social media (authors' own)

Dimensions of work	Description
1. Work	Presenting and exhibiting the work output (product, service, art, performance).
2. Worker	Projecting elements of people at work, such as expertise, identity, managerial style, skills, assets, experiences and relationships.
3. Work process	Providing the recipient access to the process of the making, sharing ideas and knowledge, and giving advice.
4. Experience of work	Showing the meaning of work and particularly how it is experienced by workers, through its affective, expressive, embodied and aesthetic dimensions.
5. Work context	Describing the organizational life and showing the environment in which work unfolds, its spatial and material setup.

[2] We should note that this separation in five categories is more analytical than empirical. Indeed, posts like the examples we are presenting here offer the possibility of combining several of these dimensions.

shared by themselves—can present their work by reporting their achievements. For example, an ethnographer provides a textual account of the milestones completed (fieldwork and interviews), while an accountant posts a picture of her computer screen and describes the finality of what she is doing.

In traditional workspaces such as corporate offices, workers have different opportunities to show their achievements to their peers and managers, for example, during joint work sessions, meetings, formal presentations or informal interactions. Their work might also be visibilized through internal communication channels, such as an Intranet or a newsletter. By showing their work on public social media, workers are not limited to a specified showcase opportunity targeting a predefined audience. They can reach users sharing the same interests, even if they do not know them (or if their profiles are not connected), by using hashtags in their posts. Hashtags, which are commonly used on most social media platforms, is a convention developed by users to self-categorize their posts by adding the '#' sign in front of keywords (e.g. *'#work'*). They affect the visibility of post, as users can access all posts containing the same hashtag by clicking on them. They therefore facilitate the articulation of collective narrative activities on a specific topic, which can lead to open conversations between users sharing the same interests. For example, the hashtags #planting and #farm on a post published by a farmer has the potential to reach a community of farmers outside the boundaries of the user's personal and professional networks, thereby extending the possibility of showing and discussing each other's work results.

As for artists and creative workers, they are not only showcasing their pieces of art or sharing pictures taken during an exhibition or a show but are also performing directly on social media. For example, a performance artist posts a photo of an intervention in the urban public space documenting its performance as it is happening. Similar to the *Instagram* post above where a videoconferencing platform is used while working with the LEGO blocks, in this example, the art performance is not only reproduced on social media afterwards but actually 'taking place' *in parallel* on the street and on social media. This is a good illustration of how social media is not only a stage for self-presentation but actually constitutes a workspace, a space where work is conducted and performed. What seems obvious for people whose work entails a 'performance' aspect, such as video bloggers and cam stars who perform and conduct their work on video platforms, is also true for other workers from various fields. Indeed, when professionals expose their work on social media and ask the crowd for feedback and advice, they are performing aspects of their work on social media.

2. Worker

Working out loud on social media is also about presenting oneself in relation to one's work, either through selfies, pictures of the worker in action, or textual descriptions of expertise, specificities, skills or managerial style. For example, a naval mechanic shares a picture showing himself in his work environment while he is repairing a boat engine. By doing so, he shows sides of him that are rarely seen by others, since his work setting and practices are hardly accessible to anyone besides those who put a foot on this specific boat.

Public social media provide a space to create and express professional identities in more flexible ways than what is possible or permitted in traditional workspaces. Workers deliberately choose what they make visible in order to define themselves as members of specific groups or categories or to identify the distinctive traits that define them at work. For example, the hashtag *#tradergirl* is used by a trader in her posts not only to reflect a professional identity but also to affirm a sense of distinctiveness by categorizing herself as a girl in a male-dominated profession. In other cases, these identity markers are not directly work-related, but are self-used to define the person at work. For example, when a graphic designer presents herself with the hashtag *#workingmom*, she is not only referring to her as a worker but calling forth another facet of the life in relation to work. While considering herself as a working mom might also be expressed in various ways in traditional physical workspaces, social media facilitates this as they allow for representing in an effective and visual way what, specifically, the person wants to showcase about the juxtaposition of identities and roles (e.g. by showing a picture of herself working with her child playing beside her).

Showing oneself at work does not necessarily imply the crafting and promotion of an 'ideal version' of the self. When they are working out loud, workers are also—and often—revealing aspects of themselves that are flawed and publicly displaying moments of failure and self-doubt at work, much like they could do informally with some of their colleagues in traditional workspaces. For example, a teaching assistant shares a selfie showing his discouraged face as he admits, in the comments, that his procrastination has put him in a difficult situation where he is overworked. This practice is particularly pronounced among artists such visual artists, photographers or painters (see e.g. https://vivian-fu.tumblr.com/). Making their imperfections visible on social media can thus be seen as one of the various micro practices through which new subjectivities as artists are enacted (Bonneau et al., 2018).

3. Work Process

Workers also expose their ways of doing things, including the ordinary and ephemeral aspects of their work. They share details about the work as it is unfolding and show sketches, intermediary products, incomplete versions and work in progress. They document the various steps of their work processes and, by doing so, share tacit knowledge and test ideas. For example, a designer shares early versions of sketches of her design, asking her followers/her community for feedback. Workers also reveal their workarounds (see Sachs, 1995) and the little solutions they devise to solve their daily problems. An example of this in our material is the case of an administrative assistant who shows her email interface and explains that she sends messages to herself to remind her of important things.

These posts provide an exclusive access to behind-the-scenes work and informal work processes that are not part of anybody's job description but which are crucial for the achievement of an individual work task. In some cases, the posts even highlight elements central for the collective functioning of the organization. For example, an accountant provides a glimpse into her work process as she explains the various steps of the work of account reconciliation. While traditional workspaces show many traces of work processes such as those sketches or paper piles, social media rematerializes those traces and turns the inside of the workspace outside, thereby extending it to a greater audience and also allowing for new possibilities for the work process to be documented and reassembled, illustrating a new modality of "spacing" organizations across space and time (Vásquez & Cooren, 2013) through the use of social media.

4. Experience of Work

Workers not only document how they work but also how they experience life at work. Hence, social media represent a rich site to explore the subjective and experiential side of work and organizations. This is what we are seeing in the content we are analyzing: part of the workers' subjective experiences at work, as they are seeing it and choosing to expose it.

For example, the fun and informal aspects of work are the social side of the mundane life at work and office humor, such as in an example where an office worker shows how her colleagues decorated her work environment for her birthday. We also get to grasp the aesthetic side of organizations and its atmosphere, which is conveyed through pictures, descriptions, storytelling and contextual hashtags, such as *#havingfunatwork* or *#companyculture*. Other broad hashtags, such as *#accountinglife*, echo the mundanity of work and can also be interpreted as evoking what users associate with their daily experience of work, hence constituting a form of meta-reflection on the post itself.

Through those posts we gain an understanding of the workspace as it is enacted and lived by the employees, providing possibilities to also express forms of resistance or consent to organization-based identities that have been identified in organizational analysis of traditional work spaces (e.g. Wasserman & Frenkel, 2011).

Working out loud is also a way to render explicit the affective and expressive aspects of work including 'how it feels to work here' (e.g. Warren, 2002). We found a great number of expressive posts in which workers verbalize and exteriorize their emotions and feelings, whether positive (e.g. joy and happy moments) or negative (e.g. boredom, stress, anger or sadness). For example, a nurse explains how she felt when she had to put a patient in restraints and the emotional tensions she experienced. As such, social media makes visible elements of work that otherwise remain hidden or are not explicitly addressed. Through working out loud, those elements of work are not only made explicit but are also explicitly 'linked' to the actual workspace and thus might become a topic of open discussion among members of the actual work organization. As such, social media adds an additional space where employees can express their emotional experience of work that, in turn, might lead to changes in the actual work space and culture.

5. Work Context

Workers also describe and show the environment in which work unfolds, its spatial and material setup. They not only reveal the specific materiality associated to different work activities or professions but also how these elements are used, the bricolage that is sometimes needed to complete a task, the gestures and series of actions associated to using these tools. For example, a web developer shows his work environment and tools, consisting of several computer screens used simultaneously and displaying code that he is currently programming.

These posts allow to situate the work activities within the larger context in which they occur and to identify the material, temporal and spatial connections among those activities.

For example, the use of hashtags *#working* and *#Sunday* along with a picture of a bottle of champagne on a work table reinforce the statement made about the temporality of work and the conditions in which work happens. Visualizing this on social media extends the work context into the online space rendering social media into a work context themselves.

Discussion

The empirical example provided in Fig. 3.1 along with the description of other working out loud posts that we find on social media illustrate how social media platforms make possible new hybrid forms of visibilizing and materializing work, combining finished work outputs (product, service, art, performance), the process, context and experience shaping the production of this work and the workers themselves. More precisely, we have shown that social media make visible our five work dimensions (work, worker, work process, experience of work and work context), which include elements that are usually hard to reveal in an explicit or formalized way (such as mundane aspects of work). This is the case because they do not generate tangible manifestations (such as service work), they are related to work activities that would not 'naturally' be visible to the public in the first place (such as backstage work) or they otherwise tend to remain hidden, private or difficult to share in traditional workspaces (such as emotions and inner thoughts). Social media afford aesthetic and expressive functions that can be put to use by workers to visibilize such elements, or present them in a different way, to a different public. The use of visual features, for instance, provides an immediate, multisensory impact (Whiting, Roby, Symon, & Chamakiotis, 2018, p. 193; Endrissat, Islam, & Noppeney, 2016) even for elements that are difficult to verbalize or 'textualize'.

Because "work is, in a sense, always invisible to everyone but its own practitioners" (Nardi & Engeström, 1999), workers 'dramatize' their work in the form of digital texts and images to make it visible (Leonardi, 2014). In that sense, we propose that these dimensions of work are made material or even rematerialized through social media, hence supporting our initial proposal that these platforms are not only a communication tool or a vehicle for branding, but have an active contribution to the accomplishment of work, elevating them to workspaces. More generally, this new way of talking about work and performing work with social media represents, in our view, a new way of working, which comes with new practices (e.g. Aroles, Mitev, & de Vaujany, 2019). For instance, when workers are documenting their achievements on social media, they create a trace of their work in the form of a digital post, which not only materializes the work but also provides an opportunity to reflect on it, get feedback and potentially provide a source of inspiration or help for others who might be facing similar challenges in their work.

Given the properties of social media, such posts also open the door to impromptu conversations with people the workers may or may not know, conversations that in turn can spark further ideas, reflections and action. Even more: unless they are consciously deleted by users, these posts—which often, as we illustrated—capture ephemeral experiences and fleeting moments *and* keep them visible for a longer time than what could be achieved otherwise. Could this help workers think through of what they are doing and understand better the challenges they might be facing, while serving a basis for creating connections? We suggest that this (re) materialization can afford the production of reflective artifacts about work, which can be used by workers to make sense of their work, while also opening these inner reflections to others, outside the boundaries of the formal organization. Hence, these posts not only have an 'attention-generating' or self-promoting function but also allow workers to be more conscious of their own experience and might encourage other users to discuss and also reflect about it, either in the comments directly in the post or using the same hashtags, allowing a form of "reflexive sociability" (Frosh, 2015, cited in Locatelli, 2017).

In the following sections, we will see how these observations echo three key ideas found in the literature on workplace studies, organization studies as well as space design, when it comes to the notion of workspace. As we will discuss, these parallels may help in identifying future avenues for research on social media as workspaces. First, as workplace studies and computer-supported collaborative work studies have highlighted, the workplace is a site where work is performed (location). Then, as studies on the design of workspaces reveal, design dimensions and affordances play a key role in influencing what can happen and what can be done in the workspace, pointing to the importance of the characteristics of the workspace (properties). Finally, we link our findings to processual and sociomaterial approaches to space, which put forth the notion that a workspace is never simply 'out there', as a container in which 'things' happen: rather, space, the people who inhabit it and what they do in it are mutually influencing each other, all the while constituting each other (constitutive nature). By highlighting the links between our findings and these three strands of research, we not only reflect on what constitutes a workspace but also add to this understanding by showing how working out loud practices contribute to the constitution of social media as a workspace.

Social Media as a Site Where Work Is Taking Place (Location)

In the ethnographically informed studies of work, the workplace refers to the physical settings in which work activities 'naturally' occur. For sociologists of work and organizational ethnographers, a workplace is a field site for the study of organizational life and how work is actually accomplished (Strauss, 1985). Hence, the study of a workplace allows the researchers to situate the work activities within the larger context in which they occur and to identify the material, temporal and spatial connections among those activities. If we look more specifically at workplace studies (Heath, Knoblauch, & Luff, 2000; Schmidt, 2000), which build on the ethnographic tradition and involve doing fieldwork within an organization or work practice, the workplace is a localized worksite or a set of worksites in a particular work domain. In the seminal studies that have shaped this field, exemplified by the Lancaster University's interdisciplinary study of air traffic control (Harper, Hughes, & Shapiro, 1989) and the study of the London Underground control room (Heath & Luff, 1992), the workplace is "delimited by situation relevant boundaries, such as physical, technological, organizational, institutional, or geographic borders" (Blomberg & Karasti, 2013, p. 385).

As computer systems have over the years become part of the mundane fabric of work and organizations, the work context became also of interest to ethnographers interested in analyzing the use of technology at work as well as developers who need to take this context into account when designing organizational information systems. From the moment when, in 1984, Irene Greif and Paul Cashman coined the term computer-supported cooperative work (CSCW) to describe the multi-disciplinary discipline involving both the study of cooperative work per se and the construction of systems that can support cooperative work, the work context was always part of the agenda and the research questions. Indeed, the emphasis put on the work context was instrumental to the development of important concepts in CSCW, such as "awareness" (Heath & Luff, 1992), "articulation work" (Schmidt & Bannon, 1992) and "situated action" (Suchman, 1987), to name but a few.

The settings in which early CSCW researchers examined work were not always tied to a single physical place. When studying the operations room of an airline, Suchman (1996) also included other sites for the airline's operations at the main airport, other airlines' territories at this same airport, other airports with which members of the operations room interact, and other related locations. Here, we can note a shift from the 'workplace' to the term 'workspace'. The 'shared workspace' not only refers to the main workplace in its own right but also includes a larger network of environments that constitutes the distributed setting of a specific work activity.

With the advances made on the technological side, physical workspaces now represent only partially the settings in which work occur. Activities are partly or completely conducted in digitally mediated environments (technological platforms, online spaces, mobile device infrastructures, mixed reality environment, etc.). In the computer science (CS) and information systems (IS) literature, the term 'shared workspace' is used to designate computer-based systems that support information sharing and collective work in a group across space and time (Ellis, Gibbs, & Rein, 1991). Hence, a workspace, especially if it involves online components, is not spatially and temporally bounded. It is, by definition, more distributed and open-ended and, therefore, goes beyond the traditional workplace (at home, on the road, in cafes, in coworking spaces, etc.). This reflects the increasingly heterogeneous, distributed, online, mobile, nomadic and networked quality of many work activities conducted these days (e.g. Aroles et al., 2019; Ciolfi & De Carvalho, 2014; Kingma, 2019).

While traditional workspaces might be delimited by physical and geographical boundaries, corporate virtual environments can be delimited by organizational boundaries (when the employer provides the platforms and functionalities to be used by the employees). With public social media, we note that these boundaries tend to become more open and fluid. Hence, social media platforms constitute a site where work happens (and can be studied), like the work settings described in workplace studies and CSCW. As our empirical examples suggest, when workers, professionals and artists share elements related to their work, social media takes on the form similar to "third places" (Oldenburg, 1999) where work and community building takes place that we usually find in the home (first place) or workplace (second place). Understood as third places, we can see that social media provide people to engage in activities they usually do at work, and also offer new potentialities. In the same way that "liminal spaces" allow workers to operate in parallel with more formal organizational spaces (Concannon & Nordberg, 2018), workers can use public social media to momentarily suspend their allegiances to their 'home' organization or to identify with other communities.

Hence, what is shared on social media is not disconnected from the traditional physical workspace: it is positioned as fully complementing that workspace, while allowing other practices, such as connecting with a wider audience that may benefit the work and the worker (something that would not necessarily be possible in a traditional workspace). For that reason, we even posit that the workspace created on social media is not limited to being an extension of traditional/physical workspaces: both workspaces should rather be understood as linked to each other in a dialectic relationship. Working out loud also highlights that workers not only follow officially encouraged New Ways of Working including mobile or telework, but actively take initiative and explore New Ways of Working through social media use thereby shifting part of their work to new workspaces.

However, the boundaries of social media workspaces are more fluid, situating them within a "network composed of fixed and moving points including spaces, people and objects" (Burrell, 2009, p. 189, cited in Marwick, 2014, p. 116). This fluid and networked nature is in part a consequence of social media affordances, which we will discuss in the next section.

Social Media and the Characteristics of Workspaces (Properties)

In spite of the proliferation of non-traditional work arrangements, the literature on spaces and design reminds us that the material properties of workspaces impact the work that is done as well as the experience of work (e.g. Elsbach & Pratt, 2007). Elsbach and Bechky (2007) have presented a framework describing the instrumental, symbolic and aesthetics functions of office design, in order to show which design choices can be made to optimize these functions. For example, they explain how specific room designs (e.g. round, curtained team rooms with rolling white boards and pivoting screen projector screen that can cover entrance way) can be used to optimize not only the instrumental functions of the workspace (i.e. improve decision making, collaboration) but also its symbolic function (i.e. affirm individual distinctiveness, group status) as well as its aesthetics functions (i.e. allows for customized aesthetic experience, inspires place attachment). Hence, the managers responsible for the decisions regarding room design are also defining the functions of a workspace. For instance, architecture and interior forms can be manipulated to facilitate supervision and also to communicate what kind of social activity is appropriate within the workspace (Baldry, 1997). In other words, spatial configurations mediate social relations in specific ways (Dale & Burrell, 2008).

Halford (2004) uses the expression "social landscape" to describe such interplay between space and social relations. For instance, it is easier for workers to sit with friends (or away from managers) in some spatial configurations as opposed to more restrictive ones. Fayard and Weeks (2007) have relied on environmental affordances to show how the way the physical spaces are designed can have a substantial impact on the patterns of informal interaction and communication that occur there. The concept of affordances, drawn from ecological psychology (Gibson, 1979) and later adopted in design studies (Norman, 1988), provides a lens to consider how the material and social characteristics of an environment jointly shape the perceptions and actions of actors. In the same manner, the concept of affordances allows us to grasp the potentialities and constraints of digital space design and functions. Highlighting their relational aspect, Treem and Leonardi (2012) situate affordances as the variable process that mediates between properties of an artifact (features) and what subjects do with the properties of an artifact (outcomes). The perceptibility, accessibility and understandability of an artifact's features vary between subjects and depending on the context of use, creating a range of possible outcomes (Evans, Pearce, Vitak, & Treem, 2017). The concept of "imagined affordances" also captures such variability by considering the ways in which the technology is imagined by its users (Nagy & Neff, 2015).

In the context of social media, affordances are enabled by the functionalities of the platforms, but they are enacted through their situated uses (Bucher & Helmond, 2017). Just like the managers responsible for the decisions regarding office design are also defining the functions of a workspace, the platforms' owners are controlling the functionalities that define the instrumental, symbolic and aesthetics functions of social media as a workspace. However, these functionalities can be shaped and appropriated in a variety of ways by social media users. Treem and Leonardi (2012) identified four affordances of social media that distinguish them from other communication technologies commonly used in organizations: visibility, persistence, editability and association. As we have tried to show in the description of our empirical examples, workers can use the visibility affordance of social media to express their inner thoughts, struggles, reflections and much more. Indeed, social media can provide an emotionally supportive environment where workers can 'blow off steam' and receive support through comments from other users that are not directly involved in their struggles. The higher level of openness and the 'many-to-many' communication patterns inherent to social media platforms put no a priori limits in terms of an audience, which results in a broader reach. Contributions to social media (posts, status updates, comments, etc.) are visible to all who have access to the user's profile, as opposed to email, where the visibility of a message is limited to those to whom the message was addressed.

Working Out Loud Practices on Social Media and the Active Production of the Workspace (Constitutive Nature)

Work practices are not only structured by what would be an 'exterior' workspace: they are also creating the workspace (Dale & Burrell, 2008). In other words, rather than being a 'container' for practices, workspaces are socially produced and constituted through practices. This leads us to the broader notion of space, which is in the backdrop of this reflection on workspaces. To study work and organization from a spatial perspective is of great interest to scholars of organization studies (e.g. Beyes & Holt,

2020; Dale, 2005; Dale & Burrell, 2008, 2010; de Vaujany & Mitev, 2013; Kornberger & Clegg, 2004; Taylor & Spicer, 2007; Van Marrewijk & Yanow, 2010; Vásquez & Cooren, 2013; Wasserman & Frenkel, 2011), who usually conceive of space not as deterministic but as processual and brought into being through social relations (Lefebvre, 1991; Massey, 2005). Accordingly, space does not consist "only of physical structures but is part of the inter-subjective and subjective realms that make up our social relations. And in turn, the physical world made social comes to constitute people through its very materiality" (Dale & Burrell, 2008, p. 1).[3] Hence, examining workspaces implies paying attention to the "relations between lived work practices and the material environments they inhabit" (Suchman, 1996, p. 35). We hence borrow from these studies the general idea that workspaces should not be viewed in fixed terms, but that they are continuously redefined and produced through the interactions that workers have with each other and with their environment co-constituting each other.

Empirical examples of working out loud posts suggest that through the practices of working out loud, five dimensions of work are not only visibilized and made material (or rematerialized) but have an active contribution to the accomplishment of work, at the same time epitomizing a new way of working. If people turn to public social media for a variety of uses, they also use them to talk about their work; even more, what they do on social media is not just about sharing information about their work but also composed of work-related activities 'in themselves'. More generally, this new way of talking about work and performing work with social media represents not only a new way of working but a new social practice that produces and makes up social media as a new workspace. In a time when technology tends to dissolve work and organizations, the practice of working out loud serves as an illustration of what Halford (2005) has termed the re-spatialization of work and organization. Extending her focus from physical places to social media, our argument is that through the use of technology and the practice of working out loud, work gets

[3] See also Dale (2005) and Orlikowski (2007) for the entanglement of the social and the material in "sociomateriality", and Vásquez and Cooren (2013, p. 25) for "space as sociomaterial interrelations".

re-spatialized and rematerialized on social media thereby constituting social media as a new space of work.

Conclusion

By studying what people in work situations are doing on social media, and more specifically, by focusing on practices of working out loud, we have proposed that we can access five key dimension of work including the work, the worker, the work process, the work experience and the work setting. By combining these dimensions, we can consider social media platform not merely as communication tool or vehicle for self-promotion but rather as a genuine workspace where people perform and accomplish their work, exhibit and document their work process, where we learn about the atmosphere and emotional experience of work and the work setting. At the same time, public social media extends the traditional notion of workspace through is specific affordances and fluid boundaries, making the workspaces accessible not only for the people who work there but to a larger audience. They present a degree of informality and openness that might be difficult to find inside the organizational realm, while it might also be sought for by workers, and which might even be becoming even more important in the context of the current intensification of work.

This presents an unprecedented opportunity for research to explore questions of workspace through public social media accounts. For example, building on research that has highlighted the role of workspaces for identity building (e.g. Petriglieri & Petriglieri, 2010), future research could explore the possibilities that social media as workspace provides us an opportunity to try out and experiment with new or different digital identities and professional selves that we might be too shy to express in 'analog' worlds. This is not dissimilar to the literature that has explored the notion of 'online persona' and has discussed how online activity offers the potential to try out and express new identities and personas (Marshall, Moore, & Barbour, 2015). In a similar vein, building on research that has highlighted the role of workspaces on identity regulation and resistance (e.g. Hancock & Spicer, 2011; Wasserman & Frenkel, 2011), research can explore the opportunities of social media for workplace resistance and emancipation, for example, by considering in greater details the ways in which workers narrate and distance themselves from their workspace. As opposed to a traditional workplace, social media as workspace is not a mandatory place but provides the possibilities for new forms of community and emancipatory actions similar to third or liminal places (Shortt, 2015). As such, social media can be seen as a space of potentialities. More actions can emerge, such as opportunities for extra-organizational collaboration and knowledge sharing, as well as new risks and dangers. As the consequences of working out loud are not well documented yet, we invite future research to explore what is achieved through working out loud in the long term. Finally, as in all other workspaces, social media as workspace is prone to questions of power and privilege (Fleming & Spicer, 2014). For example, social media platform providers have repeatedly closed the accounts of artists whose art has been deemed as too provocative, censoring the work and silencing her voice (Lefebvre, 2016). Other examples suggest that social media is not a workspace that enforces equality but instead privileges celebrity accounts over regular accounts (Cath-Speth, 2019).

To conclude, much can be learned about work when we turn to public social media with a qualitative and 'thick data' approach. Although limited in terms of empirical demonstration, our argument has tried to illustrate the ample opportunities opened by considering social media as a workspace, where New Ways of Working are taking place and constituting—as much as they are constituted by—the space in which they are taking place. In a context where work and working may be in transformation, we consider that it is of primordial importance to inquire into the daily experiences and ordinary practices of workers: beneath the surface of their banality, the material shared on social media demonstrates the unfailing inventiveness of workers. While understanding New Ways of Working might be achieved through a variety of research projects, we argue that focusing on practices of working out loud that document work 'in situ' on social media might be one of the most fruitful paths to follow.

References

Aroles, J., Mitev, N., & de Vaujany, F. X. (2019). Mapping themes in the study of new work practices. *New Technology, Work and Employment, 34*(3), 285–299.

Baldry, C. (1997). The social construction of office space. *International Labour Review, 136*(3), 365–378.

Beyes, T., & Holt, R. (2020). The topographical imagination: Space and organization theory. *Organization Theory, 1*, 1–26.

Blomberg, J., & Karasti, H. (2013). Reflections on 25 years of ethnography in CSCW. *Computer Supported Cooperative Work, 22*(4–6), 373–423.

Bonneau, C., Endrissat, N., & Sergi, V. (2018). Imperfect is the new perfect: The documentation of work on social media. In *Standing conference on Organizational Symbolism (SCOS). Theme: Wabi-sabi—Imperfection, Incompleteness and Impermanence in Organizational Life*, Tokyo, Japan, August 19.

Bonneau, C., & Sergi, V. (2017). Work-related image sharing on Instagram : Implication for the understanding of social media affordance of visibility. In P. Kommers (Ed.), *Proceedings of the international conference ICT, Society, and Human Beings 2017* (pp. 226–230). Lisbon, Portugal.

Boyd, D. M., & Ellison, N. B. (2008). Social network sites: Definition, history, and scholarship. *Journal of Computer-Mediated Communication, 13*(1), 210–230.

Bucher, T., & Helmond, A. (2017). The affordances of social media platforms. In J. Burgess, T. Poell, & A. Marwick (Eds.), *The SAGE handbook of social media*. London and New York: Sage Publications.

Casilli, A., & Posada, J. (2019). The Platformization of labor and society. In M. Graham & W. H. Dutton (Eds.), *Society and the Internet; How Networks of information and communication are changing our lives* (2nd ed., pp. 293–307). Oxford: Oxford University Press.

Cath-Speth, C. (2019, February 12). Platform patricians and platform plebs: How social media favours the famous. *New Statesman, NS Tech*, Guest Opinion. Retrieved from https://tech.newstatesman.com/guest-opinion/social-media-celebrities

Ciolfi, L., & De Carvalho, A. F. P. (2014). Work practices, nomadicity and the mediational role of technology. *Computer Supported Cooperative Work: An International Journal, 23*(2), 119–136.

Concannon, M., & Nordberg, D. (2018). Boards strategizing in liminal spaces: Process and practice, formal and informal. *European Management Journal, 36*(1), 71–82.

Dale, K. (2005). Building a social materiality: Spatial and embodied politics in organizational control. *Organization, 12*(5), 649–678.

Dale, K., & Burrell, G. (2008). *The spaces of organisation and the organisation of space: Power, identity and materiality at work*. Basingstoke, UK: Palgrave Macmillan.

Dale, K., & Burrell, G. (2010). 'All together, altogether better': The ideal of 'community' in the spatial reorganization of the workplace. In A. van Marrewijk & D. Yanow (Eds.), *Organizational spaces. Rematerializing the workaday world* (pp. 19–40). Cheltenham, UK: Edward Elgar.

de Vaujany, F.-X., Dandoy, A., Grandazzi, A., & Faure, S. (2018). Experiencing a new place as an atmosphere: A focus on tours of collaborative spaces. *Scandinavian Journal of Management., 35*(2), 101030.

de Vaujany, F. X., & Mitev, N. (2013). Introduction: Space in organizations and sociomateriality. In F. X. de Vaujany & N. Mitev (Eds.), *Materiality and space: Organizations, artefacts and practices* (pp. 1–24). Basingstoke, UK: Palgrave Macmillan.

Duffy, B. E., & Schwartz, B. (2018). Digital 'women's work?': Job recruitment ads and the feminization of social media employment. *New Media & Society, 20*(8), 2972–2989.

Ellis, C. A., Gibbs, S. J., & Rein, G. L. (1991). Groupware: Some issues and experiences. *Communications of the ACM, 34*(1), 35–58.

Elsbach, K. D., & Bechky, B. A. (2007). It's more than a desk: Working smarter through leveraged office design. *California Management Review, 49*(2), 80–102.

Elsbach, K. D., & Pratt, M. G. (2007). The physical environment in organizations. *Academy of Management Annals, 1*(1), 181–224.

Endrissat, N., Islam, G., & Noppeney, C. (2016). Visual organizing: Balancing coordination and creative freedom via mood boards. *Journal of Business Research, 69*(7), 2353–2362.

Endrissat, N., & Sergi, V. (2017). The artist is (hyper)present. Performing and exhibiting cultural work on social media. In *Conference of the CAMEo Research Institute for Cultural and Media Economies: Mediating Cultural Work: Texts, Objects and Politics*, Leicester, UK.

Evans, S. K., Pearce, K. E., Vitak, J., & Treem, J. (2017). Explicating affordances: A conceptual framework for understanding affordances in communication research. *Journal of Computer-Mediated Communication, 22*(1), 35–52.

Fayard, A.-L., & Weeks, J. (2007). Photocopiers and water-coolers: The affordances of informal interaction. *Organization Studies, 28*(5), 605–634.

Fleming, P. (2014). When 'life itself' goes to work: Reviewing shifts in organizational life through the lens of biopower. *Human Relations, 67*(7), 875–901.

Fleming, P., & Spicer, A. (2014). Power in management and organization science. *The Academy of Management Annals, 8*(1), 237–298.

Fuchs, C. (2014). *Digital labour and Karl Marx*. New York and London: Routledge.

Gershon, I. (2016). I'm not a businessman, I'm a business, man' typing the neoliberal self into a branded existence. *HAU: Journal of Ethnographic Theory, 6*(3), 223–246.

Gibson, J. J. (1979). *The ecological approach to visual perception*. Boston, MA: Houghton Mifflin.

Halford, S. (2004). Towards a sociology of organizational space. *Sociological Research Online, 9*(1), 13–28.

Halford, S. (2005). Hybrid workspace: Re-spatialisations of work, organisation and management. *New Technology, Work and Employment, 20*(1), 19–33.

Hancock, P., & Spicer, A. (2011). Academic architecture and the constitution of the new model worker. *Culture and Organization, 17*(2), 91–105.

Harper, R. H. R., Hughes, J. A., & Shapiro, D. Z. (1989). Working in harmony: An examination of computer technology in air traffic control. In *ECSCW'89: Proceedings of the first European conference on Computer Supported Cooperative Work* (pp. 73–86). Gatwick, London.

Heath, C., Knoblauch, H., & Luff, P. (2000). Technology and social interaction: The emergence of workplace studies. *British Journal of Sociology, 51*(2), 299–320.

Heath, C., & Luff, P. (1992). Collaboration and control: Crisis management and multimedia technology in London underground control rooms. *Computer Supported Cooperative Work, 1*(1–2), 69–94.

Hine, C. (2015). *Ethnography for the Internet: Embedded, embodied and everyday*. London: Bloomsbury Publishing.

Kaplan, A. M., & Haenlein, M. (2010). Users of the world, unite! The challenges and opportunities of social media. *Business Horizons, 53*, 59–68.

Kingma, S. (2019). New ways of working (NWW): Work space and cultural change in virtualizing organizations. *Culture and Organization, 25*(5), 383–406.

Kornberger, M., & Clegg, S. R. (2004). Bringing space back in: Organizing the generative building. *Organization Studies, 25*(7), 1095–1114.

Kuhn, K. M., & Maleki, A. (2017). Micro-entrepreneurs, dependent contractors, and instaserfs: Understanding online labor platform workforces. *Academy of Management Perspectives, 31*(2), 183–200.

Laestadius, L. (2017). Instagram. In A. Quan-Haase & L. Sloan (Eds.), *The SAGE handbook of social media research methods* (pp. 573–592). Thousand Oaks, CA: Sage.

Latzko-Toth, G., Bonneau, C., & Millette, M. (2017). Small data, thick data: Thickening strategies for trace-based social media research. In A. Quan-Haase & L. Sloan (Eds.), *The SAGE handbook of social media research methods* (pp. 199–214). Thousand Oaks, CA: Sage.

Lefebvre, H. (1991). *The production of space*. Oxford, UK: Blackwell.

Lefebvre, S. (2016, March 10). Forbidden fruit: Why provocative art and Instagram don't mix. *The Guardian*. Retrieved from https://www.theguardian.com/artanddesign/2016/mar/10/stephanie-sarley-provocative-art-instagram-blood-oranges-feminism-sexuality

Leonardi, P. M. (2014). Social media, knowledge sharing and innovation: Toward a theory of communication visibility. *Information Systems Research, 25*(4), 796–816.

Leonardi, P. M., & Meyer, S. R. (2015). Social media as social lubricant: How ambient awareness eases knowledge transfer. *American Behavioral Scientist, 59*(1), 10–34.

Leonardi, P. M., & Vaast, E. (2017). Social media and their affordances for organizing: A review and agenda for research. *The Academy of Management Annals, 11*(1), 150–188.

Locatelli, E. (2017). Images of breastfeeding on Instagram: Self-representation. *Social Media and Society, 3*(2), 1–14.

Majchrzak, A., Faraj, S., Kane, G. C., & Azad, B. (2013). The contradictory influence of social media affordances on online communal knowledge sharing. *Journal of Computer-Mediated Communication, 19*(1), 38–55.

Marshall, D. P., Moore, C., & Barbour, K. (2015). Persona as method: Exploring celebrity and the public self through persona studies. *Celebrity Studies, 6*(3), 288–305.

Marwick, A. E. (2014). Ethnographic and qualitative research on Twitter. In K. Weller, A. Bruns, J. Burgess, M. Mahrt, & C. Puschmann (Eds.), *Twitter and society* (pp. 109–122). New York: Peter Lang.

Massey, D. (2005). *For Space*. Thousand Oaks, CA: Sage.

Miles, M. B., Huberman, A. M., & Saldana, J. (2013). *Qualitative data analysis: A methods sourcebook*. Thousand Oaks, CA: Sage Publications.

Nagy, P., & Neff, G. (2015). Imagined affordance: Reconstructing a keyword for communication theory. *Social Media + Society*, *1*(2), 2056305115603385.

Nardi, B. A., & Engeström, Y. (1999). A web on the wind: The structure of invisible work. *Computer Supported Cooperative Work, 8*(1), 1–8.

Norman, D. A. (1988). *The psychology of everyday things*. New York: Basic Books.

Oldenburg, R. (1999). *The great good place: Cafes, coffee shops, bookstores, bars, hair salons, and other hangouts at the heart of a community*. Boston, MA: Da Capo Press.

Ollier-Malaterre, A., Rothbard, N. P., & Berg, J. M. (2013). When worlds collide in cyberspace: How boundary work in online social networks impacts professional relationships. *Academy of Management Review, 38*(4), 645–669.

Oostervink, N., Agterberg, M., & Huysman, M. (2016). Enterprise social media: Practices to cope with institutional complexity. *Journal of Computed-Mediated Communication, 21*(2), 156–176.

Orlikowski, W. J. (2007). Sociomaterial practices: Exploring technology at work. *Organization Studies, 28*(9), 1435–1448.

Petriglieri, G., & Petriglieri, J. L. (2010). Identity workspaces: The case of business schools. *Of Management Learning & Education, 9*(1), 44–60.

Pigg, S. (2014). Coordinating constant invention: Social media's role in distributed work. *Technical Communication Quarterly, 23*, 69–87.

Sachs, P. (1995). Transforming work: Collaboration, learning, and design. *Communications of the ACM, 38*(9), 36–44.

Salovaara, P. (2015). What can the coworking movement tell us about the future of workplaces. In *Leadership in spaces and places* (pp. 27–48). Cheltenham, UK: Edward Elgar Publishing.

Schmidt, K. (2000). The critical role of workplace studies in CSCW. In P. Luff, J. Hindmarsh, & C. Heath (Eds.), *Workplace studies: Rediscovering work practice and informing design* (pp. 141–149). Cambridge, UK: Cambridge University Press.

Schmidt, K., & Bannon, L. (1992). Taking CSCW seriously: Supporting articulation work. *Computer Supported Cooperative Work, 1*(1), 1–33.

Scholz, T. (2012). *Digital labor: The Internet as playground and factory*. London and New York: Routledge.

Sergi, V., & Bonneau, C. (2016). Making mundane work visible on social media: A CCO investigation of working out loud on Twitter. *Communication Research and Practice, 2*(3), 378–406.

Sergi, V., & Bonneau, C. (2017). As I see life at work: Sharing work experiences on social media. In *33rd EGOS Colloquium, Sub-theme 61: Viewing the Unseen Organization in Practice*, Copenhagen, Denmark.

Shortt, H. (2015). Liminality, space and the importance of 'transitory dwelling places' at work. *Human Relations, 68*, 633–658.

Strauss, A. (1985). Work and the division of labour. *Sociological Quarterly, 26*(1), 1–19.

Suchman, L. (1987). *Plans and situated actions: The problem of human-machine communication*. Cambridge, UK: Cambridge University Press.

Suchman, L. (1996). Constituting shared workspaces. In Y. Engeström & D. Middleton (Eds.), *Cognition and communication at work* (pp. 35–60). Cambridge, UK: Cambridge University Press.

Taylor, S., & Spicer, A. (2007). Time for space: A narrative review of research on organizational spaces. *International Journal of Management Reviews, 9*(4), 325–346.

Treem, J. W., & Leonardi, P. M. (2012). Social media use in organizations: Exploring the affordances of visibility, editability, persistence, and association. *Communication Yearbook, 36*, 143–189.

Van Marrewijk, A., & Yanow, D. (2010). Introduction. The spatial turn in organizational studies. In A. Van Marrewijk & D. Yanow (Eds.), *Organizational spaces. Rematerializing the workaday world* (pp. 1–16). Cheltenham, UK: Edward Elgar.

Vásquez, C., & Cooren, F. (2013). Spacing practices: The communicative configuration of organizing through space-times. *Communication Theory, 23*(1), 25–47.

Warren, S. (2002). Show me how it feels to work here: Using photography to research organizational aesthetics. *ephemera, 2*(3), 224–245.

Wasserman, V., & Frenkel, M. (2011). Organizational aesthetics: Caught between identity regulation and culture jamming. *Organization Science, 22*(2), 503–521.

Whiting, R., Roby, H., Symon, G., & Chamakiotis, P. (2018). Participant-led video-diaries. In A. Bryman & D. A. Buchanan (Eds.), *Unconventional methodology in organization and management research*. Oxford: Oxford University Press.

4

Institutionalizing Crowdwork as a Mode of Employment: The Case of Crowdworkers in Nigeria

Ayomikun Idowu and Amany Elbanna

Introduction

Crowdwork is a new form of work and employment that has recently been identified as holding potential to reduce the rising unemployment in both developing and developed countries (Forde et al., 2017; ILO, 2018; Kuek et al., 2015). It presents a digital platform-mediated model for the sourcing of work from a large number of defined or undefined individuals. Based on one type of the crowdsourcing model, it involved paid work with financial remuneration exchanged in full over digital platforms. From the employers' perspective, crowdwork provides a functional task-oriented sourcing of labor and access to a global pool of highly

A. Idowu (✉)
University of Sussex Business School, Brighton, UK
e-mail: A.IDOWU@SUSSEX.AC.UK

A. Elbanna
Royal Holloway, University of London, London, UK
e-mail: AMANY.ELBANNA@RHUL.AC.UK

N. Mitev et al. (eds.), *New Ways of Working*, Technology, Work and Globalization,
https://doi.org/10.1007/978-3-030-61687-8_4

skilled workers with low organizational, legal and employment commitment (Boudreau & Lakhani, 2016; Ford, Richard, & Ciuchta, 2015). While it is a temporary model of sourcing tasks, recent surveys and studies show that it is rising in popularity and is being adopted by workers as a form of full-time, long-term employment.

While it is difficult to determine the number of individuals adopting this form of employment, different surveys have highlighted the exponential growth of crowdwork in both the developed and developing worlds (Berg, 2015; Dølvik & Jesnes, 2018; Huws, Spencer, & Joyce, 2016; ILO, 2018). From a societal perspective, the global reach of digital work platforms and the rapid adoption of crowdwork have led national and international organizations, such as the International Labor Organization, European Parliament and the World Bank, to recently consider it a new form of work (Forde et al., 2017; ILO, 2018; Kuek et al., 2015). Indeed, governments and policy makers, in both developed and developing countries, embraced it as a unique source of employment that breaks geographical boundaries and provides workers with an open and immediate access to the global employment market and hence provides a novel solution to reduce problems of unemployment, particularly in developing countries (Barnes, Green, & de Hoyos, 2015; Kuek et al., 2015; Leimeister, Zogaj, & Durward, 2016; Zakariah, Janom, & Arshad, 2016).

While the high level of adoption of crowdwork might help to reduce the enduring problem of unemployment in developing countries, the sustainability of this adoption, as a long-term source of employment, needs critical examination for theoretical and practical reasons. First, previous research into technology innovation and adoption has highlighted that the availability and initial adoption does not unproblematically translate into sustainable use (Avgerou & Li, 2013; Walsham & Sahay, 2006). Indeed, research has shown that sustainability does not necessarily accompany technology adoption and many technologies are adopted and abandoned even when it allows business and individuals to partake in global business networks (Kenny, 2006). Second, there seems to be a contradiction between the nature of the temporary assignments offered to crowdworkers on digital platforms and the proposition that it could serve as a long-term mode of employment for workers. Third, the current thinking of crowdwork as a global model of employment on global digital platforms seems to suggest the irrelevance of local settings. This opposes the research that highlights the importance of local context in technology adoption and use in general and the challenge of making a technology work in practice, overtime and in local settings (Braa, Monteiro, & Sahay, 2004), particularly in developing countries (Avgerou & Walsham, 2018). Indeed, previous research has highlighted the efforts it takes to adopt and adapt technology in local contexts and achieve institutionalized use that persists over time (Braa et al., 2004).

This study aims to explore the lived experiences of crowdworkers in order to examine their shared practices in achieving long-term crowdwork. We adopted an inductive research approach and collected rich data from different sources including interviews, participant observations, social media monitoring and platform observations. Data collection took place in Nigeria, which is one of the largest countries in Africa with a significantly high unemployment rate (over 40%) and where crowdwork is promoted by government and international donors as a source of employment. Examining crowdwork in Nigeria can enhance our understanding of crowdworkers' experience and their practices in a developing country context where unemployment rates are alarmingly high and there is a significant need for new employment models. It could serve as an exemplary and revelatory case study (Darke, Shanks, & Broadbent, 1998; Patton, 1990) that could shed light on crowdwork in Africa and the developing world where there is a dearth of studies on New Ways of Working (Graham, Hjorth, & Lehdonvirta, 2017).

This study reveals that working on global digital platforms—while having a global reach—does not neutralize the impact of the local setting surrounding crowdworkers. Importantly, it shows the work crowdworkers do for crowdwork to become a long-term mode of employment. We identify five interconnected social and material strategies that crowdworkers adopt, namely assembling diverse digital workplace, self-provision and co-production of infrastructure, piecing financial systems, achieving digital legitimacy and integrating traditional business norms into digital work.

By adopting the perspective of crowdworkers and examining a case taking place in developing country, this study contributes to the literature in three ways. First, it enriches the literature on crowdwork by offering a much-needed, in-depth view on how crowdworkers, through their practices, make a long-term living from crowdwork. This addresses scholarly calls for the examination of workers' perspective and experience of employment in the digital economy, especially in developing countries (Graham et al., 2017). Second, it proposed a novel understanding of long-term crowdwork as the creation of proto-institution and empirically demonstrates its dimensions and processes. It shows that crowdwork is socially and materially constructed and is context specific. This finding advances the conceptual development of crowdwork as a new mode of employment. This is important as work is a core activity in society and plays an important social, economic and psychological role in everyday lives and is a significant determinant of mental health and wellbeing (Cole, 2007). Accordingly, understanding crowdworkers' experience provides important insight for international funders and policy makers. Third, the study also contributes to the literature on institutional work. We extend this literature to a new setting for work that is mediated by digital platforms and occurs beyond the traditional and formal boundaries of organizations. As we examine a new digital work setting, our study provides an empirically supported examination of the creation of a new institution that is not necessarily disruptive but rather complementary and sometimes helps maneuvering around existing institutional arrangement.

The chapter is organized into seven sections. Following the introduction, the second section discusses the crowdsourcing literature and its existing bias toward the employer's perspective, which leaves a gap in our understanding of crowdsourcing work. The third section presents the theoretical lens for this research while the fourth one outlines the research methodology including the research context, data collection and data analysis. The fifth section presents the research findings in terms of the social and material strategies that crowdworkers employ to sustain their employment on digital platforms. The sixth section discusses the finding and the contribution of this research. The final section concludes the chapter.

Crowdsourcing and Crowdworkers

Crowdsourcing is a new form of digital labor that harnesses input from large-scale decentralized contributors through open calls (Brabham, 2008; Morris, McDuff, & Calvo, 2014). Regarding remuneration, the crowds could be compensated through tangible monetary payment or intangible means (Howe, 2006). Crowdwork is one type of crowdsourcing where employment occurs on digital platforms and workers exchange digital work for agreed financial payment. Crowdwork tasks can be classified as micro tasks and macro tasks (Ikediego, Ilkan, Abubakar, & Bekun, 2018). Micro tasks are small, repetitive tasks requiring very limited skills to complete while macro tasks take more time to complete, require domain specific skills and are highly remunerated in comparison to micro tasks.

Crowdwork is based on flexible, short-term, casual labor where workers are not in permanent employment with any particular employer or digital platform. Hence, it is argued that there is little employment security, steady income stream and legal protection for workers (Aloisi, 2016). In this regard, it has created a controversy in the public and the research domain. Authors point to the power imbalance between employers and workers arguing that exploitation might occur as workers have little or no bargaining power, which enables employers to exploit them by paying them the legal minimum for the tasks they complete (Berg, 2015; Fuchs, 2013). Other authors argue that crowdwork empowers workers with flexibility and autonomy to work anytime and anywhere (Deng, Joshi, & Galliers, 2016; Sánchez, Gimilio, & Altamirano, 2015; Zyskowski, Morris, Bigham, Gray, & Kane, 2015).

Crowdwork research is lacking empirical research and conceptual development (Howcroft & Bergvall-Kåreborn, 2018; Wood, Graham, Lehdonvirta, & Hjorth, 2019; Zhao & Zhu, 2014). Indeed, studies that examine crowdworkers and how they organize this type of digital work remain scant (Barnes et al., 2015; Heeks, 2017; Howcroft & Bergvall-Kåreborn, 2018). Hence, there is little understanding of the dynamics of crowdwork as a new form of employment. Research has yet to understand how crowdworkers experience work on digital platforms and how they organize their working lives when adopting it as a mode of employment, in particular as a long-term employment.

While it is believed to hold potential for developing countries to open up global labor market and increase employment opportunities, little research has been conducted in this context. Crowdworking research in developing countries has also been limited to largely involving theoretical discussions and hypothetical propositions lacking empirical studies. However, authors continue to advance the hypothetical argument that the increased access to computers, smartphones and the Internet in the developing world would straightforwardly increase the adoption of different crowdsourcing types, including crowdwork (Gillwald, Mothobi, & Schoentgen, 2017). They also argue that crowdwork has the potential to be an important alternative source of employment for individuals in developing countries (Lehdonvirta & Ernkvist, 2011; Taeihagh, 2017). There is a need for in-depth understanding of how crowdworkers in developing countries organize their work and life to make crowdwork a source of long-term employment if we take crowdwork seriously as a possible source of employment and a way to reduce their alarmingly high unemployment burden.

Research Methods

Research Setting

Data collection took place in Nigeria. Nigeria is the most populous country and largest economy in Africa with a population of more than 190 million individuals (Nakpodia, Adegbite, Amaeshi, & Owolabi, 2018; National Bureau of Statistics, 2017). The country has over 40% unemployment or underemployment among population of the working age (National Bureau of Statistics, 2017) with little hope of finding a decent paying job in a formal sector that is commensurate with their education (Adekola, Allen, Olawole-Isaac, Akanbi, & Adewumi, 2017; Olotu, Salami, & Akeremale, 2015). Nigeria is estimated to have 150 million mobile phone users and 98.3 million active Internet users (Nigerian

Communication Commission, 2018). Considering its large population, high percentage of unemployment, proliferation of mobile use and the availability of Internet, Nigeria presents a relevant and important context for research on crowdwork in a developing country. Examining crowdwork in Nigeria helps flesh out its employment potential in a developing country context, which could inform the current debate in this regard.

Research Approach and Data Collection

We adopted an inductive interpretive approach that aims to "piece together people's words, observations and documents into a coherent picture expressed through the voices of the participants" (Trauth & Jessup, 2000, p. 54). Data were collected from a variety of sources including interviews, website reviews, observations and informal conversations, open online blogs, social media groups and online discussion threads. Regarding interviews, 38 in-depth (some unstructured and others semi-structured) interviews were conducted with 35 participants. The first interviews were followed by a number of follow-up interviews to clarify and extend upon ideas. The participants comprised 23 male and 12 females aged between 22 and 46 years.

The participants of the study were selected through purposeful sampling. Purposeful sampling is based on selecting participants based on the particular characteristics and objectives of the study and is widely used in qualitative research (Guetterman, 2015). The inclusion criteria of the participants were based on (1) being involved in crowdsourcing activities for a minimum of two years and (2) being engaged in paid macro-crowdwork as full-time employment and main source of income. These criteria were important in ensuring that participants have enough experience of crowdsourcing and they are knowledgeable enough to provide reliable account of its stability as an employment mode (Hodkinson, 2008).

The interviews were open-ended allowing for divergence and spontaneity with questions arising from conversations with the respondents. This provided an opportunity to gather and explore the life experience of participants and allow new discoveries to emerge (Guetterman, 2015). Familiarity of one of the authors with the context of Nigeria helped in creating a repertoire with interviewees and increasing the participants' confidence, openness and trust (Myers, 2013; Myers & Newman, 2007). This facilitated the expression of candid views, which enhanced the richness and quality of the collected data (Myers, 2013). The interviews were conducted through Skype voice call, in English, which is the official language of Nigeria. All interviews were digitally recorded and transcribed verbatim.

The data collection was carried out in three phases. The pilot phase was carried out between December 2017 and January 2018 with a total of six participants interviewed. The pilot study was helpful as the participants were responsive, reflective and articulate in expressing their ideas. This helped gaining an initial understanding of crowdsourcing in Nigeria and developing the research design. The second and third stages were carried out between June 2018–August 2018 and October–November 2018 with respectively 18 and 12 in-depth semi-structured interviews.

Interview questions and conversations during the two phases were focused on gaining a clear understanding of their social and work practices, behavior, perception of self, the activities they engage in, how and why they engage in these practices. We also asked questions about their feeling and aspirations. Interviews lasted between 50 and 120 minutes with an average of 75 minutes, while follow-up interviews lasted between 15 and 30 minutes. According to Charmaz (2006), critical issues and ideas might emerge during subsequent interviews and therefore the interviewers can make a step toward pursuing these leads. In this case, further interviews were conducted with three interviewees alongside various email exchanges with several interviewees to get insight and clarifications into issues that were not discussed and/or were not clear in the first interviews.

Informal visits and observations of crowdworkers in their workspace were conducted. Rich data were collected as we were "given free rein to observe whatever [we] like" (Myers, 2013, 140) and ask questions. Observations of crowdworkers in their natural setting (workplace) allowed physical confirmation and documentation of the set-up of their workspace, how they organize their work, their routine and relationship with other workers. The conversations we had during the observations were about their day-to-day routines, the challenges they encounter, the disposition to their work, the effect of the work on their lives, their experiences with employers on the platforms, their workspace, how they bid for work online and manage their work, the management of their time, objects in their work environment and their attitude to crowdwork. Visiting the workplace of crowdworkers was essential in providing insight and details of their working environment and has informed the examination of their need to create a physical workplace to supplement their digital work and provide a socially accepted façade for their digital platform work. The data from the interviews were supplemented and triangulated with data gathered from open online blogs, social media groups and online discussion threads in addition to examining the participants' profiles on crowdsourcing websites.

Data Analysis

After each interview, the respondents were given pseudonyms to protect their identity. Our analysis followed the inductive and thematic approach that aims to allow data to speak for itself while constantly organizing them into themes. This is consistent with the guidelines of conducting interpretive case study research (Klein & Myers, 1999; Walsham, 1995, 2006).

Our initial data analysis involved an open and inductive coding approach (Hodkinson, 2008; Vaast & Walsham, 2011). Codes and themes were developed through reflecting on the content of the interviews, explicitly guided by participants' quotes from the interview (Braun & Clarke, 2006; Braun, Clarke, & Terry, 2014) and triangulated with other sources of data to enhance theoretical validity (Venkatesh, Brown, & Bala, 2013). These were discussed between the research team and agreed upon in order to improve internal validity (Feagin, Orum, & Sjoberg, 1991). This allowed us to discover the amount of work the crowdworkers do on and off the digital platform that make their temporary work rather stable. Informed by the lens of institutional work, we organized the emerging codes into five themes that make the sub-sections in the analysis section of this chapter. The research findings elaborate on these themes and the involved categories by including sample quotes that add rich insight into the experience of crowdworkers (Koch, Leidner, & Gonzalez, 2013). To assess our research approach, we relied on Klein and Myers' (1999) principles of interpretive research, which have become the standard for evaluating interpretive case study in IS research.

The Creation of an Institution

To present our findings, we first provide in this section an overview of the theoretical concepts that our analysis resonates with. This is related to institutional creation and institutional work.

Institutions are "multi-faceted, durable, social structures, made up of symbolic elements, social activities, and material resources" (Scott, 2001, p. 49). Institutions exist within and across formal organizations and in society. They are commonly understood as taken-for granted and enduring social patterns that could go through periods of stability and change (Zietsma & Lawrence, 2010). Institutional theorists identified institutional carriers that endure stability, including norms and symbols, routines, rules, standards and material objects (Mayernik, 2016). While traditional institutional theorists have explained change as an exogenous force that disturbs the reproduction of institutions, a stream of research in organization studies has embraced agency and the effort required to create, disrupt or stabilize institutions. This stream focuses on actors' work to create, maintain or disrupt institutions in what is termed institutional work (Lawrence, Leca, & Zilber, 2013; Lawrence, Suddaby, & Leca, 2011). Institutional work is defined as "the purposive action of individuals and organizations aimed at creating, maintaining and disrupting institutions" (Lawrence & Suddaby, 2006). It presents the "enabling work" that allows actors to create stability in their work environment (Dacin, Goodstein, & Scott, 2002; Lawrence et al., 2013). In this regard, actors play a central role as producers and carriers of institutions (Zilber, 2002). The term "institutional work" also reflects a connotative connection between work and effort where "the notion of work connects effort to a goal, and thus institutional work can be understood as a physical or mental effort done in order to achieve an effect on an institution or institutions" (Lawrence, Suddaby, & Leca, 2009, p. 15).

The notion of institutional work shifts the research attention from the stability implied in the organization to the work done to create, maintain and disrupt institutions and the activities enacted everyday by individuals (Lawrence & Suddaby, 2006). In this regard, institutional work is situated as actors reflexively engage with institutions that surround them in order to gain or sustain legitimacy (Lawrence et al., 2011). The subjective meanings individual actors derive from their institutional environment have a significant impact on the institutional work they engage in (Zilber, 2002).

The primary goal of research in institutional work is to develop a situated, inductive, empirically grounded understanding of the effort, activities and strategies that people employ to affect any of the three broad categories of institutional work, namely creating, maintaining or disrupting institution (Lawrence et al., 2009; Lawrence & Suddaby, 2006). The occurrence of institutional work is facilitated by various mechanisms. Suddaby and Viale (2011) provide four mechanisms through which institutional work occurs: (1) actors use their legitimacy and expertise to confront incumbent institutional arrangements and to introduce new ones; (2) actors take advantage of their skill and social capital to recruit new actors and introduce new identities; (3) actors redraw boundaries of their field by introducing new rules and standards; and (4) actors create a new social order in their field by reproducing social capital.

Studying the creation of institutions through the lens of institutional work allows focusing on understanding "actors who attempt to create new institutions, the conditions under which they do so, and the strategies they employ" (Lawrence et al., 2009, p. 8). So, the focus is on "why, how, when, and where actors *work at creating* institutions" (ibid., p. 10). Indeed, it shifts scholarly attention to the activities of actors in creating new practices and institutions (Greenwood, Suddaby, & Hinings, 2002) and the origin, emergence and creation of new practices in institutional arrangements (Lounsbury & Crumley, 2007; Scott, 2001).

New institutions arise when organized actors with sufficient resources see an opportunity to realize interests that they highly value (DiMaggio, 1988). The creation of institutions has been achieved in cases when members of society justify the need of a particular institution and the role it plays to fulfill their need (Farny, Kibler, & Down, 2018). Institutions can also be created through layering, which involves the creation of new institutions on top and alongside structures of existing institutions (Mahoney & Thelen, 2010, pp. 15–16). An institution created through this means however retains the characteristics, rules and norms of the former institution (Gains & Lowndes, 2014). Streeck and Thelen (2005) reveal how new institutions are created when institutional actors engage in political contestation with dominant powers and boundaries of existing institutional arrangement. Farrell and Héritier (2003) also revealed how change in formal institution can give rise to the creation of informal institutions.

The Institutionalization of Crowdwork

This section describes the institutional work undertaken by crowdworkers in Nigeria to construct crowdwork as a proto-institution. It reveals the strategies they undertake to create crowdwork as a semi-stable, long-term employment. These strategies include assembling diverse digital workplaces, self-provision and co-production of communication infrastructure, piecing together financial systems from available technology, achieving digital legitimacy and adopting traditional business norms in managing customers' relations. These strategies are highly interlinked and are presented and discussed below in a separate format for analytical clarity and presentation convenience.

Assembling Diverse Digital Workplaces

In order to improve their chances to sustain work, crowdworkers subscribe to different digital platforms for crowdwork. They do so in order to broaden their opportunity to find employers. In this regard, they create several accounts in different digital platforms. They also orientate their profile in each platform to what they believe suits the employers base of each platform and the types of tasks that are typically posted on that platform. In addition, they also create different accounts on the same digital platform to project different profiles and set of skills. They also subscribe to different access points for the same platforms and/or use different platforms that have different access points (i.e. web and mobile). This means that they need to navigate through a number of different digital work settings, digital design environments, payment protocols, interacting with different platform algorithms and employers. Respondents revealed that it is not unusual for crowdworkers to juggle between several jobs on multiple platforms simultaneously in an effort to earn sustainable income. They do this while considering the platform algorithm and how each platform matches employees to tasks. In this regard, they separate their skills across profiles and platforms in order to get better matches to employers and tasks and hence improve their chances to get more work and sustain their employment. This was explained vividly by Fred, a crowdworker for five years:

> *I do my work across three accounts… have two accounts on (platform) and one on (Second platform). One is for my main software work, I've had it for over 5 years….the second one is for Writing task, I have good ratings on both profiles but I try to specialize a profile for a certain type of task, it's easier when you build your profile based on a specific skill. I use the (second Platform) because job post there are mainly for design, so I use it to get design Jobs…This work involves juggling across different platforms and tools, for example I use the sites, mobile apps… there are lots of environment I have to work in at the same time, that's the work.*

While juggling between digital platforms, crowdworkers also learn when to use each platform; by understanding in which digital platform they have higher chances of getting work on, they make themselves available on these platforms more frequently and while others are supplementary. Aisha, a crowdworker for two years explains that she uses four platforms as follows:

> *I have profile on Four platforms, I have a profile on Fiverr,* Freelancer.com, *Upwork and Crowdflower. I am active on all four; freelancer and Fiverr are my main ones, they're always open on my laptop and phone. Upwork and Crowdflower, I use about three days a week.*

Self-Provision and Co-Production of Communication Infrastructure

Nigeria has problems with the distribution and availability of electrical power and insufficient power supply (USAID, 2018). Power blackouts are not uncommon and can last for days and sometimes months. For example, in January 2018, the entire country had a power outage (Olawoyin, 2018) and, in June 2018, all nation's power plants collapsed causing another blackout in the country (Cox, 2018). To overcome this limitation, crowdworkers generate their own electricity through the purchase of electrical generators, inverters and solar panels.

Another common problem in Nigeria with regards to Internet is its availability. A number of Internet service providers (ISPs) have reasonable plans for power supply backup, but this does not ensure that there is always Internet connectivity, which results in interrupting crowdwork. Also, subscribers are usually not informed about scheduled maintenance plans which can leave them without Internet access for an unknown period of time. Crowdworkers typically only discover that they are without Internet connection when they try to access the Internet for work.

In order to ensure uninterrupted connectivity, workers subscribe simultaneously to multiple Internet Service Providers (ISPs) in order to alternate between them in case there is a problem with one. Emeka, crowdworker for five years explained:

> *Right now, I have subscription to three Internet networks so that I can easily continue with my work by switching between the Internet networks in case one of the networks has a problem, I have the second one to fall back on…this happens a lot (Emeka, five years).*

Piecing Together Financial Systems from Available Technologies

Crowdworkers in Nigeria experience problems transferring income earned in foreign currencies on digital platforms to their local bank accounts. Ideally platforms provide facilities through popular payment options like *PayPal*, bank transfers and *Skrill* to enable workers access to their earnings. But due to financial restrictions by *PayPal*, banks and financial services like *Visa* and *MasterCard* on accounts registered in Nigeria (Counted & Arawole, 2015; Efobi, Beecroft, & Osabuohien, 2014), workers are not able to transfer earnings into their local bank accounts. This resulted in the creation of alternative payment and transaction methods. These methods include using multiple *PayPal* accounts and using virtual debit/credit cards through *Payoneer*. *Payoneer* "is an Internet-based financial services business that allows users to transfer money and receive payments through re-loadable prepaid credit/debit cards" (Siddiqui & Akram, 2015). Olawunmi, a six-year crowdworker revealed:

> *for PayPal I have two accounts also, one is international that I bought from someone in America and manage it using VPN to link to my payoneer card, the other is a Nigerian PayPal.*

Crowdworkers also engage in the practice of transferring their funds among a number of payment platforms in search for less expensive transactions and exchange rates. Workers revealed that digital platforms charge exorbitant transfer fees and offer unfavorable exchange rates. In order to get their income, workers use social media platforms, mainly *Facebook* and *Twitter* to market and trade these earnings. Crowdworkers advertise the availability of their funds to potential buyers who may need foreign currencies; funds are advertised after they have been transferred to a *PayPal* or *Payoneer* account. *PayPal* accounts used to retain foreign currency are usually bought from or opened by friend and families who live overseas. Crowdworkers perform these financial trade operations on social media as an extension of their work activities. This strategy of institutional work expands the workplace across different existing digital financial platforms and appropriating social media to be another financial platform. This is best articulated by Lolade, who has been a crowdworker for six years:

> *the problems with PayPal here…our money can't be [transferred] into our bank account, we have to get people who need foreign currency and PayPal to buy*

things abroad and sell the funds to them and get Naira (local currency.... So, where else seem appropriate than social media so that I can reach a wider audience of people, usually I meet some on Facebook. I just post it on my Facebook page that I have this amount in dollar to sell and people contact me, and we negotiate the exchange rate. That's the main ways I meet people that buy my PayPal, Skrill and Payoneer credits[fund]).

Achieving Digital Legitimacy

Power structure exists in every institution and crowdsourcing is no exception. Digital platforms are engrained with complex algorithms that rank workers based on their skills, experience, previously conducted work, among other parameters. This ranking is used to recommend workers to prospective employers. This ranking, produced by algorithmic calculations, is presented as a measure of crowdworkers' ability to satisfactorily complete a specific task. Crowdworkers in Nigeria find that the higher a worker ranks, the higher the chances of employment are and that a crowdworker does not stand a chance if their ranking is low. Daniel, a crowdworker for over six years, has expressed this view saying: *"you are invisible to employers with low rating".*

Full-time crowdworkers in their quest for sustained employment and through experimentations and discussions with colleagues recognize the algorithmic demands of the digital platform and their correlation to the likelihood of getting employed. Interestingly, they compare this algorithmic ranking to the long-standing tradition of the employment institution and find that it is similar to the practices of job interviews and CV writing. Ola, a crowdworker for seven years, expressed that:

these websites work like real-life, when you go for an interview, the higher your qualification and experience, the better your chances of getting the job and that also determine your pay. It just happen that in this case, it's online and an algorithm determines that....People talk to you nicely and with respect when you have a good profile and ranking, because I think there's a perception that you are good at what you do and they (employers) want to work with the best guys on the website.

However, crowdworkers also realize the possibility of and need to "work on the system" and "play the algorithm" to increase their ranking. They find this as a way not only to increase their employability but also to obtain a bargaining power over employers. This view has been expressed as follows:

> *Now I can bargain prices with client, that's not something I had the luxury of when I first started, I can tell them my price and what time I can deliver their work (Monica, three years).*

Adopting Traditional Business Norms in Managing Customers' Relations

The high stakes and pressure of sustaining earnings and full-time employment on digital platform have encouraged crowdworkers to experiment with it and find ways to maneuver around the institutional boundaries of the algorithm in order to find practical solutions. Hence, they build long-term relationships with employers on and surprisingly largely outside the digital platform, compete to be the first to bid, bid low on projects and also compete to deliver faster than requested. For example, some crowdworkers share their email, *Skype* ID and phone numbers with employers to enable contact outside of the platforms. These off-platform communications can be used to get more jobs and be paid directly, thereby circumventing the restrictions and also charges on digital platforms. The building of long-term relationship outside the platform has been a recurring theme in interviews and was expressed by Joseph and Adesola as:

> *I have their [employer] contacts now, …so I build relationship with this kind of people[employers], so when they need my services, they have to call me or send message to me through WhatsApp so that I can do the job for them (Joseph, six years).*

> *[Y]ou must always keep close relationship with them [employers]… always tell them you're available after working for them and then capitalize on it to use it judiciously so that we can keep a constant, close relationship with our client [employer], …so that many time they come back and say I need a job, get it*

done…they can easily come back to you, so we maintain a relationship, a solid one (Adesola, two years).

This practice is sometimes initiated by employers requesting off-platform contact or could be part of the work being offered:

[T]here are some jobs you need to do, you just have to exchange contact, its normal, … probably I have to design a website for you, you have to register my email on your WordPress before I could have access, I have to exchange contact…he (employer) told me he wouldn't want to be communicating so much on the platform, can I give him my email or my skype ID and I did, and we communicate on skype and sometimes he pays directly to my account (Apostle, six years).

Crowdworkers who are new to the digital platforms find the need to build their platform reputation. They achieve this by underbidding on projects in order to accumulate positive reviews and gain influence. Hence, they purposely offer their services for lower prices as compared to other workers on the platform. An indicative sample is expressed below:

I just take the projects at annoyingly lower rates just so that I can build my ranking and profile on the website, I knew once I have a higher project completion rate and reviews, I'll be able to charge more (Ola, seven years).

To further improve their algorithmic ranking, crowdworkers, particularly those who are new to the digital platform, offer to conduct and finish jobs in a much shorter period of time than requested by the employer. They believe that this underbidding gives them a favorable position on the platform. Participants have commonly expressed this view; Blessing captured this strategy:

I will offer them a quicker response time, like if you want the job done in three days, I will tell you I can do it in a day or two (Blessing, two years).

Crowdworkers maintained the view that bidding low and offering faster delivery on projects allow them to compete through accumulating good rating and thus improve their ranking on the crowdsourcing digital platform. Hence, they continued this practice.

Discussion and Contribution

There is an exponential growth in crowdwork and growing belief that it creates a global labor market that could reduce the problem of unemployment, particularly in developing countries. However, beyond surveys, research has yet to provide a deep understanding of the phenomenon from the crowdworker's perspective. Our research aims to contribute to the latter through shedding light on the lived experiences of crowdworkers in the context of developing countries. It critically examines the view that it could be adopted as a long-term mode of employment and specifically answers the question: how do workers adopt crowdwork as a model of full-time long-term employment? Empirically, it examined the lived experience of crowdworkers in Nigeria, which is one of the largest developing countries in terms of population with a significantly high rate of unemployment. The theoretical lens of institutional work emerged during the analysis and provides a cohesive explanation of what people do in their attempt to achieve permanent institutional arrangements (Lawrence et al., 2011, 2013; Lawrence & Suddaby, 2006). Accordingly, it served as a suitable case study to closely examine the proposition of crowdsourcing as a source of sustainable employment particularly in the context of developing countries, which could inform the current debate in this regard.

This research shows the effort it takes for crowdwork to create crowdwork as a long-term employment. It reveals that crowdworkers create crowdwork as an institution in its own right with its norms, resources, routines and arrangements. In establishing its social activities and material resources as an institution (Scott, 2001; Zietsma & Lawrence, 2010), crowdworkers are impacted by and negotiate with different existing institutions and technologies. These include state regulations and infrastructure, existing digital institutions including payment platforms and social media financial systems in addition to digital platforms of work with their dynamics and operations.

This study shows the effort, strategies and "purposive action" crowdworkers employ in order to establish crowdwork as an institution with its normative and regulative elements (Lawrence & Suddaby, 2006), thus transcending social, technical, political and economic constraints of existing institutions. It identifies five interlinked and overlapping social and material strategies crowdworkers adopt to create the "crowdsourcing institution". They highlight the important role of context in the examination of the potential of crowdwork employment. It highlights that long-term employment in local settings is an achievement and not a given immediately driven from the global reach and settings of digital platforms. The institutionalization practices crowdworkers engage in to create crowdwork as a long-term employment are essentially social and material, involving a large number of technologies in addition to social, legal and societal considerations. This conceptual development contributes to the crowdsourcing literature that has underexamined crowdworkers' perspective and insufficiently theorized crowdsourcing (Howcroft & Bergvall-Kåreborn, 2018; Zhao & Zhu, 2014).

This study shows that crowdworkers in Nigeria are engaged in auxiliary work outside digital platforms to generate electricity and ensure the availability of access to the internet and mobile services. In doing so, they complement the country's existing communication infrastructure. They also expand and redefine the country's financial system infrastructure to include the appropriation of social media as a marketplace to advertise and trade currencies. This appropriation required collective engagement and the cooperation of several parties to operate successfully. This finding shows that although crowdsourcing is an individualistic form of work, the homogeneity of challenges and context in which workers operate sets in motion cooperation between workers and other parties to use different financial digital platforms and also appropriate other platforms such as social media to act as parallel and/or alternative to existing institutions. This points to both the creation of a new institutional arrangement by actors justifying the need for it (Farny et al., 2018) and creating parallel institutional arrangements alongside existing ones (Lawrence & Suddaby, 2006; Mahoney & Thelen, 2010). The creation of an informal financial system could be a matter of concern in terms of risks, its legal and regulatory implications. In the context of Nigeria however, bypassing or avoiding organized institutional arrangements by creating parallel "self-governing economic, socio-cultural and juridical system" is an everyday practice that assert individual and collective agency in closing gaps in state's resources (Osaghae, 1999).

The study also showed that crowdworkers are involved in assembling diverse digital platforms and profiles in their attempt to create a digital workplace that is capable of sustaining full-time and long-term employment and income. This finding extends the understanding of the material and social arrangement of crowdwork. It shows that digital spaces of work are not separate objects from the social and institutional spaces and that they impact each other. This finding supports the view that advocates the value of examining them together and not in separation (Orlikowski, 2007).

Our study shows that crowdworkers in Nigeria are involved in a mix of platform and algorithmic workarounds and traditional business networking. Previous research approached workspace in crowdsourcing as confined to the digital platforms where workers and employers meet (Deng & Joshi, 2016; Forde et al., 2017). This study extends this view by uncovering the business networking crowdworkers pursue on and off the digital platform to build rapport and sustainable relationship with clients. The unintended consequence of these institutional work practices will be its negative effect on the profitability and long-term survival of digital platforms as the number of transactions and overall revenue decrease.

The study points to the power and influence dynamics of digital platforms driven by the reputation system. Our findings revealed that crowdworkers are involved in algorithmic management to increase their reputation and gain higher status on the digital platform, which in turn increases their chances of employment and income sustainability. Although previous research examined the influence and role played by algorithmic ranking in various digital platforms (Eslami, Vaccaro, Karahalios, & Hamilton, 2017; Jøsang, 2007; Jøsang, Ismail, & Boyd, 2007), our findings show that not only do algorithms influence crowdworkers' employability but crowdworkers also 'play the algorithm' on and off the digital platform to gain high rankings and power. The institutional work of attaining power does not renounce the reputation system of the platforms but involves creating new practices that help crowdworkers attain a privileged position within the power structure.

Our study also contributes to advancing the application of the theoretical lens of institutional work (Lawrence et al., 2013; Lawrence & Suddaby, 2006). It extends this research to a new setting for work that is mediated by digital platforms and occurs beyond the traditional formal organizational boundaries. As we examine a new digital work setting, our study provides an empirically supported examination of the digital, physical and mental work required to create a new institution in this new digital work setting. It empirically showed that the creation of the crowdwork institution is not necessarily disruptive to existing institutions but could take place through complementing and incrementally building new institutions alongside or within existing institutional arrangements (Mahoney & Thelen, 2010).

In terms of the implications of research on practice, this study provides an in-depth understanding of the contextual factors that impact the adoption of crowdwork and its effect on workers in the context of a developing country. Hence, our research in this context could be relevant not only to academia but also to key stakeholders including government, development agencies in addition to digital platform owners and employers. This supports policy makers in their effort to promote this new type of digital work to solve the unemployment problem. It also provides platform owners with a much-needed understanding on the lived experience of crowdworkers and the practical problems they face in their attempt to adopt it for longer term as a mode of employment. This insight allows the rethinking of the business model of digital platforms and the refinement of digital platforms to cater for its adoption for full-time employment.

Conclusion, Limitations and Further Research

The study shows that while crowdworking on digital platforms has been lauded for its potential ability to transcend geographical boundaries (Berg, 2015; Kuek et al., 2015; Zakariah et al., 2016), it remains subject to the social, political and technological conditions of the users' environment. This is consistent with previous research that examined other systems and technological adoption and use to highlight the importance of the local context (Avgerou & Walsham, 2018; Braa et al., 2004). Research assumes that crowdworkers have the "freedom to choose when and where to work, how long to spend and what work to perform" (Kleemann, Voß, & Rieder, 2008, p. 154). Our study argues that these are not inherent characteristics of crowdwork but context-specific practices. Our study shows that while these characteristics exist in principle, crowdworkers in Nigeria who adopt crowdsourcing as an employment mode and source of living do not enjoy much of this freedom as they are constrained by existing institutions. They work from professional offices for long hours and compete on digital platforms over availability, speed of respond, prices and delivery time. In their local context, crowdworkers are engaged in auxiliary work to create their physical and digital workplace. They also create the necessary infrastructure for their work and engage with the digital platforms algorithms to gain power and better opportunities.

Research has examined the quality of crowdwork (Allahbakhsh et al., 2013; Daniel, Kucherbaev, Cappiello, Benatallah, & Allahbakhsh, 2018) and the engagement of the crowd (Berardi, Tonelli, & Serio, 2014; Naderi, 2018). Our research complements this literature by showing that crowdsourcing work, while essentially digital, yet, involves work to stabilize many social, technological and institutional elements and that crowdworkers can only sustain their employment by doing this institutional work. While our research reveals five strategies crowdworkers employed to establish crowdsourcing as a stable institution in Nigeria, these strategies are not exhaustive. Further research might identify more or different strategies in other contexts. Indeed, "institutional work involves action that is triggered, facilitated, and constrained by the environments in which it occurs" (Lawrence & Dover, 2015). Hence, different contexts might affect institutional work differently (Battilana & D'Aunno, 2009; Wright & Zammuto, 2013).

This study focused on examining crowdsourcing work in Nigeria; future research can examine other contexts for crowdsourcing work. Indeed, while this study contributes to the filling of research gap in understanding crowdwork by examining its sustainability and the technological and economic arrangement crowdworkers do, more research is needed to examine other aspects of crowdsourcing work. While this study is limited to examining the perspective of crowdworkers, further research could examine multiple perspectives. Indeed, future research can shed valuable insight into this area by conducting a comparative study of employers, digital platforms and workers perspectives.

In conclusion, the sustainability of crowdsourcing employment is not readily available through the existing platforms as research and different international and development organizations perceive it. On the contrary, it takes significant work from crowdworkers to institutionalize it into a sustainable mode of employment. Organizations that aim to support crowdsourcing work as sustainable source of employment need to facilitate the occurrence of this institutional work.

References

Adekola, P. O., Allen, A. A., Olawole-Isaac, A., Akanbi, M. A., & Adewumi, O. (2017). Unemployment in Nigeria; A challenge of demographic change? *International Journal of Scientific Research in Multidisciplinary Studies ISROSET, 2*(5), 1–9.

Allahbakhsh, M., Benatallah, B., Ignjatovic, A., Motahari-Nezhad, H. R., Bertino, E., & Dustdar, S. (2013). Quality control in crowdsourcing systems: Issues and directions. *IEEE Internet Computing, 17*(2), 76–81.

Aloisi, A. (2016). Commoditized workers: Case study research on labor law issues arising from a set of "on-demand/gig economy" platforms. *Comparative labor Law and Policy Journal, 37*(3), 620–653.

Avgerou, C., & Li, B. (2013). Relational and institutional embeddedness of Web enabled entrepreneurial networks: Case studies of entrepreneurs in China. *Information Systems Journal, 23*(4), 329–350.

Avgerou, C., & Walsham, G. (2018). *Information technology in context: Studies from the perspective of developing countries*. Abingdon, UK: Routledge.

Barnes, S. A., Green, A., & de Hoyos, M. (2015). Crowdsourcing and work: Individual factors and circumstances influencing employability. *New Technology, Work and Employment, 30*(1), 16–31.

Battilana, J., & D'aunno, T. (2009). Institutional work and the paradox of embedded agency. In T. B. Lawrence, R. Suddaby, & B. Leca (Eds.),

Institutional work: Actors and agency in institutional studies of organizations (pp. 31–58). Cambridge, UK: Cambridge University Press.

Berardi, M., Tonelli, M., & Serio, L. (2014). Crowdsourcing in developing countries: A possible model to co-create with the poor. In M. Gudic, A. Rosenbloom, & C. Parkes (Eds.), *Socially responsive organizations and the challenge of poverty* (pp. 253–263). Chicago, IL: Greenleaf Publishing.

Berg, J. (2015). Income security in the on-demand economy: Findings and policy lessons from a survey of Crowd workers. *Comparative Labor Law and Policy Journal, 37*, 543–576.

Boudreau, K., & Lakhani, K. (2016). To answer the most vexing innovation and research questions, crowds are becoming the partner of choice. In V. Grewal-Carr & C. Bates (Eds.), *The three billion enterprise crowdsourcing and the growing fragmentation of work*. London: Deloitte Consulting LLP.

Braa, J., Monteiro, E., & Sahay, S. (2004). Networks of action: Sustainable health information systems across developing countries. *MIS Quarterly, 28*(3), 337–362.

Brabham, D. (2008). Crowdsourcing as a model for problem solving: An introduction and cases. *Convergence, 14*(1), 75–90.

Braun, V., & Clarke, V. (2006). Using thematic analysis in psychology. *Qualitative Research in Psychology, 3*(2), 77–101.

Braun, V., Clarke, V., & Terry, G. (2014). Thematic analysis. In P. Rohleder & A. Lyons (Eds.), *Qualitative research in clinical and health psychology* (pp. 95–114). Basingstoke, UK: Palgrave Macmillan.

Charmaz, K. (2006). *Constructing grounded theory: A practical guide through qualitative analysis*. Thousand Oaks, CA: Sage.

Cole, K. D. (2007). *Good for the soul: The relationship between work, wellbeing and psychological capital, Doctoral Dissertation*. Canberra, Australia: University of Canberra.

Counted, A. V., & Arawole, J. O. (2015). We are connected, but constrained: Internet inequality and the challenges of millennials in Africa as actors in innovation. *Journal of Innovation and Entrepreneurship, 5*(3), 1–21.

Cox, J. (2018, June 16). Power out Nigeria plunged into darkness by power grid meltdown as millions watched World Cup build-up on TV. *The Sun*.

Dacin, T. M., Goodstein, J., & Scott, R. W. (2002). Institutional theory and institutional change: Introduction to the special research forum. *Academy of Management Journal, 45*(1), 45–56.

Daniel, F., Kucherbaev, P., Cappiello, C., Benatallah, B., & Allahbakhsh, M. (2018). Quality control in crowdsourcing: A survey of quality attributes, assessment techniques, and assurance actions. *ACM Computing Surveys, 51*(1), 1–40.

Darke, P., Shanks, G., & Broadbent, M. (1998). Successfully completing case study research: Combining rigour, relevance and pragmatism. *Information Systems Journal, 8*(4), 273–289.

Deng, X., & Joshi, K. D. (2016). Why individuals participate in micro-task crowdsourcing work environment: Revealing crowd workers' perceptions. *Journal of the Association for Information Systems, 17*(10), 648–673.

Deng, X., Joshi, K. D., & Galliers, R. D. (2016). The duality of empowerment and marginalization in microtask crowdsourcing: Giving voice to the less powerful through value sensitive design. *MIS Quarterly, 40*(2), 279–302.

DiMaggio, P. (1988). Interest and agency in institutional theory. In L. G. Zucker (Ed.), *Institutional patterns and organizations: Culture and environment* (pp. 3–22). Cambridge, MA: Ballinger.

Dølvik, J. E., & Jesnes, K. (2018). *Nordic labour markets and the sharing economy: report from a Pilot project.* Copenhagen, DK: Nordic Council of Ministers.

Efobi, U., Beecroft, I., & Osabuohien, E. (2014). Access to and use of bank services in Nigeria: Micro-econometric evidence. *Review of Development Finance, 4*(2), 104–114.

Eslami, M., Vaccaro, K., Karahalios, K., & Hamilton, K. (2017). Be careful; Things can be worse than they appear: Understanding biased algorithms and users' behavior around them in rating platforms. In *International Conference on Web and Social Media*, Montreal, Canada, May 15–18, 62–71.

Farny, S., Kibler, E., & Down, S. (2018). Collective emotions in institutional creation work. *Academy of Management Journal, 62*(3), 765–799.

Farrell, H., & Héritier, A. (2003). Formal and informal institutions under codecision: Continuous constitution-building in Europe. *Governance, 16*(4), 577–600.

Feagin, J. R., Orum, A. M., & Sjoberg, G. (Eds.). (1991). *A case for the case study*. Raleigh, NC: University of North Carolina Press Books.

Ford, R. C., Richard, B., & Ciuchta, M. P. (2015). Crowdsourcing: A new way of employing non-employees. *Business Horizons, 58*(4), 377–388.

Forde, C., Stuart, M., Joyce, S., Oliver, L., Valizade, D., Alberti, G., et al. (2017). *The social protection of workers in the platform economy. Study for the European Parliament's Committee on employment and social affairs*, Study IP/A/EMPL/2016-11. Brussels: European Union.

Fuchs, C. (2013). Class and exploitation on the Internet. In T. Scholz (Ed.), *Digital labor: The Internet as playground and factory* (pp. 211–224). New York & London: Routledge.

Gains, F., & Lowndes, V. (2014). How is institutional formation gendered, and does it make a difference? A new conceptual framework and a case study of police and crime commissioners in England and Wales. *Politics & Gender, 10*(4), 524–548.

Gillwald, A., Mothobi, O., & Schoentgen, A. (2017). *What is the state of micro-work in Africa? A view from seven countries*. Policy Paper Series no 5. Cape Town, South Africa: Research ICT Africa.

Graham, M., Hjorth, I., & Lehdonvirta, V. (2017). Digital labour and development: Impacts of global digital labour platforms and the gig economy on worker livelihoods. *Transfer: European Review of Labour and Research, 23*(2), 135–162.

Greenwood, R., Suddaby, R., & Hinings, C. R. (2002). Theorizing change: The role of professional associations in the transformation of institutionalized fields. *Academy of Management Journal, 45*(1), 58–80.

Guetterman, T. C. (2015). Descriptions of sampling practices within five approaches to qualitative research in education and the health sciences. *Educational Psychology Papers and Publications. 263, 16*(2), Article 25. Retrieved from https://digitalcommons.unl.edu/cgi/viewcontent.cgi?article=1275&context=edpsychpapers

Heeks, R. (2017). *Decent work and the digital gig economy.* Working Paper 2. Manchester: Global Development Institute.

Hodkinson, P. (2008). Grounded theory and inductive research. In N. Gilbert & P. Stoneman (Eds.), *Researching social life* (pp. 98–117). Thousand Oaks, CA: Sage.

Howcroft, D., & Bergvall-Kåreborn, B. (2018). A typology of crowdwork platforms. *Work, Employment and Society, 33*(1), 21–38.

Howe, J. (2006). The rise of crowdsourcing. *Wired Magazine, 14*(6), 1–4.

Huws, U., Spencer, N. H., & Joyce, S. (2016). *Crowd work in Europe: Preliminary Results from a survey in the UK, Sweden, Germany, Austria and the Netherlands.* Commissioned report, Foundation for European Progressive Studies. Hatfield, UK: University of Hertfordshire and Uni Europa, Uni Global Union.

Ikediego, H. O., Ilkan, M., Abubakar, A. M., & Bekun, F. V. (2018). Crowdsourcing (who, why and what). *International Journal of Crowd Science, 2*(1), 27–41.

ILO. (2018, February 15–17). Job quality in the platform economy, In *2nd meeting of the global commission on the future of work*. Geneva: International Labour Organization.

Jøsang, A. (2007). Trust and reputation systems. In A. Aldini, R. Gorrieri, & F. Martinelli (Eds.), *Foundations of security analysis and design IV* (pp. 209–245). Berlin: Springer.

Jøsang, A., Ismail, R., & Boyd, C. (2007). A survey of trust and reputation systems for online service provision. *Decision Support Systems, 43*(2), 618–644.

Kenny, C. J. (2006). *Overselling the Web: Development and the Internet*. Boulder, CO: Lynne Reiner Publishers.

Kleemann, F., Voß, G. G., & Rieder, K. (2008). Un(der) paid innovators: The commercial utilization of consumer work through crowdsourcing. *Science, Technology & Innovation Studies, 4*(1), 5–26.

Klein, H. K., & Myers, M. D. (1999). A set of principles for conducting and evaluating interpretive field studies in information systems. *MIS Quarterly, 23*(1), 67–93.

Koch, H., Leidner, D. E., & Gonzalez, E. S. (2013). Digitally enabling social networks: Resolving IT–culture conflict. *Information Systems Journal, 23*(6), 501–523.

Kuek, S. C., Paradi-Guilford, C., Fayomi, T., Imaizumi, S., Ipeirotis, P., Pina, P., et al. (2015). *The global opportunity in online outsourcing*. Washington, DC: The World Bank.

Lawrence, T., & Dover, G. (2015). Place and institutional work: Creating housing for the hard-to-house. *Administrative Science Quarterly, 60*(3), 371–410.

Lawrence, T., Leca, B., & Zilber, T. B. (2013). Institutional work: Current research new directions and overlooked issues. *Organizational Studies, 34*(8), 1023–1033.

Lawrence, T., & Suddaby, R. (2006). Institutions and institutional work. In S. Clegg, C. Hardy, T. Lawrence, & W. Nord (Eds.), *Handbook of organisational studies* (2nd ed., pp. 215–254). London: Sage Publications.

Lawrence, T., Suddaby, R., & Leca, B. (2011). Institutional work: Refocusing institutional studies of organization. *Journal of Management Inquiry, 20*(1), 52–58.

Lawrence, T. B., Suddaby, R., & Leca, B. (2009). Introduction: Theorizing and studying institutional work. In T. B. Lawrence, R. Suddaby, & B. Leca (Eds.), *Institutional work: Actors and agency in institutional studies of organizations* (pp. 1–27). Cambridge, UK: Cambridge University Press.

Lehdonvirta, V., & Ernkvist, M. (2011). *Knowledge map of the virtual economy: Converting the virtual economy into development potential.* Washington, DC: The World Bank.

Leimeister, J. M., Zogaj, S., & Durward, D. (2016). New forms of employment and IT: Crowdsourcing. In R. Blanpain, F. Hendrickx, & B. Waas (Eds.), *Bulletin of comparative labour relations series, new forms of employment in Europe* (pp. 23–41). Alphen aan den Rijn, The Netherlands: Kluwer Law International.

Lounsbury, M., & Crumley, E. T. (2007). New practice creation: An institutional perspective on innovation. *Organization studies, 28*(7), 993–1012.

Mahoney, J., & Thelen, K. (2010). A theory of gradual institutional change. In J. Mahoney & K. Thelen (Eds.), *Explaining institutional change* (pp. 1–37). New York: Cambridge University Press.

Mayernik, M. (2016). Research data and metadata curation as institutional issues. *Journal of the Association for Information Science Technology, 67*(4), 973–993.

Morris, R., McDuff, D., & Calvo, R. (2014). Crowdsourcing techniques for affective computing. In R. A. Calvo, S. D'Mello, J. Gratch, & A. Kappas (Eds.), *The Oxford handbook of affective computing* (pp. 384–394). Oxford, UK: Oxford University Press.

Myers, M. D. (2013). *Qualitative research in business and management.* Thousand Oaks, CA: Sage.

Myers, M. D., & Newman, M. (2007). The qualitative interview in IS research: Examining the craft. *Information and Organization, 17*(1), 2–26.

Naderi, B. (2018). Who are the crowd workers? In B. Naderi (Ed.), *Motivation of workers on microtask crowdsourcing platforms* (pp. 17–27). New York: Springer.

Nakpodia, F., Adegbite, E., Amaeshi, K., & Owolabi, A. (2018). Neither principles nor rules: Making corporate governance work in Sub-Saharan Africa. *Journal of Business Ethics, 151*(2), 391–408.

National Bureau of Statistics. (2017). *Nigeria labour force survey 2017.* Abuja, Nigeria: National Bureau of Statistics. Retrieved August 24, 2018, from http://www.tradingeconomics.com/nigeria/unemployment-rate

Nigerian Communication Commission. (2018). *Internet users in Nigeria hit 98.3 million.* Abuja, Nigeria: Nigerian Communications Commission. Retrieved August 24, 2018, from https://www.ncc.gov.ng/thecommunicator/index.php?option=com_contentandview=articleandid=1623:internet-users-in-nigeria-hit-98-3-millionandcatid=20andItemid=141

Olawoyin, O. (2018, January 3). Nigeria experiences: Total power outage across country. *Premium Times.*

Olotu, A., Salami, R., & Akeremale, I. (2015). Poverty and rate of unemployment in Nigeria. *International Journal of Management and Business, 2*(1), 1–2.

Orlikowski, W. J. (2007). Sociomaterial practices: Exploring technology at work. *Organization Studies, 28*(9), 1435–1448.

Osaghae, E. E. (1999). Exiting from the state in Nigeria. *African Journal of Political Science/Revue Africaine de Science Politique, 4*(1), 83–98.

Patton, M. Q. (1990). *Qualitative evaluation and research methods.* Thousand Oaks, CA: Sage Publications.

Sánchez, D. Á., Gimilio, D. P., & Altamirano, J. I. (2015). Crowdsourcing: A new way to citizen empowerment. In F. J. Garrigos-Simon, I. Gil-Pechuán, & S. Estelles-Miguel (Eds.), *Advances in crowdsourcing* (pp. 73–86). New York: Springer.

Scott, W. R. (2001). *Institutions and organizations* (2nd ed.). Thousand Oaks, CA: Sage.

Siddiqui, M. A., & Akram, M. (2015). PASSMA: Fingerprint payment system: A new way to e-pay. *International Journal of Computer and Information Technology, 4*(6), 942–948.

Streeck, W., & Thelen, K. A. (Eds.). (2005). *Beyond continuity: Institutional change in advanced political economies.* Oxford, UK: Oxford University Press.

Suddaby, R., & Viale, T. (2011). Professionals and field-level change: Institutional work and the professional project. *Current Sociology, 59*(4), 423–442.

Taeihagh, A. (2017). Crowdsourcing, sharing economies and development. *Journal of Developing Societies, 33*(2), 191–222.

Trauth, E. M., & Jessup, L. M. (2000). Understanding computer-mediated discussions: Positivist and interpretive analyses of group support system use. *MIS Quarterly, 24*(1), 43–79.

USAID. (2018). *Nigeria: Power Africa fact sheet* [Press release]. Washington, DC: USAID. April 4. Retrieved from https://www.usaid.gov/power-africa/nigeria

Vaast, E., & Walsham, G. (2011). Grounded theorizing for electronically mediated social contexts. *European Journal of Information Systems, 22*(1), 9–25.

Venkatesh, V., Brown, S. A., & Bala, H. (2013). Bridging the qualitative-quantitative divide: Guidelines for conducting mixed methods research in information systems. *MIS Quarterly, 37*(1), 21–54.

Walsham, G. (1995). Interpretive case studies in IS research: Nature and method. *European Journal of Information Systems, 4*(2), 74–81.

Walsham, G. (2006). Doing interpretive research. *European Journal of Information Systems, 15*(3), 320–330.

Walsham, G., & Sahay, S. (2006). Research on information systems in developing countries: Current landscape and future prospects. *Information Technology for Development, 12*(1), 7–24.

Wood, A. J., Graham, M., Lehdonvirta, V., & Hjorth, I. (2019). Networked but commodified: The (dis) embeddedness of digital labour in the gig economy. *Sociology, 53*(5), 931–950.

Wright, A. L., & Zammuto, R. F. (2013). Wielding the willow: Processes of institutional change in English county cricket. *Academy of Management Journal, 56*(1), 308–330.

Zakariah, Z., Janom, N., & Arshad, N. H. (2016). Crowdsourcing to uplift the lifestyle of low-income community. *Advanced Science Letters, 22*(5–6), 1658–1661.

Zhao, Y., & Zhu, Q. (2014). Evaluation on crowdsourcing research: Current status and future direction. *Information Systems Frontiers, 16*(3), 417–434.

Zietsma, C., & Lawrence, T. B. (2010). Institutional work in the transformation of an organizational field: The interplay of boundary work and practice work. *Administrative Science Quarterly, 55*(2), 189–221.

Zilber, T. B. (2002). Institutionalization as an interplay between actions, meanings, and actors: The case of a rape crisis center in Israel. *Academy of Management Journal, 45*(1), 234–254.

Zyskowski, K., Morris, M. R., Bigham, J. P., Gray, M. L., & Kane, S. K. (2015). Accessible crowdwork?: Understanding the value in and challenge of microtask employment for people with disabilities. In *18th Association for Computing Machinery Conference on Computer Supported Cooperative Work & Social Computing*, Vancouver, BC, Canada, March 14–18, 1682–1693.

Part II

New Ways of Working and Collaborative Spaces

5

Materiality as Ingredients of Events: Comprehending Materiality as a Temporal Phenomenon in a Makerspace

Anthony Hussenot

Introduction

In organization studies, the research stream called sociomateriality has been a clear signal of the interest of scholars in the role of materiality in the making of social life (Jarzabkowski & Pinch, 2013). The debate has mainly been about a shift in the understanding of the social and the material from a weak relational ontology (Slife, 2004)—also called weak sociomateriality (Jones, 2014)—to a strong relational ontology (Slife, 2004)—also called strong sociomateriality (Jones, 2014). To date, in the weak relational ontology, the social and the material are imbricated, but remain distinct, merely interdependent phenomena (Leonardi, 2010, 2011, 2013; Leonardi & Barley, 2008, 2012). Conversely, the strong relational ontology has stated that the social and the material are

A. Hussenot (✉)
Université Côte d'Azur, Nice, France
e-mail: Anthony.hussenot@univ-cotedazur.fr

N. Mitev et al. (eds.), *New Ways of Working*, Technology, Work and Globalization,
https://doi.org/10.1007/978-3-030-61687-8_5

entangled, and gain status only through their interpenetration (Orlikowski, 2006, 2007, 2010; Orlikowski & Scott, 2008, 2013; Shotter, 2013). Following this latter approach, "each thing, including each person, is first and always a nexus of relations [...] They start out and forever remain in relationship" (Slife, 2004, p. 159).

By taking the social and the material as taken-for-granted elements, scholars of the weak relational ontology have mainly focused on their interaction and their co-influence, but do not consider organization as a becoming process in which the social and the material are intertwined and constantly co-produced. Conversely, the strong relational ontology has offered interesting insights to understanding how the social and the material emerge in practices, but scholars have struggled to elude a substantive perspective consisting of the separation between the social and the material. Therefore, research has provided very little insight on the relational ontology of the social and the material as a becoming process (Cecez-Kecmanovic, Galliers, Henfridsson, Newell, & Vidgen, 2014; Kautz & Jensen, 2013). In most studies, they remain two distinct elements in the foreground to enable the study (Cecez-Kecmanovic et al., 2014), while the matter of organization has not really been considered. In fact, most research in this research stream does not question the matter of organization.

This shortcoming refrains us from understanding the role of materiality in the emergence of organizational phenomena, especially in a context of "projectification" of work and society (Jensen, Thuesen, & Geraldi, 2016), in which the organization is not a stable entity, but a constantly emerging and evolving phenomenon. In such a context, activities are more and more based on multiple and temporary projects requiring situated rules, roles, tools, objects and so on. Ways of working such as freelancing (Burke, 2015), coworking (Spinuzzi, 2012), the maker movement (Anderson, 2012; Dougherty, 2012) and digital nomadism (Makimoto & Manners, 1997) are examples of this projectification of work leading to the constant re/definition of organizational phenomena. In such phenomena, the social and the material are not stable, separated and given; they are always in state of becoming as they are constantly re/defined through situated practices. More precisely, in such project-based ways of working and organizing, the organization is not defined as a stable structure but by temporalities, that is, a situated and shared definition and configuration of past, present and future events related to the activity, that enable actors to coordinate and act (Hussenot & Sergi, 2018).

With the aim to offer some insights about how materiality participates in the making of organizational phenomena, I focus on the relation between materiality and organizational temporality. By providing insights about the relation between materiality and organizational temporality, my goal is to contribute in our understanding about organization and organizing in the context of "projectified" ways of working as well. More precisely, I rely on an events-based approach (Hernes, 2014a, 2014b; Hussenot, 2019; Hussenot, Hernes, & Bouty, 2020; Hussenot & Missonier, 2016) to study how materiality participates in the re/definition of organizational temporality. Based on the philosophies of Bergson (1889, 1896, 1907) and Whitehead (1920, 1929, 1938), this view proposes to understand materiality as tangible elements of the passage from the flux of indivisible experience to an intelligible reality. In such a view, the intelligible reality emerging from the materialization process is always a temporal one; as the intelligibility of the reality is in the re/definition of past, present and future events giving a sense of continuity and order to actors (Hussenot & Missonier, 2016). Consequently, materiality is here defined as the characteristics of past, present and future events—called "ingredients of events" by Whitehead (1929)—participating in the shaping of organizational temporality. In turn, the re/definition of organizational temporality participates in the definition of the meaning and role of materiality. In such a view, materiality shapes and is shaped by organizational temporality.

This events-based approach of materiality is illustrated with data collected from an ethnography (Hulst, Ybema, & Yanow, 2017) about the emergence of a collective of makers, members of a makerspace. Makers are creative workers developing innovative products and services combining design, craft and high tech; a makerspace is a hub of resources for makers providing workshops, coworking spaces, fablabs, and traditional and digital tools.

This empirical illustration describes the role played by materiality—such as the building, website, interior design, furniture—in the definition of a shared history, present and anticipated future about the collective of makers. This illustration shows how materiality plays the role of "ingredients of events" characterizing the past, present and future events that define a shared organizational temporality.

The main contribution of this chapter is to suggest an events-based approach of materiality in which materiality is understood as "ingredient of events" (Whitehead, 1929). This view enables us to understand how materiality participates in the definition of the past, present and future events, and how, in turn, the materiality is defined through those events. More precisely, this events-based approach of materiality participates, firstly, in the debate about sociomateriality (Cecez-Kecmanovic et al., 2014; Kautz & Jensen, 2013) by providing an alternative view about materiality that might help scholars to overcome the latent material and social dualism. In the view suggested in this chapter, the relational ontology of the materiality and the social is specified, as materiality here is considered as defined (and participating in the definition of) through events forming the organizational temporality. In such a perspective, materiality and events have a mutual and situated constitution. Secondly, this chapter participates in the debate about organizational temporality (Chia, 2002; Hernes, Simpson, & Soderlund, 2013; Reinecke & Ansari, 2017) by highlighting the role of materiality—that is, ingredients of events—in the re/definition of past, present and future events.

The first section of the chapter discusses the literature about sociomateriality and underlines the difficulty to grasp the relational ontology between the social and the material. The second section introduces an events-based approach of materiality in order to deal with the relation between materiality and organizational temporality. The third section illustrates this temporal view of materiality by relying on an ethnography with makers. The fourth section discusses the contributions of such an events-based approach of materiality in our understanding of organization and New Ways of Working.

The Relation Between the Material and the Social in Organization Studies

For decades, materiality has been a tricky matter for organization scholars. If some scholars have tried to deal with materiality as physical entities belonging to an organization (technologies, tools, etc.), other scholars have approached this notion by conceptualizing the relation between the material and the social, regardless of ontological and theoretical stances (Carlile, Nicolini, Langley, & Tsoukas, 2013; Cecez-Kecmanovic et al., 2014; Leonardi & Barley, 2012; Leonardi, Nardi, & Kallinikos, 2012). Viewing materiality through the lens of the social and the material relation has led to at least two approaches: the weak relational ontology and the strong relational ontology (Jones, 2014; Slife, 2004).

The weak relational ontology (Jones, 2014) has focused on the materiality and the organization as discrete entities. Inspired mainly by the sociotechnical systems approach (Trist, 1981; Trist & Bamforth, 1951), scholars have dealt with the imbrication of materiality and the organization (Leonardi, 2010, 2011, 2013; Leonardi & Barley, 2008, 2012). Organization is here considered as an entity—Leonardi (2013) talks about "formal organization", while the notion of materiality refers to properties that remain unchanged from one moment to the next through different locations (Leonardi, 2013, p. 145). Thus, materiality and the organization are entities with inherent properties. Consequently, the weak relational ontology has also distinguished "human agency" from "material agency" (Leonardi, 2011). However, in some research, the status of materiality is not delimited to physical objects and can be any of "(1) matter (2) practical instantiation and (3) significance" (Leonardi, 2010).

The second approach—the strong relational ontology (Jones, 2014)—has argued that the social and the material are entangled, and gain status and role only through their intertwinement with each other in practice (Introna, 2013; Jones, 2013; Orlikowski & Scott, 2008; Shotter, 2013). This second approach is mainly anchored in agential realism (Barad, 2003, 2007), posthumanism (Pickering, 1995), Actor-Network Theory (Latour, 2005) and practice theory (Feldman & Orlikowski, 2011;

Orlikowski, 2000). Here, entities have no inherent properties (Orlikowski & Scott, 2008). Taking this entanglement perspective into account, any separation is merely analytical.

However, despite several concepts to differentiate it from the weak relational ontology, such as "inseparability", "interpenetration", "relationality", "embodiment" (Jones, 2013, p. 202), research relying on a strong relational ontology have not fully overcome the social and material dualism (Cecez-Kecmanovic et al., 2014). The demonstration from "everyday practices" remains an issue and mostly consists in providing chunks of narratives based on interviews (Cecez-Kecmanovic et al., 2014), leading to a separation between the material and the social as scholars start their account by describing taken-for-granted humans and/or non-humans. In empirical studies, the material and the social thus remain more or less separated and are placed in the foreground of the study to make it feasible (Cecez-Kecmanovic et al., 2014). Therefore, by using human and non-human distinctions, scholars can no longer follow their own logic of argument.

Considering the material and the social as mutually constitutive (Orlikowski, 2007), existing only in practices (Orlikowski & Scott, 2008), and as having no inherent properties (Orlikowski & Scott, 2008), existing "as doing" (Shotter, 2013) in their "radical otherness" (Introna, 2013), requires to overcome this latent dualism. To paraphrase Jones (2013, p. 223), it is essential to not just reflect on how "matter matters", but how the material and the social matter in practices; that is, how forms and their relations appear. To overcome this latent dualism and provide an alternative relational ontological view of materiality and organization, I suggest to apply an events-based approach to materiality. This events-based approach of materiality does not pretend to answer all the questions and shortcomings about sociomateriality, but rather aims at offering an alternative way to consider the relation between the material and the social by focusing on how materiality participates in the definition of the organizational temporality and, in turn, how materiality is defined through this organizational temporality.

Understanding Materiality from the Events-Based Approach

By relying on the events-based approach (Hernes, 2014a, 2014b, 2017; Hussenot, 2019; Hussenot et al., Forthcoming; Hussenot & Missonier, 2016), the aim is to understand how materiality characterizes the events shaping organizational temporality. The relation between time and materiality has already been highlighted in organization studies. There is a long tradition of research insisting on how time is materialized in organizations (de Vaujany, Mitev, Laniray, & Vaast, 2014). In such a tradition, artefacts materialize a natural and objective view of time in which the past, the present and the future are seen as different and discrete epochs that can be positioned along a timeline once for all. Artefacts are here used to measure, organize and evaluate activities based on this objective view of time. However, by suggesting an events-based approach to materiality, our aim is not to focus on how time is materialized but, rather, to provide insights about how materiality "does time" (Barad, 2013) and, more precisely, does organizational temporality; and how, in turn, organizational temporality participates in the definition of materiality. In such, there is a clear distinction here between time and temporality as the notion of temporality refers to a situated view of time in which the past, the present and the future events are constantly redefined and configured by actors in order to define their activity and act (Hussenot, 2019; Hussenot & Missonier, 2016).

From the Flow of Experiences to Materiality

Materiality has often been associated with the idea of "object" or "technology". For instance, the matter of materiality has been largely developed in the Information Systems field in which it has often been conflated with the notions of digital or information technologies (Cecez-Kecmanovic et al., 2014). But the notion of materiality can be envisaged more broadly, as suggested by Bergson (1896, 1907). The starting point of Bergson's philosophy is to consider life as an "indivisible movement". The notion of *durée* he coined in his early work (Bergson, 1889, 1907) expresses the idea that reality is fundamentally indivisible and always in a state of transition and progression, without any predefined stage and change. However, people need to operate separation and division in the *durée* in order to make the world tangible and intelligible. In Bergson's philosophy, materiality is this very division and separation of the flow of experiences into tangible "things".

More precisely, materiality is the "forms emerging from life" (Bergson, 1907). Materiality is thus an "individuation" process in which forms appear. It is important to note that materialization is a necessary activity for people. To experience a reality, people have no choice but to define and separate "things", that is, to define humans and non-humans, or material and social "things". Thus, materiality is what offers people the ability to make the world concrete and actionable. The materialization of the world finds its very justification in the fact that it is the only way for people to act. Materialization of the world is made to act and through action. As Bergson (1907) said: "there is no things, but there is only actions" (Bergson, 1907, p. 249). Action is central in his philosophy as everything emerges from action and is defined for action. Consequently, materiality is not the ultimate reality for actors but only "images" (Bergson 1896) made for the purpose of the action. Therefore, materiality has a tricky status in Bergsonian philosophy as there is nothing tangible in the world but materiality, and, at the same time, materiality has no inherent properties. Consequently, the reality is only perceived as images emerging from experiences.

In such a view, the social has to be understood as part of the materialization process enabling actors to collectively act. What we call the social is only the forms (rules, hierarchies, roles, statuses, etc.) re/produced from the indivisible flux of experience in order to make the actions possible. Consequently, the materialization process is the characterization of social life. This view about materiality brings interesting insights for organization scholars as it considers materiality not as physical things but as the making of an intelligible and actionable social life. This means that, for scholars, what becomes important is to understand how this materialization process occurs and how it enables actors to act.

As Bergson (1896) mentioned, we materialize the world in order to act, but this materialization process means that we have to get away from the *durée*, that is, the pure experience of the indivisible flux of life, to enter in a tangible world. However, we rarely experience the pure *durée* or the pure materiality of the world; we rather experience an in-between situation that consists in a constant re/materialization of the world. This in-betweenness consists in the constant shifting from the indivisible flux of experience to a tangible reality. More precisely, this in-betweenness is this constant re/definition of the continuity of reality, providing an intelligibility and a sense to the current reality experienced by actors. The tangible reality emerging from the materialization is thus always a temporal one for Bergson (1896, 1907), as the materialization process consists in the constant re/definition of the past and the future. In such, this temporality emerging from the materialization is what makes the current reality intelligible. This view is in line with Whitehead (1920, 1929, 1938) for whom the intelligibility of reality emerges from events and temporality as they bring a sense of order and continuity (Whitehead, 1929). In the Whiteheadian view, any phenomenon is a temporal one and is defined through events and their configuration—which he called "structure of events".

Understanding Materiality as Ingredients of Events

As a tangible reality is always temporal (Bergson, 1907), what is at stake is the role of materiality in the enactment of the past, present and future events that define this tangible reality. Following this view, the materialization process is related to events forming the temporality. For Whitehead, events are simply concrete facts, or indivisible moments, that specify the character of a place experienced (Whitehead, 1920, p. 52). More precisely, the notion of event means "to appear, to come into form" (Cooper, 2014, p. 585). In such a perspective, reality also only occurs in events and there is nothing more but events arising out of other events (Cobb, 2007). As stated by Mead (1932, p. 3) "the world is a world of events". Materiality—note that Whitehead does not employ this notion but uses the terms "object" or "entity", see below—is constituted of events and characterizes these events.

Based on this process philosophy of Henri Bergson and Alfred North Whitehead, the events-based approach suggests to understand organization as a structure of events (Hernes, 2014a, 2014b, 2017; Hussenot, 2019; Hussenot et al., Forthcoming; Hussenot & Missonier, 2016).[1] Defining organization as a structure of past, present and future events re/enacted by people means that organization is this ongoing attempt to define an intelligible ordering and continuity of activities. More precisely, the structure of events is the past, present and future events enacted in the current moment and defining the organizational temporality. In this view, the organizational temporality emerging from the structure of events is considered as the core ontological dimension defining any organizational phenomena (Hussenot, 2019). Moreover, the notion of structure should not be understood as a stable outcome defining organizational temporality; but always fragile, unstable and subject to negotiation, re/definition and re/configuration as its purpose is to define a shared understanding of the continuity and ordering of activities.

Still, what is the relationship between events and the structure of events? Actually, we rarely enact events but the characteristics of those events. These characteristics are the ingredients of events—also called "objects" by Whitehead (1920, p. 144): "namely the event is what it is, because the object is what it is". The character of events is also ascertained from the objects, as they are contained in them: "in fact the character of an event is nothing but the objects which are ingredients in it" (Whitehead, 1929, p. 144). As Marovich, a Whiteheadian philosopher, stated: "an entity means, more or less, that it has become an irreducible element in the process of becoming. It emerges, it is, an element contributory to the process of becoming. It does not emerge into static existence, as a defined substance, but into a temporal process" (Marovich, 2014, p. 112). For example, the minutes of previous meetings about a project help to characterize the current meeting, not because these minutes have inherent

[1] This events-based approach is anchored in process philosophy (Rescher, 1996, 2001). In this philosophical movement, the things have no existence in themselves, no substance, no absolute role or function, but only acquire role and status through activities. Process philosophy also prioritizes activities over substance as well as process over product (Rescher, 1996, p. 31). By prioritizing activities over substance, process philosophy recognizes entities as only existing in what is happening.

properties but because they are ingredients of past, present and anticipated events enacted by actors during the current meeting. In this, the minutes can serve as a reminder of the decisions already made and the tasks that still have to be performed. The minutes, as ingredients of events, participate in the definition and redefinition of the project itself as they enable actors to enact the structure of events that defines the ordering and the continuity of this project.

Therefore, what we call materiality is all humans and non-humans gaining a meaning and a purpose because of their role in the characterization of the past, present and future events. There is no restriction in the ability of an ingredient to characterize events. As stated by Whitehead (1929, p. 144): "the ingression of an object into an event is the way the character of the event shapes itself in virtue of the being of the object".

Understanding materiality from the Whiteheadian philosophy opens up a perspective in which materiality is seen as a complex layering of characteristics defining a structure of events. The concreteness of materiality is not in its inherent properties but in its ability to define the current moment, that is, to position it in a past, present and future. Moreover, there is no predefined relationship between ingredients of events and events. Any ingredient of events can characterize several events at the same time. An ingredient does not just belong to one event. Ingredients characterize a structure of events as a whole. Ingredients also only exist for their ability to make the current moment possible, that is, to characterize the structure of events that define reality.

Most of the philosophical roots of the strong relational ontology—such as Actor-Network Theory (Latour, 2005) and agential realism (Barad, 2003, 2007)—have claimed that entities only exist in their doing; that is, by acting and constraining others. For them, the properties of entities are simply what they do and how they are associated (Latour, 2005) or "intra-acted" (Barad, 2003) with others. Any entity is thus anything that can act and is acted upon. The perspective I have suggested is in line with these approaches and suggests to go even further by specifying the condition of existence: to exist, a "thing" has to be able to characterize events and, in doing so, participate in the constant definition of reality. Furthermore, the stability of human and non-human properties (their meaning, status, role, etc.) depends on the stability of the structure of events enacted over time. As the evolution of the structure of events always encompasses both novelty and stability (Hussenot & Missonier, 2016), the human and non-human properties evolve as well. Consequently, materiality not only defines temporality but is defined through temporality, and some characteristics can remain more or less the same, while others can change. This is why the status and the role of "things" can be more or less important, according to the role they play in the definition of the structure of events. For example, the role of minutes of meetings' project can evolve according to the way actors enact these past meetings in the current moment.

The next section introduces an empirical illustration of the matter of materiality based on the events-based approach. Based on an ethnography conducted in 2014 and 2015, this illustration shows how, from the flow of experiences, founders of a makerspace defined past, present and future events producing a shared organizational temporality, and how various artefacts participated in the definition of this temporality, while, in turn, how such artefacts were re/defined through this enactment of past, present and future events.

Empirical Illustration: IciMontreuil

This illustration is anchored into the maker movement (Anderson, 2012; Dougherty, 2012; Hatch, 2013). Makers are independent workers interested in design, craft and high tech and in developing innovative products. They might be artisans, artists, architects and others, but they define themselves as makers. They can group together in shared working spaces called makerspaces. Makerspaces provide the resources the makers need, such as workshops and tools. These working spaces also offer the opportunity for makers to meet other makers to exchange and collaborate. However, makers are not employees of these spaces; they are members paying a monthly subscription to access resources.

The empirical illustration focuses on the creation of a makerspace in Montreuil, a city in the Eastern suburb of Paris, France. Montreuil is characterized by a famous industrial and artistic past as local artists such as Charles-Emile Reynault, the Pathé brothers and George Méliés in the film industry. This artistic dynamic is still alive as a high number of creatives live in Montreuil. While no official figures exist, more than 800 artists participated in the Montreuil "Open House Day[2]" in 2014 when 166 of the city workshops opened their doors to the public. However, the past has not always been seen as a glorious part of the city's history: the collapse of industry during the 1970s and 1980s led to an economic crisis in the town, which was accompanied by high unemployment (18% in 2013) and poverty rates (27% in 2013[3]). Consequently, this deindustrialization came with poverty and poor living conditions. However, the current gentrification process has led to the revival of the local economy and the rise of a creative class (Collet, 2015).

It is in this context that two founders created in 2009 a *Facebook* group in an effort to bring creative people living in Montreuil together. Due to the 2008 economic crisis and a general lack of communication, creatives such as artists and artisans were facing difficulties in promoting their work. Their principal aim was to promote the talents of Montreuil's creative class. In 2012, the founders decided to move forward and formed a cooperative with the aim of building a 1750 m^2 makerspace called IciMontreuil. This makerspace opened in January 2013 and aimed at providing resources to makers in order to help them develop innovative products. This makerspace provides workshops, coworking spaces, a fablab, and traditional and digital tools, including Computer Numerical Control machines and 3D printers. In October 2014, more than 160 makers had already decided to join, gained access to the space's material resources, and were able to collaborate on various projects. This makerspace was an immediate success and had a large influence on the French maker movement and is still considered as a major actor in this movement. In the following sections, I introduce the development of IciMontreuil and show analytically how the founders and the makers defined some core past, present and future events shaping their organizational temporality and how various objects gained their meaning as they were ingredients of these events.

[2] "Portes ouvertes des ateliers d'artiste de Montreuil" in French.

[3] Figures taken from INSEE (French National Institute. for Statistics), see https://www.insee.fr/fr/statistiques/1405599?geo=COM-93048.

The Artistic and Industrial Past of Montreuil

As founders were developing IciMontreuil, the past of the city strongly inspired them. They have lived in this city for a while and often expressed their attachment to the city, especially its industrial and artistic inheritance. In order to give a strong meaning and purpose to their project, they anchored their project into this past. By publishing articles on their website and by giving interviews to media mentioning the influence of the past of Montreuil in their project, they were creating a historical account that served the purpose of IciMontreuil. On the IciMontreuil's website, there are plenty of references about the past of the city and how IciMontreuil is a way to walk in the footsteps of its famous artists and industrialists, such as Georges Méliés, Pathé's brothers. In such, the industrial and artistic past of Montreuil was used as a strategic resource (Foster, Coraiola, Suddaby, Kroezen, & Chandler, 2017).

However, the past is not only mobilized through narratives. Founders also relied on artefact to anchor their project in this past. For example, they decided to locate IciMontreuil in an old factory. For the founders it was a way to bring the industrial past of the city in the daily lives of the makers because, despite renovations, its old industrial architecture is still powerful. Built with small red bricks, a massive iron structure and large windows, the building is typical of the industrial era.

Moreover, this link with the past of the city is not limited to the architecture of the building. The interior architecture has been created based on the same idea. The interior architecture appears to be a tribute to the industrial past of the city as well. The workshops, the meeting rooms, the coworking spaces and so on are designed with the idea to imitate the architecture of small old workshops typical in Montreuil. In other words, the interior architecture is a way to bring this industrial past to the makers' daily life. By doing so, the founders anchored their project into this local industrial and artistic inheritance. This industrial and artistic history is then enacted as past events participating in the definition of what IciMontreuil is about. It gives a specific meaning to actors' activities and identity (Suddaby & Foster, 2017). To do this, the building and interior architecture are ingredients of these past events. There are "objects"

(Whitehead, 1929) defining the character of past events.[4] These ingredients participate in the enactment of the Montreuil past and, by doing so, the legacy on which IciMontreuil relies on.

The Present "Creative Revolution" of Montreuil

However, the founders did not only rely on the past to build the IciMontreuil's organizational temporality but on some current trends as well. To do so, the founders joined the countercultures that were burgeoning during the 2010s and anchored IciMontreuil into this context. The founders relied on trends such as the development of collaborative spaces (coworking spaces and fablabs), the DIY (do-it-yourself) and the DIT (do-it-together) countercultures. All of these movements were inspirations for the project. For example, the hashtags used to describe their *Instagram* account are *#Montreuil*, *#fablab*, *#DIY* and *#DIT*.[5] These countercultures are based on the idea that people can make what they want by constantly learning new skills, sharing knowledge and using new technologies (Anderson, 2012). Such principles were easily appropriated by the founders of IciMontreuil, who found them to be a great way of giving legitimacy to their project.

However, the founders did not ignore the importance of the city's current context. The vivid artistic and craft dynamism in Montreuil was qualified as a "creative revolution" by the founders, and the aim of IciMontreuil was to participate in this creative revolution by hosting these creative people and providing them with resources. Moreover, IciMontreuil celebrates this local artistic and craftwork scene through the organization and participation of numerous events, such as exhibitions hosted in the makerspace. For example, the founders welcome exhibitions of local artists or encourage the makers to participate in shows or competitions.

[4] For the sake of the illustration, I limit here the analysis to past events, but as mentioned earlier, ingredients of events are not ingredients of one event, but rather are always ingredients of several events.

[5] https://www.instagram.com/icimontreuil/ consulted on 23 March 2017.

All these present events are made tangible through numerous artefacts in the makerspace. For instance, visitors entering the building can see a homemade arcade video-game—a typical artefact of the DIY culture, and designed pieces of furniture and artworks; this is a way to anchor the makers' activities into the current design and artistic trends in Montreuil. In other words, these artefacts play an important role in defining the present of IciMontreuil.

The Future of Production

The past and the present of IciMontreuil are thus made tangible through various artefacts. The same can be said about the future. For instance, at the front door of the building a sign indicates what IciMontreuil is about: "Art[tisanat] + Design + Techno". This sign was installed when IciMontreuil just opened, that is, when the members were just starting to work in the makerspace. However, the first projects completed in the makerspace rarely combined these three aspects, so it was more a goal to share with the members than a matter of fact. Moreover, this way of defining IciMontreuil is linked with another founder's aim: to participate in the development of the local economy. By encouraging makers to create objects combining art, craft, design and high tech, the aim was to make sure that members' activity would participate in the local economy. It was a personal goal for the founders and is very clearly stated on their website.[6]

Another example of how future events can be characterized materially can be found in the role allocated to the fablab. The fablab (fabrication laboratory) is a workshop where makers can find all the technologies they need to craft prototypes and develop electronic parts for their products. 3D printers, laser cutters and so on are available in the fablab where makers can develop innovative products based on innovative tools. It represents the innovative and high-tech dimensions that IciMontreuil is trying to promote. This fablab was originally built in the basement of the building, just next to other workshops dedicated to wood, iron, fabric and so

[6] https://makeici.org/icimontreuil/

on. It made sense to put the fablab next to the other workshops as the makers could move easily from one workshop to another. However, the founders decided to move it to the ground floor at the centre of the building. By doing that, the fablab became the central element of IciMontreuil, representing the potential of IciMontreuil to develop future innovations. This new fablab is much bigger, much better equipped, while the founders hired a second person to assist the makers in developing their prototypes. In this, the future is not only made concrete through a narrative account but is characterized with the building of this new fablab as well. All of these artefacts participate in the definition of the organizational temporality of IciMontreuil as they were ingredients of past, present and future events. In turn, these artefacts gained a specific meaning, role and status through their ability to characterize the organizational temporality of IciMontreuil.

Discussion and Contributions

In this chapter, I have suggested to understand the relation between materiality and organizational temporality. I have proposed to understand materiality as ingredients of events. In such a perspective, the material and the social are the same process, that is, an individuation process of the flux of experiences into events. More precisely, materiality is here conceived as the character of the events shaping organizational temporalities. By employing the events-based approach to materiality, this chapter contributes, firstly, to our understanding of organization as it highlights the role of materiality in the process making of organization by showing how materiality participates in the re/definition of the structure of past, present and future events that defines the organizational temporality. Secondly, the events-based approach of materiality brings an alternative way to understand the emergence of new organizational phenomena, especially in the context of New Ways of Working and organizing. In such a view, innovative ways of working and organizing are not only about new ways of producing, communicating, collaborating and so on, but about new ways to relate with the past, the present and the future as well.

The Role of Materiality in the Making Process of Organization

By defining materiality—which can be any human or non-human actors—as the tangible ingredients of events (Whitehead, 1929) characterizing the structure of events, materiality is the concrete and tangible expression of organizational phenomena and, more precisely, its temporality. In such, "things" are tangible characteristics of events (Bono, 2014). Materiality is partly what makes the past, the present and the future tangible in the current moment. For example, in our illustration, the building is partly what makes the industrial past of Montreuil tangible. The building is an ingredient enabling the enactment of the industrial past of Montreuil by founders and makers of IciMontreuil, but the same building also participates in the enactment of the present of IciMontreuil as well, as it characterizes the current economic crisis and the "creative revolution" occurring in Montreuil. In such, the building is an ingredient for several events. Consequently, the situated history and present of IciMontreuil are partly made concrete by the founders and makers through this artefact. By insisting on the role of artefact in the re/definition of the structure of events, the chapter has shown that the materialization of the organizational temporality is not only made through narratives. As most of the research about temporality has mainly focused on narratives to deal with its re/production, an events-based approach of materiality insists on the role of any human and non-human actor (such as a building) in the re/production of the structure of events. To be more precise, materiality gains a meaning, a role and a status thanks to its ability to re/define the structure of events. For instance, the building of IciMontreuil gained a special meaning because of its ability to characterize the history of the town and the current development of IciMontreuil. Moreover, some artefacts make the enactment of a shared future possible, as the fablab did, for instance. In turn, this fablab gains its meaning, role and status because of its ability to participate in the definition of future events—such as the development of the local economy—that enable the makers to make sense of what they are doing. By being an ingredient of the future events of Montreuil, the fablab participates in the re/definition of a future enabling the makers to position their various activities in a shared temporality. It is in this sense that we can understand any human or non-human as a temporal phenomenon.

Contribution of an Events-Based Approach of Materiality in Our Understanding of the Emergence of New Ways of Working and Organizing

A second contribution of this temporal view of materiality is in its potential to follow and understand how new "things" such as categories, labels, statuses, roles emerge from New Ways of Working and organizing. The illustration based on the maker movement is an example of how any New Ways of Working leads to the creation of numerous "things" that define the organizational phenomenon itself. Creations of new "things" can also be found in other trends at work such as coworking, digital nomadism and freelancing (Hussenot & Sergi, 2018). Considering these "things" as ingredients of a structure of events (Whitehead, 1929) can enable scholars to understand how these new categories, labels, statuses, roles and so on are defined to characterize new temporalities, because with labels such as coworking and digital nomadism, actors are not only experimenting New Ways of Working, they are also re/defining the history, the present and the future of work. The events-based approach of materiality is a call for understanding how these new "things" emerge, not as disconnected from the past but as an alternative way to enact a past, a present and a future of work; and how this temporality constitutes what these New Ways of Working and organizing are. In this, an events-based approach of materiality is a call to understand how new work practices, rules, tools and so on are ingredients of events participating in the definition of new organizational temporalities.

Conclusion

In this chapter, I have suggested an events-based approach of materiality. This approach consists in understanding materiality as anything that defines the past, the present and the future of the current activity. Anchored into the process philosophy (Rescher, 1996, 2001), all the "things" of the reality are understood not as spatial and physical phenomena but as temporal ones. Materiality is ingredients of events defining a temporality. By giving to materiality such a broad meaning, anything can participate in organizational temporality. This might help to overcome the classic dualism between the material and the social by focusing instead on the role of materiality in the making process of organizational temporality. This attempt to provide an alternative view to materiality is motivated by the constant evolution of ways of working and organizing that requires to question our assumptions about what an organization is. The events-based approach of materiality can enable scholars to live, follow and transcribe those constant evolving organizational phenomena.

Acknowledgements I'm very grateful to the editors for giving me this opportunity to write this chapter. I would also like to thank Albert David and the "Cercle de l'Innovation" of the Fondation Dauphine for having partly funded this research.

References

Anderson, C. (2012). *Makers: The new industrial revolution*. New York: Random House.

Barad, K. (2003). Posthumanist performativity: Toward an understanding of how matter comes to matter. *Signs: Journal of Women in Culture and Society, 28*(3), 801–831.

Barad, K. (2007). *Meeting the universe halfway: Quantum physics and the entanglement of matter and meaning*. Durham, NC: Duke University Press.

Barad, K. (2013). Ma(r)king time: material entanglements and re-memberings: cutting together-apart. In P. R. Carlile, D. Nicolini, A. Langley, & H. Tsoukas

(Eds.), *How matter matters: Objects, artifacts, and materiality in organization studies* (pp. 16–31). London: Oxford University Press.

Bergson, H. (1889). *Essai sur les données immédiates de la conscience*. Paris: Presses Universitaires de France.

Bergson, H. (1896–1939). *Matière et mémoire*. Paris: Presses Universitaires de France.

Bergson, H. (1907–2009). *L'évolution créative*. Paris: Presses Universitaires de France.

Bono, J. J. (2014). Atomicity, conformation, enduring objects, and "things": science and science studies after the Whiteheadian turn. In R. Faber & A. Goffey (Eds.), *The Allure of thing: Process and object in contemporary philosophy* (pp. 16–35). London: Bloomsbury.

Burke, A. (Ed.). (2015). *The handbook of research on freelancing and self-employment: Shankill*. Dublin, Ireland: Senate Hall Academic Publishing.

Carlile, P. R., Nicolini, D., Langley, A., & Tsoukas, H. (2013). *How matter matters: Objects, artifacts, materiality in organization studies*. Oxford, UK: Oxford University Press.

Cecez-Kecmanovic, D., Galliers, R. D., Henfridsson, O., Newell, S., & Vidgen, R. (2014). The sociomateriality of information systems: current status, future direction. *MIS Quarterly, 38*(3), 809–830.

Chia, R. (2002). Essay: Time, duration and simultaneity: Rethinking process and change in organizational analysis. *Organization Studies, 23*(6), 863–868.

Cobb, J. B. (2007). Person-in-community: Whiteheadian insights into community and institution. *Organization Studies, 28*(4), 567–588.

Collet, A. (2015). *Rester bourgeois. Les quartiers populaires, nouveaux chantiers de la distinction*. Paris: La Découverte.

Cooper, R. (2014). Process and reality (chapter 36). In J. Helin, T. Hernes, D. Hjorth, & R. Holt (Eds.), *Process philosophy and organization studies*. Oxford, UK: Oxford University Press.

Dougherty, D. (2012). The maker movement. *Innovations, 7*(3), 11–14.

Feldman, M. S., & Orlikowski, W. J. (2011). Theorizing practice and practicing theory. *Organization Science, 22*, 1240–1253.

Foster, W. M., Coraiola, D. M., Suddaby, R., Kroezen, J., & Chandler, D. (2017). The strategic use of historical narratives: A theoretical framework. *Business History, 59*(8), 1176–1200.

Hatch, M. (2013). *The maker movement manifesto: Rules for innovation in the new world of crafters, hackers, and tinkerers*. New York, NY: McGraw-Hill Professional.

Hernes, T. (2014a). *A process theory of organization*. Oxford: Oxford University Press.
Hernes, T. (2014b). Alfred North Whitehead (chapter 16). In J. Helin, T. Hernes, D. Hjort, & R. Holt (Eds.), *Oxford handbook of process philosophy and organization studies*. Oxford, UK: Oxford University Press.
Hernes, T. (2017). Process as the becoming of temporal trajectory. In A. Langley & H. Tsoukas (Eds.), *The SAGE handbook of process organization studies* (pp. 601–607). Thousand Oaks, CA: Sage.
Hernes, T., Simpson, B., & Soderlund, J. (2013). Introduction: managing and temporality. *Scandinavian Journal of Management, 29*, 1–6.
Hulst, M. V., Ybema, S., & Yanow, D. (2017). Ethnography and organizational processes. In A. Langley & H. Tsoukas (Eds.), *SAGE handbook of process organization studies* (pp. 223–236). Thousand Oaks, CA: Sage.
Hussenot, A. (2019). *L'organisation à l'épreuve des makers. Propositions pour une approche par les événements*. Québec, Canada: Presses Universitaires de Laval.
Hussenot, A., Hernes, T., & Bouty, I. (Forthcoming). Studying organization from the perspective of the ontology of temporality: Introducing the event-based approach. In J. Reinecke, R. Suddaby, A. Langley, & H. Tsoukas (Eds.), *About time: Temporality and history in organization studies*. Oxford, UK: Oxford University Press.
Hussenot, A., & Missonier, S. (2016). Encompassing stability and novelty in organization studies: an events-based approach. *Organization Studies, 37*(4), 523–546.
Hussenot, A., & Sergi, V. (2018). Collaborating without (formal) organization: How do independent workers call into question the matter of organization? In C. Cézanne & L. Saglietto (Eds.), *Human Capital Intensive Firms*. Hershey, PA: IGI Global Edition.
Introna, L. D. (2013). Otherness and the letting-be of becoming: Or, ethics beyond bifurcation. In P. R. Carlile, D. Nicolini, A. Langley, & H. Tsoukas (Eds.), *How matter matters: Objects, artifacts, and materiality in organization studies* (pp. 260–287). Oxford, UK: Oxford University Press.
Jarzabkowski, P., & Pinch, T. (2013). Sociomateriality is 'the New Black': accomplishing repurposing, reinscripting and repairing in context. *M@n@gement, 16*(5), 579–592.
Jensen, A., Thuesen, C., & Geraldi, J. (2016). The projectification of everything: Projects as a human condition. *Project Management Journal, 47*(3), 21–34.

Jones, M. (2013). Untangling materiality. In P. R. Carlile, D. Nicolini, A. Langley, & H. Tsoukas (Eds.), *How matter matters: Objects, artifacts, and materiality in organization studies* (pp. 197–226). Oxford, UK: Oxford University Press.

Jones, M. (2014). A matter of life and death: Exploring conceptualizations of sociomateriality in the context of critical care. *MIS Quarterly, 38*(3), 895–925.

Kautz, K., & Jensen, T. B. (2013). Sociomateriality at the royal court of IS A jester's monologue. *Information and Organisation, 23*, 15–27.

Latour, B. (2005). *Reassembling the social: An introduction to actor-network theory*. Oxford, UK: Oxford University Press.

Leonardi, P., Nardi, B. A., & Kallinikos, J. (2012). *Materiality and organizing social interaction in a technological world*. Oxford: Oxford University Press.

Leonardi, P. M. (2010). Digital materiality? How artifacts without matter, matter. *First Monday*, 15(6).

Leonardi, P. M. (2011). When flexible routines meet flexible technologies: Affordance, constraint, and the imbrication of human and material agencies. *MIS Quarterly, 35*(1), 147–176.

Leonardi, P. M. (2013). The emergence of materiality within formal organization (chapter 7). In P. R. Carlile, D. Nicolini, A. Langley, & H. Tsoukas (Eds.), *How matter matters: Objects, artifacts, and materiality in organization studies*. Oxford, UK: Oxford Press University.

Leonardi, P. M., & Barley, S. R. (2008). Materiality and change: Challenge to building better theory about technology and organizing. *Information and Organization, 18*, 159–176.

Leonardi, P. M., & Barley, S. R. (2012). What's under construction here? Social action, materiality, and power in constructivist studies of technology and organizing. *The Academy of Management Annals, 4*(1), 1–51.

Makimoto, T., & Manners, D. (1997). *Digital nomad*. Chichester, UK: Wiley.

Marovich, B. (2014). Creaturely things: living matter, dead matter, and the resonance of actual entities (chapter 6). In R. Faber & A. Goffey (Eds.), *The Allure of things: Process and object in contemporary philosophy*. London: Bloomsbury.

Mead, G. H. (1932). *The philosophy of the present*. Chicago, IL: Open Court Company.

Orlikowski, W. J. (2000). Using technology and constituting structures: A practice lens for studying technology in organizations. *Organization Science, 4*(4), 404–438.

Orlikowski, W. J. (2006). Material knowing: the scaffolding of human knowledgeability. *European Journal of Information Systems, 15*, 460–466.
Orlikowski, W. J. (2007). Sociomaterial practices: Exploring technology at work. *Organization Studies, 29*(9), 1435–1448.
Orlikowski, W. J. (2010). The sociomateriality of organisational life: considering technology in management research. *Cambridge Journal of Economics, 34*(1), 125–141.
Orlikowski, W. J., & Scott, S. V. (2008). Sociomateriality: Challenging the separation of technology, work, and organization. *The Academy of Management Annals, 2*(1), 433–474.
Orlikowski, W. J., & Scott, S. V. (2013). Knowledge eclipse: Producing sociomaterial reconfigurations in the hospitality sector. In P. R. Carlile, D. Nicolini, A. Langley, & H. Tsoukas (Eds.), *How matter matters: Objects, artifacts, and materiality in organization studies* (pp. 119–141). Oxford: Oxford Press University.
Pickering, A. (1995). *The mangle of practice: Time, agency, and science*. Chicago: IL: University of Chicago Press.
Reinecke, J., & Ansari, S. (2017). Time, temporality, and process studies. In A. Langley & H. Tsoukas (Eds.), *The SAGE handbook of process organization studies* (pp. 402–416). Thousand Oaks, CA: Sage.
Rescher, N. (1996). *Process metaphysics: An introduction to process philosophy*. New York: New York State University Press.
Rescher, N. (2001). *Process philosophy: A survey of basic issues*. Pittsburgh, PA: University of Pittsburgh Press.
Shotter, J. (2013). Reflections on sociomateriality and dialogicality in organization studies: From "inter-" to "intra-thinking"… in performing practices. In P. R. Carlile, D. Nicolini, A. Langley, & H. Tsoukas (Eds.), *How matter matters: Objects, artifacts and materiality in organization studies* (pp. 32–47). Oxford, UK: Oxford University Press.
Slife, B. D. (2004). Taking practice seriously: Toward a relational ontology. *Journal of Theoretical and Philosophical Psychology, 24*(2), 158–178.
Spinuzzi, C. (2012). Working alone together: Coworking as emergent collaborative activity. *Journal of Business and Technical Communication, 26*(4), 399–441.
Suddaby, R., & Foster, W. M. (2017). History and organizational change. *Journal of Management, 43*(1), 19–38.

Trist, E. (1981). *The evolution of socio-technical systems: Conceptual framework and an action research program*. Occasional paper, Toronto: Ontario Ministry of Labour, Ontario Quality of Working Life Centre.

Trist, E. L., & Bamforth, K. W. (1951). Some social and psychological consequences of the longwall method of coal-getting. *Human Relations, 41*(1), 3–38.

Vaujany, F.-X. d., Mitev, N., Laniray, P., & Vaast, E. (Eds.). (2014). *Materiality and time. historical perspectives on organizations, artefacts and practices*. Basingstoke, UK: Palgrave Macmillan.

Whitehead, A. N. (1920). *Concept of nature*. Cambridge, UK: Cambridge University Press.

Whitehead, A. N. (1929–1978). *Process and reality*. New York, NY: The Free Press.

Whitehead, A. N. (1938). *Modes of thought*. New York, NY: The Free Press.

6

The Role of Digital Materiality for Organizing a Living Lab

Philippe Eynaud and Julien Malaurent

Introduction

Living labs gather individuals and organizations from various horizons (private, public, non-profit) in open infrastructures around common goals (Schaffers, Garcia Guzman, & Merz, 2008) to foster innovation by experimenting New Ways of Working (Almirall & Wareham, 2008). Living labs can be regarded as clusters aiming to structure collaboration on a territory through "win-win" strategies (Guzmán, del Carpio, Colomo-Palacios, & de Diego, 2013, p. 29): "living labs are facilities that provide the physical and organizational infrastructure to support efforts to involve users in innovation and product development". These facilities

P. Eynaud (✉)
Sorbonne Business School, Paris, France
e-mail: philippe.eynaud@univ-paris1.fr

J. Malaurent
ESSEC Business School, Cergy, France
e-mail: malaurent@essec.edu

N. Mitev et al. (eds.), *New Ways of Working*, Technology, Work and Globalization,
https://doi.org/10.1007/978-3-030-61687-8_6

are assumed to support interaction among stakeholders with the objective to establish connections between academic knowledge and in-situ knowledge by providing "technology-related facilities, such as technological services, training courses, dialogue cafés and other initiatives" (Guzmán et al., 2013, p. 30). However, living labs are difficult to manage. They require specific expertise and experience to manage successfully actors with different agendas, but also facilities and spatial arrangements. This new organizational form requires a detailed investigation to understand how they materialize but also how they are managed throughout their operations.

This chapter is organized as follows. The next section discusses the challenges of organizing living labs before introducing sociomateriality as a lens to analyze the role of materiality for organizing. In the third section, we discuss the case of a French organic farming living lab. This chapter concludes with a discussion on the role of digital materiality for addressing living labs issues.

Challenges of Living Labs

The concept of living lab (i.e. living laboratories) was first proposed in the 1990s by several researchers (Bajgier, Maragah, Saccucci, & Verzilli, 1991; Bengtson, 1994; Lasher, Ives, & Jarvenpaa, 1991; Mitchell, 1999) as a new approach to study innovation. The novelty relied on involving users in co-creative environments enriched by embedded technologies. Living labs are part of a renewed organizational context where members coming from various organizations work together, as a collective, and mobilize appropriate technologies. Living labs are often assimilated to other novel organizational structures such as fablabs, media labs, and hackerspaces. Thus, "living labs are innovation infrastructures within which software companies and research organizations collaborate with lead users and early adopters in creating participative strategies to define, design, develop, and validate new products and services that maximize the socioeconomic conditions of the partnership" (Guzmán et al., 2013, 29).

Living labs were institutionalized in 2006 by the European Union through the creation of a European Network of Living Labs (ENoLL). ENoLL defines living labs as "user-centered, open innovation ecosystems based on a systematic user co-creation approach, integrating research and innovation processes in real life communities and settings" (Schuurman & Tõnurist, 2016, p. 6). ENoLL recognize living labs as practice-driven fluid organizations, arenas of open innovation, and shared spaces with the objective to foster social, economic, and environmental development.

A living lab is often approached as a "third place" (Oldenburg, 1998) that is an in-between location, a neutral place, a space to foster dialogue in complement (and in reaction) to traditional professional and personal arenas. A third place is a space (physical or not) where temporary proximities can be activated. Like living labs it presents opportunities and challenges related to networking, as well as the role of information technologies in the transformation of organizational practices (Ducheneaut, Moore, & Nickell, 2007; Wakelin & Street, 2015). The notion of space, and its materiality, has also a specific role to play in living labs. Most of the time, the project is driven by a local community to address a given issue to support economic and/or social development. The creation of a living lab is therefore embedded in a specific spatial context with contingent resources. In this regard, living labs are different from clusters or industrial districts. People rally in living labs to address demand issues. Supply issues, if any, are not the focus of living labs.

Living labs are also places where heterogeneous actors can participate in design thinking activities (Gray, Mangyoku, Serra, Sánchez, & Aragall, 2014). Thus, innovation is not the sole responsibility of engineers. A large range of activities can take place in living labs, from individual activity close to DIY (Do-it-yourself) to DIWO (Do-it-with-others). This collaborative approach aims to shorten development cycles, lower risks, increase product appropriation by users, and improve innovation. Thus, "services offered by a living lab may include facilities for incubating ideas for new products and services based on the needs and desires of end-user communities, support for developing ideas, tools for validating technological solutions, and support for the wide-scale launch of products. The nature of user participation depends on the specific nature of the living lab" (Guzmán et al., 2013, p. 30).

Hence, the scope of possibilities in living labs is limitless, and idiosyncrasy is a core rule of their functioning. User involvement can be limited to the evaluation of a prototype or can be extended to the mobilization of a large crowd for the dissemination of social innovations. In the same vein, public authorities can merely play the role of facilitator or can choose to be a business and/or funding partner. Thus, it is difficult to define good practices regarding a unique business or governance model. There is no "one best way" to manage a living lab and no a priori recipe to develop a smart, universal living lab. Living labs assume "effective practices to manage the collaboration", but as shown by Guzmán et al. (2013, p. 29), there is "currently no process reference model for efficient practices to manage a living lab".

The Importance of Materiality

Sociomateriality (Leonardi & Barley, 2010; Orlikowski, 2007; Orlikowski & Scott, 2008) offers a rich analytical lens to understand the constitutive relationships between group dynamics, artefacts, spaces, and organizational legitimacy. The social and material dimensions (e.g. walls, windows, corridors, furniture) are recognized to be "entangled" (Orlikowski & Scott, 2008) or "imbricated" (Leonardi, 2011) within social practices (De Vaujany & Vaast, 2013). However, in the context of living labs, there has been, so far, limited discussion on how the materiality of a community is built and brought to life over time. Previous literature analyzing online communities has focused on the concepts of "distance" and "perceived proximity" (Wilson, O'Leary, Metiu, & Jett, 2008) and how to handle it from a practical perspective. More research is needed on the way heterogeneous groups of actors coming from different organizations deal with the construction of a group's legitimacy, organizational structure, and the development of collective practices in this context. This is an important issue given that open innovation, ideation, but also material infrastructures and collective practices, correspond to what people do in such organizational and technological environments based on situated learning dynamics (Lave & Wenger, 1991).

This leads us to define what we mean by "materiality". Leonardi and Barley argue: "Materiality matters for theories of technology and organizing because the material properties of artefacts are precisely those tangible resources that provide people with the ability to do old things in new ways and to do things they could not do before" (Leonardi & Barley, 2008, p. 161). Materiality is a concept that represents the tangible resources that provide people the ability to do things individually and collectively. However, physicality is different from materiality because the latter is related to an emergent process (Hayles, 2012). Materiality is indeed not given a priori. It emerges as the result of interactions between different elements. Materiality can also be a necessary ingredient for a community of people working on a collective assignment. It can be composed of physical artefacts (i.e. desks, meeting rooms) but also of more intangible artefacts such as working procedures, regulations, and software. In order to qualify the material properties of software (as well as platforms and apps), Leonardi (2010) uses the term "digital materiality". Leonardi posits that a new lens is indeed necessary to apprehend the organizing dynamics characterizing this specific kind of materiality—often characterized as intangible phenomena. He suggests three aspects to approach materiality: (1) matter, (2) practical instantiation, and (3) significance: "if materiality is defined simply as matter (…) digital artefacts cannot be said to have materiality. However, when materiality is understood to represent the practical instantiation and the significance of an artefact, digital artefacts can clearly be seen to have materiality" (Leonardi, 2010, p. 2). Thus, Leonardi (2010) distinguishes three dimensions to investigate digital materiality.

- *Focusing on its use*: According to Leonardi our focus should be on how digital artefacts are perceived and used. He refers to Orlikowski (2007) who defines materiality as "stuff" in order to avoid the term "object" which implies tangibility. Therefore, what "matters most about an artefact is not what it is made of, but what it allows people to do" (Leonardi, 2010, p. 5). It allows connecting the concept of materiality with the literature on affordance (Gibson, 1986).
- *Capturing its practical implications*: Digital artefacts can translate idea into action. Leonardi discusses how software can "instantiate the

abstract idea of management" (Leonardi, 2010, p. 8) to have material aspects and properties like tangible resources. Thus, it matters little "whether an artefact has matter or not" (Leonardi, 2010, p. 8). The main point is that artefact has a performative power on reality and provides people with capabilities (Pickering, 2001).

- *Giving significance*: An artefact can be "material" when "it makes a difference in the current situation" (Leonardi, 2010, p. 8). Therefore, being material is being significant. The artefact is making sense in the context where it is used (Weick, 1988) and there is consequently a need to focus on "technology-in-practice". This dimension emphasizes that an artefact can have different features and that they are not "equally significant to everyone" (Leonardi, 2010, p. 9).

In what follows, we discuss how an organic farming living lab experienced digital materiality as a way to collectively create its organizational practices, as well as its own interactional dynamics.

Melibio: An Organic Farming Living Lab in Quest of Materiality

Organizational Settings

The association *Pole Bio* has created a multi-tenant project called *Melibio* to support the spread of organic agriculture in the Massif Central region of France. This group of actors is specifically interested in meadows that are composed of a variety of flora or forage crops. It brings together a group of heterogeneous actors: researchers in biology, computer scientists, Chamber of Agriculture officials, teachers, agricultural experts, and farmers' associations. The project is supported by public funders and aims to find new and innovative agricultural techniques to handle climate change.

The common goal of the *Melibio* project is to foster innovation among farmers' communities to help them adjust organic agriculture crops. To reach this goal, the project has two objectives: the first one consists of producing a decision-making model to assist seeding. This decision-making model (named *Capflor*) will be embedded within an online platform to assist farmers in calculating the most appropriate mix for seeding flora in meadows. Farmers will have to enter local data into the software (such as location, soil type, weather conditions, etc.), and will get advice about seeding mixes. The second objective is related to the creation of a wiki-based knowledge platform to articulate both expert and lay knowledge in order to improve the collective expertise of the organic farming community in that region.

In order to reach these two objectives, the actors group have to collaborate closely despite their differences (different institutions with different interests, and geographic distance) to come up with collective and collaborative decisions. This second objective contributes to the first one because it can increase the value of *Capflor* by spreading its results on a large scale. Therefore, it appears as a key success condition to better bridge academic and lay knowledge if these recommendations are to be adopted by farmers. The living lab is also promoting a serious game for farmers. Its name is *Rami fourrager* ("fodder card game"). This simulation game (designed by academic researchers) aims to provide a situated training tool and a mean for opening discussion between farmers about their practices. It is also a way to combine scientific and practitioners' knowledge. The perspective offered by the serious game is not only top-down oriented but also bottom-up oriented. The idea is to help farmers share their knowledge with their peers, but also to enrich the online decision model *Capflor* by collecting their experience from the fields.

This chapter is based on the analysis of 35 in-depth semi-interviews with *Melibio* members as well as a number of participant observations and secondary data collected by both authors (meeting minutes, official documents, etc.). Thanks to our official integration in the group as participant observers, we were allowed to record and collect data without limitation.

Initial Unstructured Interactions

Our observations of the group's interactions reveal that the diversity of the members does not appear to be an issue. On the contrary, some actors see it as a major asset. The lack of hierarchy in the group seems also to be important for allowing the emergence of innovation. One member told us that: "The interest of the project is related to the diversity inside the group and in the fields that are investigated. We are all peers. There is no hierarchy and it is easy to communicate (…) Melibio is a very open project. You can feel it. No one is trying to dominate the collective (…) I feel safe. I have the feeling of working with skilled people who always intend to move forward. I learn a lot."

However, facilitating collaboration in such a heterogeneous group, without any physical infrastructure, is not easy. During an interview, a member expressed the following: "The evolution of the geographical perimeter of the project leads to an increase of phone conferences and a decrease of face to face meetings. That is clearly a drawback for the group's interactions". Another interviewee said something similar: "We have a problem because of the size of our territory and the geographical distances between the members. Of course, we can increase the number of phone (and video) conferences but it does not seem to be sufficient. I am a bit worried about this problem of geographical remoteness".

Throughout these statements, we can measure the importance of a common space and common infrastructures for organizing collective interactions. In what follows, we discuss how a digital artefact (Leonardi, 2010) played a major role in the construction of a group's materiality through the elaboration of a boundary object (Carlile, Nicolini, Langley, & Tsoukas, 2013).

A Collective Digital Space to Structure the Collective

At first, the heterogeneity of the group members led to a number of difficulties due to the lack of a common organizational structure, leadership, rules, and task allocation. The group also suffered from the lack of a common space to meet and exchange. A number of interviews revealed that users were confused because of the lack of a common platform to organize people's contributions, share documents, and so on. Email exchanges and online meetings were found to be insufficient. A shared physical artefact (e.g. a meeting place to meet regularly) or a digital one (e.g. an online meeting room) was missing.

Based on these observations, and in agreement with the project manager, we proposed the introduction of an online project management software system (instantiated from the *BaseCamp* platform[1]) to answer actors' quest for materiality. In what follows, we present three illustrative examples revealing the importance of this digital artefact for organizing *Melibio*'s digital lab. Each illustration corresponds to one of the three dimensions suggested by Leonardi (2010).

Focusing on Its Use

When we suggested to *Melibio* members to adopt *BaseCamp* as a common space for collaboration, most members were willing. However, some were afraid of not having the skills to handle the software. Others were worried of having to use another platform in addition to the ones they were already using. This led us to organize a series of training sessions to make everyone familiar with the artefact. During those training sessions, one member was particularly in need for support, as it seems that her only experience with digital tools was the use of emails. Additionally, she complained about the limited capacity of her mailbox as she could not send or receive large files to communicate with people located elsewhere. *Basecamp* became a tangible workaround system to bypass the limitations of her mailbox. Right after the platform's launch, she uploaded photographs of a parasite invading her meadows, and asked for advice to the group members. A discussion started and some members informed her about the procedure she should follow to eradicate it. This is an example showing how users should not limit themselves to their initial perception of the artefact but focus on its potential for use.

[1] https://basecamp.com/

Capturing the Practical Implications

When setting up the *Basecamp* platform, we realized that we could divide the collective into a maximum of ten thematic subgroups. This question of structuring the group into subgroups had never been faced before since the organization of the collective was very informal until then. One of the training sessions therefore turned into an open discussion about the subgroups: How many of them should be created? Who will moderate them? Who will be participating in each of them? Could people belong to two or three of them? Who should have access to what? We found that this practical feature had a great influence and collective decisions were taken about its organization and structure. The homepage of the platform was used to list all thematic subgroups, with the members' list and moderators. This illustrates how the practical characteristics of a digital artefact may have direct consequences on the organization of a collective.

Giving Significance

During the *Melibio* project, it was suggested that an in-depth analysis of the impact of climate change on organic farming in Southern Europe could help to anticipate the on-going transformations occurring in Massif Central. Therefore, a decision was made to recruit a trainee who would travel to Spain and Portugal to carry out an empirical investigation. A Spanish native speaker was recruited and immediately started his mission without having a chance to meet the vast majority of the group. However, the trainee used the platform to share his field notes on a daily basis, which took the form of a diary, photographs, notes from interviews with farmers, scientific reports, and personal comments. Through this particular use the platform took its full significance. Several members commented regularly on the trainee's diary and engaged in various collective conversations about the empirical findings. This contributed to a sense of collective identity.

Discussion and Conclusion

This empirical case offers several contributions. First, it illustrates the concept of digital materiality. The three dimensions suggested by Leonardi (2010) were found to be meaningful in the analysis of *Melibio* living lab. The first dimension (Focusing on its use) helped us understand how its members appropriated the tool by focusing on its affordance. The second dimension (Capturing the practical implications) guided our analysis of how the platform was approached as a performative tool—helping the group to formalize its organization. The third dimension (Giving significance) highlighted how members could make sense of the platform through engagement and exchange. The three dimensions put together helped to capture how digital materiality, in the case of *Melibio,* fostered knowledge and innovation.

Second, this case illustrates how digital materiality can substitute for physical materiality. Since the group was spread on a large territory with members working from different organizations and different agendas, the use of a digital artefact to substitute the lack of a common space was found to be a relevant alternative.

We suggest that further studies on living labs could challenge the original but provocative "Digital First" argument of Baskerville, Myers, and Yoo (2020) who claim that digital reality is created first, and physical reality second.

References

Almirall, E., & Wareham, J. (2008). Living labs and open innovation: Roles and applicability. *The Electronic Journal for Virtual Organization & Networks, 10*, 21–46.

Bajgier, S. M., Maragah, H. D., Saccucci, M. S., & Verzilli, A. (1991). Introducing students to community operations research by using a city neighborhood as living laboratory. *Operations Research, 39*(5), 701–709.

Baskerville, R., Myers, M., & Yoo, Y. (2020). Digital First: The ontological reversal and new challenges for IS Research. *MIS Quarterly*. Forthcoming.

Bengtson, P. (1994). Which comes first, internal involvement or external? *The Journal for Quality and Participation, 17*(5), 32–37.

Carlile, P., Nicolini, D., Langley, A., & Tsoukas, H. (Eds.). (2013). *How matter matters: Objects, artifacts, and materiality in organization studies*. Oxford: Oxford University Press.

De Vaujany, F.-X., & Vaast, E. (2013). If these walls could talk: The mutual construction of organizational space and legitimacy. *Organization Science, 25*(3), 713–731.

Ducheneaut, N., Moore, R. J., & Nickell, E. (2007). Virtual "third places": A case study of sociability in massively multiplayer games. *Computer Supported Cooperative Work, 16*(1–2), 129–166.

Gibson, J. J. (1986). *The ecological approach to visual perception*. Hillsdale, N.J.: Lawrence Erlbaum.

Gray, M., Mangyoku, M., Serra, A., Sánchez, L., & Aragall, F. (2014). Integrating design for all in living labs. *Technology Innovation Management Review, 4*(5), 50–59.

Guzmán, J. G., del Carpio, A. F., Colomo-Palacios, R., & de Diego, M. V. (2013). Living labs for user-driven innovation. *Research Technology Management, 56*(3), 29–39.

Hayles, K. (2012). *How we think: Digital media and contemporary technogenesis*. Chicago, IL: Chicago University Press.

Lasher, D. R., Ives, B., & Jarvenpaa, S. L. (1991). USAA-IBM partnerships in information technology: Managing the Image project. *MIS Quarterly, 15*(4), 551–565.

Lave, J., & Wenger, E. (1991). *Situated learning: Legitimate peripheral participation*. Cambridge: Cambridge University Press.

Leonardi, P. M. (2010). Digital materiality? How artifacts without matter, matter. *First Monday*, 15(6).

Leonardi, P. M. (2011). When flexible routines meet flexible technologies: affordance, constraint, and the imbrication of human and material agencies. *MIS Quarterly, 35*(1), 147–168.

Leonardi, P. M., & Barley, S. R. (2008). Materiality and change: Challenges to building better theory about technology and organizing. *Information and Organization, 18*(3), 159–176.

Leonardi, P. M., & Barley, S. R. (2010). What's under construction here? Social action, materiality, and power in constructivist studies of technology and organizing. *The Academy of Management Annals, 4*(1), 1–51.

Mitchell, W. J. (1999). *E-topia: "Urban Life, Jim—But Not as We Know It"*. Cambridge, MA: MIT Press.

Oldenburg, R. (1998). *The great good place: Cafes, coffee shops, bookstores, bars, hair salons, and other hangouts at the heart of a community*. Cambridge, MA: Da Capo Press.

Orlikowski, W. J. (2007). Sociomaterial practices: Exploring technology at work. *Organization Studies, 28*(9), 1435–1448.

Orlikowski, W. J., & Scott, S. V. (2008). Sociomateriality: Challenging the separation of technology, work and organization. *The Academy of Management Annals, 2*(1), 433–474.

Pickering, A. (2001). Practice and posthumanism: Social theory and a history of agency. In T. R. Schatzki, K. Knorr Cetina, & E. von Savigny (Eds.), *The practice turn in contemporary theory* (pp. 163–174). London: Routledge.

Schaffers, H., Garcia Guzman, J., & Merz, C. (2008). An action research approach to rural living labs innovation. In P. Cunningham & M. Cunningham (Eds.), *Collaboration and the knowledge economy: issues, applications, case studies* (pp. 617–624). Amsterdam: IOS Press.

Schuurman, D., & Tõnurist, P. (2016). Innovation in the public sector: exploring the characteristics and potential of living labs and innovation labs. Proceedings of the OpenLivingLab Days 2016, Montreal, Canada (pp. 78–90). Presented at the OpenLivingLab Days 2016.

Wakelin, K., & Street, A. (2015). An online expressive writing group for people affected by cancer: A virtual third place. *Australian Social Work, 68*(2), 198–211.

Weick, K. (1988). Enacted sense making in crisis situations. *Journal of Management Studies, 25*(4), 305–317.

Wilson, J. M., O'Leary, M., Metiu, A., & Jett, Q. R. (2008). Perceived proximity in virtual work: Explaining the paradox of far-but-close. *Organization Studies, 29*(7), 979–1002.

7

Do Coworking Spaces Promise a Revolution or Spark Revenge? A Foucauldian Spatio-Material Approach to the Re-spatialization of Remote Work in Coworking Spaces

Aurélie Leclercq-Vandelannoitte

Introduction

Organizational knowledge work has liquefied and is taking place elsewhere (Bauman, 2000; Bauman & Lyon, 2013; Salovaara, 2015), so that "work isn't where it used to be" (Blakstad, 2015). In a context of liquid modernity (Bauman, 2000), several interrelated factors are breaking down the traditional organizational boundaries, including the increased importance of knowledge work and service industries (Drucker, 1988), the development of collaborative and networking information technologies and digitization (Castells, 1996; Orlikowski, 1991), the dematerialization of processes, the growth of employees' expectations, mobility and sustainability issues and greater awareness of well-being (Urry, 2007), cost and space pressures (Halford, 2005), and work "projectification"

A. Leclercq-Vandelannoitte (✉)
IESEG School of Management, Lille, France
e-mail: a.leclercq@ieseg.fr

N. Mitev et al. (eds.), *New Ways of Working*, Technology, Work and Globalization,
https://doi.org/10.1007/978-3-030-61687-8_7

(Spinuzzi, 2015). Together these trends have prompted new working practices (Kingma, 2018), such as nomadic, mobile, flexible, distributed, remote, and tele forms of work (Sewell & Taskin, 2015). Such practices reflect work that increasingly gets performed outside typical physical, spatial, and temporal organizational boundaries (Salovaara, 2015).

From spatial, temporal, and material perspectives, organizations and the nature of work have changed dramatically, shifting from a strong centralization around the production tools and technologies of the nineteenth century to the decentralization, distantiation, and despatialization of work (Taskin, 2006, 2010), which is associated with virtualization and spatio-temporal dislocation (e.g., colocation) of managers, subordinates, and peers (Halford, 2005). Beyond virtualization and the "anytime-anywhere" rhetoric (Hislop & Axtell, 2009), we also observe a shift toward a "re-spatialization" of work in multiple, new locations (Halford, 2005), such as third workspaces (Kingma, 2016). This spatial reconfiguration (Hislop & Axtell, 20009) often results in the "hybridation" of workplaces (Halford, 2005; Kingma, 2016), such that work occurs on client premises, in traditional offices, and in third workspaces. Despite the options for dematerializing and distantiating work from its material setting, organizations seek to re-spatialize work in new places (O'Brien, 2011), re-materialize it, and finally re-embed it in formal organizational settings. For example, Yahoo and IBM have encouraged their remote employees and teleworkers to abandon homeworking and go back to the office. Third workspaces (Kingma, 2016) offer appealing alternative workplaces for organizations too, in that they provide remote employees with a more productive setting than homes and also address the changing needs of new generations of workers (Salovaara, 2015).

With a few exceptions (e.g., Halford, 2005; Hislop & Axtell, 2009; Taskin & Edwards, 2007), this spatial reconfiguration of work has been poorly theorized, leaving with no answer to questions about the meaning and implications of the re-spatialization of work, even though such practices inevitably alter the social space of organizations (Lefebvre, 1991), that is, their territoriality and materiality (Halford, 2005; Sewell & Taskin, 2015). By modifying the spatial, temporal, and material frames of work, these practices imply a "re-regulation" (i.e., reorganization of the conduct of work; Edwards, Geary, & Sisson, 2002), with various effects for social, managerial, and power relations (Dale, 2005; Dale & Burrell, 2008; Sewell & Taskin, 2015). Noting the proliferation of new places of work, this study focuses on the re-spatialization and re-regulation of remote work in coworking spaces, which companies increasingly use to re-materialize the activity of their remote employees.

Coworking spaces initially sought to appeal primarily to freelancers, entrepreneurs, start-ups, and micro-enterprises (Salovaara, 2015), but companies also find them attractive (Saiidi, 2017). Although there is no consensual academic definition of coworking, it generally constitutes a new category of flexible workspace, or third workspace (Kingma, 2016), between private homes and corporate offices. Coworking thus offers a new category of flexible work and perhaps the next generation of telework (Kingma, 2016); it designates a new form of organizing collaborative work according to a novel spatiality. By leveraging the "unoffice" (Spinuzzi, 2012a, 412), coworking becomes "part of a larger movement toward distributed work and perhaps a way to examine and predict further work trends" (Spinuzzi, 2012b). No clear typology exists, but different types of coworking spaces can be distinguished, including shared spaces (which host entrepreneurs or freelancers who initiate their development) versus coworking business spaces (which are developed by and for organizations; Kingma, 2016). The use of third workspaces is "equally divided over informal spaces and specialized business centers" (Kingma, 2016, 176; Strelitz, 2011). With these alternative workplaces, companies can re-create, at a distance, connections with remote employees, provide them with a more productive environment than home, and avoid the sense of isolation felt by many homeworkers. These spaces also may provide opportunities for autonomy, flexibility, trust, knowledge sharing, and serendipitous encounters (Kingma, 2016; Spinuzzi, 2012a, 2012b).

Even with the popular enthusiasm coworking spaces have generated, relevant organizational research remains limited (Salovaara, 2015). Studies on third spaces have developed rapidly (De Vaujany, Dandoy, Grandazzi, & Faure, 2018; Garrett et al., 2017; Garrett, Spreitzer, & Bacevice, 2017; Johns & Gratton, 2013; Waber, Magnolfi, & Lindsay, 2014); far fewer investigations consider the use of coworking spaces by companies and their employees (Kingma, 2016; Salovaara, 2015). To address this under-researched context of workplace hybridation, we investigate the physical re-territorialization of nomadic working practices (Gandini, 2015; O'Brien, 2011) in coworking spaces to determine the following: What does the re-spatialization of work in coworking spaces mean? What kind of re-regulation of work is implied by the re-spatialization of knowledge workers' activity in coworking spaces?

In this chapter, we seek to make sense of these questions by placing the re-spatialization of work within a framework of organizational politics. Based on French philosopher Michel Foucault (1970, 1973, 1977, 1980, 1985a, 1985b), we propose a symbolic/narrative, material, and experienced approach. Accordingly, we investigate the re-spatialization of activity by remote employees in coworking spaces along three dimensions: a symbolic/narrative dimension, with a consideration of space as a discursive construction; a material dimension in which space is an instrumental materialization; and an experienced dimension in which space represents an embodied experience. Next, we apply the framework to an illustrative case, detailing the experience of a company that instituted a policy for part-time work in coworking spaces among its remote knowledge workers. This example is not representative of all types of work hybridation, re-spatialization, or re-regulation of work in coworking spaces. Rather, it is indicative and illustrative (Hislop & Axtell, 2009), supporting our attempt to understand, in this specific context, what the re-spatialization of remote knowledge workers' activities in coworking spaces implies for work re-regulation (Edwards et al., 2002). We do not aim to generalize from our observations but rather to illustrate, with a specific example, the conditions, meaning, and implications of the understudied phenomenon of workplace hybridation and work re-regulation in a context marked by the re-spatialization of remote work practices.

We start with an overview of relevant literature on work distantiation, hybridation, re-spatialization, and re-regulation. We then present our conceptual framework on narrative, material, and experienced aspects of social space. The case illustration is an example of re-spatialization of the activity of remote workers in coworking spaces. We analyze how the distantiation and re-spatialization at stake in coworking spaces (used as business centers by the company) produce a specific, unsuspected disciplinarization of managerial norms. This study thus contributes to literature on de-spatialization (Taskin, 2006, 2010), re-spatialization

(Halford, 2005), and re-regulation (Edwards et al., 2002) by advancing understanding of the conditions, implications, and tensions of new places of work, as well as issuing a challenge to rethink the relations among organizational space, materiality, and management control in the context of workspace hybridation. In particular, this chapter challenges the widely assumed dichotomy between corporate and coworking values (Salovaara, 2015); instead, coworking spaces sometimes implicitly adopt and materialize corporate business values, even while using the rhetoric of purely altruistic values.

Work Distantiation, Re-spatialization, and Re-regulation

Despite their long history, traditional offices and fixed workspaces are no longer the norm (Salovaara, 2015). Distributed work practices, such as remote work, nomadism, telecommuting, telework, and project-based and virtual work (Errichiello & Pianese, 2016; Mark & Su, 2010; Spinuzzi, 2007) break down traditional spatial and temporal organizational boundaries and imply work distantiation (Taskin, 2010). This distantiation entails a qualitative shift from traditional forms of centralized social organizations toward more diffused, complex sets of social relations (Sewell & Taskin, 2015)

Research on virtual teams (Maznevski & Chudoba, 2000), homeworking, telework (Sewell & Taskin, 2015), and distributed work arrangements (Errichiello & Pianese, 2016) notes the shifts and "re-regulation" of work (Edwards et al., 2002) prompted by these practices, such as from direct supervision to distance management, from face-to-face to technology-mediated communication, and from co-located teams to virtual collaborations (Bailey & Kurland, 2002; Errichiello & Pianese, 2016). The conclusions of such studies vary though. Some investigations see telework as a way to improve autonomy, flexibility, and trust, such that it weakens power structures, loosens the reins of both managerial and peer control, and grants employees new opportunities to exercise autonomy at a distance (Felstead, Jewson, & Walters, 2003; Illegems &

Verbeke, 2004; Mello, 2007). But other findings emphasize how such practices can paradoxically link to symbolic reconstructions of norms associated with the traditional workplace, such as visibility, presence, trust, and availability (Halford, 2005; Orlikowski & Scott, 2008; Sewell & Taskin, 2015).

Remote work arrangements and virtual working have been a primary research focus (Brocklehurst, 2001; Kurland & Cooper, 2002; Sewell & Taskin, 2015); the hybridation of workplaces and re-spatialization of work in various spaces have been less studied (see Halford, 2005). In addition to supporting "anywhere–anytime" work concepts (Hislop & Axtell, 2009), information technologies can prompt spatial reconfigurations toward more hybridity (Halford, 2005; Sewell & Taskin, 2015), such that work gets performed in a mix of settings and spaces (e.g., domestic space, organizational space, and cyberspace) (Halford, 2005; Hislop & Axtell, 2009), including new places of work like third workspaces (Kingma, 2016; Oldenburg, 1989).

Yet even when they recognize the possibilities of work dematerialization and distantiation, organizations often re-embed and re-spatialize work in formal physical and material settings. For example, new technologies enable virtual organizational structures and relationships that operate with little or no face-to-face contact (Halford, 2005), such that organizations become "edgeless" and "permeable" (Davidow & Malone, 1992). Instead, organizations seem to re-embed work in formal organizational settings by requiring employees to return to headquarters or regional offices, blurring the lines between office and living spaces (Fleming & Spicer, 2004), or encouraging remote workers to adopt more formal settings like third workspaces (Kingma, 2016; O'Brien, 2011; Salovaara, 2015). Such evolutions imply, ironically, that the future of work might mean returning to the office (Huber, 2017). At Yahoo, for example, employees were banned from working from home in 2013, due to abuses of the remote work system, with the argument that "speed and quality are often sacrificed when we work from home" as explained by Yahoo CEO Marissa Mayer (Smith, 2013). After years of distantiation and dislocation of its staff through telework, Yahoo sought a re-spatialization on the company's premises because "We need to be one Yahoo!, and that starts with physically being together" (Goudreau, 2013). Similarly, IBM pioneered telecommuting in the 1990s, then rejected the trend it helped start by asking thousands of employees to return to offices. As an alternative, coworking spaces give remote or homeworking employees a more productive setting to work (Salovaara, 2015).

Thus, even as virtual work gains prominence in the popular imagination, it remains rare and unpopular among managers (Taylor & Spicer, 2007). Organizations could become boundaryless, and might benefit from doing so, yet "managers continue to require physical presence in the workplace and … performance is often judged on the amount of time spent 'at work'" (Taylor & Spicer, 2007, 332). The main challenge to distantiation and de-spatialization thus seems to derive from the altered presence and visibility of employees (Felstead et al., 2003), which results in a double loss of physical and psycho-sociological proximity and an ability to manage people (Taskin, 2010). According to Taylor and Spicer (2007), remote work is hard to implement because managing as an activity is difficult to displace. Thus, managers exhibit enduring reluctance and raise barriers to the adoption of remote work arrangements, because their managerial legitimacy and authority appear embedded in physical and psycho-sociological proximity (Halford, 2005). They also might fear losing visibility and control over employees, which may be why companies tend to re-spatialize work in more formal settings.

Furthermore, the hybridation and spatial reconfiguration of work alters employees' notions of visibility and invisibility, presence and absence, and colocation or dislocation, in both time and space and virtual or physical settings (Felstead et al., 2003; Halford, 2005). Thus, it involves a novel re-regulation of work and reorganization of the conduct of work (Edwards et al., 2002; Taskin & Edwards, 2007) that require new managerial practices, as well as revised social and power relations. We need a deeper investigation of the materiality and spatiality of new work practices (Dale, 2005), embedded in these new organizational politics, especially with regard to the way companies use coworking spaces for their own employees, in a way that tends to re-spatialize and re-materialize remote work and re-embed it in a physical space.

Conceptual Framework: A Narrative, Material, and Experienced Foucauldian Tryptic

Paradoxically, despite the importance of space in work practices (Halford, 2005), it has long been absent from research in organization studies (Sewell & Taskin, 2015). Hypermobility (Urry, 2007), liquidity (Bauman, 2000), flexibility, and the ability to work 'anytime, anyplace, anywhere' may have distracted researchers from the importance of spatial and material issues (Dale, 2005; Dale & Burrell, 2008; Halford, 2005; Sassen, 2000), even though, ironically, such practices have increased the meaning of physical places, at work and in managerial relations (Blakstad, 2015).

Although material places and the relation of physical and social space with management have not been treated conceptually at great length (Ropo, Salovaara, Sauer, & de Paoli, 2015), material aspects of organizational life, and space in particular, have regained interest in organization studies (Clegg & Kornberger, 2006; Dale, 2005; Dale & Burrell, 2008; de Vaujany & Mitev, 2013; Ropo et al., 2015; Van Marrewijk & Yanow, 2010). This so-called spatial turn, inspired by the materiality turn (Dale & Burrell, 2008; Kornberger & Clegg, 2005; Taylor & Spicer, 2007), has revived considerations of the spatial, material, and sociomaterial aspects of organizing, with the recognition that space offers a novel "source of thinking about social relations" (Sewell & Taskin, 2015, 1509). Organizational research highlights the influence of spatial and temporal dimensions on the nature and implications of work practices, proposing that the "where" and "when" intertwine to produce the "how" of working, such that "where work is done makes a difference to working practices and to organizational and personal relationships" (Halford, 2005, 20). Spatial hybridity in particular changes the nature of work, organization, and management, because they get enacted in different spaces (e.g., domestic, organizational, virtual) (Halford, 2005), leading to a re-regulation of work that involves new ways to manage and control employees (Taskin & Edwards, 2007). Furthermore, power relations are central to understanding why organizations are spatially organized in certain ways (Taylor & Spicer, 2007). For example, offices and spaces represent devices of managerial regulation (Felstead, Jewson, & Walters, 2005;

Taskin & Edwards, 2007). Therefore, re-spatialization should be embedded within an organizational politics frame. Because the spatial turn distinguishes objective, physically observable dimensions of space (architecture, design, technology) from its subjectively perceived dimension (emotionally felt by people) (Ropo et al., 2015), it demands research into both the physical design and spatial organization of work, as well as the values and symbolic meanings associated with re-spatialization, their effects on social relations and organizing at work, and the various ways space shapes power relations (Dale, 2005; Dale & Burrell, 2008; de Vaujany & Vaast, 2014; Halford, 2005; Sewell & Taskin, 2015).

We therefore propose an integrative framework, based on the spatial thinking detailed by Michel Foucault (1970, 1973, 1977, 1980, 1985a, 1985b), to conceptualize a spatial and material view of the re-spatialization of the activities of remote employees in coworking spaces. As Foucault (1980, 70) recognized: "For generations in the social science, space was treated as the dead, the fixed, the undialectical, the immobility," and yet, "space is fundamental in any form of communal life; space is fundamental in any exercise of power" (Foucault, 1984, 252). Using Foucault's integrative framework (Taylor & Spicer, 2007) enables an analysis of the significance of the physical working environment and its subjective meaning for organizational life; for Foucault (1977, 148), spaces are "mixed spaces: real because they govern the disposition of buildings, rooms, furniture, but also ideal, because they are projected over this arrangement of characterizations, assessments, and hierarchies."

In particular, Foucault's framework suggests a more inclusive reconsideration of the notion of social space (Lefebvre, 1991) because it introduces issues of power, politics, control, hierarchy, identity, and emotions that have been excluded from previous analyses of social spaces (Lefebvre, 1991). It can support further elaboration on the distantiation (Taskin, 2006, 2010), re-spatialization, and re-regulation of work, which also have not been conceptualized in prior research.

To that end, we distinguish three main periods in Foucault's thought and approach to space (Burrell, 1998): archaeological (focused on symbolic/narrative dimensions, translated into discourses, rhetoric, and discursive practices), genealogical (focused on discipline and power relations embedded in the material), and ethical (or late Foucault, with a focus on the self, experiences, modes of subjectification, agency, and resistance). As a whole, the main concepts derived from these three periods anticipate the spatial turn and also support a rethinking of social spaces (Lefebvre, 1991), which can be opaque and ambiguous—and thus difficult to investigate empirically (Dale, 2005; Taylor & Spicer, 2007). As summarized in Table 7.1, we consider space as a discursive construction, such that we emphasize the discursive practices and narratives associated with specific spatial arrangements, physical manifestations, imaginary and expected uses of space, and the legitimation processes that underlie the construction or uses of such spaces. We also consider space as an instrumental materialization, highlighting power relations, hidden control, and influential and manipulative dynamics of materializing relations and planning and configuring that space. Finally, we denote space as an embodied experience, to emphasize the ways actors care for, experience, and emotionally feel, live, appreciate, and react to space and its embedded representations.

Table 7.1 Synthesis of Foucauldian dimensions of social space (author's own)

Dimensions	Definition	Parallel with traditional dimensions of social spaces
Space as a discursive construction	Discursive practices associated with spatial arrangements, physical manifestations, imaginary aspects, legitimation processes, and expected uses of space.	Spatial practices, perceived space (Lefebvre, 1991); imagined space (Taylor & Spicer, 2007)
Space as an instrumental materialization	Power relations, hidden control, and influential and manipulative dynamics associated with the planning, design, and configuration of space.	Representations of space, conceived spaces (Lefebvre, 1991); spatial planning (Taylor & Spicer, 2007)
Space as an embodied experience	Reflexive, critical, emotional appreciation and reaction to a space and its embedded representations, providing meanings or feelings, and ways to express one's sense of self.	Spaces of representation, lived spaces (Lefebvre, 1991); practiced space (Taylor & Spicer, 2007)

With this framework, we investigate coworking spaces along three dimensions (space as a discursive construction, instrumental materialization, and embodied experience), while also taking organizational politics into account, with an illustrative example.

Illustrative Vignette

An Example of the Re-spatialization of the Activity of Remote Employees in Coworking Spaces

We investigated our research questions through the lens of a narrative, material, and experienced Foucauldian framework, in the specific context of an exploratory, qualitative case study of a Belgian consulting company (as part of a larger project on the use of coworking spaces by companies). This company introduced a policy of part-time working in coworking spaces for its remote workers. They were encouraged to work in coworking spaces located in the main cities in Belgium that the company had previously identified. We explored their practices through guided tours, observations, and interviews (with remote employees, their manager, and three coworking space operators) conducted in three coworking spaces. For our data analysis, we applied a qualitative thematic analysis with a mixed and rich thematic coding process, using Nvivo software.

The Re-spatialization of Work in Coworking Spaces as a Discursive Construction

The re-spatialization of the activity of these remote employees in coworking spaces was logically presented by the company and the coworking space operators as a way to improve their autonomy, flexibility, and working conditions. Coworking spaces were discursively constructed by the coworking space operators and the company's managers as spaces of freedom, empowerment, knowledge sharing, and trust. They were presented as a new generation of workspace, apart from the home or office, that would enhance remote employees' well-being at work by providing them with a more flexible, better adapted work environment so that they could avoid isolation, reduce commuting times, and gain autonomy. These spaces also contributed to the diffusion of a renewed organizational culture, promoting forward-thinking and the well-being and self-control of employees, thus making the company more attractive for future hires.

As a coworking space operator explained, "*these spaces provide fresh air compared to the office; they enable people to work differently, to change their posture towards work.*" They also were presented as "*spaces offering a more professional environment for nomad workers and teleworkers than the home,*" together with social connections and a community. He described these spaces as "*unexpected opportunities to unearth new markets, innovate, or collaborate in unexpected ways.*"

The Re-spatialization of Work in Coworking Spaces as an Instrumental Materialization

However, these spaces also appeared as concrete instrumental materializations (Dale, 2005) manipulated by the organization with two main objectives. The first was to create a sense of community, belonging, and togetherness among professionals, who often felt isolated (due to the enactment of materialized spaces and artifacts, as shown by the range of services offered in these workspaces). The spaces were crafted, from a material perspective, to cultivate informal relationships, socializing, information and knowledge sharing, trust, and a creative atmosphere (Fabbri & Charue-Duboc, 2013; Kingma, 2016).

The second objective was to create spaces of control that replicated office working conditions. Surprisingly, homeworking was not formally permitted in this company, so coworking spaces provided alternative places of work that encouraged productivity, responsiveness, efficiency, and control, but beyond the physical boundaries of the company. The coworking space operators worked in close collaboration with the company and the manager to develop novel, indirect *dispositifs* of management and control (e.g., indicators of presence, use of a common electronic platform, technological tools such as intense reliance on instant messaging, formalization of meetings on specific days of the week). The operator thus contributed to the re-regulation of work at distance (Taskin & Edwards, 2007). As summarized by the manager, "*The workspace is a lever of performance, a real tool of management, which, when carefully thought, can result in more efficacy.*" A coworking space operator mentioned that "*the goal is to put a toolbox at the disposal of managers to help them really manage their team at a distance.... We put at their disposal many resources on the jurisdictional and legal aspects of telework in coworking spaces and other tools of management and supervision to enable a distanced analysis of activities through the elaboration of credible and objective measures.*"

These new spaces of work thus were described as more convenient and providing more flexibility for remote employees, but they also enabled the company to exert indirect forms of control, based on presence and time management (e.g., when workers start or leave) and peer observation. Whereas third workspaces were discursively constructed as places of trust and emancipation, they were instrumentalized by the company to exert more precise control on the practices of their remote workers who are, by definition, outside of the presence of hierarchical control.

The Re-spatialization of Work in Coworking Spaces as an Embodied Experience

Finally, the enactment of these spaces produced different embodied experiences and relationships among the manager, remote employees, and coworking space operators, embedded in the way they used and perceived the spaces, which prompted some paradoxical tensions (i.e., relief or anxiety) (Sewell & Taskin, 2015). For some remote workers, the spaces recreated opportunities to signal their presence and engagement (Taskin & Edwards, 2007); for others, they introduced new constraints of availability, exposure, and visibility in third places intentionally designed for the purpose.

In the end, coworking spaces can be analyzed as materialized extensions of corporate settings at a distance, enabling work continuity, but in contradiction with the official discourse, which officially represented these new places of work as spaces of well-being, autonomy, and trust. Coworking spaces were used by the company as a way to re-spatialize and re-materialize the activity of its remote workers, "*in a context where home-work started to become widespread on Fridays*," according to one of the coworking space operators. Paradoxically, these modern workspaces, based on notions of collaboration and openness, were not exempt from more conventional forms of control.

Re-spatialization in Coworking Spaces as a Replication of Corporate Settings and Re-materialization of Remote Work

New ways of working suggest that work is mobile and unbound, but coworking spaces present an example of its re-spatialization; they thus are important places to study to understand what work in the digital age comprises. Although the current research has some limitations—we conducted an exploratory illustrative study, in the specific field of consulting (which is not representative of all professional contexts), with a single team, a single manager, and three third workspaces (which are not representative of all coworking spaces)—it also offers some novel insights. That is, even if our findings cannot be generalized, they provide a different, original angle on New Ways of Working and places of work, which highlights the ambiguities in the use of third workspaces by companies. This study contributes to a better understanding of the possible conditions and consequences of novel spatio-temporal designs and new places of work as new sources of tensions, which challenge us to rethink management control in a context of workspace hybridation, as well as the relationships among organizational space, materiality, management, and control. As Dale (2005, 651) notes, "little attention has been paid to the specific and explicit ways in which materiality is incorporated in social control, nor how forms of control are enacted and embodied on an everyday basis."

Some studies indicate that materiality is relevant for understanding changing modes of control in organizational life (Dale, 2005; Dale & Burrell, 2008; de Paoli, Sauer, & Ropo, 2019; Sewell & Taskin, 2015). Spaces also are implicated in the constitution of distinctive power relations, control, and resistance in workspaces (Dale, 2005). Dale and Burrell (2008, 43) refer, for example, to "securing" and "obscuring" power in open-plan offices and emphasize the "latent power" of any built form that is visible in everyday practices, such that the manipulation of space is "achieved through keeping occupants ignorant of the sources and the operation of power" (Dale & Burrell, 2008, 45). The qualities and positive expectations of new places of work frequently get emphasized to create attention, attraction, and enchantment—especially as corporate strategies seek an image of "having creative workspaces" (de Paoli et al., 2019). Yet as demonstrated for the context of open spaces (de Paoli et al., 2019), spatial power is often exerted through the enchanting narrative of an open culture.

In this vein, our research highlights that coworking spaces are objects of discursive constructions that do not always correspond to the material configuration and underlying power relations of the space, leading to perceived tensions in the way people interpret, integrate, and use these third workspaces in their overall workspace. In particular, our analysis of the re-spatialization of the activity of remote employees in coworking spaces, through the adoption of a Foucauldian narrative, material, and experienced framework, highlights a new form of disciplinarization, at odds with the image of coworking spaces and telework. The distantiation and re-spatialization at stake in these coworking spaces (used by the example company as business centers) involves a re-regulation of work (Edwards et al., 2002) in the form of new bureaucratic protocols that reintroduce notions of visibility and presence at a distance, as well as produce a specific disciplinarization of managerial norms of efficiency, autonomy, and accountability.

Although remote work and telework generally involve the "decoupling of work activity from one material workplace such as the office … as well as from prescribed working hours, work schedules, scripts and practices" (Tietze & Musson, 2005, 385; quoted in Taskin & Edwards, 2007), our case study reveals how the re-spatialization of remote work in coworking spaces is provoking a back movement. Paradoxically, the places we observed tended to make the activity of remote workers more predictable and reinforce the traditional bureaucratic characteristics of surveillance, visibility, and control through the "superimposition of new practices of control on existing ones" (Taskin & Edwards, 2007, 204), which are contrary to the discourses about trust, emancipation, and flexibility often put forward about and within these spaces.

The rapid development of coworking spaces instead has been characterized by a "celebratory framework," a "vibe," and an "enthusiastic claim" (Gandini, 2015, 193), largely initiated by those who run and develop these places. The founders of coworking spaces generally bring to the fore their "alternative nature" and "potential to change society," in what they call a "profound cultural revolution" (Vidaillet & Bousalham, 2020, 2). Coworking is commonly presented as a new form of work organization that enables collaboration opportunities and encourages a sense of community inside a shared space, gathering workers from different companies or even freelancers with different profiles and objectives (Johns & Gratton, 2013). Studies on coworking often tell positive stories about better opportunities for collaboration, innovation, knowledge sharing, serendipitous encounters, and creativity (Garrett et al., 2017; Johns & Gratton, 2013). Therefore, these new places convey hope, in a global context that professes to be moving work practices toward a more collaborative economy, holacracy (Bernstein, Bunch, Canner, & Lee, 2016; Robertson, 2015), liberated organizations (Carney & Getz, 2009), empowerment, and trust (Martin, Liao, & Campbell, 2013; Morris, Farrell, & Reed, 2016; Seibert, Silver, & Randolph, 2004). As such, third workspaces claim to be new places of work that make the office obsolete (Jones, Sundsted, & Bacigalupo, 2009). However, our study reveals that the coworking spaces we studied replicated the corporate world and conventional working conditions at a distance (Mello, 2007). They rematerialized remote work and generated new tensions among the narrative, discursive, and symbolic practices developed around the coworking spaces; the physical spatial design and configuration coupled with materialized forms of instrumentalization; and the underlying management system and 'hidden logic of control' they entail.

This study informs research on third workspaces, which have not been investigated in sufficient depth thus far. Nor have these new work practices been substantially contested (Lyons, 2016; Ramadier, 2017). In contrast with generally positive evaluations of the coworking movement, our study offers a different, more nuanced, critical view. Some research points to tensions and contradictions "under the surface" of coworking spaces (Gandini, 2015, 203; Vidaillet & Bousalham, 2020, 5). But few contributions actually "dwell upon empirical findings and rarely offer a critical understanding" of these places (Gandini, 2015, 194). In particular, coworking spaces have been described as spaces that evade and even transcend power relations (de Peuter, Cohen, & Saraco, 2017), such that "coworking is assumed to be benign and its operations of power are unquestioned" (De Peuter et al., 2017, 688). In line with Gandini's (2015, 203) call for organizational researchers to "seriously take into account the contradictory nature" of coworking spaces, this study seeks to detail the tensions and contradictions sometimes observed in these spaces, notably between the pretended "counter-corporate identity" of coworking and "its recapitulation of neoliberal norms" (De Peuter et al., 2017, 687). In research that identifies an opposition between coworking values and corporate norms (Spinuzzi, 2012a), a common proposition is that "those who chose coworking subscribe to coworking values, rather than corporate values" (Salovaara, 2015, 35), and recent studies show that some companies are adopting coworking values (Salovaara, 2015), as exemplified by IBM's experiment with non-territorial offices or Microsoft's reorganization of its open-plan offices. But the reverse is true as well. Our study adds depth to this assumed contrast between corporate and coworking norms and values, by showing that coworking spaces sometimes implicitly adopt and apply corporate and business values, even as they espouse a rhetoric of purely altruistic values based on openness, well-being, flexibility, and collaboration.

Accordingly, this study contributes to literature on de-spatialization (Taskin, 2006, 2010), re-spatialization (Halford, 2005), and re-regulation (Edwards et al., 2002), by providing a counterpoint to the fictional revolution of coworking, showing that some practices and management principles remain the same, or are even re-regulated and reinforced, at a distance, with the image and rhetoric of a creative, modern, liberating working space. This finding is all the more striking when we note that the activity of remote knowledge workers generally has been characterized by high skills, deregulated work, flexible arrangements, and strong commitment (Cooper & Kurland, 2002; Peters, Tijdens, & Wetzels, 2004). In turn, we call for further research that conceptualizes the underlying reasons and implications of such a re-spatialization and re-materialization of remote work.

References

Bailey, D. E., & Kurland, N. B. (2002). A review of telework research: Findings, new directions, and lessons for the study of modern work. *Journal of Organizational Behavior, 23*(4), 383–400.

Bauman, Z. (2000). *Liquid modernity*. Cambridge: Polity.

Bauman, Z., & Lyon, D. (2013). *Liquid surveillance: A conversation*. New York: John Wiley & Sons.

Bernstein, E., Bunch, J., Canner, N., & Lee, M. (2016). Beyond the holacracy hype. *Harvard Business Review, 94*(7), 38–49.

Blakstad, S. H. (2015). Work isn't where it used to be. In A. Ropo, P. Salovaara, E. Sauer, & D. De Paoli (Eds.), *Leadership in spaces and places*. Cheltenham: Edward Elgar Publishing.

Brocklehurst, M. (2001). Power identity and new technology homework: Implications for 'new forms' of organizing. *Organization Studies, 22*(3), 445–466.

Burrell, G. (1998). Modernism, postmodernism and organizational analysis: The contribution of Michel Foucault. In A. McKinlay & K. Starkey (Eds.), *Foucault, management and organizational theory (chapter 2)*. London: Sage.

Carney, B. M., & Getz, I. (2009). *Freedom, Inc.: Free your employees and let them lead your business to higher productivity, profits, and growth*. New York: Crown Business.

Castells, M. (1996). *The rise of the network society, vol. 1* (The information age: Economy, society and culture). Oxford: Blackwell Publishing.

Clegg, S., & Kornberger, M. (Eds.). (2006). *Space, organization and management theory*. Copenhagen: Copenhagen Business School Press.

Cooper, C. D., & Kurland, N. B. (2002). Telecommuting, professional isolation, and employee development in public and private organizations. *Journal of Organizational Behavior, 23*(4), 511–532.

Dale, K. (2005). Building a social materiality: Spatial and embodied politics in organizational control. *Organization, 12*(5), 649–678.

Dale, K., & Burrell, G. (2008). *The spaces of organisation and the organisation of space: Power, identity and materiality at work*. Basingstoke: Palgrave Macmillan.

Davidow, W., & Malone, M. (1992). *The virtual corporation*. London: Harper Collins.

de Paoli, D., Sauer, E., & Ropo, A. (2019). The spatial context of organizations: A critique of 'creative workspaces'. *Journal of Management & Organization, 25*(2), 331–352.

de Peuter, G., Cohen, N. S., & Saraco, F. (2017). The ambivalence of coworking: On the politics of an emerging work practice. *European Journal of Cultural Studies, 20*(6), 687–706.

De Vaujany, F. X., Dandoy, A., Grandazzi, A., & Faure, S. (2018). Experiencing a new place as an atmosphere: A focus on tours of collaborative spaces. *Scandinavian Journal of Management, 35*(2), 101030.

de Vaujany, F.-X., & Mitev, N. (2013). *Materiality and space. Organizations, artifacts and practices*. London: Palgrave.

de Vaujany, F. X., & Vaast, E. (2014). If these walls could talk: The mutual construction of organizational space and legitimacy. *Organization Science, 25*(3), 713–731.

Drucker, P. (1988). The coming of the new organization. *Harvard Business Review, 66*(1), 45–53.

Edwards, P., Geary, J., & Sisson, K. (2002). New forms of work organisation in the workplace: Transformative, exploitative, or limited and controlled? In G. Murray, J. Bélanger, A. Giles, & P.-A. Lapointe (Eds.), *Work and employment relations in the high-performance workplace*. London: Continuum.

Errichiello, L., & Pianese, T. (2016). Organizational control in the context of remote work arrangements: A conceptual framework. In S. Widener, M. Epstein, & F. Verbeeten (Eds.), *Performance measurement and management control: Contemporary issues* (Vol. 31, pp. 273–305). Bingley, UK: Emerald Publishing.

Fabbri, J., & Charue-Duboc, F. (2013). The role of physical space in collaborative workspaces hosting entrepreneurs: The case of the beehive in Paris. In F. de Vaujany & N. Mitev (Eds.), *Materiality and space. Organizations, artefacts and practices* (pp. 117–134). Basingstoke: Palgrave Macmillan.

Felstead, A., Jewson, N., & Walters, S. (2003). Managerial control of employees working at home. *British Journal of Industrial Relations, 41*(2), 241–264.

Felstead, A., Jewson, N., & Walters, S. (2005). *Changing places of work*. London: Palgrave.

Fleming, P., & Spicer, A. (2004). You can check out any time you want, but you can never leave: Spatial boundaries in a high commitment organization. *Human Relations, 57*(1), 75–94.

Foucault, M. (1970). *The order of things: An archaeology of the human sciences*. London: Tavistock.

Foucault, M. (1973). *The birth of the clinic*. London: Tavistock.

Foucault, M. (1977). *Discipline and punish: The birth of the prison*. New York: Random House.

Foucault, M. (1980). *Power/knowledge*. London: Harvester Wheatsheaf.

Foucault, M. (1984). Space, knowledge and power. In P. Rabinow (Ed.), *The Foucault reader*. New York: Pantheon.

Foucault, M. (1985a). *The use of pleasure: The history of sexuality, volume 2*. New York: Pantheon.

Foucault, M. (1985b). *The care of the self: The history of sexuality, volume 3*. New York: Pantheon.

Gandini, A. (2015). The rise of coworking spaces: A literature review. *Ephemera – Theory and Politics in Organization, 15*(1), 193–205.

Garrett, L. E., Spreitzer, G. M., & Bacevice, P. A. (2017). Co-constructing a sense of community at work: The emergence of community in coworking spaces. *Organization Studies, 38*(6), 821–842.

Goudreau, J (2013). Back to the Stone Age? New Yahoo CEO Marissa Mayer bans working from home. *Forbes*, 6.

Halford, S. (2005). Hybrid workspace: Re-spatialisations of work, organisation and management. *New Technology, Work and Employment, 20*(1), 19–33.

Hislop, D., & Axtell, C. (2009). To infinity and beyond? Workspace and the multi-location worker. *New Technology, Work and Employment, 24*(1), 60–75.

Huber, K. (2017). Does the future of work mean returning to the office? *CGTN News Channel*, 7 July.

Illegems, V., & Verbeke, A. (2004). Telework: What does it mean for management? *Long Range Planning, 37*(4), 319–334.

Johns, T., & Gratton, L. (2013). The third wave of virtual work. *Harvard Business Review, 91*(1), 66–73.

Jones, D., Sundsted, T., & Bacigalupo, T. (2009). *I'm outta here! How coworking is making the office obsolete*. Austin, TX: Not an MBA Press.

Kingma, S. (2016). The constitution of 'third workspaces' in between the home and the corporate office. *New Technology, Work and Employment, 31*(2), 176–193.

Kingma, S. (2018). New Ways of Working (NWW): Work space and cultural change in virtualizing organizations. *Culture and Organization, 25*(5), 1–24.

Kornberger, M., & Clegg, S. (2005). Bringing space back in organizing the generative building. *Organization Studies, 25*(7), 1095–1114.

Kurland, N. B., & Cooper, C. D. (2002). Manager control and employee isolation in telecommuting environments. *The Journal of High Technology Management Research, 13*(1), 107–126.

Lefebvre, H. (1991). *The production of space*. Oxford: Blackwell.

Lyons, D. (2016). *Disrupted, my misadventure in the start-up bubble*. Verlag: Hachette Books.

Mark, G., & Su, N. M. (2010). Making infrastructure visible for nomadic work. *Pervasive and Mobile Computing, 6*(3), 312–323.

Martin, S., Liao, H., & Campbell, E. (2013). Directive versus empowering leadership: A field experiment comparing impacts on task proficiency and proactivity. *Academy of Management Journal, 56*(5), 1372–1395.

Maznevski, M., & Chudoba, K. (2000). Bridging space over time: Global virtual team dynamics and effectiveness. *Organization Science, 11*(5), 473–492.

Mello, J. (2007). Managing telework programs effectively. *Employee Responsibilities and Rights Journal, 19*(4), 247–261.

Morris, J., Farrell, C., & Reed, M. (2016). The indeterminacy of 'temporariness': Control and power in neo-bureaucratic organizations and work in UK television. *Human Relations, 69*(12), 2274–2297.

O'Brien, M. (2011). *Finding a home for the "digital nomad". New forms of identity and work in relation to mobile media and public space*. Retrieved July 2, 2013, from http://www.michelleobrien.net/wpcontent/uploads/2011/10/OBRIEN_Home_digital_nomad.pdf

Oldenburg, R. (1989). *The great good place: Cafes, coffee shops, community centers, beauty parlors, general stores, bars, hangouts, and how they get you through the day*. New York: Paragon House.

Orlikowski, W. J. (1991). Integrated information environment or matrix of control? The contradictory implications of information technology. *Accounting, Management and Information Technologies, 1*(1), 9–42.

Orlikowski, W. J., & Scott, S. V. (2008). Sociomateriality: Challenging the separation of technology, work and organization. *Academy of Management Annals, 2*(1), 433–474.

Peters, P., Tijdens, K., & Wetzels, C. (2004). Employees' opportunities, preferences, and practices in telecommuting adoption. *Information & Management, 41*(4), 469–482.

Ramadier, M. (2017). *Bienvenue dans le nouveau monde, comment j'ai survécu à la coolitude des startups*. Paris: Premier Parallèle.

Robertson, B. (2015). *Holacracy: The new management system for a rapidly changing world*. New York: Henry Holt and Company.

Ropo, A., Salovaara, P., Sauer, E., & de Paoli, D. (2015). *Leadership in spaces and places*. Cheltenham, UK; Northampton, MA: Edward Elgar Publishing.

Saiidi, U. (2017). Coworking spaces aren't just for entrepreneurs anymore. *CNBC News Channel*, 1 Sept. Retrieved October 11, 2018, from https://www.cnbc.com/2017/09/01/coworking-spaces-arent-just-for-entrepreneurs-anymore.html

Salovaara, P. (2015). What can the coworking movement tell us about the future of workplaces? In A. Ropo, P. Salovaara, E. Sauer, & D. De Paoli (Eds.), *Leadership in spaces and places* (pp. 27–48). Cheltenham, UK, and Northampton, MA: Edward Elgar Publishing.

Sassen, S. (2000). Excavating power. *Theory, Culture and Society, 17*(1), 163–170.

Seibert, S., Silver, S., & Randolph, W. (2004). Taking empowerment to the next level: A multiple-level model of empowerment, performance, and satisfaction. *Academy of Management Journal, 47*(3), 332–349.

Sewell, G., & Taskin, L. (2015). Out of sight, out of mind in a new world of work? Autonomy, control, and spatiotemporal scaling in telework. *Organization Studies, 36*(11), 1507–1529.

Smith, K. (2013). Here's the confidential memo Yahoo sent employees about working from home. *Business Insider*, 23 Sept. Retrieved May 24, 2018, from https://www.businessinsider.com/yahoo-working-from-home-memo-2013-2?IR=T

Spinuzzi, C. (2007). Guest editor's introduction: Technical communication in the age of distributed work. *Technical Communication Quarterly, 16*(3), 265–277.

Spinuzzi, C. (2012a). Working alone together: Coworking as emergent collaborative activity. *Journal of Business and Technical Communication, 26*(4), 399–441.

Spinuzzi, C. (2012b). *Writing: Working alone, together* [blog], 30 May. Retrieved January 22, 2019, from http://spinuzzi.blogspot.com/2012/05/writing-working-alone-together.html

Spinuzzi, C. (2015). *All edge: Inside the new workplace networks*. Chicago, IL: University of Chicago Press.

Strelitz, Z. (2011). *Why place still matters in the digital age. Third place working in easy reach of home*. Business Report, ZZA Responsive User Environments.

Taskin, L. (2006). Télétravail: Les enjeux de la déspatialisation pour le management humain (online). *Revue Interventions économiques, 34*(2), 73–94.

Taskin, L. (2010). Déspatialisation: Un enjeu de gestion. *Revue Française de Gestion, 36*(202), 61–76.

Taskin, L., & Edwards, P. K. (2007). The possibilities and limits of telework in a bureaucratic environment: Lessons from the public sector. *New Technology, Work and Employment, 22*(3), 195–207.

Taylor, S., & Spicer, A. (2007). Time for space: A narrative review of research on organizational spaces. *International Journal of Management Reviews, 9*(4), 325–346.

Tietze, S., & Musson, G. (2005). Recasting the home–work relationship: A case of mutual adjustment? *Organization Studies, 26*, 1331–1352.

Urry, J. (2007). *Mobilities*. Cambridge, UK: Polity.

Van Marrewijk, A. V., & Yanow, D. (2010). *Organizational spaces. Rematerializing the workaday world*. Cheltenham, UK: Edward Elgar.

Vidaillet, B., & Bousalham, Y. (2020). Coworking spaces as places where economic diversity can be articulated: Towards a theory of syntopia. *Organization, 27*(1), 60–87.

Waber, B., Magnolfi, J., & Lindsay, G. (2014). Workspaces that move people. *Harvard Business Review, 92*(10), 69–77.

8

More than Perks and a Shared Office: How Coworking Spaces Participate in Entrepreneurs' Resource Acquisition

Kutay Güneştepe, Zehra Topal, and Deniz Tunçalp

Introduction

Since first established in San Francisco in 2005 by Brad Neuberg (Rus & Orel, 2015), coworking spaces have flourished in different cities of the world, offering a place to work, convene, and socialize for their residents. These places host companies from different sizes in various businesses in a shared physical layout, fostering their interaction and engagement. This physical proximity is expected to facilitate communication and collaboration among its residents and at the same time coworking spaces establish themselves as hubs for attracting people with cognitive proximity (Capdevila, 2013, 2015). Moreover, coworking spaces enable the sharing of goods and services that may otherwise be underutilized (Bouncken & Reuschl, 2016; Capdevila, 2013) and, therefore, offer affordable levels of office cost for their users (Spinuzzi, 2012).

K. Güneştepe (✉) • Z. Topal • D. Tunçalp
Istanbul Technical University, Maslak, Turkey
e-mail: topalz@itu.edu.tr

N. Mitev et al. (eds.), *New Ways of Working*, Technology, Work and Globalization,
https://doi.org/10.1007/978-3-030-61687-8_8

The popularity of coworking spaces has attracted the interest of social scientists as an interesting phenomenon, offering different research questions such as knowledge creation dynamics and innovation practices in localized communities (Capdevila, 2013, 2015), new and changing work practices (Mariotti, Pacchi, & Di Vita, 2017; Mitev, de Vaujany, Laniray, Bohas, & Fabbri, 2018), community-building in a workplace (Garrett, Spreitzer, & Bacevice, 2017; Mitev et al., 2018), emotions experienced in a coworking atmosphere (de Vaujany, Dandoy, Grandazzi, & Faure, 2019), and developing entrepreneurial skills through learning in coworking spaces (Bouncken & Reuschl, 2016; Butcher, 2018; Fuzi, 2015). Studies have indicated that while initial users of coworking spaces were mostly self-employed people and freelancers, they have increasingly become the primary choice of startups and entrepreneurs (Capdevila, 2015; Mitev et al., 2018; Moriset, 2014).

Entrepreneurs are known to have scarce resources (Chang & Chen, 2020; Lee, 2017) for reaching their goals and exploiting or developing opportunities in uncertain conditions. They have to seek, generate, accumulate, and mobilize different tangible and intangible resources (Jones, Macpherson, & Jayawarna, 2014; Lee & Shaw, 2016). Entrepreneurial enthusiasm is not enough to overcome the problems of the entrepreneurial situation. They need to both conform to their broader context and, at the same time, be innovative in their businesses to meet the expectations of their stakeholders (De Clercq & Voronov, 2009). In parallel to this pursuit of entrepreneurs, coworking spaces appear more than brick-and-mortar office buildings, as they also provide several tangible and intangible resources. Existing studies focus on different aspects of coworking spaces attracting entrepreneurs. However, how coworking spaces support entrepreneurs to acquire resources is poorly explored. In this chapter, our objective is to focus on this question to uncover the dynamics involved.

In our study, we used the "capital" framework from Bourdieu (1986), which has been widely employed by many scholars to explain how entrepreneurs acquire different forms of resources (e.g., De Clercq & Voronov, 2009; Jones, Macpherson, & Thorpe, 2010; Lee & Shaw, 2016; Stam, Arzlanian, & Elfring, 2014). This framework identifies various forms of capital, such as economic capital, social capital, cultural capital, and symbolic capital. According to this perspective, actors use different forms of capital as a "capacity to produce profits and to reproduce itself" (Bourdieu, 1986, 241). Bourdieu (1986) argues that economic capital is the most obvious one among the others that could be quickly and directly convertible into money. However, intangible forms of capital are also critical, and they may also be converted into economic capital. We argue that coworking spaces offer various tangible and intangible types of resources that can be converted into one and other. Bourdieuan concepts help scholars to examine intersubjective and interdependent social phenomena better (Özbilgin & Tatli, 2005).

In this chapter, we carry out a Bourdieuan analysis of the entrepreneurial situation in coworking spaces (Drakopoulou-Dodd, McDonald, McElwee, & Smith, 2014) and conducted a qualitative study in the two most prominent coworking spaces in Istanbul, namely Alpha and Beta (pseudonyms). Both of these coworking spaces are close to central business districts of Istanbul and privately owned. One of these coworking spaces is part of a coworking space chain in Istanbul, and the other one is a university-affiliated coworking space located inside the main campus. We selected these coworking spaces as our polar cases (Eisenhardt & Graebner, 2007), as they have distinctly different characteristics that may help us to broaden our perspective toward other varieties of coworking spaces.

Our findings indicate that coworking spaces allow entrepreneurs to cultivate tangible and intangible sources of capital. They access these resources through various mechanisms supported by coworking spaces. Some of these mechanisms allow accumulating more than one type of capital. The relationships between these mechanisms and sources of capital are drawn as a framework and described in detail.

The study has various contributions, as it offers a novel framework by adopting Bourdieu's capital framework, and emphasizes the critical dependence on the context:

First, this study provides a novel framework involving a "multiplicity of relations" (Everett, 2002, 57) between different aspects of coworking spaces and the resource acquisition of their inhabitants. Our study follows that coworking spaces are not just "workforce containers" (Reuschke, 2016, 379), and understanding them requires a more comprehensive analysis (Tatli, Vassilopoulou, Özbilgin, Forson, & Slutskaya, 2014).

Our framework emphasizes the richness and complexity of relations inside coworking spaces. We believe scholars studying this domain can elaborate further on these relations, which may foster further empirical work about entrepreneurship in and around coworking spaces. Moreover, our approach to coworking phenomena and findings can guide practitioners better understand the role of coworking spaces for their individual members, organizations, and the surrounding regional entrepreneurship ecosystems.

Second, our study offers a novel adaptation of Bourdieu's capital framework in the analysis of coworking spaces. Although social capital is used broadly in the entrepreneurship literature (Stam et al., 2014), there are very few examples that consider the symbolic and the cultural capital (e.g., De Clercq & Voronov, 2009; Lee & Shaw, 2016). Therefore, this study is one of the early examples covering all forms of capital, as introduced by Bourdieu, and it also provides a new perspective on how entrepreneurs gain and exploit different forms of capital.

Third, as our study involves two polar cases, we can account for a diversity of coworking spaces and different entrepreneurial situations. While most entrepreneurship studies quantitatively analyzed the field-level (Drakopoulou-Dodd et al., 2014), we take an organizational level of analysis. Entrepreneurship and its context are "too dynamic and complex" (Neergaard & Ulhøi, 2006, 4). Collecting empirical data from two coworking spaces with interviews, observations, and secondary data sources, we can capture complexity (Johnstone, 2006) regarding the focal phenomenon (Denzin & Lincoln, 2005).

In this chapter, we first introduce Bourdieu's framework regarding the sources of capital and present the entrepreneurship literature regarding different forms of capital. Following that, we describe the design of the study and how we analyzed our empirical data. In the next section, we draw a framework based on our results, showing various mechanisms supported by coworking spaces to access sources of different forms of capital. Then we conclude the manuscript with possible directions for future research.

Forms of Capital for Entrepreneurs

According to Bourdieu, field actors struggle to accumulate different forms of capital to reach their interests (Bourdieu, 1993). Capital can be in objectified or embodied forms (Bourdieu, 1986), and the most prominent forms of capital in entrepreneurship literature are economic, social, cultural, and symbolic capital (Lee & Shaw, 2016). Moreover, all of these forms of capital are accumulated in time and can be transformed into one another (Bourdieu, 1986, 1993) (Table 8.1).

Economic capital is more about tangible forms of capital that cover monetary and material wealth that are easy to value (Everett, 2002). While this type of capital is foundational and pervasively studied in the literature, other forms of capital need to be considered separately without essentially reducing it to economic capital (Bourdieu, 1986). In parallel to this definition, economic capital can be exemplified as money (e.g., Vershinina & Rodgers, 2020) or other forms of financial assets such as housing (Reuschke, 2016).

Social capital is about having a network that provides (potential) resources to its members (Bourdieu, 1986). Specifically, being a member of a group is crucial in the performance of entrepreneurs (Aldrich & Zimmer, 1986) and, therefore, social capital is widely examined by scholars focusing on entrepreneurship and small businesses (Stam et al., 2014). Individuals' possession of social capital is considered based on the size of their network and mostly analyzed quantitatively (e.g., Burt, 1997; Stam et al., 2014). Nevertheless, there are also several qualitative studies acknowledging entrepreneurs not as heroic actors, but as individuals who network for the growth of their business (Anderson, Drakopoulou-Dodd, & Jack, 2010; Drakopoulou-Dodd & Anderson, 2007). For example,

Table 8.1 Bourdieu's framework of capital (adapted from Bourdieu, 1986)

Economic capital	Social capital	Cultural capital			Symbolic capital
		Embodied cultural capital	Objectified cultural capital	Institutionalized cultural capital	

Lehner (2014) has studied how social capital relates to opportunity and gets transformed into economic capital with crowdfunding by entrepreneurs.

The third form of capital is cultural capital, which is about education, experiences, and learning. Bourdieu defines three forms of cultural capital, "embodied, objectified, and institutionalized" (Bourdieu, 1986). Embodied cultural capital is mostly converted from an external source, like the society and the social class of the individual, and internalized unconsciously. Moreover, embodied capital requires time to transmit or to acquire (Bourdieu, 1986). In the case of entrepreneurship, embodied cultural capital manifests itself as knowing and acting according to field norms. This corresponds to entrepreneurs trying to be innovative and different from their competitors in order to align with the expectations of investors and other stakeholders (De Clercq & Voronov, 2009).

The second type of cultural capital is objectified cultural capital, which represents a materialized form of cultural capital that is transmitted with objects (Bourdieu, 1986). This is different from the economic capital corresponding to the value of a particular object. Objectified cultural capital covers the capital required to appropriate and use an object according to its specific purposes (Bourdieu, 1986). For instance, this type of cultural capital can be objectified by having a design of an entrepreneur's office space like other startup founders (De Clercq & Voronov, 2009).

The last type of cultural capital is institutionalized cultural capital that indicates the competency of the bearer of culture, such as a certificate of academic qualification (Bourdieu, 1986). It is the institutionalized cultural capital that enables comparisons between the qualifications of different parties and allows determining conversion rates between cultural capital and economic capital (Bourdieu, 1986). For example, Lee and Shaw (2016) examined different entrepreneurship training programs for professional higher technicians and non-professionals. Their findings show that professionals possess valuable non-material capital in comparison to non-professionals.

The fourth form of capital presented by Bourdieu (1986) is symbolic capital, which accumulates with gaining recognition (Bourdieu, 1993). Therefore, prestige, reputation, and fame are types of accrued symbolic capital. In case possession of other forms of capital is considered legitimate, they convert into symbolic capital (Everett, 2002). Therefore, symbolic capital can be identified as "the amalgam of and key to the deployment of all other forms capital" (Özbilgin & Tatli, 2005, 861). In the entrepreneurship literature, scholars refer to symbolic capital to reveal values and meanings ascribed by incumbents of the entrepreneurial field. For example, entrepreneurs try to be reputable to be considered by investors and convince them to invest money in a business that has a lot of uncertainties (De Clercq & Voronov, 2009; Lee & Shaw, 2016). They may aim to establish a workplace that reflects the image of an enjoyable, less-formal work atmosphere (Lee & Shaw, 2016), or employ past cultural markers to be recognized across transnational entrepreneurial fields (Vershinina & Rodgers, 2020).

Methodology

To reveal how coworking spaces support entrepreneurs to acquire resources, we conducted qualitative research (Dyer & Wilkins, 1991) in two coworking spaces of Istanbul with distinct characteristics, namely Alpha and Beta (pseudonyms). We selected these coworking spaces as our polar cases (Eisenhardt & Graebner, 2007), as they have distinctly different characteristics that may help us to broaden our perspective toward other varieties of coworking spaces. Alpha is part of a coworking space chain that is well known for its inspiring office design and community-building activities. It provides private offices, fixed and nomad desks to freelancers, self-employed professionals, and entrepreneurs running various businesses. Beta is a university-affiliated coworking space, as it is owned by the management company of the university science park. It is located on the university campus at a convenient location. As it is part of the science park, it is subject to particular legislation that regulates what activities can be performed in science parks and entails a level of tax exemption for the companies residing in the area. Accordingly, companies working at Beta need to be technology companies and are admitted after a strict evaluation process. Thus, Beta hosts entrepreneurs, their startup teams, and the business development staff of a few big corporations. Due to regulations, no self-employed professionals or freelancers are allowed. Selecting two polar coworking spaces with diverse characteristics provided us the opportunity to make a "broader exploration" (Eisenhardt & Graebner, 2007, 27).

The data collected for this chapter is part of a larger research program on coworking spaces lead by the second author. We collected data from several sources, such as observations, interviews, and archival data. The first and third authors of this study have participated directly in the management of the university science park. The second author has no affiliation with either coworking space. Her outsider status enabled the cross-checking of the analysis and the interpretation of the data, enhancing the validity of our study. Our primary data source for this study is interview data and participant observations. Before starting the interviews, the second author, who is not affiliated with either coworking space, performed participant observation to understand implicit and explicit aspects of the research context (DeWalt & DeWalt, 2011) in both places for two and a half months. Extensive field notes were taken during this period regarding the physical aspects of the spaces, interactions between residents, and events organized in these spaces.

We carried out 14 semi-structured interviews (Fontana & Frey, 2005), and these interviews lasted between 10 and 65 minutes, with an average of 45 minutes. All interviewees were informed about the study and asked for permission for recording during the interview. We did snowball sampling and asked each interviewee to introduce others. All interview records were transcribed verbatim. In Alpha, we also interviewed the management team of the facility, an angel investment network, a freelancer, and a law company, to balance our perspective and data access for both locations.

The transcribed interviews, compiled field notes, and observations were synthesized and then organized around emergent themes after cycles of coding. The first two authors coded the data through open coding separately. Then categories and themes were developed, discussed, and questioned until agreement (Eisenhardt, 1989). We continuously discussed our ideas while forming the codes, categories, and themes through an iterative and recursive coding process ending with the consensus of all authors. Then we drew links between themes and different forms of capital as introduced by Bourdieu (1986). These themes emerged from the data and were reinforced with the literature. We examined the data in detail to relate these themes and our theoretical framing. Therefore, throughout the analysis process, emergent ideas were critically compared with the literature (Anderson et al., 2010). This constant comparative approach to data analysis (Alvesson & Skoldberg, 2000; Glaser & Strauss, 1967; Silverman, 2000) involves an iterative reviewing of the data with emerging categories and themes (McKeever, Jack, & Anderson, 2015). Table 8.2 shows our categories and themes generated through the inductive process.

Although two authors had managerial access to one of the coworking spaces, our case-based approach in this study may not be considered as action research, as we were not implementing any action at Beta based on our inquiry (Coghlan & Brannick, 2005). With a comparative case approach, we explored the accounts of members of both spaces. To enhance our methodological reflexivity (Johnson & Duberley, 2003), the

Table 8.2 Categories and themes generated from empirical data (authors' own)

Cost reduction
Saving time through proximity
Savings through sharing economy
Savings through tax advantages
Entrepreneurial community
Common attitudes and behaviors among entrepreneurs
Emotional support
Proximity facilitating interaction among entrepreneurs
Entrepreneurial learning
(In)formal meetings facilitating access to knowledge
Events facilitating access to knowledge
Networking
Proximity to potential customers
Proximity to qualified workforce and professionals
Workplace facilitating interaction with outsiders
Property features
Nice architectural design
Office design and location impressing customers
Office design and location satisfying employees' expectations
Venture recognition
Admission after an evaluation process
Building trust through the coworking space's recognition
PR support through the coworking space's recognition

second author conducted the primary data collection with interviews and participant observation in both settings. The ethnographic observations in Alpha and Beta of the second author are supplemented with the participant observations of the other two authors in Beta (Skrutkowski, 2014). During the analysis phase, we critically considered our epistemic reflexivity (Johnson & Duberley, 2003) and tried to avoid possible biases arising from our social positions and past experiences. We discussed our interpretations and preferences to naturalize our presuppositions. We scrutinize our findings by triangulating different sources of data (Yin, 1994). Although we tried to hold methodological and epistemic reflexive positions, our accounts in this study may still reflect our socially derived self-image and are open to academic scrutiny.

Findings and Discussion

Our results indicate coworking spaces do play a role in obtaining different forms of capital for entrepreneurs. Coworking spaces support entrepreneurs to access both objectified and embodied forms of capital through different mechanisms. Moreover, various forms of capital available in coworking spaces are convertible to other ones, so gathering a form of capital may indirectly allow entrepreneurs to gain another. The links between our analytical themes and different forms of capital are shown in Fig. 8.1.

Cultural Capital

Coworking spaces are meeting hubs of entrepreneurs and field incumbents. In this study, we find that cultural capital is acquired by, and transmitted to entrepreneurs, through the social communities residing in, and the physicality of, the workplace that conveys this culture. In coworking spaces, several mechanisms support acquiring cultural capital, and it requires time and long-lasting relations with the embedded context.

Coworking spaces catalyze community-building by bringing like-minded people together (Capdevila, 2013). Communities emerge through the proximity, and organized events in these workplaces that

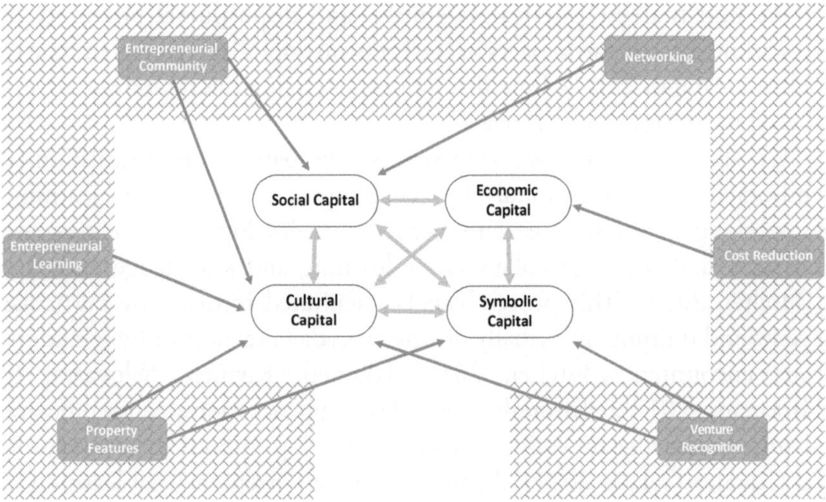

Fig. 8.1 Mechanisms to access resources by coworking spaces (authors' own)

facilitate interaction and are also promoted by emotional support among the residents (Garrett et al., 2017). Members have shared dispositions and behaviors (Anderson et al., 2010; Garrett et al., 2017) that foster the accumulation of cultural capital (Tatli et al., 2014). Moreover, community-based cultivation occurs unconsciously through being a member of a social group having a collective identity. Regarding the community in our empirical context, interviewees mentioned:

> *Working with other startups in the same collaborative space and knowing that everybody is working is an unconscious source of motivation. I think this point is so crucial.* (Interview, CSB-2)

> *People can rent a bigger office at a different location, nevertheless you prefer to be in this place when you consider the communication and socialization in here.* (Interview, CSA-4)

> *In startups, we always have hidden problems, and they [non-entrepreneurs] do not understand how we feel. For example, we think our cash flow is problematic; we cannot pay salaries; will our money be transferred or not. In here, they [entrepreneurs] understand you and mostly better than yourself.* (Interview, CSB-5)

We find that the physical, cognitive, and dispositional proximity in coworking spaces participates in the transmission of an embodied state of cultural capital. This is done through experiencing the shared values and shared meanings at a workplace.

We also find that coworking spaces take part in the acquisition of embodied cultural capital by enabling entrepreneurial learning. Coworking spaces support entrepreneurs to develop new practices and business skills through collaborative learning and knowledge exchange (Butcher, 2018). This process can be facilitated formally by particular events and training, informally during everyday practices or by serendipitous encounters (Butcher, 2018; Jakonen, Kivinen, Salovaara, & Hirkman, 2017). Through these learning occasions, entrepreneurs acquire knowledge on various topics and develop embodied cultural capital (Karatas-Özkan, 2011). As an example of entrepreneurial learning in our research context, interviewees mentioned:

> *For example, there is an event called the Founders Club here. Founders meet monthly for training and discuss subjects extensively.* (Interview, CSB-4)
>
> *Last Friday, a friend came [coworker in the same place] and asked you are doing this, and we need such thing […] in case they have questions, and if it is our area of specialization, we try to help them in 10 minutes while drinking coffee.* (Interview, CSB-2)

Entrepreneurial learning is different from acquiring cultural capital through the embedded community and is more about accumulating knowledge regarding entrepreneurial issues such as business opportunities, management experiences, and gathering resources. Moreover, acquiring or transmitting knowledge occurs through (in)formal meetings or events with a plan or a topic. So, this source of capital accumulation is a more conscious activity.

Our empirical data also show that coworking spaces enable entrepreneurs to acquire cultural capital by supporting the employee's image of entrepreneurs through property features. Employees' image of entrepreneurs is related to the collection of functional and symbolic benefits gathered through employment in a company, and attributes of a workplace play a role in developing a better image (Lievens & Highhouse, 2003).

For example, entrepreneurs exploit the design and location of the office space "that aligns with the field's current fashion" to collect objectified cultural capital (De Clercq & Voronov, 2009, 405). In line with this, we find that coworking spaces provide a workplace that supports the venture's image as an employer to gather cultural capital in a materialized form. The interviewees mentioned:

> *When an employee comes, and we say look, this is the place where you will work, she/he is happy. They value the job position here. If it is at Oto Sanayi [an underdeveloped district that was first established to host car maintenance and repair shops], it is hard to accept the offer.* (Interview, CSB-1)
>
> *People who are coming for a job interview like this place and find it fancy.* (Interview, CSB-2)

In our empirical context, both of the coworking spaces are close to central business districts and are very well known for their fancy office design. The location of coworking spaces and their internal designs are influential on people. So being located in such a place represents the objectified cultural capital of an entrepreneur.

In our empirical study, we find that entrepreneurs accumulate cultural capital also through venture recognition. When a coworking space "officially recognized [and] guaranteed competence" (Bourdieu, 1986, 248) of an entrepreneur, it transmits institutionalized cultural capital. Examples of institutionalized cultural capital are credentials like educational qualifications (e.g., Shaw, Gordon, Harvey, & MacLean, 2013; Vershinina, Barrett, & Meyer, 2011) or professional certifications (Lee & Shaw, 2016) of entrepreneurs. In our empirical context, one of the coworking space, Beta, selects ventures after an evaluation process. This process includes assessments of the entrepreneur's qualifications to perform an R&D project and run a company in a scalable manner. The recognition as being the member of Beta is described as the following:

> *This place is Turkey's advanced level entrepreneurship center. There are several bright people. [...] These ventures are selected and filtered. They are very successful.* (Interview, CSB-4)

Here, I meet with several people contributing intellectually because they are all handpicked, and everybody wants to be successful. (Interview, CSB-4)

Therefore, selecting a venture to the coworking space indicates that the entrepreneur has some sort of qualifications, and the others recognize this approval.

Social Capital

People collect and aggregate social capital through networks of relationships and membership in a group. For entrepreneurs, cofounders gather and keep social capital through having a variety of connections with different characteristics. For example, Stam et al. (2014) found that while weak indirect connections and network diversity increase the performance at the early stages of ventures, they make use of strong ties and network size at a later stage. The relations forming social capital can exist between entrepreneurs, customers, suppliers, and investors (Aldrich & Zimmer, 1986). Among these parties, the effects of relations differ, whether they are between entrepreneurs or between entrepreneurs and non-entrepreneurs (Burt, 1997).

In our empirical context, both of the coworking spaces host an entrepreneurial community. These community members have different backgrounds, and they run ventures in various business areas. However, they have characteristic patterns of work, such as dealing with uncertainty, growing their business, selling their products, and finding financial support. They build relations as an entrepreneurial community:

For instance, we utilize social relations. [...] For example, [an entrepreneur] that we meet at a happy hour gave us a contact at [name of a company]. On another occasion, [someone else] told us I could meet with this person. Like sharing a common fate of people who are walking on the same road. (Interview, CSA-5)

After a while, daily talks evolve into a conversation about whether you are growing, if you are well, etc. You say we have such and such problems. If this problem is something that I can help with, you say I know this guy who can help you. (Interview, CSB-4)

When the social proximity arising from the community meets with the physical proximity in coworking spaces, entrepreneurs build relationships fostering collaboration (Parrino, 2015). Similarly, we explore that coworking spaces enable relationships in the entrepreneurial communities and leverage social capital.

Another type of connection in coworking spaces appears between entrepreneurs in the community and non-entrepreneurs. Entrepreneurs and other coworkers can build fruitful relationships, such as a cofounder developing a relationship with a business development expert of a big company or a freelancer in the same coworking space. Moreover, the events taking place in coworking spaces and visitors coming to these places allow entrepreneurs to extend their relationships. In this study, we aggregated such activities under networking.

In both of the coworking spaces in this study, there are representatives of big corporations working close to the entrepreneurs, self-employed professionals, and investors. Alpha also hosts freelancers. The big corporations locate their representatives to build customer-supplier relationships or collaborate with entrepreneurs. Independent professionals provide different services to entrepreneurs such as consultancy on law or patents, design support, and so forth. Investors aim to work closely with entrepreneurs to identify successful ones and extend their portfolio through making investments.

The relationships with customers and suppliers are essential for entrepreneurs as they provide strategic information for their business, such as forecasting future demand and develop new products (Adler & Kwon, 2002) or better manage the added value through suppliers (Hormiga, Batista-Canino, & Sanchez-Medina, 2011). Relationships with investors, furthermore, provide various resources and advice on many issues (Katila, Rosenberger, & Eisenhardt, 2008). Developing relationships with investors through casual meetings can be more efficient and helps to reach better outcomes and firm performance (Hallen & Eisenhardt, 2012). Coworking spaces facilitate developing such relationships between entrepreneurs and with other residents through networking. As mentioned by the interviewees,

> *The manufacturing team of [a big corporation] told us their needs and made some requests…through this person I understand the needs more clearly.* (Interview, CSB-3)
>
> *What we are doing well at this place is … meeting supply with demand. For example, to the ones who ask if this team can reply to your request, or if you two meet, you will be a great team or such and such. Of course, [as an investor network] doing such things is not our primary objective, but as we meet several others and [Alpha] is sharing space … we do this voluntarily.* (Interview, CSA-1)

As in these examples, informal meetings in coworking spaces facilitate entrepreneurs' timely reach to resources that allow them to control external resources without losing their flexibility (Stam et al., 2014).

Outsider visits and events organized in these coworking spaces also allow building connections with potential partners, customers, or investors. These occasions could be the first touchpoint of entrepreneurs to distant social circles. Interviewees mentioned such spontaneous interactions:

> *There are visitors from outside Turkey who want to understand the entrepreneurship ecosystem in Turkey…all of these people start to come [to Alpha].* (Interview, CSA-1)
>
> *For example, when we were not at a coworking space, we considered this ecosystem as much as our immediate network. Here you meet with people with very different profiles that you cannot meet at a coffee shop, or let's say at any other place.* (Interview, CSB-5)

Such weak links gained at events provide flexibility to new ventures and can become strong ties in time.

Economic Capital

Economic capital is essential for new ventures (Chandler & Hanks, 1998), and savings appear as a critical form of economic capital that is employed to reach the objectives of a new venture (Pret, Shaw, & Drakopoulou-Dodd, 2016). Moreover, this kind of economic capital is widely preferred by entrepreneurs as it lessens the external financial needs (Kim, Aldrich, & Keister, 2006). We find that coworking spaces can help entrepreneurs to access economic capital by reducing their costs.

First of all, similar to their counterparts around the world (e.g., Merkel, 2015; Spinuzzi, 2012), coworking spaces in this study offer affordable prices when compared to renting a private office at similar locations with the same office services. Assembling several working units in a facility allows adopting a sharing economy as several functions can be provided more cheaply through economies of scale. Entrepreneurs exploit this financial resource by running their business in coworking spaces. For example, one of the interviewees mentioned:

> *Rental prices are too high in Istanbul. [...] In addition to overhead costs, there are other expenses such as when I choose this place, I have to purchase a table, a seat. Therefore, there appears a huge gap in the budget.* (Interview, CSA-3)

The collaborative working space, comprising fixed and nomad desks, also includes basic furniture in both of the coworking spaces. So, users of this space do not need to spend money on office furniture for their new ventures. Moreover, coworking members do not pay extra overhead expenses, labor costs for cleaning and security, or some value-added benefits such as hot drinks, soft drinks, and so on as all of them are included in the monthly rental price. As one interviewee told us,

> *As a small company, we did not look for someone to work for office services, let's say cleaning, preparing tea and coffee... it is not easy to hire someone just for these services.* (Interview, CSB-2)

Another mechanism to reduce costs is the tax advantage of carrying out your business in a coworking space. Tax incentives play a role in entrepreneurial decisions as it creates economic value through maximizing their income (Parker, 2003). Entrepreneurs from both coworking spaces mentioned such tax advantages. Whereas these tax advantages are regulation-driven and country-specific, it is a standard governmental policy around the world. In Turkey, you need to pay a stoppage tax to run a business when you are renting an office from a real person. The regulation is such that you do not need to pay this tax when you locate your business in coworking spaces. You can also claim back VAT tax as the coworking space is invoicing you the rental service with VAT. This is the case for both of the coworking spaces in the study. Interviewees mentioned:

> *I asked for the rental price of an office place in Gayrettepe [a central district close to the location of Alpha], and they told me 1500 Turkish Lira plus stoppage tax.* (Interview, CSA-3)
>
> *At a starting point, it [being a member of a coworking space] sounds very reasonable to us because […] invoiced amount can be deducted from VAT tax.* (Interview, CSA-5)

Moreover, because of its affiliation with the university and the science park, Beta offers additional tax benefits. Technology ventures in this place do not pay corporation tax, as they carry out technology development with officially registered projects. Furthermore, employees in these companies do not pay income tax, which means they get their gross salary as net income. As one of the interviewees stated,

> *We chased membership of the science park for a long time because tax advantages were very crucial for us.* (Interview, CSB-4)

We also find that coworking spaces reduce costs by saving time through proximity to several services. Coworking spaces host self-employed professionals and several companies that could help entrepreneurs. This proximity makes it possible for entrepreneurs to get various services without spending too much time and effort. For example, a visual communication designer working with entrepreneurs in Alpha mentioned that

> *I am staying here and working with my design tablet, and people come and ask what are you doing, are you designing something, our company needs such a thing, are you interested in doing it.* (Interview, CSA-4)

Likewise, the prototyping lab in Beta makes it easy to reach several manufacturing services. One of the interviewees said:

The AR glasses that we have sent to our customers have some missing parts. We promptly talked with [the company running the lab] and asked them to print [these parts]. (Interview, CSB-2)

Such cost reductions allow entrepreneurs to spend money on other activities such as sales and marketing, to grow their business.

Symbolic Capital

Symbolic capital is the most valuable form of capital (Everett, 2002), as it represents the legitimacy of accumulated capitals in other forms. As a consequence of high uncertainty and a lack of past results, it is challenging for entrepreneurs to gather resources (Zott & Huy, 2007). Therefore, entrepreneurs use symbolic communication to gain trust and convince resource holders of their potential future performance (Aldrich & Ruef, 2006). There are various symbolic actions such as endorsement by approved bodies that helps to build a reputation (Rao, 1994) or having an office with properties such as location, décor, and furnishing that indicate a professional management approach in an organization (Zott & Huy, 2007). Entrepreneurs also make use of such activities to accumulate social capital and gain legitimacy.

In this study, we find that coworking spaces help entrepreneurs to cultivate symbolic capital through venture recognition and property features. As mentioned earlier, Beta is part of the management company of a university science park. This university is well known for its engineering background and one of the oldest technical schools in the world. Moreover, this university science park is one of the top-performing science parks in Turkey. Beta is associated with the science park and was selected through an evaluation of its technology development plans. This process implies a recognition of the sophistication or the potential of the technology projects of Beta members. One of the interviewees said:

The trust issue is problematic. Unfortunately, customers consider foreign companies, like a German or a US-based company, and even when they are a startup, differently. Nevertheless, trust in Turkish companies is very different.

They do not believe in you. They cannot be sure and do not want to support you. Here we get the approval of the school. Here we are backed by [the name of the university]. (Interview, CSB-6)

Gaining legitimacy and trustworthiness through recognition supports entrepreneurs to reach resources, such as human resources, customers, and investors. Moreover, the fame of the coworking spaces also provides some status:

I think the increase in recognition of [Beta] also increases the recognition and trustworthiness of the companies here. For example, when I visit a customer and say I am at [Beta], it develops trust. (Interview, CSB-3)

Besides venture recognition, features of a property may cultivate symbolic capital (e.g., Elsbach, 2004; Zott & Huy, 2007). Coworking spaces are famous for their "fascinating" (de Vaujany et al., 2019, 2) interior designs, and their location choices also bring symbolic meanings (Spinuzzi, 2012). Such property features are prominent in our empirical data as

When you come to [Alpha], the place has a spirit. It impresses you so much. You don't expect it and say, wow! When you enter, there are high ceilings and brick walls, for example, a renovated hood of a Volkswagen hanging on the wall, etc. (Interview, Alpha-1)

[Alpha] has a ready-made design, a spirit… like an old factory, new customers visiting us like it so much. (Interview, Alpha-4)

When you invite customers, they are impressed [by the place], and they say there is something important here. (Interview, Beta-1)

In both of the coworking spaces, entrepreneurs are able to impress their customers and employees with the symbolic capital gathered through the coworking space and atmosphere.

Conclusion

In this study, we explore how coworking spaces support entrepreneurs to acquire tangible and intangible resources. Entrepreneurs need different resources to grow their business, and they frequently choose coworking spaces as their office location. However, what coworking spaces contribute to entrepreneurs' resource acquisition has not been fully examined before. By using Bourdieu's capital framework, we identified different mechanisms supported by coworking spaces that help entrepreneurs accumulate various forms of capital. Accordingly, we draw a framework to locate relations between these mechanisms and sources of capital (see Fig. 8.1).

We believe our study shows the richness and complexity of relations in coworking spaces supporting how entrepreneurs deal with uncertainty and lack of resources. This study has practical implications in terms of helping practitioners to understand what coworking spaces provide to entrepreneurs. Moreover, this study provides a perspective about entrepreneurs' resource acquisition activities and could foster similar Bourdieuan analyses in cultivating resources in other settings. In addition to this, while it is hard to reach generalizable results with a qualitative study, our deliberative selection of two fundamentally different cases helps us to cover as much variety as we can and develop a comprehensive framework.

Our findings are open to development with further inquiry. For example, as entrepreneurs can acquire different forms of capital, and they are convertible into each other (Tatli et al., 2014), the mechanisms used to obtain more than one type of capital in our framework could be the result of such conversions. Our cross-sectional analysis and results can be developed with a longitudinal study to reveal how one source of capital is transformed into other forms and with which mechanisms as time unfolds. The conversion of one source of capital into another form is understudied in the literature (Pret et al., 2016), and its temporal analysis could reveal different patterns of activities employed for such transformations.

The COVID-19 pandemic is going to impact the demand for coworking spaces, as there are increased concerns for contacting other people in shared spaces because of the risk of cross-contamination and sanitation of surfaces. How COVID-19 will influence the social norms, economy, will leave traces in the symbols and culture of social communities, impact the availability and appropriation of social, cultural, and economic capital and impact coworking spaces need further inquiry.

Moreover, there are different types of coworking spaces with varying business models and missions, as in our empirical context and mentioned in the literature (de Vaujany et al., 2019). These differences may arise from several reasons, such as the broader social context or material characteristics of these spaces. Therefore, comparative analysis of coworking spaces could give more information regarding idiosyncratic aspects of coworking spaces in providing resources to entrepreneurs.

References

Adler, P. S., & Kwon, S. W. (2002). Social capital: Prospects for a new concept. *Academy of Management Review, 27*(1), 17–40.

Aldrich, H. E., & Ruef, M. (2006). *Organizations evolving* (2nd ed.). Thousand Oaks, CA: Sage.

Aldrich, H. E., & Zimmer, C. (1986). Entrepreneurship through social networks. In D. L. Sexton & R. W. Smilor (Eds.), *The art and science of entrepreneurship* (pp. 3–23). Cambridge, MA: Ballinger Publishing Company.

Alvesson, M., & Skoldberg, K. (2000). *Reflexive methodology. New vistas for qualitative researchers.* Thousand Oaks, CA: Sage.

Anderson, A. R., Drakopoulou-Dodd, S., & Jack, S. (2010). Network practices and entrepreneurial growth. *Scandinavian Journal of Management, 26*(2), 121–133.

Bouncken, R. B., & Reuschl, A. J. (2016). Coworking-spaces: How a phenomenon of the sharing economy builds a novel trend for the workplace and for entrepreneurship. *Review of Managerial Science, 12*(1), 317–334.

Bourdieu, P. (1986). The forms of capital. In J. G. Richardson (Ed.), *Handbook of theory and research for the sociology of education* (pp. 241–258). Westport, CT: Greenwood.

Bourdieu, P. (1993). *The field of cultural production.* Cambridge, UK: Polity Press.

Burt, R. S. (1997). The contingent value of social capital. *Administrative Science Quarterly, 42*, 339–365.

Butcher, T. (2018). Learning everyday entrepreneurial practices through coworking. *Management Learning, 49*(3), 327–345.

Capdevila, I. (2013). Knowledge dynamics in localized communities: Coworking spaces as microclusters. Retrieved from SSRN https://ssrn.com/abstract=2414121 or https://doi.org/10.2139/ssrn.2414121

Capdevila, I. (2015). Coworking spaces and the localized dynamics of innovation in Barcelona. *International Journal of Innovation Management, 19*(3), 1540004.

Chandler, G. N., & Hanks, S. H. (1998). An examination of the substitutability of founders' human and financial capital in emerging business ventures. *Journal of Business Venturing, 13*(5), 353–369.

Chang, Y., & Chen, M. (2020). Creative entrepreneurs' creativity, opportunity recognition, and career success: Is resource availability a double-edged sword? *European Management Journal.* In press. https://doi.org/10.1016/j.emj.2020.03.004

Coghlan, D., & Brannick, T. (2005). *Doing action research in your own organization* (2nd ed.). London: Sage.

De Clercq, D., & Voronov, M. (2009). Role of cultural and symbolic capital in entrepreneurs' ability to meet expectations about conformity and innovation. *Journal of Small Business Management, 47*(3), 398–420.

de Vaujany, F. X., Dandoy, A., Grandazzi, A., & Faure, S. (2019). Experiencing a new place as an atmosphere: A focus on tours of collaborative spaces. *Scandinavian Journal of Management, 35*(2), 101030.

Denzin, N., & Lincoln, Y. S. (2005). Introduction: The discipline and practice of qualitative research. In N. Denzin & Y. S. Lincoln (Eds.), *The Sage handbook of qualitative research* (3rd ed., pp. 1–32). Thousand Oaks, CA: Sage.

DeWalt, K. M., & DeWalt, B. R. (2011). *Participant observation: A guide for fieldworkers* (2nd ed.). New York, NY: Altamira Press.

Drakopoulou-Dodd, S., McDonald, S., McElwee, G., & Smith, R. (2014). A Bourdieuan analysis of qualitative authorship in entrepreneurship scholarship. *Journal of Small Business Management, 52*(4), 633–654.

Drakopoulou-Dodd, S. L., & Anderson, A. R. (2007). Mumpsimus and the mything of the individualistic entrepreneur. *International Small Business Journal, 25*(4), 341–360.

Dyer Jr., W. G., & Wilkins, A. L. (1991). Better stories, not better constructs to generate better theory: A rejoinder to Eisenhardt. *Academy of Management Review, 16*(3), 613–619.

Eisenhardt, K. M. (1989). Building theories from case study research. *Academy of Management Review, 14*(4), 532–550.

Eisenhardt, K. M., & Graebner, M. E. (2007). Theory building from cases: Opportunities and challenges. *Academy of Management Journal, 50*(1), 25–32.

Elsbach, K. D. (2004). Interpreting workplace identities: The role of office décor. *Journal of Organizational Behavior, 25*(1), 99–128.

Everett, J. (2002). Organizational research and the praxeology of Pierre Bourdieu. *Organizational Research Methods, 5*(1), 56–80.

Fontana, A., & Frey, J. H. (2005). The interview: From neutral stance to political involvement. In N. K. Denzin & Y. S. Lincoln (Eds.), *The Sage handbook of qualitative research* (3rd ed., pp. 695–728). Thousand Oaks, CA: Sage.

Fuzi, A. (2015). Coworking spaces for promoting entrepreneurship in sparse regions: The case of South Wales. *Regional Studies, Regional Science, 2*(1), 462–469.

Garrett, L. E., Spreitzer, G. M., & Bacevice, P. (2017). Co-constructing a sense of community at work: The emergence of community in coworking spaces. *Organization Studies, 38*(6), 821–842.

Glaser, B., & Strauss, A. (1967). *The discovery of grounded theory*. London: Weidenfeld & Nicolson.

Hallen, B. L., & Eisenhardt, K. M. (2012). Catalyzing strategies and efficient tie formation: How entrepreneurial firms obtain investment ties. *Academy of Management Journal, 55*(1), 35–70.

Hormiga, E., Batista-Canino, R. M., & Sanchez-Medina, A. (2011). The impact of relational capital on the success of new business startups. *Journal of Small Business Management, 49*(4), 617–638.

Jakonen, M., Kivinen, N., Salovaara, P., & Hirkman, P. (2017). Towards an economy of encounters? A critical study of affectual assemblages in coworking. *Scandinavian Journal of Management, 33*(4), 235–242.

Johnson, P., & Duberley, J. (2003). Reflexivity in management research. *Journal of Management Studies, 40*(5), 1279–1303.

Johnstone, B. A. (2006). Ethnographic methods in entrepreneurship research. In H. Neergaard & J. P. Ulhøi (Eds.), *Handbook of qualitative research methods in entrepreneurship* (pp. 97–121). Cheltenham, UK: Edward Elgar.

Jones, O., Macpherson, A., & Jayawarna, D. (2014). *Resourcing the startup business: Creating dynamic entrepreneurial learning capabilities*. London: Routledge.

Jones, O., Macpherson, A., & Thorpe, R. (2010). Learning in owner managed small firms: Mediating artefacts and strategic space. *Entrepreneurship and Regional Development, 22*(7–8), 649–673.

Karatas-Özkan, M. (2011). Understanding relational qualities of entrepreneurial learning: Towards a multi-layered approach. *Entrepreneurship and Regional Development, 23*(9–10), 877–906.

Katila, R., Rosenberger, J., & Eisenhardt, K. M. (2008). Swimming with sharks: Technology ventures and corporate relationships. *Administrative Science Quarterly, 53*(2), 295–332.

Kim, P. H., Aldrich, H., & Keister, L. (2006). Access (not) denied: The impact of financial, human, and cultural capital on entrepreneurial entry in the United States. *Small Business Economics, 27*(1), 5–22.

Lee, R. (2017). *The social capital of entrepreneurial newcomers: Bridging, status-power and cognition*. Basingstoke, UK: Palgrave Macmillan.

Lee, R., & Shaw, E. (2016). Bourdieu's non-material forms of capital: Implications for startup policy. *Environment and Planning C: Politics and Space, 34*(8), 1734–1758.

Lehner, O. M. (2014). The formation and interplay of social capital in crowdfunded social ventures. *Entrepreneurship and Regional Development, 26*(5–6), 478–499.

Lievens, F., & Highhouse, S. (2003). The relation of instrumental and symbolic attributes to a company's attractiveness as an employer. *Personnel Psychology, 56*(1), 75–102.

Mariotti, I., Pacchi, C., & Di Vita, S. (2017). Coworking spaces in Milan: Location patterns and urban effects. *Journal of Urban Technology, 24*(3), 47–66.

McKeever, E., Jack, S., & Anderson, A. (2015). Embedded entrepreneurship in the creative re-construction of place. *Journal of Business Venturing, 30*(1), 50–65.

Merkel, J. (2015). Coworking in the city. *Ephemera: Theory and Politics in Organization, 15*(1), 121–139.

Mitev, N., de Vaujany, F., Laniray, P., Bohas, A., & Fabbri, J. (2018). Coworking spaces, collaborative practices and entrepreneurship. In K. Riemer, S. Schellhammer, & M. Meinert (Eds.), *Collaboration in the digital age* (pp. 15–43). Cham, Switzerland: Springer Verlag.

Moriset, B. (2014). *Building new places of the creative economy. The rise of coworking spaces*. 2nd Geography of Innovation International Conference 2014, Utrecht University, Utrecht, 23–25 January 2014, 24.

Neergaard, H., & Ulhøi, J. P. (2006). Introduction: Methodological variety in entrepreneurship research. In H. Neergaard & J. P. Ulhøi (Eds.), *Handbook of qualitative research methods in entrepreneurship* (pp. 1–14). Cheltenham, UK: Edward Elgar.

Özbilgin, M., & Tatli, A. (2005). Book review essay: Understanding Bourdieu's contribution to organization and management studies. *Academy of Management Review, 30*(4), 855–877.

Parker, S. C. (2003). Does tax evasion affect occupational choice? *Oxford Bulletin of Economics and Statistics, 65*(3), 379–394.

Parrino, L. (2015). Coworking: Assessing the role of proximity in knowledge exchange. *Knowledge Management Research and Practice, 13*(3), 261–227.

Pret, T., Shaw, E., & Drakopoulou-Dodd, S. (2016). Painting the full picture: The conversions of economic, cultural, social and symbolic capital. *International Small Business Journal, 34*(8), 1004–1027.

Rao, H. (1994). The social construction of reputation: Certification contests, legitimation and the survival of organizations in the American automobile industry: 1895–1912. *Strategic Management Journal, 15*(S1), 29–44.

Reuschke, D. (2016). The importance of housing for self-employment. *Economic Geography, 92*(4), 378–400.

Rus, A., & Orel, M. (2015). Coworking: A community of work. *Teorija in Praksa, 52*(6), 1017–1038.

Shaw, E., Gordon, J., Harvey, C., & MacLean, M. (2013). Exploring contemporary entrepreneurial philanthropy. *International Small Business Journal, 31*(5), 580–599.

Silverman, D. (2000). *Doing Qualitative Research: A Practical Handbook.* London: Sage.

Skrutkowski, M. (2014). Doing research in your own organization: Being native, going stranger. In E. Jeanes & T. Huzzard (Eds.), *Critical management research: Reflections from the field* (pp. 101–118). London: Sage.

Spinuzzi, C. (2012). Working alone together: Coworking as emergent collaborative activity. *Journal of Business and Technical Communication, 26*(4), 399–441.

Stam, W., Arzlanian, S., & Elfring, T. (2014). Social capital of entrepreneurs and small firm performance: A meta-analysis of contextual and methodological moderators. *Journal of Business Venturing, 29*(1), 152–173.

Tatli, A., Vassilopoulou, J., Özbilgin, M., Forson, C., & Slutskaya, N. (2014). A Bourdieuan relational perspective for entrepreneurship research. *Journal of Small Business Management, 52*(4), 615–632.

Vershinina, N., Barrett, R., & Meyer, M. (2011). Forms of capital, intra-ethnic variation and Polish entrepreneurs in Leicester. *Work, Employment and Society, 25*(1), 101–117.

Vershinina, N., & Rodgers, P. (2020). Symbolic capital within the lived experiences of Eastern European migrants: A gendered perspective. *Entrepreneurship and Regional Development, 32*(1–2), 1–16.

Yin, R. K. (1994). *Case study research: Design and methods* (2nd ed.). Newbury Park, CA: Sage Publications.

Zott, C., & Huy, Q. (2007). How entrepreneurs use symbolic management to acquire resources. *Administrative Science Quarterly, 52*(1), 70–105.

Part III

New Ways of Working and Telework

9

From De-materialization to Re-materialization: A Social Dynamics Approach to New Ways of Working

Michel Ajzen

Introduction

For several decades, a large number of work transformations have taken place in our societies, inter alia globalization, flexibilization, digitalization or virtualization (Huws, 2014). These changes contributed to the emergence of New Ways of Working (NWW) (Taskin, Ajzen, & Donis, 2017). Among the practices associated to NWW (Ajzen, Donis, & Taskin, 2015), telework has been of great interest for scholars who questioned the effects of such practices on organizational outcomes. However, these effects remain diversified and mostly unexplained (De Menezes & Kelliher, 2011; Martin & MacDonnell, 2012). For instance, little is known about the social dynamics that occur from the introduction of teleworking practices to their effective uses by social actors. To do so, this chapter aims to reintroduce the political dimension underlying these social dynamics by questioning how the implementation of teleworking

M. Ajzen (✉)
Université Catholique de Louvain, Louvain-la-Neuve, Belgium
e-mail: Michel.ajzen@uclouvain.be

N. Mitev et al. (eds.), *New Ways of Working*, Technology, Work and Globalization,
https://doi.org/10.1007/978-3-030-61687-8_9

practices—as a part of a broader NWW project—leads to a redefinition of what is work and how workers might behave in this context (Gomez, 2006; Gomez & Jones, 2000; Reynaud, 2004, 2007; Reynauld & Richebé, 2009).

Based on a case study conducted within a company located in Belgium, the chapter highlights to what extent the introduction and the development of telework practices have resulted in different ways of organizing work. The analysis shows the emergence of different effects such as a reconfiguration of responsibilities, a transformation of control and an evolution of coordination modes leading to a redefinition of what is work in this new context.

This transformation entails a process of work de-materialization that, among others, individualized and invisibilized work(ers). This process can be depicted, for example, by a feeling of isolation or uselessness, an instrumentalization of interactions, the lack of consideration for some work activities, the rise of results-based management practices as well as individual strategies to maximize time and space in order to comply with new managerial expectations.

More interestingly, the results show a counter-movement of re-materialization through which work(ers) become more visible. Here, actors aim to re-materialize social relations at the workplace through different means such as the virtualization of exchanges (*WhatsApp* groups), by being present at work at particular moments, by planning future face-to-face interactions, by defining rules of coordination, and also by giving more visibility to work produced remotely. These strategies, either individual or collective, intend to re-materialize work(ers) by affirming a particular vision of work in terms of objective, subjective and collective dimensions of work.

As a result, the contribution of the chapter is twofold. First, it explores the political dimension underlying the process of building social relationships in organizations by questioning how and why telework—as a part of NWW project—is regulated by actors. While questioning this process, I find that the introduction of NWW practices leads to new social dynamics aiming to both question and re-appropriate managerial injunctions. Second, it questions these re-appropriations through a re-materialization process. The findings highlight a new responsibility for employees to manage a tension between individual performance—through the maximization of time and space—and the collective maintaining of a social community at work.

A Changing World of Work

Over the last decades, the world of work has faced profound transformations through the globalization of markets, the flexibilization of work and employment, the financialization of management, the digitalization of work processes and the individualization of employment relations (Taskin et al., 2017). These changes have shaped the so-called New Ways of Working. The origin of these changes might be credited to the emergence of computer technologies in the early 1960s which have quickly constituted a source of competitive advantage for many companies (Huws, 2013) as the more advanced the technologies are, the more they reduce production costs (e.g. automation). In the same vein, the development of Information and Communication Technologies (ICTs) in the following decades has led to the standardization of employment processes that enable organizations to reduce labor costs by relocating their activities (Huws, 2014). This trend was reinforced in the early 1990s through the intervention of European and international institutions to promote the increase of capital concentration, market deregulation and free movement of capital and people around the world. Even though the globalization was already underway, it is currently supported and promoted by a strong political discourse that aims to define a new worker: prototypical, interchangeable, speaking the main international languages and able to mobilize ICTs. As a result, competition within labor markets increases at the same time as the geographical distance between skills decreases (Huws, 2014; Thorne, 2005). This has led to a de-industrialization as well as the disappearance of regional or national expertise in favor of a more competitive workforce in other parts of the world (Huws, 2014).

In this context of globalization, the call for more external flexibility (e.g. flexibility of employment status and of systems of production) has been justified by many employers as a need to be adaptable and responsive to market requirements. This has led to the emergence of new forms of employment (Eurofound, 2015). Besides, since ICTs are increasingly transportable and accessible, a similar justification has been used to introduce internal flexibility at the company level (Nydegger & Nydegger, 2010; Richter, Meyer, & Sommer, 2006; Vakola & Wilson, 2004); this involves a set of flexible practices related to working time, workspace, work organization and wages (de Nanteuil, 2004; Vendramin & Valenduc, 2002). Consequently, the organization's physical boundaries have gradually blurred and become porous. This usually referred to as the virtualization of organizations (Bell & Kozlowski, 2002; Breu & Hemingway, 2004; Vartiainen, 2006) which can be characterized by virtual spaces facilitating interactions between actors and simultaneously making geographically remote resources more accessible (Shekhar, 2006).

Toward a New World of Work?

Although NWW can be approached as a consequence of the societal and organizational trends discussed above, they perhaps paradoxically also carry a wish to work differently by breaking with the traditional ways of organizing work (e.g. bureaucracy, managerial control and rigidity), contest an antinomic perspective of the relation between work and life by proposing a more holistic approach (e.g. work-life balance arrangements and autonomy) and offer more voice to workers by introducing more participative work methods (Taskin et al., 2017).

NWW can be defined as a set of practices combining: '(a) spatial and temporal flexible work practices; (b) specific organizational configurations of work; (c) participative and collaborative management practices [and], drawing on the extended use of ICTs' (Taskin et al., 2017, 70). In their literature review, Ajzen et al. (2015) list the different practices usually associated to these NWW components. Among the spatial and temporal flexible work practices, we find teleworking from home, co-working spaces or satellite offices but also, shared desk and/or clean-desk policies. The work configurations are mostly represented by open-spaces, virtual teams and (semi-)autonomous teams. Finally, the participative and collaborative management practices are characterized by different practices such as knowledge management, management by objectives, project management, collaborative autonomy, participative autonomy or total quality management.

However, one can wonder whether organizations are simply disguising something old as something new. Taking a quick look at these practices one could argue that they are not really 'new'. For instance, open-spaces, participative management or management by objectives have existed since the 1950s (Haigh, 2012; van Meel, 2011) and teleworking since the early 1970s (Nilles, 1998). So, what is really new with NWW? The possible answer to this question is twofold. First, according to Taskin (2012), NWW can be seen as a synergistic bundle of practices aligned with organizational strategies, rather than an accumulation of practices over time. Second, NWW conveys a management philosophy promoting democracy, empowerment, transparency and well-being at work (see e.g. Kelliher & Richardson, 2012; Peters, Poutsma, Van Der Heijden, Bakker, & De Bruijn, 2014; Taskin et al., 2017).

Telework as a Spearhead for NWW

Telework might include old-fashioned management practices far from a 'new world of work'. Bergum (2007) showed that the annual number of scientific publications on telework had steadily decreased since the mid-1990s, questioned this lack of interest and suggested that (1) telework had failed to reach stakeholders' expectations and was not used anymore; (2) telework was so embedded in daily work practices than the prefix 'tele' disappeared; and (3) telework had evolved and was taking a different form.

The first cannot be supported since research shows that telework has increased over time (e.g. Eurofound, 2010; Eurofound & the International Labour Office, 2017). The other two suggestions are relevant, particularly the third one. Considering the massive use of ICTs such as smartphones, online communication and collaborative tools (*Lync, Skype, FaceTime, Slack*, etc.), the huge growth of Wi-Fi spots in public areas and 4G/5G data connections, it is easy to be connected everywhere all the time. These facilities were already used by mobile workers such as sales representatives, multi-site managers or trainers (see Felstead, Jewson, &

Walters, 2005; Gareis, Lilischkis, & Mentrup, 2006) in the early 2000s, now these tools are widely used. We have all observed people working with their laptops and mobile phones in coffee shops, trains, airports, cars and homes. Telework embodies NWW as it breaks with the traditional Taylorist/Fordist forms of management in favor of a more agile model using spatio-temporal flexible practices and recent ICT tools (Kelliher & Richardson, 2012).

One can argue that telework represents a spearhead for NWW as it combines different NWW components described above: it is often accompanied by a transformation of workspaces (e.g. open-space, clean-desk and share-desk) either as a means or as a purpose (Bosch-Sijtsema, Ruohomäki, & Vartiainen, 2010; Taskin & Ajzen, 2015); it offers opportunities to manage working time more flexibly and therefore work-life balance; since control cannot be exerted through physical proximity, other ways to monitor work are used such as management by objectives; depending on the type of work and the frequency of use, telework supports virtual collaboration.

Taskin (2011, 73) proposes the following definition: 'Telework refers to the exercise of a professional activity, completely or partly, performed remotely (i.e. not in the immediate vicinity of where the result is expected and not in the physical presence of managers monitoring work) through ICT tools'. This definition highlights three key elements characterizing telework: work performed remotely, frequency of use and use of ICTs.

Among the different forms of remote work, homeworking is undoubtedly the most popular practice (see Kowalski & Swanson, 2005; Sullivan, 2003; Verbeke, Schultz, Greidanus, & Hambley, 2008). However, other places can be used to work remotely such as a co-working space which refers to an office with temporary workstations and shared facilities (Johnson, 2003) or a satellite office, which is company-owned (Kurland & Bailey, 1999; Tremblay, Chevrier, & Di Loreto, 2007; Verbeke et al., 2008). A third type of remote work has been depicted by Nilles (1998) as a '*tutti frutti*' practice. This refers to the combination of different places such as a home, a co-working space, a satellite office but also a hotel, a station hall, an airplane, a train and so on (Kingma, 2018). This practice is associated to nomadic workers (Felstead et al., 2005; Holm & Kendall, 2008; Vartiainen, 2006).

The second element that characterizes telework is its frequency of use. It can be characterized both in terms of time and regularity. Time refers to the proportion of working time performed remotely. Some authors propose the following typology (Halford, 2005; Hanhike & Gareis, 2004) based on time: occasional telework (less than 20%), alternating telework (between 20% and 90%) or permanent telework (more than 90%). I can also add the regularity of use since telework can be used on a structured basis (e.g. every Tuesday), on a flexible basis (e.g. ad hoc) or on a more hybrid basis while combining structured and flexible frequencies.

Finally, the last element characterizing telework is the use of ICTs. Telework is different from other work configurations from home (e.g. crafts persons and artisans) which do not require intensive ICT use to communicate and collaborate with colleagues remotely, to manage information, acquire knowledge or facilitate decision-making (Bobillier-Chaumon, 2003).

Rethinking Teleworking Through Social Dynamics: A Critical Research Perspective

There are many studies which study the effects of telework at different analytical levels: societal (Kurland & Bailey, 1999; Nilles, 1998), organizational (Felstead et al., 2005; Kelliher & Richardson, 2012; Pyöriä, 2011; Tietze & Musson, 2010) and individual (Child & Rodrigues, 2005; Harris, 2003). The effects of telework at these different levels are extremely varied (Boell, Cecez-Kecmanovic, & Campbell, 2016; De Menezes & Kelliher, 2011; Martin & MacDonnell, 2012) and causal relationships difficult to demonstrate; indeed, I argue here that telework needs to be understood through a dynamic relationship of interdependence rather than of causality. This suggests that the context in which telework is implemented in terms of frequency, workplaces and ICT use plays a crucial role in how it impacts both companies and individuals.

Considering the context means addressing the social dynamics involved in the managerial goals of introducing telework and how it is actually implemented and performed: whether this is agreed with unions' representatives or a managerial policy is decided unilaterally, or there are informal arrangements between workers and managers (see Martinez & De Schampheleire, 2005). It is also likely that practices differ, to varying degrees, from the content of an agreement or arrangement. As Lallement (2007) and Cushen and Thompson (2012) observed, there are gaps between prescribed and real work. Prescribed work refers to managerial norms on what is expected, normal or desired. These 'operating precepts' aim to define rules on how work has to be performed (Léonard, 2015). However, rules may be applied differently when work is actually performed: workers face situations where rules are not adequate or do not exist, often deal with the inconsistency between rules and the reality of work, and regulate work activities by producing, maintaining or modifying rules through different strategies (Reynaud, 2004).

According to Reynaud (2004), rules produced by social actors can be considered as a set of normative standards named 'convention', or a system of rules which provides information on expected behaviors. A convention gives sense to action in terms of what is assumed as 'normal' or not (Gomez, 2006). Therefore, I see the implementation of telework as (re)defining work through a (new?) normative framework about expected behaviors in the 'new world of work' (see e.g. Taskin & Gomez, 2015) and explore this in a case study next.

Toward a New World of Work: The *Barzel* Case

Barzel (not its real name) is an international company located in 80 countries around the world. The international headquarters are located in the US from where they manage more than 50,000 employees worldwide. Our case study focuses on the Belgian branch located in Brussels where 165 white-collar workers are employed. Among the different teams, there are three main occupations: administrative (Admin); sales representatives and technical experts (TechniCom); and support such as HR, finance, legal or IT teams (Support). A total of 31 semi-structured interviews were conducted with 17 employees, 8 managers, 2 team leaders and 4 union representatives from 3 Admin teams, 2 TechniCom teams and 5 Support teams. Interviews lasted from 25 minutes to 90 minutes (66 minutes average) and were recorded and transcribed. NVivo 11 was used to analyze the empirical material through a thematic analysis and a conceptual categorization (Paillé & Mucchielli, 2012). The interviews were carried out in French and the quotations in this chapter were translated and anonymized and some are included below to describe the case study.

The introduction of telework is part of a larger managerial project that aims to transform the traditional ways of working by introducing more spatial and temporal flexibility of work.

> *I think that teleworking is originally part of a will to increase flexibility within the company. This is in line with the evolution of the world and society, with a new mindset and with the aspirations of new workers. Therefore, by providing more flexibility, work is carried out at different times, and is organized differently with respect to particular requirements or job needs related to the employee's occupation.* (Jack, HR Manager)

It started with the transformation of the workspaces from individual offices to 'flexdesk' which refers to an open-space where belongings have to be removed on a daily basis. The aim was to reduce costs related to workspaces. In the past, employees were in separate offices with a maximum of six persons and managers had their own personal office. At the same time, management promoted agility rather than specialization to ensure more flexibility within some teams. In 2014, telework was introduced for one day per week maximum.

Originally, the HR manager intended to reach a collective agreement on telework with workers' representatives. However, the proposal was deemed unacceptable for three reasons: access to telework depended on abandoning clocking in which allows workers to get compensation for overtime; workers had to use their own equipment (laptop, internet, etc.); and the allowance for the use of their own tools was perceived as insufficient. The HR manager decided to stop the bargaining process and implement a teleworking policy unilaterally. Despite the protests of workers' representatives, especially on abandoning the clocking in system, employees started to sign individual arrangements to access telework. Over time, the number of teleworkers has increased and therefore, the number of workers still using the traditional clocking system has decreased (12% in 2017). The HR manager decided that all employees should abandon clocking in at the end of 2017. In the meantime, telework has been expanded to two days per week.

A Managerial Project Facing the Reality of Work: From Global to Local Regulations

Before the formal introduction of telework, the practice was already used by some employees either to respond to job requirements (as for managers or TechniCom workers) or for exceptional personal matters (e.g. to take care of a sick child or when faced with a public transport strike). This informal use of telework highlights how social actors produce rules to organize their own activity. By then specifying teleworkers' rights and obligations, the management policy produced new rules aiming to define how telework has to be performed. Nevertheless, these rules are locally interpreted by social actors.

Even though the management policy defines telework as a work realized at home with a maximum of two regular days per week, the results show that other workplaces are used by employees (e.g. satellite offices, customers' offices, hotel rooms, airport halls or holiday homes). Regarding the frequency of use, it varies across teams and ranges from a maximum of one regular or variable day at home per week to a maximum of two days at the office (for TechniCom workers).

> *I can work for Holland from here … I am from Southern Europe and at one point I had to leave for three weeks in Southern Europe and I just had to take my laptop from here and I was able to work from there without anyone realizing that I was not even here. (…) And now we have another colleague, he has a house in Dublin. And sometimes, when he goes there, he takes two weeks off and he works for two weeks. So, he goes to the office in Dublin with his laptop, he logs in and he works. I'm sure they do it elsewhere too.* (Charlotte, Employee)

Similarly, both access to telework and technical support have been interpreted locally. For instance, a few managers circumvent the rule prescribing a trial period before authorizing a worker to telework, either by increasing or reducing the amount of time regarding job requirements. In the same vein, IT employees provide technical support to teleworkers informally. Considering that supplying ICT tools and providing support are part of company's duties, they circumvent the rules.

> *We cannot manage their equipment so they have to find solutions for the connection, this is not too difficult to do but sometimes, some bugs appear. And then, even if we cannot, we feel obliged to provide support on personal laptops. (…) But we are not supposed to provide the support. But otherwise people cannot work anymore from home.* (Gio, Employee)

Telework meant abandoning clocking in, and as a result the notion of working time is now perceived as less important than before. For most teams, working time is not 'working the right number of hours' any longer but 'doing the tasks that have to be done', even if this involves managing work (mostly emails) in the evening, at weekends or during holidays. The control of working time became obsolete and was replaced by management by objectives as the main mode of control. No matter the time spent on tasks, the job has to be done. This shift has been possible as the company uses software to monitor workloads instantly. Control of work is not an issue as it is expected that everyone is responsible for managing time, space and workloads efficiently.

> *It's a possibility, but I think the real control is about whether the work has been done or not. This is the new philosophy with telework. In the past, you had the clocking machine and you had to do your working hours, and if you had done these, it was fine. You could be busy working or sleeping, it did not matter. Now, control is on the work realized at the end of the month, it has to be done, and if it's done, it's good. It's another philosophy.* (Loulou, Employee)

Telework is perceived as providing better opportunities to manage the work-life balance. For instance, most employees report how telework is particularly useful to take care of children after school, to arrange appointments with doctors, banks or public authorities during business hours, to receive a home delivery, to do the shopping, or to still work when sick and able to work remotely. Nevertheless, this flexibility is supported by a principle of productivity. Indeed, actors are not completely free since they are expected to act in order to comply with what a 'good' teleworker is:

> *As part of the Program, a teleworker must demonstrate his performance; be a good manager of time, workload and goals; be motivated and responsible; be attentive to working hours and productivity; be results oriented, focus on priorities and deadlines; be able to work autonomously and without supervision (…) More importantly, the teleworker must be committed to making the system work.* (Barzel's Telework Policy, p. 5)

In this context, time, space and physical presence are less important as long as the objectives are achieved. However, this is not entirely appropriated by all workers. Some of them develop strategies to demonstrate to colleagues and managers that they are really busy working. These signals take different forms such as responding quickly to emails, starting a chat through company communication platforms, spontaneously sending a list of expected and realized tasks to the manager, letting the manager knows if they need to be temporarily absent during business hours, justifying their request for telework or limiting the use of telework by being at the office when the manager is on-site or for some meetings.

> *When I work from home, I always respond very quickly to emails I receive. Even faster than if I were here [at the office]. Yes, this aims to show that I am active and that I am busy working.* (Carine, Employee)

When questioning the way managers organize (tele)work, I found that it is mainly managed by teams' members. But, in a few cases, the manager maintains control over the organization of work. Moreover, the introduction of telework has led to the emergence of rules regarding the virtual or physical presence at work. For instance, there is an implicit rule that at least one person has to be present in each team every day in order to ensure physical duty cover. This may constrain access to telework in smaller teams, and may also make it difficult to arrange meetings. Another example is the arrangement of meetings. In some teams, they do not pay attention to physical presence since remote employees can be virtually present. But, in other teams, it is expected that everyone is physically present when a meeting is organized, whether telework was planned or not. This is why some teams have chosen a day of presence and/or have encouraged to preferably telework or not on a regular day. Nevertheless, in a few cases, some employees prefer to assess the cost-benefit ratio of their presence before deciding to change or cancel their teleworking day.

> *No, or I ask if it is really compulsory, I evaluate the importance of the meeting. There are some meetings like the daily group 'huddle' meetings where it is not necessary to be present for example, you can call or simply give your feedback by email and you do not have to be there. On the other hand, there are other formal meetings where you could say is it absolutely necessary to be there or ask if it is important for me to be there, or whether I can be updated by others. And if it's really important, yes … then you have to cancel your homeworking day.* (Cléo, Employee)

This re-organization of work also affects the coordination and social cohesion between workers. For most employees, the number of face-to-face contacts has decreased. Some employees explain that when they work from home, they don't feel the 'workplace atmosphere' and feel that they are missing some information.

> *And, at that moment, you are alone at home, isolated and there is nobody who will call you or send an email because you are not at work. So, yes, it's easier to work because you're not disturbed, but it also means that you're more isolated.* (Elkin, Employee)

By contrast, some employees, mostly TechniCom workers, claim that communication has changed, rather than the number of contacts, by becoming more virtual. When introducing telework, *Barzel* implemented a company chat system called *Lync* and expected that everyone used this communication platform. However, while the use of *Lync* is compulsory in some teams, it is left to employees' discretion in others. Moreover, whereas some employees (mostly mobile workers and managers) assert that it is important to be always 'online', available and contactable when working remotely, for others, a new rule has emerged in order to not disturb colleagues who are teleworking. Telework is understood as an opportunity to better manage workflows during the week by choosing which tasks to perform at home (mainly tasks requiring concentration); escape the open-office perceived as disruptive; 'get away from the workplace atmosphere'; 'take a breather'; or 'control my time'. Therefore, some workers limit the number of remote interactions to urgent matters or short questions and use face-to-face interactions when colleagues are back in the workplace.

> *In theory, you can be reached at home but I work on the principle that, here, in our case, in our small team, we try to make telework day really productive and so, this means that if we have a small delay, we prefer, unless it is urgent, to take care of the colleague's helpline phone so that she is able, at home, to make the most of her work, in order to provide a breath of fresh air until she comes back at the office.* (Tchitchel, Employee)

As a result, employees organize their presence at work by scheduling their next interactions, arranging meetings with colleagues and changing or canceling the teleworking day if needed, in order to be present with colleagues and take time for collaboration. This shows that face-to-face interactions are preferred to virtual communication. This is why most interviewees declare that two telework days per week is a maximum in order to be with colleagues.

> *But more than two days, I think it would be difficult. (…) Here, there are employees who work with other colleagues anyway, so there is a moment I guess, the communication (…), if these employees do not see each other anymore, it will not help because doing everything by phone is difficult. When there are critical meetings, no one wants to do it by phone because we don't see body language, we don't feel what is going on, we don't have the atmosphere.* (Jay, Employee)

It's funny to observe because in the past we just said "goodbye, see you tomorrow" but now, you can see they think "oh yes tomorrow, I have to call you if I need this." So yes, in their behavior, there is clearly a change. (Bernard, Employee)

Even though face-to-face interactions are preferred to virtual exchanges, the work requirements may imply to use *Lync* in order to provide or get information but also to keep in touch with colleagues. For instance, a few groups of teammates have found an informal and local arrangement aiming to provide information from the 'daily huddle' meetings to their remote colleagues through *Lync*. Moreover, another communication tool spontaneously emerged: *WhatsApp*. This chat system, mainly used in private lives, is not a company tool and its use not mandatory but appears as 'self-evident' within some teams. The increased use of *Lync* or *WhatsApp* helps remote workers to remain a part of this social community. Although *WhatsApp* may be used for professional purposes, in this context, it is mostly used for private matters such as jokes, recipes, gardening advice or holiday photographs.

Maybe it affects the team spirit, maybe the human touch is something that participates in the team spirit. If you do not have these contacts, it's not the same team spirit. But you can have WhatsApp groups or another major communication platform where you can share fun little things, your experiences. If you do not have that then you have nothing to create a team. So, I think that more days at home can affect team spirit. (Audrey, Employee)

(…) yes, we are at home but we have less contact with our colleagues in Brussels, we do not know what is happening there … oh yes, maybe it's good … In the past, we sent emails every day with all the points but it takes time and then someone said: "via WhatsApp, we create a Barzel's group and everyone people may join it" … oh yes, yes, it's a good idea. (Julien, Employee)

The use of these communication systems may be helpful to reinforce social cohesion, and they are also used for remote collaboration, even at the workplace.

I have one colleague at work, for example Dante, it happens that he is in the office right next to me, he is in the landscape, he is right in front of me and he sends me anyway a little 'Lync' saying "Léon, I finished to work on the file, you can see the report" instead of coming and tell me "Léon, the file is ready, you can check it". (Léon, Manager)

We use Lync, it's easy, if I need someone, an information, I can see if the person is available because he has given his availability status: 'available', 'off-line'... you can ask a question, you get a quick answer and you continue your work. We use it while we are teleworking but also when we are here ... as we are working on different floors. (Roger, Employee)

The results show that the implementation of telework changes the traditional ways to organize work. This leads to social dynamics in how NWW are performed and are discussed in the next section.

Discussion: Re-materialization of Work as a Consequence of the De-materializing Effects of Telework?

Transformation of Normative Frameworks: From Presence to Performance

Our findings, about how telework changed ways of working in our company case study, raise the following question: What are a 'good' worker and a 'good' work?

Before the introduction of telework, the physical presence and visibility of employees were crucial (except for TechniCom workers). The convention on expected behaviors was that 'you must be in the office and work your hours'. The implementation of telework has altered this convention since the concept of working time and working space are questioned. This led to several transformations in terms of individual and collective work organization: the content of work is now partly or totally transportable; workplaces are depersonalized; the clocking in system that was the main managerial control tool is gone; since time is no longer the reference, control has moved from time to results; physical presence is no longer relevant due to remote work but visibility may be physical or virtual. The convention has changed to 'organize yourself but be productive'. The principles of physical presence and visibility have been replaced by a principle of performance. In other words, it is now expected that (a good) worker manages his/her time and space in order to be efficient.

This evolution of the normative framework is consistent with the social dynamics I observed. Indeed, it is in the name of performance that I observed: individual and collective re-appropriation of time and space (e.g. emails in the evenings or during holidays, working in trains, not wasting time commuting to attend meetings); manipulating access to telework for some employees (e.g. extension or reduction of the trial period); a reconfiguration of responsibilities (e.g. giving more room to individuals or team members to organize telework); or the emergence of new team coordination mechanisms (e.g. 'do not disturb' or 'physical duty cover').

One generally expects that the introduction of new management practices changes work organization; however, the implementation of NWW practices also transforms attitudes toward work by altering normative frameworks, especially on time and space. In the next section, I discuss how the NWW transformation of organizational normative frameworks redefines the appropriate behaviors to adopt, work and attitudes toward work.

From Time to Results: Toward an Invisibilization of Work(ers)?

Beyond the abandonment of the clocking in system, the shift of control from time to results means that the number of working hours has become irrelevant. This means that overtime is not paid or even considered as employees are responsible for managing their working time. Controlling the 'bottom-line' is preferred to controlling work. This managerial expectation seems to be accepted by employees who claim that only results matter now and that it is their responsibility to manage time and space accordingly.

This new 'philosophy' leads to the invisibilization of work and people in space and time. Alongside the erosion of temporal norms, employees have to deal with the workload anywhere and anytime. Even though it is more common for TechniCom workers and some managers to handle their emails outside working hours (Haddon & Brynin, 2005), this trend has spread among others. Managing emails during evenings, weekends and holidays is often perceived by employees as a positive behavior in that they can deal with small requests or keep themselves up to date (Felstead et al., 2005; Vega, 2003). To what extent does dealing with emails 'outside' working hours become a new norm? Since control is based on the bottom-line, to what extent are efforts to achieve objectives taken into account?

One answer might be that telework frees up time to focus on work activities that matter, those which make it possible to achieve the objectives. However, some tasks are no longer considered as 'work' (e.g. emails or phone calls outside working hours and coordination with colleagues) but as intermediary steps, activities that have to be done in order to achieve the objectives and make 'productive' work visible. As Huws explains (2014), the invisibilization process affects not only workers but also work. In the *Barzel* context, this process might be reinforced by a work organization that promotes agility over specialization.

New Responsibilities, More Individualities: Every Man for Himself?

It is now expected that everyone manages their own time and space in order to reach the objectives. As a consequence, the social dynamics have become more individualized. Indeed, my findings reveal that some employees feel isolated, invisible or useless when they work remotely. In the same vein, other workers explain that they don't feel the 'workplace atmosphere' and feel that they are missing some information. Although this confirms previous research results (see Golden, 2007; Harris, 2003; Vega, 2003; Wilks & Billsberry, 2007), my findings also show that the number of contacts between colleagues has not only decreased but has also become more depersonalized. Face-to-face contacts are less numerous, more selective and partially replaced by virtual exchanges (Kingma, 2018). Moreover, since the online messaging service was implemented

(*Lync*), employees use it to contact their colleagues rather than interacting face-to-face. In some cases, it does not matter who is on the other side of the computer, only the answer matters. To some extent, this might be compared to a Chatbot, an artificial intelligence program which responds autonomously to users' requests. The research conducted by Harris (2003) and Thorne (2005) demonstrates that interactions have become less relational and more transactional.

This individualization trend is also reinforced by the reconfiguration of responsibilities which expects that everyone complies with the new convention. This is strongly supported by a managerial rhetoric defining what is a 'good' (tele)worker. For instance, the company teleworking policy defines a teleworker as someone competent, responsible, productivity-conscious, autonomous, results-oriented and flexible. This concurs with Thorne (2005), Walker (2006) and Huws (2014) who argue that the virtualization of organizations tends to profile a prototypical worker as responding to managerial injunctions of empowerment, autonomy and flexibility, sometimes referred to as an 'intrapreneur'. While the reconfiguration of responsibilities may offer more autonomy to employees, it also puts the weight of results on individuals' shoulders (Bélanger & Thuderoz, 2010). This represents a managerial intent to shape identities at work (Alvesson & Willmott, 2002). The way 'intrapreneurs' comply with this managerial rhetoric by deserting offices, working outside working hours, attending or not a meeting, defining rules on remote availability and so forth may refer to a process of disciplinarization through which actors are 'free' to decide how to comply with the new norm (Taskin & Raone, 2014).

Re-materialization as a Vision of Work

In the previous sections, I observed that the introduction of telework has led to the emergence of social dynamics aiming to (re)define what is a new 'normal' way of working. My findings show how telework both individualized and invisibilized work(ers). While questioning the underlying rationalities of such social regulations, one can observe that these dynamics comply with a new normative framework defining the performance as the ultimate end of all actions. By focusing on the bottom-line, other dimensions of work are neglected (e.g. coordination, collaboration, social support and working time) or are instrumentalized (e.g. Chatbot). This shows that the humanity of work and at work has declined in order to comply with a financialized management oriented toward managing results instead of work and people (Batt & Appelbaum, 2013). As a result, beyond operational tools, managerial techniques and work processes, this new norm leads to what I call the de-materialization of work. This refers to a process through which work becomes less tangible, less visible, less material, less collective, less 'human'.

Interestingly, I observed a counter-movement through which employees resist this de-materialization. My findings show different behaviors aiming to reinvest the office in order to seek social connections, collegiality, and maintain team cohesion (e.g. by changing or canceling the teleworking day in order to be present with their teammates). Moreover, since face-to-face coordination is preferred to virtual interactions, employees develop collective strategies in order to maintain social communities at the workplace as well as solidarity between themselves. I also observed individual strategies aiming to make work and people more visible while working remotely through 'signaling strategies' (Taskin & Edwards, 2007; Taskin & Raone, 2014), for example, attending or not attending certain meetings, being at the office when the manager is on-site, sitting at different workstations depending on who is present on-site and responding quickly to emails. Furthermore, the introduction of a physical duty cover at the workplace in each team—ensuring that a minimum of one team member is present at work—is evidence of a wish to convey the message that the team is active, available, responsive and present for others.

This illustrates the existence of individual and collective strategies reinforcing a different vision of work not only by reshaping solidarity within and between teams but also by giving more visibility to work and people. Reinvesting the work offices as a social space, scheduling interactions and meetings or using *Lync* or *WhatsApp* devices in order to keep in touch and maintain social communities at work represent a process of re-materialization. By doing so, employees assert a vision of work made of non-depersonalized and physical interactions, collective cohesion and solidarity. In other words, they bring a sensitivity to the richness of work which cannot be resumed to the bottom-line. This supports the work of Gomez (2013) and Taskin and Dietrich (2016) who use a humanistic multidimensional perspective to take into account not only the objective dimension of work (e.g. results, time and space) but also its collective (e.g. identification, collaboration, social support and solidarity) and subjective (e.g. resistance, emancipation, fairness, recognition and gratitude) dimensions. NWW may empower people to manage their own time and space and provide more opportunities in terms of work-life balance, but this cannot be done at the cost of a de-materialized work.

In my case-study findings, the individual and collective strategies aiming to re-materialize work are not in contradiction with the new convention. In fact, these social dynamics occur because employees comply with the injunction of performance. Nevertheless, this shows how managerial injunctions are collectively questioned and locally re-appropriated, and demonstrates how actors contribute to the shaping of the new convention by (re-)defining under what conditions the performance should be reached. Workers are dealing with the tension between developing strategies to manage time and space efficiently and strategies to maintain social communities at work; and this has become their responsibility. Before the introduction of NWW practices, the company provided a work environment where collaboration, face-to-face interactions and social cohesion were supported by proximity between employees. Since the workspaces and interactions have become depersonalized and the responsibility for work and employment relations more individualized, this has led to a new responsibility to keep work a meaningful and social experience in which workers can be fulfilled.

Research has shown that NWW is far from keeping all its promises. Instead of providing more autonomy, NWW practices may lead to the reinforcement of control (Bélanger, Giles, & Lapointe, 2002; Geary & Dobbins, 2001; Proenca, 2010; Taskin & Edwards, 2007). Instead of providing more participation, this may lead to more disciplinarization (Edwards & Collinson, 2002; Leclercq-Vandelannoitte, Isaac, & Kalika, 2013). Autonomy, empowerment and the new responsibilities bestowed to workers do not seem to represent a humanist approach but rather a perversion and instrumentalization of a democratic and humanistic ideal (see Ajzen et al., 2015; Taskin & Ajzen, 2015). This phenomenon characterized by Alvesson and Spicer (2012) as a 'stupid' functionalistic approach to management seems to tie with another societal trend, the financialization of management (Batt & Appelbaum, 2013; Chiapello, 2015). In other words, workers have the right to organize individually or collectively their work and their social interactions, as long as they comply with the (imposed) corporate strategy that involves meeting (imposed) goals and, of course, this is their responsibility.

Of course, this skeptical perspective on NWW needs to be moderated. Indeed, it is more likely that, for instance, telework leads to a better way to manage work and life by giving more autonomy to workers and that autonomous teams provide more democracy and participation. However, this managerial rhetoric often based on catchy concepts such as 'autonomy', 'empowerment', 'work-life balance', 'freedom', 'democracy', 'trust', 'respect', 'collaboration' or 'participation' has to be questioned in terms of ends. Is it a management philosophy or a new way to exert power? The answer to this question cannot be black or white but it invites researchers and practitioners to be wary of this managerial rhetoric, to become aware of the social dynamics that occur when NWW practices are implemented and to understand to what extent this 'new' world of work transforms the very defintion of what (a) work(er) is (Ajzen et al., 2015; Taskin et al., 2017).

To conclude this discussion, I would like to consider what the future of work might look like by using two scenarios: pessimistic and optimistic. The pessimistic scenario might lead to what Baruch (2000) calls the 'Autistic Society', a society of egotistic, atomized and isolated individuals for whom collaboration is essentially perceived in an instrumental and strategic way and is related to the rise of the 'intrapreneur'. By contrast, the optimistic scenario might be that NWW practices offer such opportunities that workers could manage the tension between performance and social cohesion at work (collegiality, solidarity, collaboration). Management might then (re)consider work as a multifaceted concept in which the collective and subjective dimensions of work are as important as the objective dimension (Gomez, 2013; Taskin & Dietrich, 2016). Nevertheless, it might be more relevant to think about a third scenario, more realistic, which combines features of both extremes. Time will tell…

Conclusion

In this chapter, I proposed to reintroduce the political dimension underlying the social dynamics that occur when an NWW project is implemented. The aim was to discuss how it leads to a redefinition of what work is and how workers are expected to behave in this new work environment. Our findings and discussion of the *Barzel* case demonstrated how the introduction of teleworking practices—as a part of an NWW project—re-organizes work, transforms control norms and reconfigures responsibilities. The discussion further highlights how these changes, beyond organizational practices, transform the normative framework or 'convention' by redefining what work should be and how workers should behave.

The discussion provides contributions to the understanding of the social regulation of NWW. I illustrate empirically the importance of going beyond the managerial rhetoric and study to what extent this new world of work challenges the 'old' world of work. My findings suggest an individualization and invisibilization of work(ers) which I call a 'de-materialization process'. This relates to the financialization of management through which the management of results is preferred to the management of work(ers). In other words, work is only perceived through its objective and rational dimension. Another finding is a counter-movement of 're-materialization', through which actors are able to resist this managerial project by collectively defining an alternative way to comply with the new convention by reinvesting the office, arranging coordination and interactions, developing signaling strategies, but by asserting a humanist vision of work. Finally, the findings show how introducing NWW practices implies a new responsibility for employees to manage the tension between individual performance and the collective maintaining of a social community at work.

Rather than depicting a widespread trend, this chapter aims to illustrate to what extent the implementation of NWW practices may lead to a particular process of de-materialization but also how actors are able to define strategies aiming to resist such process by re-affirming an existing work community, which I called 're-materialization'. Finally, this chapter provides some avenues for further critical research to understand to what extent NWW denotes a disciplinarization process or offers some paths for emancipation. We call for further contextualized and qualitative research about how the tension is managed and how this affects the (re) construction of identity at work.

Acknowledgments This chapter has been written during a three-month visiting stay at the Michael Smurfit Business School (University College Dublin). I would like to warmly thank colleagues from 'HRM & Employment Relations' for insightful discussions and in particular Prof. John Geary for his valuable feedback on a previous version of this chapter.

References

Ajzen, M., Donis, C., & Taskin, L. (2015). Kaléidoscope des nouvelles formes d'organisation du travail: L'instrumentalisation stupide d'un idéal collaboratif et démocratique. *Gestion 2000: Management & Perspective, 32*(3), 125–147.

Alvesson, M., & Spicer, A. (2012). A stupidity-based theory of organizations. *Journal of Management Studies, 49*(7), 1194–1220.

Alvesson, M., & Willmott, H. (2002). Identity regulation as organizational control: Producing the appropriate individual. *Journal of Management Studies, 39*(5), 619–644.

Baruch, Y. (2000). Teleworking: Benefits and pitfalls as perceived by professionals and managers. *New Technology, Work and Employment, 15*(1), 34–49.

Batt, R., & Appelbaum, E. (2013). *Impact of financialization on management and employment outcomes.* Upjohn Institute Working Paper 13–191. Kalamazoo, MI: W.E. Upjohn Institute for Employment Research.

Bélanger, A., Giles, A., & Lapointe, P.-A. (2002). *Work and employment relations in the high-performance workplace.* London: Continuum.

Bélanger, J., & Thuderoz, C. (2010). Le répertoire de l'opposition au travail. *Revue Française de Sociologie, 51*(3), 427–460.

Bell, B., & Kozlowski, S. (2002). A Typology Of Virtual Teams: Implications for effective leadership. *Group Organization Management, 27*(1), 14–49.

Bergum, S. (2007). What has happened to telework? Failure, diffusion or modification? *The Journal of E-Working, 1*(February), 13–44.

Bobillier-Chaumon, M. E. (2003). Evolutions techniques et mutations du travail: émergence de nouveaux modèles d'activité. *Le Travail Humain.*, *66*(2), 161–192.

Boell, S. K., Cecez-Kecmanovic, D., & Campbell, J. (2016). Telework paradoxes and practices: The importance of the nature of work. *New Technology, Work and Employment, 31*(2), 114–131.

Bosch-Sijtsema, P. M., Ruohomäki, V., & Vartiainen, M. (2010). Multi-locational office workers in the office: Navigation, disturbances and effectiveness. *New Technology Work and Employment, 25*(3), 183–195.

Breu, K., & Hemingway, C. (2004). Making organisations virtual: The hidden cost of distributed teams. *Journal of Information Technology, 19*, 191–202.

Chiapello, E. (2015). Financialisation of valuation. *Human Studies, 38*(1), 13–35.

Child, J., & Rodrigues, S. (2005). Social identity and organizational learning. In M. Easterby-Smith & M. Lyles (Eds.), *Handbook of organizational learning and knowledge management* (pp. 305–329). Oxford: Blackwell Publishing.

Cushen, J., & Thompson, P. (2012). Doing the right thing? HRM and the angry knowledge worker. *New Technology, Work and Employment, 27*(2), 79–92.

De Menezes, L. M., & Kelliher, C. (2011). Flexible working and performance: A systematic review of the evidence for a business case. *International Journal of Management Reviews, 13*(4), 452–474.

Edwards, P., & Collinson, M. (2002). Empowerment and managerial labor strategies. *Work and Occupation, 29*(1), 271–290.

Eurofound. (2010). *Telework in the European Union*. Dublin: European Foundation for the Improvement of Living and Working Conditions.

Eurofound. (2015). *New forms of employment*. Luxembourg: Publications Office of the European Union.

Eurofound & the International Labour Office. (2017). *Working anytime, anywhere: The effects on the world of work*. Luxembourg: Publications Office of the European Union and Geneva: International Labour Office.

Felstead, A., Jewson, N., & Walter,s, S. (2005). *Changing places of work*. New York: Palgrave Macmillan.

Gareis, K., Lilischkis, S., & Mentrup, A. (2006). Mapping the mobile eworkforce in Europe. In J. Andriessen & M. Vartiainen (Eds.), *Mobile virtual work. A new paradigm?* (pp. 45–69). Heidelberg: Springer.

Geary, J., & Dobbins, T. (2001). Teamworking: A new dynamic in the pursuit of management control. *Human Resource Management Journal, 11*(1), 3–23.

Golden, T. (2007). Co-workers who telework and the impact on those in the office: Understanding the implications of virtual work for co-worker satisfaction and turnover intentions. *Human Relations, 60*(11), 1641–1667.

Gomez, P.-Y. (2006). Information et conventions. Le cadre du modèle général. *Revue Française de Gestion, 32*(160), 217–240.

Gomez, P.-Y. (2013). *Le travail invisible. Enquête sur une disparition*. Paris: François Bourin éditeur.

Gomez, P.-Y., & Jones, B. C. (2000). Conventions: An interpretation of deep structure in organizations. *Organization Science, 11*(6), 696–708.

Haddon, L., & Brynin, M. (2005). The character of telework and the characteristics of teleworkers. *New Technology, Work and Employment, 20*(1), 34–46.

Haigh, G. (2012). *The office*. Melbourne: The Miegunyah Press.

Halford, S. (2005). Hybrid workspace: Re-spatialisations of work, organisation and management. *New Technology, Work and Employment, 20*(1), 19–33.

Hanhike, T. & Gareis, K. (2004). *Modelling ework - Towards a better understanding of information technology's impact on workplaces and work locations*. 22nd Annual International Labour Process Conference, Amsterdam, 2004.

Harris, L. (2003). Home-based teleworking and the employment relationship. Managerial challenges and dilemmas. *Personnel Review, 32*(4), 422–437.

Holm, J., & Kendall, G. (2008). Working on the move: Subverting the logic of non-space. In D. Hislop (Ed.), *Mobility and technology in the workplace* (pp. 27–39). New York: Routledge.

Huws, U. (2013). Working online, living offline: Labour in the internet age. *Work Organisation, Labour & Globalisation, 7*(1), 1–11.

Huws, U. (2014). *Labor in the global digital economy: The Cybertariat Comes of Age*. New York: Monthly Review Press.

Johnson, L. (2003). *The co-workplace. Teleworking in the neighborhood*. Vancouver: UBC Press.

Kelliher, C., & Richardson, J. (2012). *New ways of organizing work: Developments perspectives and experiences*. New York: Routledge.

Kingma, S. (2018). New ways of working (NWW): Work space and cultural change in virtualizing Organizations. *Culture and Organization*, 1–24.

Kowalski, K., & Swanson, J. (2005). Critical success factors in developing teleworking programs. *Benchmarking, 12*(3), 236–249.

Kurland, N., & Bailey, E. (1999). The advantages and challenges of working here, there, anywhere, and anytime. *Organizational Dynamics, 28*(2), 53–68.

Lallement, M. (2007). *Le travail. Une sociologie contemporaine*. Paris: Gallimard - Collection Folio Essai.

Leclercq-Vandelannoitte, A., Isaac, H., & Kalika, M. (2013). *Travail à distance et e-management. Organisation et contrôle en entreprise*. Paris: Dunod.

Léonard, E. (2015). *Ressources Humaines. Gérer les personnes et l'ordre social dans l'entreprise*. Louvain-la-Neuve, Belgium: De Boeck.

Martin, B. H., & MacDonnell, R. (2012). Is telework effective for organizations? A meta-analysis of empirical research on perceptions of telework and organizational outcomes. *Management Research Review, 35*(7), 602–616.

Martinez, E., & De Schampheleire, J. (2005). *Télétravail et négociation collective*. Brussels: Lettre d'information Travail, Emploi, Formation - ULB, 4.

de Nanteuil, M. (2004). *Europe at a time of flexibility*. Brussels: European Trade Union Institute (ETUI) & The National Institute for Working Life and The Swedish Trade Unions in Co-operation (SALTSA).

Nilles, J. M. (1998). *Managing telework. Strategies for managing the virtual workforce*. New York: John Wiley Sons Inc.

Nydegger, R., & Nydegger, L. (2010). Challenges in managing virtual teams. *Journal of Business & Economics Research, 8*(3), 69–82.

Paillé, P., & Mucchielli, A. (2012). *L'analyse qualitative en sciences humaines et sociales* (3ème éd.). Paris: Armand Colin.

Peters, P., Poutsma, E., Van Der Heijden, B., Bakker, A., & De Bruijn, T. (2014). Enjoying new ways to work: An HRM-process approach to study flows. *Human Resource Management, 53*(2), 271–290.

Proenca, T. (2010). Self-managed work teams: An enabling or coercive nature. *International Journal of Human Resource Management, 21*(3), 337–354.

Pyöriä, P. (2011). Managing telework: Risks, fears and rules. *Management Research Review, 34*(4), 386–399.

Reynaud, J.-D. (2004). *Les règles du jeu. L'action collective et la régulation sociale*. Paris: Armand Colin.

Reynaud, J.-D. (2007). *Le conflit, la négociation et la règle*. Toulouse: Octares Editions.

Reynauld, J.-D., & Richebé, N. (2009). Rules, conventions and values: A plea in favor of ordinary normativity. *Revue Française de Sociologie, 5*(50), 3–35.

Richter, P., Meyer, J., & Sommer, F. (2006). Well-being and stress in mobile and virtual work. In J. Andriessen & M. Vartiainen (Eds.), *Mobile virtual work. A new paradigm?* (pp. 231–252). Heidelberg: Springer.

Shekhar, S. (2006). Understanding the virtuality of virtual organizations. *Leadership and Organization Development Journal, 7*(6), 465–483.

Sullivan, C. (2003). What's in a name? Definitions and conceptualisations of teleworking and homeworking. *New Technology, Work and Employment, 18*(3), 158–165.
Taskin, L. (2011). *Despatialisation: Enjeux organisationnels et managériaux. Perspective critique et études de cas sur la transformation du contrôle dans le cadre du télétravail à domicile.* Saarbrücken: Editions Universitaires Européennes.
Taskin, L. (2012). New ways of organizing work. Developments, perspectives and experiences. *Management Learning, 43*(4), 467–469.
Taskin, L., & Ajzen, M. (2015). *Managing sustainable and innovative workplaces: NWOW, towards sustainable organizational performance?* Louvain-la-Neuve: Louvain School of Management Research Institute, Université Catholique de Louvain.
Taskin, L., Ajzen, M., & Donis, C. (2017). New ways of working: From smart to shared power. In V. Muhlbauer & W. Harry (Eds.), *Redefining management. Smart power perspectives* (pp. 65–79). London: Springer.
Taskin, L., & Dietrich, A. (2016). *Management humain: Pour une approche renouvelée de la GRH et du comportement organisationnel* (Manager RH). Brussels: De Boeck Supérieur.
Taskin, L., & Edwards, P. K. (2007). The possibilities and limits of telework in a bureaucratic environment: Lessons from the Public Sector. *New Technology, Work and Employment, 22*(3), 195–207.
Taskin, L., & Gomez, P. Y. (2015). Articuler la théorie de la régulation social et l'approche conventionnaliste en gestion pour comprendre l'échec d'un projet de changement organisationnel? Illustration par la mise en place du télétravail dans deux administrations publiques belges. *@GRH, 1*(14), 99–128.
Taskin, L., & Raone, J. (2014). Flexibilité et disciplinarisation: repenser le contrôle en situation de distanciation. *Economies et Societes, 3*(1), 35–69.
Thorne, K. (2005). Designing virtual organizations? Themes and trends in political and organizational discourses. *Journal of Management Development, 24*(7), 580–607.
Tietze, S., & Musson, G. (2010). Identity, identity work and the experience of working from home. *Journal of Management Development, 29*(2), 148–156.
Tremblay, D.-G., Chevrier, C., & Di Loreto, M. (2007). *Le télétravail comme nouvelle forme d'organisation du travail.* Montréal: Chaire Bell en technologies et organisation du travail, Université de Québec a Montréal.
Vakola, M., & Wilson, I. (2004). The challenge of virtual organization: Critical success factors in dealing with constant change. *Team Performance Management, 10*(5/6), 112–120.

Van Meel, J. (2011). The origins of new ways of working: Office concepts in the 1970s. *Facilities, 29*(9/10), 357–367.

Vartiainen, M. (2006). Mobile virtual work - concepts, outcomes and challenges. In J. Andriessen & M. Vartiainen (Eds.), *Mobile virtual work. A new paradigm?* (pp. 13–34). Heidelberg: Springer.

Vega, G. (2003). *Managing teleworkers and telecommuting strategies*. Westport, CA: Praeger.

Vendramin, P., & Valenduc, G. (2002). *Technologies et flexibilité. Les défis du travail à l'ère du numérique*. Entreprise & Carrière, Editions Liaisons: Reuil-Malmaison.

Verbeke, A., Schultz, R., Greidanus, N., & Hambley, L. (2008). *Growing the virtual workplace*. Cheltenham: Edward Elgar.

Walker, H. (2006). The virtual organization: A new organizational form? *International Journal of Networking and Virtual Organisations, 3*(1), 25–41.

Wilks, L., & Billsberry, J. (2007). Should we do away with teleworking? An examination of whether teleworking can be defined in the new world of work. *New Technology, Work and Employment, 22*, 168–177.

10

Work/Non-work? Laminated Boundary-Tensions and Affective Capabilities: A Case of Mobile Consulting

Natalie Paleothodoros

Introduction

This chapter draws on a case of materiality in the digital age, a case of mobile consulting, to shed light on how new sorts of work/non-work boundary-tensions emerge, overlap and become 'laminated'. This chapter reports on a consulting firm referred to via the pseudonym *MobileCom*, which had no head office and employees organized themselves via Instant Messaging (IM) on their mobile phones. Although working with mobile phones is not 'new', the case demonstrates how relations come together in IM practice to produce new sorts of boundary-tensions, which has material consequences for organizing. IM technologies differ from previous technologies offered by smartphones such as text and email; they are instant, visible and knowable in new ways. With consultants' billable hours depending on a world of speed, affective relations and intensification at a distance, at all times and in all spaces, the case offers a suitable

N. Paleothodoros (✉)
University of York, Leyland, UK
e-mail: natalie.paleothodoros@york.ac.uk

N. Mitev et al. (eds.), *New Ways of Working*, Technology, Work and Globalization,
https://doi.org/10.1007/978-3-030-61687-8_10

way of highlighting the sociomaterial construction of new work/non-work boundary-tensions. This matters because as technology evolves so do our boundaries. This chapter offers an important contribution not only by examining how IM technologies shape boundaries given the rise of mobile work and virtual teams but also by articulating an alternative way to conceptualize boundaries as boundary-tensions, a framework to better understand how New Ways of Working and boundaries shape one another.

The tensions involved in boundary organizing with mobile phones are well-documented in the literature, and maintaining boundaries between work/non-work is considered increasingly problematic. Yet, the concept of work/non-work 'boundaries' is also problematic. First is the assumption that boundaries are pre-existing.

In the literature on work/non-work boundaries, studies often draw on the influential work of Nippert-Eng (1996) who developed the theory of boundary work to make sense of how people manage their work/non-work boundaries, developing analysis around boundary theory, border theory and human agency perspectives (Senarathne Tennakoon, Silveira, & Taras, 2013). Scholars have produced valuable insights into mobile technology, focusing on the impact of its functions (Middleton & Cukier, 2006) and borders (Wajcman, Bittman, & Brown, 2008) on user experiences (Matusik & Mickel, 2011); and highlighting some of the paradoxes of attempting to manage work/non-work boundaries via mobile phones (Jarvenpaa & Lang, 2005). Whereas these insights are undoubtedly useful in understanding how individuals manage work/non-work tensions, boundaries are treated as something that already exists and that people 'manage'; the focus is on human agency. But what about if we ask questions about how these boundaries matter in the first place? Where do these tensions come from? And how do they become meaningful embodied concepts?

Barad (2003, 815) would argue boundaries emerge through agential intra-actions, rather than merely human activities. She would also argue that it is not the boundary itself but the relations that 'matter'. If we are to understand, not boundaries, but 'boundary-tensions', then a different point of departure is needed: one which takes a relational ontology and explores tensions (relations) instead of boundaries as entities.

Sociomaterially does just this: it offers a relational ontology for examining not just the social or the material as separate entities, but the sociomaterial relations that reconstitute our world (i.e. boundary-tensions) in practice. Researchers taking a sociomaterial perspective recognize that the social and material are embedded and entangled in practices with affective consequences or capabilities across bodies and things (Dale & Latham, 2015; Katila, Laine, & Parkkari, 2019; Pullen, Rhodes, & Thanem, 2017). The literature taking a sociomaterial approach to mobile phones and boundary-tensions sheds light on the sociomaterial aspects and affective capabilities of mobile phones and boundary organizing: how peoples' norms, values, human perspectives, performances, action-possibilities become reconstituted in practice (Cousins & Robey, 2015; Hislop et al., 2015; Orlikowski, 2007; Symon & Pritchard, 2015). These studies add an understanding of how meaning changes as part of this process, with consequences for work/non-work time. Boundaries are not something that we just 'manage', they act upon on us too. Boundaries are not fixed, nor separable, yet we feel the tensions.

This brings us to the second and perhaps more pertinent issue addressed in this chapter: the assumption that boundaries are even present at all. Boundaries are generally still treated as existing. What if the problem is that boundaries are no longer present? We used to assume particular and separable time-spaces of work/non-work but now we do not. Now we find our spatiotemporal and technological arrangements ambiguous, overlapping and dynamic. What does it mean when all of these relations are overlapping, concurrent, multiple? Layered, 'laminated'[1] perhaps? And what are the affective consequences of this?

This chapter, therefore, takes a different point of departure in examining boundary-tensions being sociomaterially constructed. It is not centred on boundaries in and of themselves, but rather how relations come together to construct new sorts of tensions. Thus, the key concerns of this chapter are how new sorts of boundary-tensions emerge and what their affective consequences are. I ask three questions.

[1] After the sociologist Erving Goffman, see Collins (1980).

How are boundary-tensions sociomaterially constructed?
What happens when boundary-tensions become layered, multiple and concurrent? Laminated?
And what are the affective consequences?

Work/Non-work Boundaries

Researchers agree that boundaries are important ways of distinguishing between social groups or entities, such as work/non-work, and have categorized boundaries in many different ways. Notably, the literature on boundaries challenges assumptions around boundaries being stable or unambiguous (Perrow, 1986; Scott, 1998; Weick, 1979), with common assumptions being that work/non-work boundaries are socially constructed, complex and always changing (Montgomery & Oliver, 2007; Wadel, 1979). For example, Wadel (1979, 365) argued that work is socially constructed and that work/non-work boundaries are continuously changing, making them significant to New Ways of Working:

> (1) activities we term work in our own society are continuously changing: new types of activities are continuously included under the concept, while others are excluded, and (2) the way in which we characterize work activities and distinguish them from non-work activities is continuously changing.

Understandably, many work/non-work boundary studies thus draw on ideas from boundary theory, heavily influenced by Nippert-Eng (1996) and Ashforth, Kreiner and Fugate (2000), whereby human agency is seen as central to the shaping of people's boundaries. For example, the work/non-work boundary is often seen as enacted via people's day to day choices and behaviours (Montgomery & Oliver, 2007). Boundaries are therefore often thought of in terms of preference or style and literature tends to outline ways in which these preferences or styles are managed, reinforcing human agency (Kreiner, Hollensbe, & Sheep, 2009; Rothbard, Phillips, & Dumas, 2005). Contextual factors are also often taken into consideration, the assumption being that individual people's contextual factors, such as social life inside and outside of the family, will also impact on the work/non-work boundary; and that the work/non-work boundary is not actually split into two so easily, the boundary is more complex depending on the individuals' context. Further, over time, it is agreed that people's contextual factors (such as social and family life) change and therefore so do their ways of managing boundaries. Nippert-Eng's (1996) segmentation-integration boundary preference spectrum is often drawn on in such studies as it provides a framework for demonstrating how individuals continuously reshape their boundaries and how these, therefore, evolve. Montgomery and Oliver (2007) continue to advocate research that focuses on the social construction of boundaries, taking contextual factors into account. Further, organizations have been managing these boundaries too. For example, Fleming and Spicer (2004) demonstrated how managerial programmes are aimed at reorganizing work/non-work boundaries to control labour by encouraging private practices at work and institutional norms outside of work. It is not just individuals (human agency) that manage these boundaries but management (managerial agency) too. Whereas these lines of enquiry have made important headway in understanding the nature of work/non-work, the focus remains with human agency and social aspects of organization. There is, therefore, scope to develop a better understanding of the material aspects of organization and work/non-work boundaries.

Hernes (2004, 10) explains that "boundaries are constantly subject to construction and reconstruction". He identifies three boundary processes involved in this evolution and the effects that these boundaries can have on organization: physical boundaries, represented by material infrastructures and electronic resources which act as ordering devices (ways of providing rules); social boundaries, represented via social bonding which act as distinctions (ways of making identity-linkages); and mental boundaries represented via ideas that guide organized actions and act as thresholds (ways of establishing borders around inclusion/exclusion). This framework provides scope to pay attention to how the material can be understood as meaningful in the evolution of work/non-work boundary processes, without returning to social and technological determinism.

Sociomateriality

> It is through specific agential intra-actions that the boundaries and properties of the "components" of phenomena become determinate and that particular embodied concepts become meaningful. (Barad, 2003, 815)

Ultimately, Barad (2003) is concerned with how boundaries come to be meaningful or how they come to 'matter'. Barad's (2003, 815) relational ontology based on 'intra-action' offers an understanding in contrast to the common notion of 'interaction' "which presumes the prior existence of independent entities".

Advocates of sociomateriality have taken up this relational ontology whereby the material and social are understood as mutually enacting and have been concerned with the way materials are organized by relations and how materials organize relations in return (Dale, 2005; Orlikowski & Scott, 2015; Parmiggiani & Monteiro, 2018). Through this ontology, the material is not treated merely as a tool for social tasks. The social and material are instead seen as inherently inseparable, as they already comprise a set of configurations, they are already interrelated and entangled in practices (Introna, 2009; Orlikowski, 2007; Suchman, 2007). Orlikowski and Scott (2008) argue that we need to move away from the language of 'mediation' and 'enabling', whereby relationships are thought of as 'moulded into networks' (a one-way relationship where entities are mediated or enabled into being), towards a language of 'intermediation', focusing analysis on practices (with two-way relationships where entities are always co-constitutive of each other). Thus, instead of considering boundaries as prior structures, they become understood as 'performed relations' (Pickering, 1995). The implications for organizations are important as these practices do not just mediate work, they perform organizational realities (Orlikowski & Scott, 2008).

People and things only exist in relation to each other (Cooper, 2005); distinctions between the social and material are analytical only and boundaries are thus sociomaterial. All bodies and things are entangled processes with the ability to affect and be affected (Pullen et al., 2017). Katila et al. (2019) draw attention to how 'affect' can be thought of as an intensity or energy set across sociomaterial entanglements, that is bodies and things. Dale and Latham (2015, 166) highlight that, due to multiple ways in which relations come together, we see multiple differences of affects or 'embodiments' of meaning in their various interrelationships with materiality.

Accordingly, this chapter follows suit and draws on the relational ontology based on intra-actions offered by Barad (2003) and others in taking a sociomaterial approach to thinking about boundaries. In this way, boundaries cannot be thought of as separate, pre-existing and interacting; that is coming together to interact or mediate a particular end, and then post-interaction continues without consequence. Instead, entities intra-act or intermediate, implying that they aren't separable, but engaged in a two-way, a co-constitutive, entanglement which (re)organizes the relations involved; that is there are affective consequences for boundary-tensions, their meaning and practice. It is thus through intra-actions that boundary-tensions are constructed. In doing so, we can examine not only what relations are present, but how they are sociomaterially constructed, and, over time, how this process might (re)organize relations in return.

Mobile Phones

Research has demonstrated that usage of mobile phones during working hours results in the work/non-work boundary becoming blurred or unclear and that there is a great deal of variability of lived experience between users and how they use mobile phones to manage boundaries, emphasizing human agency (see Hislop et al., 2015; Hislop & Axtell, 2011; Matusik & Mickel, 2011; Mazmanian, Yates, & Orlikowski, 2006; Middleton & Cukier, 2006; Wajcman et al., 2008).

Many studies have been concerned with the paradoxical nature of mobile phones, smartphones and BlackBerrys; and the conflicts between individual/group interests (Bader & Kaiser, 2017; Jarvenpaa & Lang, 2005; Mazmanian, Orlikowski, & Yates, 2013). For example, Mazmanian et al. (2006, 5) described how *BlackBerry* users have "underlying expectations of one another" and similarly, Middleton (2007, 3) demonstrated that "mobile technologies both empower and enslave users ... and blur the boundaries between private and public space". Further, Matusik and Mickel (2011) described conflict for employees who on the one hand felt pressure from work colleagues to be accessible and responsive at all times (which created boundary problems during private time), whilst on the other hand felt pressure from family and friends to be accessible and responsive at all times (which created boundary problems at work). In light of these tensions, Turkle (2008) drew attention to the material and argued that digital communications are essentially changing the way we relate to each other and our devices. Orlikowski (2007) went on to demonstrate how email practices redefined work/non-work boundaries, internally between employees, and explained that emails are 'pushed', over time reinforcing an addictive relationship between employees and their *CrackBerrys*. More recently, there have been attempts to bridge social and material relations with human agency perspectives on boundaries. For example, Hislop et al.'s (2015) paper bridged socio-technical relations with boundary work theory to position technology as a product of human interpretations. Symon and Pritchard (2015) established that mobile phones involve identity work, whereby employees 'perform' being contactable and responsive. Cousins and Robey (2015, 35) demonstrated how specific affordances or 'action possibilities' of mobile technologies might be implicated in work-life boundary-management practices.

What is clear from these studies is the paradoxical nature of work/non-work boundary organizing and that we should be focusing on tensions. From triangulating the literature on mobile phones and boundaries, these paradoxes can be drawn together and categorized as tensions between empowerment/enslavement; public/private; and individual/group. These tensions are not mutually exclusive, but often interrelated, as tension in autonomy might also link to tension in separating public/private spheres. Boundary-tensions are entangled in an ongoing process, co-constructing each other.

Boundaries are not fixed, nor separable, or 'manageable'. Now we find our spatiotemporal and technological arrangements increasingly ambiguous, overlapping and dynamic. We see New Ways of Working emerge with material consequences for people organizing work/non-work time. There is ample evidence concerning the social construction of work/non-work boundaries, sociomateriality of boundaries generally, and mobile phone paradoxes or tensions. But research is less clear on how with mobile phone practices relations come together to form new sorts of tensions with affective consequences for organization and organizing; and what the material consequences are for boundary-tensions between empowerment/enslavement, public/private and individual/group. How these issues were investigated methodologically is outlined next.

Case and Method

The research aimed to advance understanding into how materiality is implicated in the organization of mobile consulting and, as such, *MobileCom* appeared to be a suitable case to investigate. Work/non-work boundaries emerged to be particularly problematic and so attention was paid to how they materialized.

At the time of the study (commencing June 2011), *MobileCom* was small, made up of a Managing Director (MD) and 15 employees and fairly new at 16 years old. *MobileCom* specialized in remote Warehouse-Management applications and consultants worked to billable hours. MobileCom consultants utilized *BlackBerry* mobiles, given to them by the MD on their employment, to communicate internally and with clients. There was no head office where consultants worked with each other on a daily basis, or daily visits to clients needed due to the remote nature of their work. There were occasions when consultants visited clients to diagnose a problem, have a face-to-face meeting and generally maintain friendly relations. Therefore most consultancy work was conducted remotely, from consultants' homes, and some work was conducted on the move or from client sites if there was a need for a visit.

MobileCom members are referred to via pseudonyms for anonymity in this chapter (see Fig. 10.1).

Design, Collection and Analysis

Data were collected with the *BlackBerry* over 18 months via participant observation, supplemented by interviews. The strategy for these specific

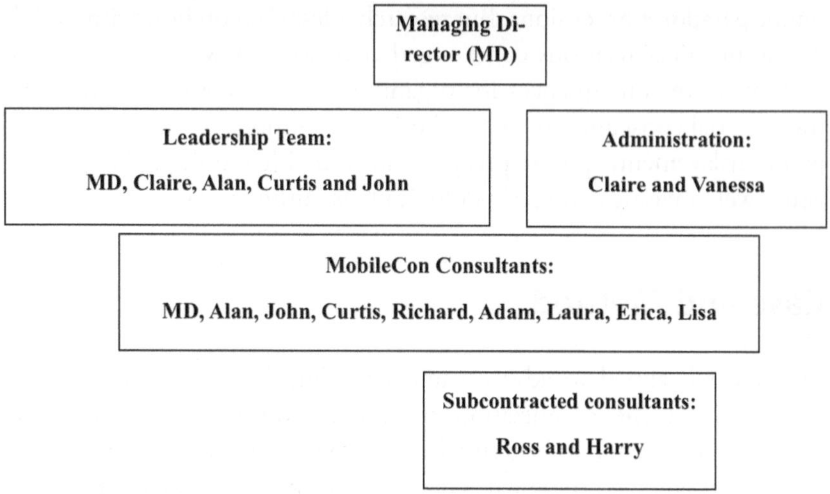

Fig. 10.1 MobileCom (author's own)

data collection methods relates to examining the role of *BlackBerry Instant Messenger* (IM), otherwise known as BBM. IM operates in three different ways: via observations, conversations and practice (users can see, talk and do). Therefore the examination of IM required observations, conversations (interviews) and practice (so that the research would encompass also seeing, talking and doing).

As *MobileCom*'s primary method of communication and organization was the *BlackBerry*, the research method for communication and organization with consultants (and clients if permitted) was also accomplished via the *BlackBerry*. There was a need to experience the "environment, problems, background, language, rituals, and social relations" (Van Maanen, 2011, 3) of *MobileCom*. An ethnographic approach was therefore employed via IM as this was considered the most appropriate way of studying and reporting on the organization. The very conditions of data collection themselves allowed the researcher to be involved in the spatiotemporal and technological arrangements also as a user. This allowed for a very specific sort of participation, even if not formally a participant observer. Ethnographic observations provided an interesting insight because the very IM technologies that afforded participation in

MobileCom's communications also afforded the research to be involved and included in formal and informal work situations as an observer which would have otherwise been missed. Ethnographic observations were also sociomaterial accomplishments.

Much of the data were collected from a distance, with some face-to-face encounters (although a small number of them in comparison with technologically intermediated encounters). Working on-the-move meant working from anywhere, therefore the research was messy and heterogeneous (Law, 2006). A critical challenge faced was the issue of 'being there'. Fincham et al. (2010, 4) raise the following significant question: "can appropriate proximity be achieved through the use of technologies or does the researcher have to be present?" During this research, being there physically was not always possible or suitable so being there was enacted via *BlackBerry*. Further, as such as there was no head office. So, if consultants were not physically present with each other or their clients, then there was nowhere for the research to be physically either. If face-to-face meetings were organized (e.g. at client sites), then observations of those meetings did take place, sporadically.

Informed consent was a governing norm in this process (Kimmel, 1988); all data were kept confidential and made anonymous before dissemination. As Reich (2015) pointed out, technologically mediated interactions often require additional sensibilities as participants often share not only work-related information with researchers but also, over time, their private lives. The research was sensitive to how consultants might have revealed private or unintended information via IM, and decisions were taken accordingly about what would and would not count as suitable data. An example of this follows in the next part of this chapter, which highlights the slippage between intended and unintended information when a consultant revealed they were 'off to the gym'. Whereas the whole conversation could not be included in this chapter as it would not have been ethically appropriate to do so, a snippet can be shared to highlight the issue.

Data were collected in three phases: initial interviews and observations with participants (via the *BlackBerry*), followed by topic-specific interviews and observations to gather information for specific tasks (via a range of materials), followed by a small number of observations and interviews that took place face to face. Each of the official or scheduled interviews or observations took about an hour and they add up to over 150 hours of interaction. A host of informal interactions also took place such as sharing of images, music, jokes via IM or other materials observed such as email competitions for the best office gadget or most 'manly' meal choices for the annual Christmas party. They also took the form of conference calls, company documentation, testing of new systems and, as time moved on, informal social gatherings (either online or in-person). The researcher attempted to remain participative in all the latest developments of *MobileCom* to gain insight and understanding into the role of the material in the organization of boundaries.

I analysed the data with thematic analysis (Van Maanen, 1979). I undertook Bazeley's (2013) method of initial exploration followed by data refinement as a systematic process of data analysis. I generated open codes by labelling, defining and categorizing similarities in the data that took place. Thereafter, I employed data reduction by combining or eliminating open codes as a form of analysis which "refines, iterates, and revises frameworks" (Miles, in Van Maanen, 1979, 122). I then established links between the data and developed into themes, providing a means for interpretation and conceptualization.

Boundaries at a Distance?

The data demonstrate that IM technologies allow the reconstitution of boundary-tensions through three themes: speed; making affective relations predominate; and intensification, each with material consequences for tensions between empowerment/enslavement, group/individual interests and public/private spheres.

Speed: And the Consequences for Empowerment/Enslavement

MobileCom consultants maintained urgent, conjoined and collaborative ways of working. They did not work from a centralized location and often worked with limited face-to-face interactions. They utilized multiple electronic means such as *Skype*, screen-sharing technologies, online shared diaries and, most prominently, *BlackBerry* IM. IM was instrumental in organizing and ordering work at a distance. Although the consultants had previously also used email and text capabilities of smartphones, they were distinctively different to IM technologies. The main distinction was speed: IM technologies were instant, eliminating text and email delays. The consultants explained that the text function of mobile phones had its flaws. Examples included lost messages in poor signal areas, only a small number of characters being available to send a text and, generally, often having the same response rate as emails. As one consultant explained:

> *Email is too distant as a communication method as often hours can be lost in between exchanges. If I'm working at a client site on a project, fast email response is simply not possible ... except for perhaps during dinner breaks ... Although then I will often have to network with clients.*
>
> *Telephone calls are too intrusive... I don't really want to bother people when they're working, especially with particular clients! Anyway, no one answers the phone anymore!*
>
> *Same with texts—you can ignore them or get to them later ... if you remember!* (Curtis, telephone interview)

As ordering devices, something was missing from these forms of communication. In taking a close look at IM, something else is accomplished. IM offered a real-time service that came with real-time urgency due to the instantaneous nature of the communication it afforded. IM technologies also rendered users visible in new ways and knowable via new forms of information (as Zuboff, 1985, might say), again they reinforced the need for speed. When IM users received an instant message, their devices flashed and made a different noise and colour in comparison to having received a text or email. Once an IM user received the message, a D for delivered appeared next to the message and once the user read the message, an R for read appeared. When a user was responding, the other person in the conversation saw that a message was being written at that time 'writing message' and three dots are displayed until the message is finished and sent:

…

During observations, consultants demonstrated urgency in responding to IM messages due to the status of 'D' which changed to 'R' once the recipient read it; the consultants explained it was hard to ignore due to its highly visible nature. Furthermore, the 'writing message' feature extended the visibility of the IM user in an even more pressured manner and ordered the user to respond quickly, without taking too long to think about their response to a message once they started it. The instantaneous script of the feature also pushed users to finish a message they started there and then as it visibly stated *writing message*, as opposed to getting distracted or dealing with something else first and going back to it later (as with emails, for example). IM, therefore, directed users to respond to messages quickly and finish messages once they started them.

> *Yea you don't ignore BBM in the way you can a text! Once you've opened it you respond as quickly as you can*
>
> …
>
> *It's a conversation happening now*
>
> …
>
> *If someone wanted you to think about it and respond later, they'd send an email wouldn't they!*
>
> 👍 😂 (John, IM)

This urgency was experienced on numerous occasions throughout the research. The most successful way of organizing telephone calls to discuss developments was via IM rather than through responses to emails or texts (responses of which were rare from the consultants). Consultants explained that although they could open emails, read them, assess their importance and reply accordingly, with BBM they had to respond immediately because they did not want to be perceived as rude; if they were 'seen' as opening and reading the message they could not ignore it. Observations revealed that consultants responded to IM messages at all times, including weekends, whereas email trails seemed to stop:

Thanks all for the comments. I'll get back on it later. Hope everyone is having a top weekend! 🙂 (Curtis, IM)

These examples showed how boundary-tensions became meaningful for consultants through reinforcement, reaction and responsiveness. Boundaries were not already 'there' and then simply managed. Sociomaterial relations came together to produce boundary-tensions. Further, boundaries were not pre-determined by set relations. Instead, it was how relations come together and intersect that produced various interrelationships with materiality, with multiple affective consequences.

Making Affective Relations Predominate Through Organizational Symbolism: And the Consequences for Public/Private Spheres

BlackBerry IM, or BBM, users added 'friends', not colleagues. This was the description of the entity they were 'adding' to their network. In light of this, IM advocated casual, fun, friendly interactions that resembled human face-to-face interactions as opposed to the more official format of company emails. Company email tended to include users' full names and titles, with the company logo attached, and created an official framing of communication. In contrast, IM users created a personal profile, could see their 'friends' pictures and statuses, and the technology offered a variety of emojis to help construct messages. Sending pictures or videos via IM was simple and quick and was observed to be common practice in the study. In fact, no serious messages were observed. Even if the topic of the message was serious, a smiley face of some sort tended to accompany it. IM seemed to cause uneasiness about sending a message without a smiley face for the consultants. *MobileCom* was continuously engaged with the IM features of *BlackBerrys*, which in turn employed the consultants with enacting and reproducing the discourse of fun. For example, when the MD announced *MobileCom* would have a new 'Hub' office space, consultants were invited to take part in an online 'gadget competition'. Each consultant nominated the best gadgets for the new office and a winner was announced at the end. The MD bought the winning gadget for the office, bacon-flavoured envelopes.

> *I much prefer virtual gadgets to enjoy*
>
> …
>
> *Like the online competitions for best office gadget—the stuff that people sent through was hilarious. That's much more fun than actually being in an office!*
>
> …
>
> (Curtis, IM)

It quickly became apparent that social bonding, particularly closeness as a team, was something assumed to be accomplished via IM, and there were several positive anecdotes in this respect. For example, one of the research tasks set by the MD was to 'integrate a new starter' (who at the time was Laura). The idea behind the task entailed IM conversations with Laura to encourage her to use IM.

During one of the conversations, Laura stated:

> *The team itself makes it really great working here. You send a message and get a response quickly… I have never felt isolated. I might have felt isolated without it.* (Laura, telephone interview)

IM was understood as crucial to MobileCom's way of working: it constituted norms around accepted ways of working and therefore encouraging employees to use it was important. The MD explained that he always asked a member of the team to integrate a new starter via IM chats. The assumption was that they would get used to it and engage well with it. The MD explained that he had concerns about some consultants and closeness as a team:

> *[Vanessa] is still sending formal emails to consultants that can come across as quite abrupt … she's struggling to integrate … but we'll get her there.* (MD, face-to-face meeting, at the Hub)

Upon reflection, it was clear that the research had been integrated in this same way. The firm tasked Alan with integrating me into the team and I felt awkward to not knowing how to respond to an IM message in a friendly and informal tone, with a smiley face. Not only did IM play a role in spilling into 'non-work' time via the instantaneous nature of it, but because the relationship at stake was of a friendly (rather than formal) nature, this created an even stronger urge to reply. Quickly. Happily.

I observed a different set of relations when it came to IM and clients. The consultants explained that a lot of clients used email, text and phone calls, with the accompanying problems already described. However, the consultants explained that some clients also had BlackBerrys so they used IM with them. The consultants reported being able to establish different relationships with those clients when compared with clients who did not use IM.

The consultants expressed that they had much closer, friendlier and long-term relationships with clients that also used IM, frequently sharing social time with them to the extent that they considered them friends, in comparison to those clients who did not use IM. During a supplementary interview, one client from an organization referred to as 'Food' for this article (the organization manufactured food) expressed that one of the *MobileCom* consultants, Curtis, had become "Totally Foodified":

> *Yeah, he's been Foodified. It's like he's one of us! Totally Foodified! [Laughs] I was speaking to my girlfriend the other day—she works in a different department—and she didn't even realise he was a consultant, she thought he was one of ours.* (Food employee, face-to-face meeting, client site)

The client explained how he sometimes forgot Curtis was external to the firm as he had been part of the team for a long time and did not behave any differently from other Food employees. The consultants believed that they were able to develop this form of relationship because of IM:

Haha

…

we have the best relationship with them because we have an informal place to chat

…

ask quick questions about anything, see each other's statuses etc

...

we're like friends

. (Curtis, IM)

When questioned about their relationships with clients who did not use IM, consultants agreed that there was a difference:

> *Not all clients are the same, obviously. We have our good relations and our, let's say more challenging ones! But I would say that clients who also use IM are better ... I mean, we get on better. Do I think IM makes a difference in that sense? Yes, I do.* (Richard, telephone call)

Over time, IM became more than a communication tool and it changed in significance. IM acted as a gate for regulating relations through social bonding and identity-linkages. What was at stake was not just a client, a professional relationship, but a whole set of relations that resembled personal ones, which made it harder to disentangle work/non-work boundaries. Tensions between public/private spheres thus intensified, with the consequences of them being felt by users.

> *It's not just for keeping in touch, communicating—I mean, it is—but it's also about relationships. Over time, it becomes about relationships.* (Alan, telephone call)

Intensification Through Simultaneous Tasking: And the Consequences for Group/Individual Interests

Over the duration of the study I found that consultants formed clear, although unspoken, rules about the organization of IM which acted as a guide for actions at a distance. These rules encompassed negotiating being visible and accountable online, being friendly and approachable in responses, and being speedy in responsiveness.

Consultants described occasions when they were physically located with clients and had to decide on where their visibility and accountability mattered more: online via IM presence or physically in their presence. The consultants were aware of the MD's expectations and had developed rules around communicating speedily:

> *We've been given the things [BlackBerrys]. And they're pretty cool. But make no mistake; we know how to use them. Like, really use them! It's all about being seen and being seen quickly!* (Alan, telephone call)

Nevertheless, consultants resisted and formed their own sense of control; something that the Managing Director (MD) was very aware of, as he explained:

> *There is a lot of trust involved. I'm not sure about Alan sometimes, I'm sure I call him and I can hear background noise. But I've got to trust him.* (MD, telephone call)

For example, during a conference call with *MobileCom* an MD heard an ice-cream van in the background. The MD asked who was 'out at the park' and, whilst everyone laughed, no one admitted to it, it created a tense moment. There were tensions around work time-space. Even though all time-space was 'work time-space' (responsiveness at all times), there appeared to be tensions with social time-space (i.e. social noise). The implications seemed contradictory: there were no boundaries but there were clear tensions.

The consultants described a set of unwritten rules around acceptable negotiations of speedy and informal communication. For example, when an IM message was received, the name and picture of the sender were displayed along with the first line of the message. Due to the size of the *BlackBerry* screen, usually, six to eight words could be viewed on display before opening a message, which meant that often employees made assumptions about its importance/urgency. Although BBM created a sense of urgency, *MobileCom* consultants were very busy and often managed multiple relations simultaneously. Therefore their sense of urgency was relationally constructed, rather than a given state. For example, a consultant explained:

It's quite normal to resist replying if I need to … I can try … but I feel uneasy about it … because we all know that we do this … we know each other are there and that not replying is a choice … so there better be a good reason for it. There's no hiding! (John, telephone call)

Consultants reported the importance of avoiding the 'ping', which is to send a loud vibrating noise through to the person whose attention is required. Even when a *BlackBerry* was not set to vibrate upon message alerts, the 'ping' is scripted to vibrate nevertheless. For example, if a user sent a message and it was not responded to quickly enough then a ping was sent to remind the recipient to respond. The ping was almost an 'angry' function, so much so that multiple pings were not sent to a user (only one at a time).

Negotiating practices emerged whereby consultants pinged someone simply to get their attention with the addition of a smiley face to confirm the pings' friendly nature. For instance, Alan was rushing to the airport and sent an IM message explaining that he would send a ping when ready for a telephone interview:

Just getting to the airport now will ping you in a bit 🙂. (Alan, IM)

In this instance, the ping that followed was not an angry ping, but a friendly ping. However, Alan was not able to send more than one ping, so the person pinged needed to watch the *BlackBerry* closely for further instructions. Losing concentration was not an option so as not to miss the telephone interview.

On occasions, consultants broke or renegotiated the rules. For example, Alan confessed towards the end of a phone call:

Right, cheers—I'm off to the gym! (Alan, telephone call)

Although, it appeared that this was not an intended confession:

Hey! Just realised … did I tell you I sneaked off to the gym this afternoon???? (Alan, IM)

Although Alan's IM profile status at the time stated he was "working on the big rollout", in reality, he was off to the gym. Yet as long as Alan remained connected whilst at the gym, he was efficiently online. Alan's IM constituted him present in an otherwise absent environment. In doing so, Alan remained close with clients and consultants (and the MD). The *BlackBerry* established itself as a durable supplement to maintaining work at a distance.

The rules of being visible and accountable online, being friendly and speedy in responsiveness, also acted as thresholds of inclusion and exclusion. Following the rules meant inclusion in multiple ways whilst simultaneously threatening exclusion. For example, consultants following the rules set by the MD internalized them and thus were included in the MD's description of "how we do things"; whereas members of the team who did not quite fit in and communicate as expected were seen as challenging members who needed ordering into being. Not enrolling risked exclusion. However, some of the internal IM negotiations such as going to the gym included consultants but excluded the MD to some extent. Firstly, the MD was not excluded entirely as he was aware or suspicious of some of the negotiations and, secondly, through IM practice, exposure was always a threat. In a similar way, Alan had become too speedy, too informal in his practice and he let it 'slip' that he was off to the gym. Thus, IM also negotiated the boundaries in consultants' lives. It acted as a negotiator that included or excluded. At any moment boundaries were reconfigured, overlapping and constituted New Ways of Working, thinking, doing. Thus, IM presented a particular set of inclusion/exclusion challenges for *MobileCom* internally.

Externally, however, IM practices afforded an alternative set of challenges. Expectations varied and were even more problematic. Being responsive, visible, accountable and legitimately online was not the same across all clients and multiple versions of relations emerged. With clients who used IM, consultants described acceptance into back-stage domains that they struggled to access without IM. They explained how they were able, over time, to develop a relationship that was more fruitful, long-term and profitable. On the other hand, with clients that did not use IM, *MobileCom* consultants did not have such access:

> *Yeah so clients that don't use BBM … we have to go through more formal procedures to talk to them—like email or call (laughs) … it's a pain, sure.* (Alan, telephone call)

When speaking with clients, they echoed these sentiments. However, clients also explained that when consultants worked remotely and sent them a message, if they did not respond quickly, the consultants would be frustrated. Yet when I spoke with the very same clients, they explained how they would also be frustrated if a consultant was physically present working with them on their time but was also responding to another client:

> *You don't want someone here on your time … you're being charged … but they're constantly on messenger talking to other clients … potentially even competitors.* (Client, face-to-face meeting, client site)

The very idea of being present, visible, legitimate and responsive was, therefore, a muddy one, meaning different things to different people in different time-spaces. Consultants reported not just multi-tasking, but simultaneous-tasking their communications, often they worked on site but still needed to respond to consultants or (other) clients via IM. This posed several issues for MobileCom trying to satisfy multiple relations and demands. As the stakes were higher with IM relationships, IM had intensified affective consequences. The issue was not about work/non-work boundaries: it was about the layering of different aspects of organizing which used to be distinguished and separated as now concurrent and multiple, or laminated.

Discussion and Conclusion

This chapter opened up research questions around how work/non-work boundary-tensions are sociomaterially constructed; what happens when relations are multiple, concurrent and layered; and what the affective consequences are. While there is a robust literature addressing tensions involved in managing work/non-work boundaries, especially when working with mobile phones, researchers tend to treat boundaries as entities, existing, to be 'managed'. Existing research was less clear how boundary-tensions are constructed in the first place. This study demonstrates that for many clear-cut work/non-work boundaries no longer exist, and therefore the notion of work/non-work boundaries is problematic. It is instead relations that are of importance; and how these come together to constitute new sorts of tensions around work/non-work.

The findings establish a set of co-constitutive relations in the organization of mobile consulting; and demonstrates how new sorts of boundary-tensions around work/non-work become meaningful. What becomes important is the layering of tensions and how this has affective consequences in the way consultants responded to and were entangled with IM technologies. These consequences are fluid, continuously reconstituted and multiple, with no one version of events. What is evident in the data is tension, intensification and speed up. Not only are boundaries non-existent as inseparable aspects of life are happening at the same time and space, but the tensions we feel from these relations become laminated with intensifying affects: they overlap, they are layered with affective consequences. It is these tensions, therefore, not boundaries as existing entities that we should be paying attention to.

First of all, it is clear that work/non-work is increasingly problematic and the smartphone plays a role in constituting this tension. This lends support to common perceptions around boundary organizing being problematic and adds details of how material aspects become constitutive of boundary-tensions. What this study has added is an insight into how boundary-tensions become meaningful as part of a set of sociomaterial relations and intra-actions, supporting and extending the work of scholars such as Orlikowski and Scott (2015) who are developing a sociomaterial narrative of organization. By examining the role of IM, the research has added an alternative viewpoint to established understandings of organizational boundaries which highlight some of the complexities or tensions that were previously hidden. The ethnographic methods employed also set apart the research from predecessors such as Orlikowski (2007) who based their findings on qualitative interviews. The ability to observe and practice IM, to be affectively involved in the process, as well as interview consultants about it, has been instrumental in shedding light on boundary-tensions and their affective capabilities.

Secondly, the instantaneous nature of IM is intensifying boundary problems as multiple relations come together to construct new sorts of boundary-tensions. Over time, IM orders particular messages, images, emotions to be performed within and across relations which become reconstitutive of what work/non-work means and how boundary-tensions around that meaning are performed. Looking at IM extends Orlikowski's (2007) prior discussion around norms and values becoming reconstituted via *BlackBerry* email by demonstrating that IM is intensifying this process. Further, by extending the analysis beyond internal communication of an organization to include clients, the analysis demonstrates even further the intensification of what Orlikowski (2007) previously described as something more is at stake with clients. This intensification spills over into work/non-work boundary-tensions, adding another perspective to struggles of empowerment/enslavement, public/private and individual/group interests via the empirical nuances that constitute the IM.

Thirdly, the analysis demonstrates how the interplay between social and material entities can be captured via sociomateriality. It is evident that material aspects co-construct boundary-tensions in their entanglement with social and mental practices. What is striking is that the predominant mode of establishing and maintaining consulting relationships can be found at the intersection of the material, social and psychological; and that these continuously renegotiate boundary-tensions around empowerment or enslavement, what is public or private and what are individual or group interests.

The idea that boundaries co-exist is not new. Hernes (2004) pointed to this with his social, mental and physical boundary types. This study, however, adds the affective consequences of boundary-tensions, rather than boundaries, co-existing: at their intersection we see relations come together to produce new meaning and therefore new sorts of boundary-tensions. Beyond the co-existence of boundary-tensions, we can see these become laminated with intensifying affects. What is evident over time is a change in relations, and workflow; a monetary outcome between consultants and with their clients. As the consultants expressed themselves, more fruitful, long-term relationships with clients were accomplished via IM.

Finally, the nature of reconfigurations to work/non-work boundary-tensions is multiple and fluid. Whereas the MD put IM in place to structure and control work in a particular way, unintended practices emerged which had consequences for IM relations and became (re)constitutive of multiple consequences. It is not just a case of IM reconstituting work/non-work but of IM being reconstitutive of a whole set of affective relations around what work/non-work means. This includes but is not limited to the following: (a) the reconstitution of what people mean, of the tensions between what it means to be professional, a colleague or a friend; (b) the reconstitution of what it means for how communication (of words, images, jokes) is enacted; and (c) the renegotiation of what BBM means to consultants in this practice. Each consultant had one *BlackBerry*: one device for personal and work contacts, rather than having separate phones for work/non-work. *BlackBerry* orders don't know rules or boundaries between work/non-work so they push through regardless. Consultants could switch off their phones but they didn't. The order of work, formal and informal rules around it, relationships, internally and externally, and boundaries, sociomaterial, were (re)constituted via the practice of BBM. There emerges a whole set of becoming something other than before, extending Turkle's (2008) observations around us becoming something else through our interactions with technology.

Overall, it is evident that IM was implicated in the sociomaterial construction of boundary-tensions and, in the process, reorganization of consulting relations, of consultants and consulting. Intended rules were continuously (re)negotiated, (re)practised, and these included some and excluded others. There are distinctions between what Wright (1973) would call intended and accidental functions and these distinctions play out in IM practice. The findings demonstrate that, whereas the MD's aim was maintaining close relations, internally and externally, and making sure employees did work, agency cannot only be attributed to a manager, or person (to the MD, consultants and clients). Agency is enacted through relations, by pulling actors and artefacts together via the way things are structured; materiality pulls things into position, but this is not the end of the story. Instead, the findings demonstrate the rules around power in the ways individuals, groups and materialities navigate their interests and between their private/public spheres.

The tensions outlined of empowerment/enslavement, public/private spheres and group/individual interests are similar to findings documented in the literature, with a greater intensification evident when looking at the 'Instant' in the Messaging. Bloom (2015) already warned us that work-life balance is a fallacy that can never be accomplished in contemporary capitalism; and the issue of intensification is now on the rise, with technologies being put in place to enhance this (Bloomfield & Dale, 2015). The fallacy thus becomes even more pertinent, there can never be a balance, that's why we talk of boundaries and why they have received so much attention.

However, as demonstrated in this chapter, even boundaries themselves are problematic. Not only are they not fixed, separable and distinguishable; they are no longer present. The consequences of spillovers between boundaries which used to entail separate domains are multiple and intensifying. Now we are faced with boundary-tensions which are ambiguous, overlapping and dynamic. With all of these relations overlapping, concurrent and multiple, we feel the consequences of layered tensions, creating a laminated and intensifying affect.

The relevance of intensification extends beyond the IM in this case to the whole host of Instant Messaging platforms available, including *WhatsApp*, *I-Message*, *Facebook Messenger*, *LinkedIn Messenger* to name a few; as well as beyond a variety of virtual and mobile platforms that have emerged in organizational life and share the instant characteristic. The instant in communication has spilled over into every domain of life. Intensification is thus a very real threat to boundaries. Negotiations between relations are perpetual as new forms of tensions and meaning around work/non-work are continuously renegotiated and reconstituted. And this process of relations and relating will never be finished, with meaning only ever being a 'temporary stopping place' (Cooper, 2006). These concerns and their importance thus ever remain, increase and intensify with our ever-changing and intensifying spatiotemporal and technological arrangements, and their related affective capabilities.

References

Ashforth, B. E., Kreiner, G. E., & Fugate, M. (2000). All in a day's work: Boundaries and micro role transitions. *Academy of Management Review, 25*(3), 472–491.

Bader, V., & Kaiser, S. (2017). Autonomy and control? How heterogeneous sociomaterial assemblages explain paradoxical rationalities in the digital workplace. *Management Revue, 28*(3), 338–358.

Barad, K. (2003). Posthumanist performativity: Towards an understanding of how matter comes to matter. *Signs, 28*(3), 801–831.

Bazeley, P. (2013). *Qualitative data analysis: Practical strategies*. London: Sage.

Bloom, P. (2015). Work as the contemporary limit of life: Capitalism, the death drive, and the lethal fantasy of 'work-life balance'. *Organization Studies, 23*(4), 1–9.

Bloomfield, B., & Dale, K. (2015). Fit for work? Redefining 'normal' and 'extreme' through human enhancement technologies. *Organization Studies, 22*(4), 552–569.

Collins, R. (1980). Erving Goffman and the development of modern social theory. In J. Ditton (Ed.), *The view from Goffman* (pp. 170–209). Basingstoke: Palgrave Macmillan.

Cooper, R. (2005). Peripheral vision: Relationality. *Organization Studies, 26*(3), 1689–1710.

Cooper, R. (2006). Making present: Autopoiesis as human production. *Organization, 13*(1), 59–81.

Cousins, K., & Robey, D. (2015). Managing work-life boundaries with mobile technologies. *Information Technology & People, 28*(1), 34–71.

Dale, K. (2005). Building a sociomateriality: Spatial and embodied politics in organizational control. *Organization, 12*(5), 649–678.

Dale, K., & Latham, Y. (2015). Ethics and entangled embodiment: Bodies–materialities–organization. *Organization, 22*(2), 166–182.

Fincham, B., McGuiness, M., & Murray, L. (2010). *Mobile methodologies*. Basingstoke: Palgrave Macmillan.

Fleming, P., & Spicer, A. (2004). 'You can checkout anytime, but you can never leave': Spatial boundaries in a high commitment organization. *Human Relations, 57*(1), 75–94.

Hernes, T. (2004). Studying composite boundaries: A framework of analysis. *Human Relations, 57*(1), 9–29.

Hislop, D., & Axtell, C. (2011). Smartphones during work/non-worktime: A case study of mobile, non-managerial workers. *Information and Organization, 21*(1), 41–56.

Hislop, D., Axtell, C., Collins, A., Daniels, K., Glover, J., & Niven, K. (2015). Variability in the use of mobile ICTs by homeworkers and its consequences for boundary management and social isolation. *Information and Organization, 25*(4), 222–232.

Introna, L. D. (2009). Ethics and the speaking of things. *Theory, Culture and Society, 26*(4), 25–46.

Jarvenpaa, S. L., & Lang, K. R. (2005). Managing the paradoxes of mobile technology. *Information Systems Management, 22*(4), 7–23.

Katila, S., Laine, P. M., & Parkkari, P. (2019). Sociomateriality and affect in institutional work: Constructing the identity of start-up entrepreneurs. *Journal of Management Inquiry, 28*(3), 381–394.

Kimmel, A. (1988). *Ethics and values in applied social research* (Vol. 12). Thousand Oaks, CA: Sage.

Kreiner, G. E., Hollensbe, E. C., & Sheep, M. L. (2009). Balancing borders and bridges: Negotiating the work-home interface via boundary work tactics. *Academy of Management Journal, 52*(4), 704–730.

Law, J. (2006). *Making a mess with method.* Lancaster: Department of Sociology, Lancaster University. Version of 19 January 2006. Retrieved March 2020, from http://www.heterogeneities.net/publications/Law2006MakingaMesswithMethod.pdf

Matusik, S. F., & Mickel, A. E. (2011). Embracing or embattled by converged mobile devices? Users' experiences with a contemporary connectivity technology. *Human Relations, 64*(8), 1001–1030.

Mazmanian, M., Orlikowski, W. J., & Yates, J. (2013). The autonomy paradox: The implications of mobile email devices for knowledge professionals. *Organization Science, 24*(5), 1337–1357.

Mazmanian, M., Yates, J., & Orlikowski, W. (2006). *Ubiquitous email: Individual experiences and organizational consequences of BlackBerry use.* Proceedings of the 65th Annual Meeting of the Academy of Management, Atlanta GA, August 11–16.

Middleton, C. A. (2007). Illusions of balance and control in an always-on environment: A case study of BlackBerry users. *Continuum: Journal of Media and Cultural Studies, 21*(2), 165–178.

Middleton, C. A., & Cukier, W. (2006). Is mobile email functional or dysfunctional? Two perspectives on mobile email usage. *European Journal of Information Systems, 15*(3), 252–260.

Montgomery, K., & Oliver, A. L. (2007). A fresh look at how professions take shape: Dual-directed networking dynamics and social boundaries. *Organization Studies, 28*(5), 661–687.

Nippert-Eng, C. (1996). *Home and work: Negotiating boundaries through everyday life*. Chicago, IL: University of Chicago Press.

Orlikowski, W. J. (2007). Sociomaterial practices: Exploring technology at work. *Organization Studies, 28*(9), 1435–1448.

Orlikowski, W. J., & Scott, S. V. (2008). Sociomateriality: Challenging the separation of technology, work and organization. *The Academy of Management Annals, 2*(1), 433–474.

Orlikowski, W. J., & Scott, S. V. (2015). Exploring material-discursive practices. *Journal of Management Studies, 52*(5), 697–705.

Parmiggiani, E., & Monteiro, E. (2018). The nested materiality of environmental monitoring. *Scandinavian Journal of Information Systems, 27*(1), 33–54.

Perrow, C. (1986). *Complex organizations - a critical essay* (3rd ed.). New York: McGraw-Hill.

Pickering, A. (1995). *The mangle of practice: Time, agency, and science*. Chicago, IL: The University of Chicago Press.

Pullen, A., Rhodes, C., & Thanem, T. (2017). Affective politics in gendered organizations: Affirmative notes on becoming - woman. *Organization, 24*, 105–123.

Reich, J. A. (2015). Old methods and new technologies: Social media and shifts in power in qualitative research. *Ethnography, 16*(4), 394–415.

Rothbard, N. P., Phillips, K. W., & Dumas, T. L. (2005). Managing multiple roles: Work-family policies and individuals' desires for segmentation. *Organization Science, 16*(3), 243–258.

Scott, W. R. (1998). *Organizations – Rational, natural and open systems* (4th ed.). Englewood Cliffs, NJ: Prentice Hall.

Senarathne Tennakoon, U. K. L., Silveira, G. J. C., & Taras, D. G. (2013). Drivers of context-specific ICT use across work and nonwork domains: A boundary theory perspective. *Information and Organization, 23*(2), 107–128.

Suchman, L. A. (2007). *Human–machine reconfigurations: Plans and situated actions*. Cambridge: Cambridge University Press.

Symon, G., & Pritchard, K. (2015). Performing the responsive and committed employee through the sociomaterial mangle of connection. *Organization Studies, 36*(2), 241–263.

Turkle, S. (2008). Always-on/always-on-you: The tethered self. In K. Blair, R. M. Murphy, & J. Almjeld (Eds.), *Handbook of mobile communication studies* (p. 121). Boston, MA: Cengage Learning.

Van Maanen, J. (1979). *Qualitative methodology*. London: Sage.

Van Maanen, J. (2011). *Tales of the field* (2nd ed.). Chicago, IL: University of Chicago Press.

Wadel, C. (1979). The hidden work of everyday life. In S. Wallman (Ed.), *Social anthropology of work* (pp. 365–384). London: Academic Press.

Wajcman, J., Bittman, M., & Brown, J. E. (2008). Families without borders: Smartphones, connectedness and work–home divisions. *Sociology, 42*(4), 635–652.

Weick, K. E. (1979). *The social psychology of Organising* (2nd ed.). New York: Random House.

Wright, L. (1973). Functions. *The Philosophical Review, 82*(2), 139–168.

Zuboff, S. (1985). Automate/informate: The two faces of intelligent technology. *Organizational Dynamics, 14*(2), 5–18.

Part IV

New Ways of Working and Organizational Spaces

11

Space for Tensions: A Lefebvrian Perspective on New Ways of Working

Andrea Simone Barth and Susanne Blazejewski

Introduction

To meet the challenges of the changing organizational environment, companies are increasingly implementing New Ways of Working (NWW). NWW refer to new spatiotemporal working practices that aim at improving flexibility, collaboration, innovation, efficiency, and autonomy of employees (Hackl, Wagner, Attmer, & Baumann, 2017; Kingma, 2018; Leede, 2017). In order to put NWW ideas into practice, a growing number of companies are changing their 'traditional' workspaces to 'new' workspaces, which are intended to facilitate and shape working behavior. However, NWW seem to have controversial outcomes and effects. Despite positive contributions to organizational life, research reveals contradictions and tensions in the way employees, managers, and organizations develop, enact, and respond to NWW (Brunia, de Been, & van der

A. S. Barth (✉) • S. Blazejewski
Department of Business Management, Alanus University of Arts and Social Sciences, Alfter, Germany
e-mail: andrea-simone.barth@alanus.edu; susanne.blazejewski@alanus.edu

N. Mitev et al. (eds.), *New Ways of Working*, Technology, Work and Globalization,
https://doi.org/10.1007/978-3-030-61687-8_11

Voordt, 2016; Hodgson & Briand, 2013; Kingma, 2018; Putnam, Myers, & Gailliard, 2014). Although organizational scholars point to tensions, contradictions, and paradoxes associated with NWW concepts, the relevance of the organizational space in integrating, producing, and handling tensions in organizations appears to be underexplored and has not yet received enough attention in scholarly debate. In this conceptual paper, we propose a theoretical framework on space and tensions in organizations in order to allow a deeper examination of the tensions and contradictions associated with NWW and its spaces.

We draw on Lefebvre's (1974/1991) theory of spatial production to conceptualize organizational space and inform it with considerations of paradox theory (Lewis, 2000; Lüscher & Lewis, 2008; Smith & Lewis, 2011) regarding the emergence and handling of tensions in organizations. Lefebvre's theory is particularly relevant for the study of contradictions in organizational space, as he highlights the ongoing struggles related to space and refers to the tensions involved in spatial production (Spicer & Taylor, 2006; Zhang, Spicer, & Hancock, 2008). Paradox theory, on the other hand, offers a powerful lens for a deeper understanding of the dynamics of organizational tensions (Schad, Lewis, Raisch, & Smith, 2016). Therefore, the paradox perspective allows theorizing and valuable insights into the controversies and unexpected outcomes associated with new workspaces.

First, we will introduce Lefebvre's (1974/1991) theory of spatial production and then briefly outline the theoretical groundwork of paradox studies on dynamics of tensions in organizations. Second, we discuss the linkages between space and tensions in organizations. Finally, we apply this theoretical lens to new workspaces and draw some conclusions.

Organizational Space: A Lefebvrian Perspective

In the last decades there has been a growing interest among organizational scholars in studying organizational space and engaging spatial settings in the study of organizations (Clegg & Kornberger, 2006; Mitev & Vaujany, 2013; Taylor & Spicer, 2007; van Marrewijk & Yanow, 2010).

Space is more and more understood as being central to organizations (Dale & Burrell, 2008). In response to the prior lack of interest in the spatial and material reality of organizations, scholars now aim at establishing an understanding of organizations as "material, spatial ensembles" (Kornberger & Clegg, 2004, 1095). Henri Lefebvre's (1974/1991) theory of spatial production has increasingly been used as analytical framework by organizational scholars to conceptualize space (e.g. Dale & Burrell, 2008; Kingma, Dale, & Wasserman, 2018; Taylor & Spicer, 2007; Wasserman, 2011; Wasserman & Frenkel, 2015), and more recently to explore dynamics in modern and new workspaces (Dale, 2005; Kingma, 2018; Wasserman & Frenkel, 2011, 2015). Lefebvre (1974/1991) goes beyond the—at that time dominant—perspective of space as a 'mental thing' and argues that space is socially produced. Lefebvre is known for his work on urbanism, dialectical materialism, and social space with which he has also largely contributed to Marxist theory. Particularly, his focus on the everyday life and his emphasis on the role of space in the reproduction of social relations of production have attracted renewed scholarly interest over the last decade. In his book *The Production of Space* Lefebvre aims at developing a unitary theory of space and emphasizes the dialectical character of space, thereby highlighting the social (spatial) practices inherent to the forms of space. He introduced the 'spatial triad' which describes three epistemologically different but complementary perspectives of spatial production—the conceived, perceived, and lived space. The three processes of spatial production underlie a trialectic relationship which means that three spaces are not isolated from another, but in a dynamic, sometimes contradictory, interplay and mutually dependent. However, in contrast to (and as a critique of) Hegelian dialectic, none of these dimensions can be considered as the absolute origin, as a 'thesis', and neither does the triad result in a synthesis as in the Hegelian system. The three moments are constantly in interaction and "going from conflict to alliance and back again" (Lefebvre, 1992/2004, 12). Every dimension contributes in different ways to the production of space "according to their qualities and attributes, according to the society or mode of production in question, and according to the historical period" (Lefebvre, 1974/1991, 46). Lefebvre (1974/1991, 34) argues that "social space works (along with its concept) as a tool for analysis of society" and every society produces its own spaces with its specific "modes of production and specific relations of production". Every organization may be considered as a 'society' and thus produces its own space with its own modes of (re-)production of social relations.

Lefebvre's theory is particularly interesting for studying tensions in organizational space, as it highlights the ongoing struggles related to space and refers to the contradictions involved in spatial production (Zhang et al., 2008). First, space is considered as "embodiment of relations of consistent struggle" between those who are in power to control space and those who "take advantage of the freedom which might be found in a space" (Spicer & Taylor, 2006). Second, as already mentioned, Lefebvre (1974/1991) distinguishes between three forms of spatial production that in a trialectical relationship constitute space. Third, Lefebvre is particularly interested in the history of space and how space changes over time. He argues that "a new space cannot be born (produced) unless it accentuates differences" (Lefebvre, 1974/1991, 52). Consequently, in the organizational context, workspaces such as new offices and corporate buildings cannot be established without producing contradictions since they often build on existing and populated spaces. Following Lefebvre, particular attention should be on the relation (and struggles) between the plans and daily use of organizational space, and also on space as means of power and control in organizations. Especially with regard to new workspaces, we find the trialectical relationship between the three forms of spatial production an interesting starting point for the analysis of tensions and contradictions associated with such spaces.

Organizational Tensions: A Paradox Perspective

The study of organizational tensions, contradictions, dialectics, and paradoxes has increased substantially in the past decade (Putnam, Fairhurst, & Banghart, 2016; Schad et al., 2016). Interdisciplinary work has also put forward multiple theories and perspectives for examining organizational tensions (Putnam et al., 2016). Among studies that are concerned with tensions in organizations, there is an increasing body of literature that applies a paradox lens on tensions. Paradox studies offer analytical insights into an array of organizational tensions such as tensions of cooperation and competition, exploration and exploitation, purpose and profit, stability and change (Schad et al., 2016). The theoretical work by Smith and Lewis (2011), Lüscher and Lewis (2008), and Lewis (2000) provides the foundation of paradox theory and is concerned with the question of how organizations can attend to competing demands simultaneously. It offers a powerful lens for analyzing dynamics of tensions and strategies to handle contradictory demands in organizations.

The Emergence of and Responses to Tensions in Organizations

Smith and Lewis (2011, 382) define paradox as "contradictory yet interrelated elements that exist simultaneously and persist over time". They argue that organizational paradoxical tensions often remain latent, becoming salient particularly under conditions of plurality, change, scarcity or through individual cognitive efforts. Schad et al. (2016, 7) emphasize that even though paradox involves a "dynamic and constantly shifting relationship between alternative poles, the core elements remain". Whereas Schad et al. (2016) identify the contradiction and the interdependence as the core elements of paradox, they treat persistence of paradox as given and as prerequisite. In particular, the persistence of paradox over time caught our interest but is as yet theoretically underexplored. What makes contradictions persevere in organizations? In their study, Cnossen and Bencherki (2018) asked how organizations persist over time and thereby pointed to the role of space in making 'endurance' of organizing possible. Linking their findings to concepts of paradoxes in organization, we assume that space plays a role in making contradictions persist in organizations over time.

When tensions become salient in organizations, the issue of how to handle tensions arises. Responses to tensions can be manifold (for overview, see e.g. Putnam et al., 2016; Schad et al., 2016). Those preferred from a paradox perspective are constructive 'both/and' responses that encourage actors to embrace and accept tensions and its competing forces

(Lewis, 2000; Smith & Lewis, 2011). In contrast to constructive responses, destructive responses are characterized by an 'either/or' thinking and involve defensive mechanism such as projecting, repressing, withdrawal, regression, reaction forming, ambivalence (Vince & Broussine, 1996), selection of one pole over the other (Seo, Putnam, & Bartunek, 2004) as well as separation through source splitting and dividing of contrary forces (Poole & van de Ven, 1989). In particular, scholars in this field have highlighted the individual actors' capabilities, cognition, and emotional responses in rendering paradoxes salient and in handling tensions over time (e.g. Miron-Spektor, Ingram, Keller, Smith, & Lewis, 2017). Spatial responses to tensions such as spatial separation and integration have been mentioned (Poole & van de Ven, 1989) only in passing rather than explored thoroughly.

So far, space and the linkages between organizational space and tensions have not received much scholarly attention in paradox studies yet. Fairhurst and Putnam (2014) note that paradox research needs more attention to the objects, bodies, spaces, and places in which discourse interfaces with materiality. In particular, as paradox scholars call for novel theoretical and methodological approaches in research on organizational tensions (Schad et al., 2016), exploring organizational tensions from a spatial perspective may contribute to this call and offer a novel understanding of the emergence and handling of tensions in organizations.

Linkages Between Tensions and Space in Organizations

In this section we discuss the linkages between space and tensions in organizations (for overview, see Table 11.1). We conceptualize space based on Lefebvre's (1974/1991) work and inform it with considerations of paradox theory (Lewis, 2000; Lüscher & Lewis, 2008; Smith & Lewis, 2011) regarding the emergence and responses to tensions. We will structure the following discussion in accordance with Lefebvre's spatial triad and elaborate on dynamics of organizational tensions for each of the three spaces.

Table 11.1 Linkages between spatial production and tensions in organizations (authors' own)

	Spatial production	Actors	Tensions in space
Conceived space	Discourse over space; concepts, plans, and ideas of space	Planners of space (architects, managers, engineers,...)	***Integration***: Integration of tensions in organizations through spatial discourse and planning
Perceived space	Embodiment of spatial discourse and everyday manifestation; (re) production of space	All actors involved in the materialization of space and daily organizational 'reality'	***Materialization and everyday experience***: Daily spatial practices may render tensions salient, (re)produce tensions
Lived space	Users' interpretations of space; (sensory) experiences based on associated images and symbols	Users of space	***Sense-making***: Sense-making of tensions through interpretations and personal images; re-interpretation of contradictory spaces

Conceived Space: Integration of Tensions in Organizational Space

The conceived space is the space of scientists, planners, urbanists, and engineers (Lefebvre, 1974/1991, 38). Lefebvre (1974/1991, 39) emphasizes that this space is the "dominant space in any society". It "reflects the priorities of the dominant group, and [...] is affected by the social position of those in power" (Wasserman & Frenkel, 2015, 1488); thereby it maintains the "relations of production" and represents the "'order' which those relations impose" (Lefebvre, 1974/1991, 33). In the organizational context, it represents the dominant architectural and managerial discourse over space, also regarding the 'appropriate' and 'ideal worker' (Wasserman & Frenkel, 2015). The conceived space constitutes formal social relations and hierarchies in organizational life. It can be defined as the conceptualized or planned space that is constructed from abstract representations, codifications, and systems of verbal (and intellectually worked out) signs (Lefebvre, 1974/1991).

Within the conceived space, tensions become integrated in the organization through discourses over space. Paradox theory assumes that organizational tensions are always both, inherent and socially constructed (Smith & Lewis, 2011). They are by nature latent—environmental factors, cognitive abilities, or relational dynamics can render tensions salient (Fairhurst & Putnam, 2014; Schad et al., 2016; Smith & Lewis, 2011). Smith and Lewis (2011, 389) state that "contradictory yet interrelated elements [are] embedded in organizing processes". Consequently, through the spatial planning (conceived space) contradictions may be embedded in organizational life and persist over time in their material manifestations. As already mentioned, the conceived space represents the architectural and managerial discourse, which involves the managerial expectations, ideas, and concepts of work and organizing. Paradoxes and tensions related to these managerial and architectural concepts may appear in discourse over space. For example, in a study on the formation and theorization on modern architecture Jones, Maoret, Massa, and Svejenova (2012) illustrate the discourse of architects over competing logics and artefactual codes that guide modern architecture. Their findings suggested that opposing forces and pluralism were integral to architectural planning. For example, modern architects combined concepts that "anchored distinct logics such as nature, art, and human with technical and economic" (Jones et al., 2012, 1538) and used multiple and contrary materials and technologies. Putnam et al. (2016, 13) conceive discourse as "a key to how paradox forms and operates" and emphasize that it "sets the condition for how actors appropriate contradictions in organizational processes".

As mentioned earlier, paradox scholars suggest different approaches for managing paradoxes. These approaches can be translated into spatial responses that can be rather polarizing (aiming at selecting one pole over the other) or integrative and bring competing poles together. For example, in Jones et al. (2012)'s study, architects finally embraced the tensions. The conflict between the logics became "a source of creative tension" for modern architecture that "integrated aspects of both logics and materials in buildings, expanding the category boundary" (Jones et al., 2012,

1523). Similarly, Kornberger and Clegg (2004, 1105) have advocated the idea of the "generative building" that "combines order and chaos". These buildings are "chaotic, ambiguous and incomplete" spaces and designed to encourage workers to be "creative and passionate" (Kornberger & Clegg, 2004, 1104). Consequently, the space allows users of space to deal with contradictions by giving them space for interaction and meaning-making. While some spaces are planned to engage users in the process of dealing with paradoxes and tensions and develop a space for dialogue, reflection, and independent sense-making (Kingma, 2016), other spaces might be rather polarizing and focusing on one pole, logic or material expression, being inflexible and repressive.

Perceived Space: Materialization and Everyday Experience of Tensions

The perceived space is produced through spatial practices (Lefebvre, 1974/1991) and refers to the "physicality of materiality" (Burrell & Dale, 2008, 7). In the organizational context, the emphasis is on the embodiment of spatial discourse and its material manifestations in organizational life. The perceived space constitutes the production and reproduction of the managerial and architectural discourse. Wasserman and Frenkel (2015, 1489) describe the perceived space as translating "the tastes of those in positions of power into material and corporeal technics. It is the disciplining space in which individuals are kept in their place and wherein their everyday activities are constrained by physical structure".

Smith and Lewis (2011) suggest that tensions become salient under conditions of plurality, change, scarcity, or through individual cognitive efforts. We would add that organizational-spatial dynamics or, more precisely, daily spatial practices can also render tensions salient in organizations. In the course of materialization and embodiment of space, organizational tensions of the conceived space also materialize and become experienced by users of space. The spatial discourse with all its contradictions becomes manifested in materialized form and (re-)produced through spatial practice. Lefebvre (1974/1991, 40) argues that "social practice presupposes the use of body". Through the body, the outside world is perceived. Consequently, also contradictions and inconsistencies of conceived space can be perceived through the body in daily practice. Lefebvre (1974/1991, 38) further emphasizes that spatial practice "propounds and presupposes" society's space "in a dialectical interaction". In organizational life, spatial practice may also differ from the ideals of the conceived space. Organizational life is full of contradictions and complexities (Smith & Lewis, 2011), hence, conceived space may in its materialized form seem not plausible in use or interfere with organizational daily reality. Examining the relationship between conceived and perceived space therefore can be informative in analyzing organizational tensions. According to Lefebvre (1974/1991), though, this is not the space for reflection or interpretation of space. Spatial practices are rather defined as routinized, that is 'thoughtless' social interactions, hence, would not include symbolic processes of sense-making of tensions.

Lived Space: Sense-Making of Tensions

The lived space is the product of the users' experiences and interpretations. This space is "lived through its associated images and symbols" (Lefebvre, 1974/1991, 39), which has the potential to also overlay physical space, "making symbolic use of its objects" (Lefebvre, 1974/1991, 39) and thus might reproduce or undermine dominant forms of spatial ordering, for example, the prescribed organizational order. This space enables an 'agentic' point of view and highlights the limitation of those in power to enforce ideas and prevalent social relations (Wasserman & Frenkel, 2015). In this space the users reflect on space, may actively question everyday spatial practice, and "take advantage of the freedoms which might be found in a space" (Spicer & Taylor, 2006) by engaging with space in a new or different form. Lefebvre (1974/1991) emphasizes that it is the space of 'users' and 'inhabitants', hence, refers to the individual experience and interpretations of space, but constructed within the social and cultural context. Consequently, lived space is produced and manifest in the experiences of those who inhabit them and can be characterized as spaces that are defined by its users.

The lived space is also the space for reflection where individual actors can ponder and thus re-interpret and re-frame tensions and paradoxes associated with workspace. Lefebvre mentions in his writings that the user has the potential to enact agency in spatial consumption through the lived space (see e.g. Lefebvre, 1974/1991, 33, 39), thus gaining some scope of action vis-à-vis the dominant space in society. Diverging spatial practices or misuse of planned spaces (Wasserman & Frenkel, 2011) may be a result of and a response to perceived contradictions. Users of space could, for example, create 'counter' images of spaces, or interpret spaces differently to the images and symbolic meaning prescribed to workspaces by the organization. These 'personal' images and different interpretations of space might be a way of handling and making sense of tensions. Take for example the image of a hospital. A hospital, in its original meaning, is related to 'hospitality'. Applying this image to a publicly operated hospital that is working to capacity where the staff is overburdened with work may create a contrary image. Probably users of space (such as patients) will recognize the discrepancies between an image of a hospital as a place of 'hospitality' and their perceived diverse 'reality' and interpret the hospital space differently, hence, create a new image of the place. Such a new image may also lead to different expectations toward actors operating in this space and changing practices in space. As a caveat, Smith and Lewis (2011) emphasize that sense-making of tensions (e.g. create counter-images of spaces) requires the individual's cognitive ability to recognize such tensions in the first place. Space thus, first of all, needs to be brought to attention and lifted out of spatial routines. Users might require a certain 'space' or 'time' in which they can recognize and reflect on their spatial consumption and the tensions involved in space.

New Workspaces

In this section we apply the theoretical framework developed above to spaces of NWW in organizations, which we refer to as 'new workspaces'. Although a variety of organizations in diverse industries are currently going through a transition and adapting NWW, we are going to focus on office work only. Our analysis is based on a review of the literature on

NWW and associated tensions and provides first insights as a basis for further empirical work. As already mentioned, Lefebvre's spatial triad underlies a trialectical relationship, which means that the three spaces are not isolated from another, but in a dynamic, sometimes contradictory, interplay and mutually dependent. Consequently, in our analysis we acknowledge dynamics of tensions within, but also at the intersection of the spatial triad. Though, we will structure the discussion according to the three spaces and in this course particularly pay attention to (1) the embeddedness of contradictions in new workspace concepts; (2) tensions arising through the practice of new workspaces; (3) the aestheticization of new workspaces.

The Embeddedness of Contradictions in New Workspace Concepts

When looking at new workspaces from a 'conceived space' perspective, we find contradictions already embedded in spatial concepts. New workspaces can be characterized as highly 'organized spaces', which embody certain conceptualizations in materialized form (Dale & Bureell, 2008, 9). These conceptualizations are created through discourses over space by actors who are responsible for planning organizational space such as architects, construction engineers, but also managers, consultants, designers, and artists. In particular, managerial discourse regarding ideal concepts of organizing and work in the 'new economy' such as NWW builds the basis for spatial conceptualizations. NWW originate from the idea that employees are able to work independent of time and place, being supported by a flexible working environment which is facilitated by information technologies (Blok, Groenesteijn, Schelvis, & Vink, 2012; Leede, 2017; Veldhoen, 2004). Beyond workplace flexibility, NWW imply also flexibility in structuring organizations (Townsend, McDonald, & Cathcart, 2016) which serve to dynamically adapt to changes in the market, and support collaboration and innovation among employees (Stryker, Santoro, & Farris, 2012). However, scholars mention tensions and controversies inherent in these NWW concepts and ideas, for example, between autonomy and control (Hodgson & Briand, 2013; Putnam et al., 2014), work and non-work (Putnam et al., 2014; Richman, Civian, Shannon, Jeffrey Hill, & Brennan, 2008), or collaboration and individualization (Hodgson & Briand, 2013; Pearce & Sims Jr, 2002; Pearlson & Saunders, 2001). As an example, tensions of autonomy and control arise through NWW, that is between the need to control working hours, autonomy in choosing the physical location for working, or task contingencies (e.g. peaks and demands, part-time and full-time work, and job sharing/rotation).

Regarding the spatial dimensions of NWW, contradictory relationships also seem to be embedded in architectural concepts of new workspaces. For example, new workspaces usually offer functional work areas that are designed to promote different and contrary work activities, for instance, some requiring more concentration (e.g. silent zones in which communication among employees is prohibited), others more communication (e.g. activity-based workplaces). Myerson and Ross's (2003) book *The Twenty-First Century Office* captures emerging themes and ideas in office architecture and interiors across organizations internationally. This is a description of the "unneighborly" office concept:

> The concept scheme [...] describes the future workplace as having a number of defining characteristics, most notably a generosity of social space with transparent meeting rooms devoid of technology to reinforce face-to-face contact and dialogue. This idea of the office as social landscape is reinforced by a blurring of the distinction between inside and outside: gardens form part of the work environment and fibrous-membrane interior walls support hydroponic plants. Individual work shells provide private enclosures but can be grouped into unneighborly clusters for open team working.

Concepts of unneighborly offices are working with the opposites 'inside' and 'outside' and intentionally integrate them in spatial plans. Another workspace concept is the 'nomadic' office. Myerson and Ross (2003) describe it as follows:

> The project proposes a club room for people from the same industry to touch down, socialize, eat and work. Interior spaces are graded from semi-public to confidential. 'Eat-work pods' are designed for non-confidential

> encounters; 'four-poster' spaces are transparent but provide complete audio privacy. This is a concept that crosses the office with nightclub, blurring the boundaries between work and play, public and private.

In this spatial concept the opposing relationship between work and non-work and public and private is addressed and actively integrated in architectural concepts of workspaces. Take the example of the nightclub: by incorporating aesthetics and symbols of nightclubs, spatial planners aim at creating innovative and hybrid atmospheres that blur the boundaries between private and public, or work and non-work life. How will these spaces affect working life? How to behave in a 'nightclub'-office atmosphere? As mentioned in the quote, the 'nomadic' office is expected to create collaboration among users of the space. Though, beyond the 'socializing' aspects, a nightclub involves much more practices that, however, can be contradictory to 'office' practices in terms of social distance, privacy, and so on. Therefore, a spatial concept that crosses two diverse spaces may lead to other, maybe unexpected outcomes and practices.

As illustrated, some new workspace concepts seem to be built on the integration of opposing forces, and such oppositions even bring these workspaces to life. The 'nomadic' office space (Myerson & Ross, 2003) involves already concrete spatial layouts of how the ideas of "blurring the boundaries between work and play, public and private" will be translated into space. Planners have defined spaces that consist of places for socializing such as the 'eat-work-pods' which are separated from the 'four posters' spaces for audio-privacy. Whereas the conceptual approach emphasizes the blurring lines between contradictory elements and suggests an integration of both poles ('both/and'), the plans for the concrete physical implementation ('materialization of space') separate the opposing elements, assigning them to different spaces within the office space ('either/or'). In contrast, with the neighborly office concept, planners seem to have implemented a 'both/and' solution. Spatial elements can be easily modified by users of space, for example, individual work shells can be grouped into neighborly clusters. These examples illustrate that contradictions are already embedded in spatial architectural concepts. The question is are they becoming 'reality' and persist through materialization in organizational space.

Tensions Arising Through Practice in New Workspaces

Research reveals tensions and contradictions in the 'perceived' (new) workspaces that become salient in the ways that employees, managers, and organizations enact and respond to NWW and its spaces (Ayoko & Hartel CE, 2003; Brunia et al., 2016; Hodgson & Briand, 2013; Holland & Bardoel, 2016; Putnam et al., 2014; Stea, Foss, & Christensen, 2015). Putnam et al. (2016) show that new workplace arrangements often fail to align with increased flexibility. Van Steenbergen, van der Ven, Peeters, and Taris (2018) also identified paradoxes in their findings related to new flexible workplaces. They argue that "NWW can simultaneously be beneficial (i.e., lead to a decrease in mental demands and workload) and detrimental (i.e., lead to decreases in autonomy and possibilities for professional development) for employees". NWW should provide more responsibility and autonomy to employees; however, instead of an increase in autonomy, employees report a decreased level of autonomy (van Steenbergen et al., 2018). Also, empirical studies have shown that employees who hold autonomy in scheduling time and place of work have longer workweeks and spend even more time on work activities (van Echtelt, Glebbeek, & Lindenberg, 2006).

Furthermore, new workspaces are expected to foster employees' engagement and identification with the company, and sustain the shared awareness of the ongoing activities at the organizational level. Therefore, in new workspaces elements that signal structural boundaries to collaboration, such as hierarchies and functional silos, are (spatially) eliminated (Elsbach & Bechky, 2007). However, scholars suggest that due to the lack of workplace personalization brought by nomadic work practices, workspaces might even lower individual feelings of belonging and distinctiveness (Elsbach & Bechky, 2007). Lack of personalization in new workspaces, thus, might endanger the organizational attachment and commitment of knowledge workers.

Among that, employees in workspaces with desk-sharing solutions ('hot-desking') tend to enact territorial behaviors, such as claiming space, systematically selecting the same work location, and using portable artifacts to mark their territory (Brown, Lawrence, & Robinson, 2005; Kim,

Candido, Thomas, & Dear, 2016). As a result, new workspaces might be paradoxically perceived as isolating, as knowledge workers established psychological distance from each other through territorial behaviors (Wohlers & Hertel, 2017) and the social identification process is altered. Contrary to the expectations, new workspaces might lower the interactions among employees. Research has thus reported a deterioration of relationships with coworkers and supervisors (Golden, 2006; Sardeshmukh, Sharma, & Golden, 2012), or negative emotions such as loneliness (Mann & Holdsworth, 2003). Svensson (2011) shows that flexible working conditions lead to lower level of trust among colleagues. Kingma (2018, 16) describes in his study on NWW at *Beware* that some employees also "felt social insecurity related to hot-desking, because of a decreased predictability of physical closeness of colleagues, as well as the permanent visibility to all. Some expressed the feeling that they were 'constantly being watched'". Also, the option to work at home was turned into a fixed day for homeworking, making employees less flexible and unavailable for office-based activities. A paradoxical situation becomes salient through spatial practice: the intended workplace flexibility results in reduced flexibility.

These examples illustrate how, in perceived space, concepts of NWW and their spatial implementation produced tensions and contradictions. Spatial practices thus can reveal paradoxical relationships that either are already embedded in new workspace concepts (conceived space) or result from differences between organizational activity and conceptualized physical workspace. Through materialization of spatial concepts, managerial and architectural ideas become 'reality' and users of space might be confronted with a working environment that contradicts with their daily spatial practice. In particular, oppositions and contradictory relationships of conceived space might be embodied by users in a way that counteract the initial ideas of how spaces were planned to be used. Take the example of office space that integrates design elements of a nightclub (Myerson & Ross, 2003). These contradictory spaces could also lead to contradictory and 'non-office-appropriate' practices, such as flirting, hanging around, or drinking alcohol at the workplace (see e.g. Fleming, 2007).

Aesthetícization of New Workspaces

The lived space is the space of 'imagination'. Users of space interpret space differently, based on their ongoing experiences of space and internalized norms and identities. These interpretations in turn have consequences for and influence their spatial practices. Therefore, diverse spatial practices and unexpected effects can also be explained by contradictions in lived space. Particularly, in new workspaces the conscious design of the aesthetic and sensory experience has gained momentum. Scholars specifically point to the 'aestheticization' of and increased symbolism in the workplace (Cairns, 2002; Dale & Burrell, 2008; Gagliardi, 1990; Strati, 1995). Organizations show increased efforts to influence the 'lived' experiences of users of space. Paoli, Sauer, and Ropo (2017, 8) illustrate that office images of new and creative workspaces "were different from regular offices as they were far more colorful, artistic, informal and playful, even childish". New workspaces include creative and playfully designed spaces that incorporate diverse themes and images from non-work-related social fields and resemble non-work-related spaces such as restaurants, bars, living rooms, or playgrounds (de Paoli et al., 2017). Van Marrewijk (2010) demonstrates how spatial planning affects the lived space of individuals, the emotions, and also their working behaviors. He explores the aesthetic experience of employees in two different corporate buildings. Aestheticization positively affected the organizational change process and the relocation from the old to the new corporate building (from the 'beasty' building to the 'beautiful' building). Organizational space thus has not only a productive function, but provides an all-round sensual experience laden with symbolism (Berg & Kreiner, 1990) that influences and affects users of space.

Though, actors' images of the organization and its space may diverge. Taylor and Spicer (2007) argue that spatial imaginaries that are propagated by managers and those circulated by employees may be different. Whereas managers may describe the company as an 'innovation space', employees compare the company with a totalitarian regime. Spatial imaginary that is mobilized in the new workplace emphasizes, for instance, 'openness', 'creativity', and 'fluidity', does not necessarily correspond to the interpretations of the users of space. Hatch (1990) argues that open plan offices are planned to symbolize 'openness' and 'accountability', but perhaps are interpreted by employees as spaces of exposure and control. Therefore, a living room atmosphere in the office may not lead to 'home'- or 'living room'-related spatial practices, because users of space interpret spaces differently. Consequently, the manager's intention to blur the boundaries between home and work might not put into practice. On the contrary, users of space will on a daily basis be confronted with a 'paradoxical' reality in which experiences are inconsistent with spatial design.

The lived space is also the place for reflection where individuals may make sense of tensions. Kingma (2018) states in his study on NWW that the lived space reveals the meaningful way of working, which may contrast with the conceived space, but may also overcome contradictions between conventional routines and the ideals of NWW. The lived space thus enables the user of space to 'handle' tensions and deal with contradictions of the perceived or conceived space, for example, through metaphors and personal images. According to paradox theory, responses to tensions, however, can be manifold; hence, interpretations and sense-making strategies to handle contradictions in organizational space differ. Although scholars have emphasized the lived space as a space associated with struggle and resistance (Wasserman, 2011; Zhang et al., 2008), Kingma (2018) found that employees are able to create 'harmony' through images and interpretations of space. He stresses that "the creative appropriation of new designs in the lived space involves a broader range of equally significant but moderate re-interpretations and modifications". Further, he states that in the lived space users explore and define the symbolic order of NWW.

However, in order to deal with contradictions, we point to Smith and Lewis (2011) who emphasize that sense-making requires the individual's cognitive ability to recognize such tensions in the first place. We suggest that in aestheticized spaces (such as new workspaces) not only cognitive skills are required, but also aesthetic or sensory knowing is required to make sense of space and associated contradictions. Scholars have highlighted that aesthetic knowledge enables us to see our environment in a new and different way (John, 2001; Taylor, 2016). Therefore, in addition to cognitive skills, aesthetic skills can inform cognition and may render spatial tensions salient and/or enable to engage with space in a reflective way.

Conclusion

In this chapter, we used Lefebvre's (1974/1991) theory of spatial production and paradox theory (Lewis, 2000; Lüscher & Lewis, 2008; Smith & Lewis, 2011) to first outline the linkages between space and tensions in organizations. Furthermore, we have applied this framework to tensions recognized in literature on NWW. Based on Lefebvre's spatial triad, we discuss how tensions become integrated into organizations through spatial concepts, how tensions are rendered salient through spatial practices, and how users of space can make sense of tensions in the lived space.

This chapter makes two main contributions: first, the literature on tensions in NWW lacks an examination of the spatial dimension. Previous studies in NWW either focus on specific practices of NWW such as homeworking, telecommuting, hot-desking, and so on or consider only the physical space and material objects in their analysis. A Lefebvrian perspective, though, unites mental, physical, and material space and highlights the various modes of spatial production. Such an approach enables a novel perspective on inconsistencies and contradictions in NWW, as it emphasizes the diverse practices that play a role in the social creation and design of workspaces. Especially in NWW, spatial arrangements are highly organized and used to facilitate and control behavior. However, contradictions embedded in workspace concepts as well as physical workspaces that do not fit to organizational activities might explain contradictory practices and tensions in new workspaces.

With regard to the second contribution, the proposed framework allows for a systematic identification and analysis of (spatial) tensions in organizations. Since paradox scholars have called for new theoretical and methodological approaches in research on organizational tensions (Schad et al., 2016), highlighting spatial-organizational dynamics in the analysis of organizational paradox research constitutes a response to this call and points to tensions that have so far gone unnoticed by researchers.

Furthermore, as theorists emphasize 'persistence' as a core characteristic of paradox (Schad et al., 2016; Smith & Lewis, 2011), we suggest further explorations on the role of space for preserving contradictions over time and for contributing to the perception of paradox in organizations. Paying attention to the spatial and material dimension in organizing could help us better understand how tensions may be resolved, or on the contrary, how they persist in organizations over time.

References

Ayoko, O. B., & Hartel CE, J. (2003). The role of space as both a conflict trigger and a conflict control mechanism in culturally heterogeneous workgroups. *Applied Psychology, 52*(3), 383–412.

Berg, P. O., & Kreiner, K. (1990). Corporate architecture: Turning physical settings into symbolic resources. In P. Gagliardi (Ed.), *Symbols and Artifacts: Views of the corporate landscape* (pp. 41–67). London: Routledge.

Blok, M. M., Groenesteijn, L., Schelvis, R., & Vink, P. (2012). New ways of working: Does flexibility in time and location of work change work behavior and affect business outcomes? *Work, 41*(Supplement 1), 5075–5080.

Brown, G., Lawrence, T. B., & Robinson, S. L. (2005). Territoriality in organizations. *Academy of Management Review, 30*(3), 577–594.

Brunia, S., de Been, I., & van der Voordt, T. J. M. (2016). Accommodating new ways of working: Lessons from best practices and worst cases. *Journal of Corporate Real Estate, 18*(1), 30–47.

Cairns, G. (2002). Aesthetics, morality and power: Design as espoused freedom and implicit control. *Human Relations, 55*(7), 799–820.

Clegg, S. R., & Kornberger, M. (2006). *Space, organizations and management theory*. Frederiksberg: CBS Press.

Cnossen, B., & Bencherki, N. (2018). The role of space in the emergence and endurance of organizing: How independent workers and material assemblages constitute organizations. *Human Relations, 3*(1), 1057–1080.

Dale, K. (2005). Building a social materiality: Spatial and embodied politics in organizational control. *Organization, 12*(5), 649–678.

Dale, K., & Burrell, G. (2008). *The Spaces of Organisation, the Organisation of Space, Power, Identity & Materiality at Work*. Basingstoke: Palgrave Macmillan.

de Leede, J. (2017). *New ways of working practices: Antecedents and outcomes*. Bingley: Emerald Group Publishing.

de Paoli, D., Sauer, E., & Ropo, A. (2017). The spatial context of organizations: A critique of 'creative workspaces'. *Journal of Management & Organization, 1*, 1–22.

Elsbach, K. D., & Bechky, B. A. (2007). It's more than a desk: Working smarter through leveraged office design. *California Management Review, 49*(2), 80–101.

Fairhurst, G. T., & Putnam, L. L. (2014). Organizational discourse analysis. In L. L. Putnam & D. K. Mumby (Eds.), *The SAGE handbook of organizational communication: Advances in theory, research, and methods* (pp. 271–296). London: Sage.

Fleming, P. (2007). Sexuality, power and resistance in the workplace. *Organization Studies, 28*(2), 239–256.

Gagliardi, P. (Ed.). (1990). *Symbols and Artifacts: Views of the corporate landscape.* London: Routledge.

Golden, T. D. (2006). The role of relationships in understanding telecommuter satisfaction. *Journal of Organizational Behavior, 27*(3), 319–340.

Hackl, B., Wagner, M., Attmer, L., & Baumann, D. (2017). *New Work: Auf dem Weg zur neuen Arbeitswelt: Management-Impulse, Praxisbeispiele, Studien.* Wiesbaden: Springer Gabler.

Hatch, M. J. (1990). The symbolics of office design: An empirical exploration. In P. Gagliardi (Ed.), *Symbols and Artifacts: Views of the corporate landscape* (pp. 129–146). London: Routledge.

Hodgson, D., & Briand, L. (2013). Controlling the uncontrollable: 'Agile' teams and illusions of autonomy in creative work. *Work, Employment and Society, 27*(2), 308–325.

Holland, P., & Bardoel, A. (2016). The impact of technology on work in the twenty-first century: Exploring the smart and dark side. *The International Journal of Human Resource Management, 27*(21), 2579–2581.

John, E. (2001). Art and knowledge. In B. Gaut & D. Lopes (Eds.), *The Routledge companion to aesthetics* (pp. 329–352). London: Routledge.

Jones, C., Maoret, M., Massa, F. G., & Svejenova, S. (2012). Rebels with a cause: Formation, contestation, and expansion of the De novo category "modern architecture," 1870–1975. *Organization Science, 23*(6), 1523–1545.

Kim, J., Candido, C., Thomas, L., & Dear, R. d. (2016). Desk ownership in the workplace: The effect of non-territorial working on employee workplace satisfaction, perceived productivity and health. *Building and Environment, 103*, 203–214.

Kingma, S. (2018). New ways of working (NWW): Work space and cultural change in virtualizing organizations. *Culture and Organization, 41*(2), 1–24.

Kingma, S. F. (2016). The constitution of 'third workspaces' in between the home and the corporate office. *New Technology, Work and Employment, 31*(2), 176–193.

Kingma, S. F., Dale, K., & Wasserman, V. (Eds.). (2018). *Organizational space and beyond: The significance of Henri Lefebvre for organization studies.* Abingdon: Routledge.

Kornberger, M., & Clegg, S. R. (2004). Bringing space back in: Organizing the generative building. *Organization Studies, 25*(7), 1095–1114.

Lefebvre, H. (1991). *The production of space* (Vol. 142). Oxford: Blackwell. (Original work published 1974).

Lefebvre, H. (2004). *Rhythmanalysis: Space, time and everyday life.* London: A&C Black. (Original work published 1992).

Lewis, M. W. (2000). Exploring paradox: Toward a more comprehensive guide. *Academy of Management Review, 25*(4), 760–776.

Lüscher, L. S., & Lewis, M. W. (2008). Organizational change and managerial sensemaking: Working through paradox. *Academy of Management Journal, 51*(2), 221–240.

Mann, S., & Holdsworth, L. (2003). The psychological impact of teleworking: Stress, emotions and health. *New Technology, Work and Employment, 18*(3), 196–211.

Miron-Spektor, E., Ingram, A., Keller, J., Smith, W., & Lewis, M. (2017). Microfoundations of organizational paradox: The problem is how we think about the problem. *Academy of Management Journal, 61*(1), 26–45.

Mitev, N., & de Vaujany, F.-X. (Eds.). (2013). *Materiality and space: Organizations, artefacts and practices.* Basingstoke: Palgrave Macmillan.

Myerson, J., & Ross, P. (2003). *The 21st century office.* London: Laurence King Publishing.

Pearce, C. L., & Sims Jr., H. P. (2002). Vertical versus shared leadership as predictors of the effectiveness of change management teams: An examination of aversive, directive, transactional, transformational, and empowering leader behaviors. *Group Dynamics: Theory, Research, and Practice, 6*(2), 172–197.

Pearlson, K. E., & Saunders, C. S. (2001). There's no place like home: Managing telecommuting paradoxes. *The Academy of Management Executive, 15*, 117–128.

Poole, M. S., & van de Ven, A. H. (1989). Using paradox to build management and organization theories. *The Academy of Management Review, 14*(4), 562–578.

Putnam, L. L., Fairhurst, G. T., & Banghart, S. (2016). Contradictions, dialectics, and paradoxes in organizations: A constitutive approach. *The Academy of Management Annals, 10*(1), 65–171.

Putnam, L. L., Myers, K. K., & Gailliard, B. M. (2014). Examining the tensions in workplace flexibility and exploring options for new directions. *Human Relations, 67*(4), 413–440.

Richman, A. L., Civian, J. T., Shannon, L. L., Jeffrey Hill, E., & Brennan, R. T. (2008). The relationship of perceived flexibility, supportive work–life policies, and use of formal flexible arrangements and occasional flexibility to employee engagement and expected retention. *Community, Work and Family, 11*(2), 183–197.

Sardeshmukh, S. R., Sharma, D., & Golden, T. D. (2012). Impact of telework on exhaustion and job engagement: A job demands and job resources model. *New Technology, Work and Employment, 27*(3), 193–207.

Schad, J., Lewis, M. W., Raisch, S., & Smith, W. K. (2016). Paradox research in management science: Looking back to move forward. *The Academy of Management Annals, 10*(1), 5–64.

Seo, M., Putnam, L. L., & Bartunek, J. M. (2004). Dualities and tensions of planned organizational change. In A. H. van de Ven & M. S. Poole (Eds.), *Handbook of organizational change and innovation* (pp. 73–107). Oxford: Oxford University Press.

Smith, W. K., & Lewis, M. W. (2011). Toward a theory of paradox: A dynamic equilibrium model of organizing. *The Academy of Management Review, 36*(2), 381–403.

Spicer, A., & Taylor, S. (2006). The struggle for organizational space. *Journal of Management Inquiry, 27*, 325–346.

Stea, D., Foss, N. J., & Christensen, P. H. (2015). Physical separation in the workplace: Separation cues, separation awareness, and employee motivation. *European Management Journal, 33*(6), 462–471.

Strati, A. (1995). Organizations viewed through the lens of aesthetics. *Organization, 3*(2), 209–218.

Stryker, J. B., Santoro, M. D., & Farris, G. F. (2012). Creating collaboration opportunity: Designing the physical workplace to promote high-tech team communication. *IEEE Transactions on Engineering Management, 59*(4), 609–620.

Svensson, S. (2011). Flexible working conditions and decreasing levels of trust. *Employee Relations, 34*(2), 126–137.

Taylor, S., & Spicer, A. (2007). Time for space: A narrative review of research on organizational spaces. *International Journal of Management Reviews, 9*(4), 325–346.

Taylor, S. S. (2016). Overcoming aesthetic muteness: Researching organizational members' aesthetic experience. *Human Relations, 55*(7), 821–840.

Townsend, K., McDonald, P., & Cathcart, A. (2016). Managing flexible work arrangements in small not-for-profit firms: The influence of organisational size, financial constraints and workforce characteristics. *The International Journal of Human Resource Management, 28*(14), 2085–2107.

Van Echtelt, P. E., Glebbeek, A. C., & Lindenberg, S. M. (2006). The new lumpiness of work: Explaining the mismatch between actual and preferred working hours. *Work, Employment and Society, 20*(3), 493–512.

Van Marrewijk, A. (2010). The beauty and the beast: The embodied experience of two corporate buildings. In A. Van Marrewijk & D. Yanow (Eds.), *Organizational spaces. Rematerializing the workaday world* (pp. 96–115). Cheltenham: Edward Elgar Publishing.

Van Marrewijk, A., & Yanow, D. (Eds.). (2010). *Organizational spaces: Rematerializing the workaday world.* Cheltenham: Edward Elgar Publishing.

Van Steenbergen, E. F., van der Ven, C., Peeters, M. C. W., & Taris, T. W. (2018). Transitioning towards new ways of working: Do job demands, job resources, burnout, and engagement change? *Psychological Reports, 121*(4), 736–766.

Veldhoen, E. (2004). *The art of working.* The Hague: Sdu Uitgevers.

Vince, R., & Broussine, M. (1996). Paradox, defense and attachment: Accessing and working with emotions and relations underlying organizational change. *Organization Studies, 17*(1), 1–21.

Wasserman, V. (2011). To be (alike) or not to be (at all): Aesthetic isomorphism in organisational spaces. *International. Journal of Work Organization and Emotion, 4*(1), 22–41.

Wasserman, V., & Frenkel, M. (2011). Organizational aesthetics: Caught between identity regulation and culture jamming. *Organization Science, 22*(2), 503–521.

Wasserman, V., & Frenkel, M. (2015). Spatial work in between glass ceilings and glass walls: Gender-class intersectionality and organizational aesthetics. *Organization Studies, 36*(11), 1485–1505.

Wohlers, C., & Hertel, G. (2017). Choosing where to work at work—Towards a theoretical model of benefits and risks of activity-based flexible offices. *Ergonomics, 60*(4), 467–486.

Zhang, Z., Spicer, A., & Hancock, P. (2008). Hyper-organizational space in the work of J. G. Ballard. *Organization, 15*(6), 889–910.

12

Beyond Flexibility: Confronting Conceived and Lived Spaces of New Ways of Working

Grégory Jemine, Sophie Fauconneau-Dufresne, François Pichault, and Giseline Rondeaux

Introduction

Over the last decade, a strong managerial interest has grown for projects aiming at modernizing workspaces and work practices in various third-sector organizations. These projects, clustered under the label "New Ways of Working" (NWW), commonly involve an ambition to redesign organizational space (De Leede, 2017; Kingma, 2018). This chapter holds that all NWW projects share a strikingly similar conception of organizational space, to the point that, when one speaks of an "NWW workspace", it has become relatively easy for an informed observer to get an idea about what the characteristics of such a workspace might be. Most

G. Jemine (✉) • S. Fauconneau-Dufresne • F. Pichault • G. Rondeaux
Université de Liège, Liège, Belgium
e-mail: gjemine@uliege.be; f.pichault@uliege.be; g.rondeaux@uliege.be

N. Mitev et al. (eds.), *New Ways of Working*, Technology, Work and Globalization,
https://doi.org/10.1007/978-3-030-61687-8_12

often, NWW projects feature open spaces, non-attributed desks, and particular care for workspace design in general. A new ideal-type of space seems to emerge, which represents a new standard in contemporary workspace design that is often referred to as "agility", "modernity", or "flexibility". As a consequence, in several sectors and companies, we observe a paradigm shift from traditional space allocation—linked to people's job and status—to fluid, activity-based, deterritorialized, and horizontal forms of space organization (Blok, Groenesteijn, Van den Berg, & Vink, 2011; Vos & van der Voordt, 2002).

Although this transition has been hinted in many papers exploring NWW projects, little is actually known about how those normative conceptions of space are translated into projects of organizational change. Moreover, few studies have attempted to compare the discursive and "conceived" spaces of NWW with the concrete and "lived" workspaces resulting from the deployment of NWW projects (Lefebvre, 1991). Therefore, our aim is to question the translation process of a discursive ideal type of space into concrete devices and practices in organizations. First, the ideal-type of workspace carried out by NWW promoters will be described. We argue that this ideal-type is structured around four key dimensions that are deterritorialization (space does not belong to particular individuals), differentiation (space is separated in zones that have their own specific purpose), fluidity (space is inhabited by mobile users), and horizontalization (space is devoid of any hierarchical symbol). Second, this chapter offers a longitudinal and comparative investigation of two companies which have deployed this ideal-type through a change project involving a complete revamping of their workspaces. Building on the widely accepted claim that change management is a determining factor weighing on a project's outcome, the choice has been made to select two case studies which have adopted radically different approaches to change. In a third part, we examine how employees reacted to their newly redefined workspaces, and how their actual practices in their "lived space" (Lefebvre, 1991) may differ from the discursive ideal-type of NWW.

The Ideal-Typical Workspace of NWW

In line with previous research on the matter (Kingma, 2018), we hold that, despite local variations that may promote some features over others, NWW discourses generally entail homogenous elements of normative nature about how organizations should design their workspaces. The ideal-type suggested in this chapter draws both on managerial texts, through which ideas about how organizational workspace should be designed are first formulated, and scientific insights and studies of existing NWW projects. On this basis, we suggest that NWW conveys a four-dimensional ideal-type of space that builds on deterritorialization, activity-based work, fluidity, and horizontalization.

The first of those dimensions, which we have, in line with the works of Léon (2010), labeled "deterritorialization", relates to the abolition of a relation of ownership between individuals and specific areas of the workspace. In the eyes of the promoters of NWW, the attribution of specific places, zones, or offices to dedicated individuals or teams is a practice that has to be questioned and should ideally be discontinued (Creighton, 2014; Van Koetsveld & Kamperman, 2011). To designate this abolition phenomenon of designated territories, NWW promoters commonly refer to more fashionable labels such as "flex desk" or "flexible desking". Many NWW projects that have been studied by academics have featured a move towards such deterritorialized layouts of workspaces, albeit to different degrees (Kingma, 2018; Lansdale, Parkin, Austin, & Baguey, 2011).

In the managerial literature on NWW, the argument that the entirety of the workspace should belong to all employees was initially founded on economic motivations. It is even common for NWW promoters to openly admit that moving towards flex desk solutions may result in a considerable financial gain for companies (Van Koetsveld & Kamperman, 2011). However, through the years, managers and consultants have attempted to demonstrate how such deterritorialized workspaces could also benefit employees, notably through a discourse advocating workspace differentiation. It has become commonplace in NWW projects to design the workspace as being a set of "focus zones", "bubbles", "collaboration rooms", "touchdowns", and "brainstorm rooms", among others.

The term "activity-based workplace" has been coined to designate such environments (Hoendervanger, De Been, Van Yperen, Mobach, & Albers, 2016). A common argument to be found in the NWW literature is that such differentiation of the workplace allows for employees to choose a working spot that best suits their current needs and is in accordance with the task they are doing (Van Koetsveld & Kamperman, 2011; Wyllie, Greene, Nagrath, & Town, 2012).

This emphasis on activity-based working and on the diversity of spatial arrangements allowed authors to distinguish NWW projects from former attempts to implement "bare" flex-desking solutions. As we mentioned, it is hard to see how the deterritorialization of the workspace in itself could hold any advantages for the employees. Academic literature has repeatedly emphasized that such "flexible desking" solutions were perceived negatively by the workers and had a series of negative consequences on them (Lansdale et al., 2011; Léon, 2010). It is indeed difficult to see why employees would rejoice to be deprived from their own space and forced to move from one workstation to another if every workstation has the same characteristics. Attempts to move towards "flexible desking" environments have therefore received a fair share of criticism and have been described as solutions that were solely motivated by financial considerations. However, the intent of NWW promoters was to demonstrate that the equation could change as soon as the workplace was depicted not as a sum of identical and non-attributed workstations, but rather as a collection of working zones conceived to best suit the various activities of the workers (Van Koetsveld & Kamperman, 2011). In NWW managerial books and texts, the combination of workspace deterritorialization and differentiation is depicted as a "win-win" solution that is satisfactory for both the employer and the employees.

A third dimension of the NWW ideal-type of workspace emerged as a somewhat mechanical result of the two first. A deterritorialized and diversified workspace can only work at one fundamental condition: its inhabitants have to be mobile. The very logic of "activity-based" working is that employees are supposed to travel from one workstation to another, depending on what they have to do. The workspace itself should become fluid, made of ongoing and continuous movement. What is a condition for the system to operate has often been depicted by NWW promoters as an "opportunity" or an "advantage" for the workers: employees have now the "valuable" possibility to be highly mobile and work "anywhere" depending on their preferences and needs (Bijl, 2011; Van Koetsveld & Kamperman, 2011).

Those three dimensions—deterritorialization, differentiation, and fluidity—form a consistent and characteristic set of principles that lie at the heart of the ideal-typical workspace of NWW. However, the survey of the NWW managerial literature reveals a fourth dimension, which we call the "horizontalization" of the workplace. To introduce this last dimension, let us recall that the initial conceptions of NWW were not primarily concerned with workspace design. Pioneer texts and books on NWW also emphasized cultural and managerial transformations of organizations (Bijl, 2011; Gates & Rasmus, 2005). Those authors claimed that symbolic separations between managers and employees should be abolished because they were unnecessary remainders of an old-fashioned hierarchical culture that was characteristic of obsolete bureaucracies (Bijl, 2011). NWW is therefore associated with a managerial project consisting in flattening hierarchies and empowering workers. With this in mind, the early designers of NWW projects suggested that everyone should comply with the new workspace rules of non-attributed offices, including the top managers. Some CEOs even willingly "played the game" of the activity-based working and argued the importance of "lead by example" in order to demonstrate the merit of their new workspace (Flamend, 2011). NWW thus promotes a horizontal vision of the workspace, in which rules are observed for everyone, regardless of the hierarchical position and status.

A four-dimensional ideal-type of the workspace that is commonly found in the NWW literature has now been described in greater length. We argue that the four identified dimensions—deterritorialization, differentiation, fluidity, and horizontalization—are constitutive of a set of discourses that prompt companies to implement NWW workspaces. Yet, how companies which claim to commit to an NWW project translate those dimensions into their actual workspaces remains an underexplored question. In organizations who have carried out NWW projects, to what extent is this ideal-type of workspace faithfully reproduced through and embedded in the concrete material settings and in the lived space?

It is through a process of organizational change that normative ideas on how space should be designed are translated into material workspaces. There is an abundant literature that emphasizes the crucial role of change management in the translation process of ideas into settings and practices (e.g. Czarniawska & Sevon, 2011; Kerber & Bueno, 2005; Pichault, 2013). According to this literature, the decisions and activities undertaken by local actors during the change process are likely to have a substantial impact on the project's outcome. To account for the translation of an ideal-type into material settings, this chapter will consider two dimensions of change management: sensegiving and enrolment. Sensegiving may be defined as the practices of strategic actors such as top management teams aiming to build and disseminate specific interpretations or "visions" within organizations (Gioia & Chittipeddi, 1991). We further borrow the concept of "enrolment" from Callon (1986) to specifically target the actors' attempts to allocate roles to others. Enrolment involves attempts to transform the interests of other actors in order to enhance alignment and increase convergence around the change (Callon & Law, 1982). In change management theories, both sensegiving and enrolment are described as practices that are likely to weigh on the project's outcome (Pichault, 2013). Based on a longitudinal and comparative study of two Belgian companies, the ambition of this chapter is to consider the translation of the NWW ideal-type of workspace into concrete material settings, by contrasting the cases on their change management process, and more specifically, on their sensegiving and enrolment practices.

Methodology

Data Collection

This chapter relies on a qualitative study of two Belgian cases that are part of a larger sample of organizations that committed to an NWW project and were studied by our research team. We deliberately selected those two organizations from our sample for two reasons. First, we assumed that the obvious contrast in their way of introducing and conducting an NWW project would ultimately result in two very different forms of lived space. We expected the change management process to be decisive in the way the ideal-type of space advocated by NWW promoters was progressively embodied into concrete spatial devices and patterns, and, ultimately, would weigh on the appropriation process of the space by the users. Secondly, in both cases, arrested and lived forms of space were observable, as the projects were implemented several years ago. We were able, in both instances, to gather data on the change management process on the one hand and on the local strategies of space appropriation in stabilized workplaces on the other hand.

Our first case study is a Belgian insurance company of approximately 4100 employees, hereinafter referred to as BIC. Our second case study is a large transport company which employs approximately 8000 workers that we will name BELTRANS. In both organizations, we performed a qualitative analysis based on observation periods of stabilized spaces (respectively 10 weeks and 20 weeks), which allowed us to account for the actual interactions between users and space in stabilized NWW environments. We also conducted semi-structured interviews with project leaders, strategic managers, middle managers, and employees (respectively 43 and 45). In both cases, those interviews spanned between two years (2014–2016 for BELTRANS) and three years (2014–2017 for BIC) in order to cover both the change management process (through interviews with project teams and top managers) and the perceptions of the lived space (of team managers and employees). The authors also relied on some internal documents—such as PowerPoint presentations, internal reports, work documents, or minutes of meetings—for complementing their dataset.

Data Analysis

Data were first summarized in the form of a separate, chronological narrative of each case. To facilitate cross-cases comparison, those narratives were ordered in three parts:

- the identification of the local, discursive ideal-type of NWW in each case (part 1);
- the activities through which the ideal-type was progressively turned into a project of organizational change, and the mechanisms of "enrolment" (Callon, 1986) that were deployed to do so (part 2);
- the employees' modes of space appropriation once the new workplace was designed and accessible (part 3).

The first part of the description aims to capture the ideal-type of NWW as it was initially designed by top management. What are the managerial intents in our cases, and how do they relate to the four-dimensional ideal-type that we have proposed earlier in the chapter? Interviews with key strategic actors (HR Director, strategic advisors, project leaders) allowed us to grasp the initial expectations of top management teams as well as their own ideal vision of the future workspace of their company. In the second part of the description, further information is given regarding the progressive creation of a project structure that was established to deploy an NWW workspace. A thematic analysis of the interviews with project leaders and project team members was performed in order to elaborate on the strategies deployed by top management to persuade others of the necessity to design new, "NWW-based" workspaces. We identified various attempts from specific actors and groups to supply "workable interpretations" that would weigh on the change management process (Gioia & Chittipeddi, 1991). In the third part, we provide in-depth descriptions of what could be named the "lived space"—the employees and local managers' behaviors and strategies within their new workspace. To that end, we relied on a set of interviews with those actors as well as on data coming from in situ observations.

Once the narratives of our cases (BIC and BELTRANS respectively) were completed, we compared our datasets with each other in a three-step process. First, we began to examine the local relevance of the theoretical ideal-type proposed above for both cases. To what extent do the projects developed by the two investigated companies share this ideal-typical conception of the workplace? Second, we briefly described change management processes with a focus on our two key dimensions: sensegiving and enrolment. For each case, we accounted for the efforts dedicated to sensegiving activities, to the work deployed by top managers to convince the rest of the organization that NWW were necessary. We then examined the various mechanisms of enrolment (such as project groups, communication activities, and enrolment attempts) that resulted from those sensegiving efforts. Finally, we analyzed the strategies deployed by employees and middle managers to reinvest their workspace in both cases, in order to compare the discursive and ideal-typical conception of space with the concrete perceptions of lived space.

A Comparison Between Two NWW Projects: Local Discourses, Sensegiving, and Enrolment

The Emergence of NWW at BIC

BIC is an insurance company employing approximately 4100 employees in Belgium. Back in 2010, a strategic reflection regarding the future organization of the company was undertaken by the Executive Board due to a combination of several factors. As the leasing terms of the two main buildings of the company, subject to a rental contract, were coming to an end, it became necessary for BIC to consider relocating its activities. Exploratory studies showed that only 58% of the working space was effectively occupied every day, suggesting that the company could drastically shrink the space needed by relying on a combination of remote working and dynamic workplaces. Growing internal and external managerial discourses denouncing the "unattractive" and "old-fashioned" image of the insurance sector as a whole also contributed to building a shared agreement among BIC top managers around the "need to change". BIC's executive committee eventually couched its managerial expectations—relocating, reducing costs, and improving the company's image—in a discourse denunciating the "old" ways of working and promoting "new" ones, hence justifying the need for the company to commit to a transformation project that was soon labeled "NWW":

> *It began with this building opportunity, but at the same time, the insurance world was changing quickly, with a new generation on the labor market, new technological possibilities (…) And our HR director immediately said, this is an excellent opportunity, not for a relocation, but for rethinking how we work. That's how it started.* (HR Strategic Advisor)

The conception of space inherent to the NWW project developed at BIC turned out to be particularly faithful to the ideal-type that was described in the introduction of this chapter. Following the strategic decision to reduce the overall working space for economic reasons, BIC's project leaders opted for promoting hot-desking and activity-based conceptions of space, and actively emphasized the new opportunities of mobility and fluidity offered by such designs. For purposes of space rationalization, workstations were designed on the basis of what was called a "0.7 ratio"—meaning that there would be seven workstations for ten employees. This led the project teams to design shared and non-attributed spaces and to edict a formal rule stating that "the whole workspace is at the disposal of all users, both employees and managers".[1] Users, then, were expected to be mobile, that is, to frequently move around in space for realizing their tasks. The workspace was split in "zones" with various properties: "quiet zones", "collaboration zones", "dynamic rooms", "decision rooms", and so on,[2] between which all users were expected to navigate depending on their tasks at hand. In this conception, space in its entirety was seen as a collective property of the whole workforce, hence devoid of territorial affectations. In other words, the workspace belonged to no one and to everyone at the same time. The same was true for the managers, up to the chief executive officer of the company who, in the new building, was not supposed to have his own office anymore. As such, BIC's case illustrates nicely the four dimensions of the ideal-type of space inherent to NWW discourses.

[1] Source: Internal document from the company: "The NWW at BIC" (2014).

[2] Source: Internal document from the company: "The NWW at BIC" (2014).

Sensegiving and Enrolment Practices at BIC

At BIC, sensegiving practices of the top managers were numerous. An initial project team, led by the HR director of the company, defined three poles constitutive of the NWW project: the "Bricks", the "Bytes", and the "Behaviors". This formulation around those "3B" allowed the project teams to delineate three distinct fields of expertise and to enroll numerous actors (around 40 people joined the project teams) with various skills and knowledge. Those "3B" teams would, in turn, be in charge of the effective deployment of the NWW project. The Bricks team, made of space designers and building specialists, was in charge of creating an "open", "flexible", and "activity-based" workplace. IT specialists gathered in the Bytes team would develop new digital tools to support remote working. Finally, the HR experts and the communication specialist forming the Behaviors team had to promote a "cultural change" in line with the new working environments. The 3Bs further had to coordinate with each other on transversal topics such as the introduction of remote working in the company or the reduction of paper use and storage.

To embody the managerial aspirations described in the previous section, discourses promoting four principles—"autonomy", "trust", "connectivity", and "results"—were actively publicized by the project teams[3]:

> *Behaviors is what matters the most to us. We do not want a Bricks & Bytes project only, that is, a modern building. It must become clear for everyone that we want a cultural change. That includes other attitudes, new conceptions of what managing a team means, autonomous and responsible people ... That will take months, even years.* (Behaviors team member)

Autonomy was defined as the opportunity for all employees to work "independently from time and space". For its part, trust was from the start promoted as a key principle that should prevail in relationships between managers and employees. The ambition of connectivity underlined the necessity for all workers to rely on the technological tools at their disposal to work remotely. Finally, the project leaders emphasized

[3] Source: Internal document from the company: "The NWW at BIC" (2014).

the necessity for all teams to evolve towards objective-based methods of control. Most of the promotion work around those four principles was achieved by the Behaviors team, who multiplied training programs, information sessions, and explanatory documents in order to disseminate those aspirations within the organization. What NWW meant at BIC was therefore rigorously framed during the change process. The combination of meaningful formulations (such as the 3B), of a heavy project structure, and of common discourses and shared beliefs formed the basics of the sensegiving activities undertaken by BIC.

Simultaneously, strong mechanisms of enrolment were deployed, with a particular awareness from the project leaders of the crucial role played by local managers:

> *Ultimately, what we are trying to accomplish here can only work if team managers are buying it. Their support is of prime importance for the NWW to come alive and last through time.* (Behaviors team member)

A detailed training plan—called a "roadmap"—was defined for both managers and employees. This roadmap entailed a "journey" involving several mandatory steps for all members of the company, such as kick-off meetings, workshops, IT training, and discussion sessions.[4] "Team agreements" sessions were further organized by the project teams. Collectively drafted during team meetings supervised by a member of the Behaviors team, those "team agreements" consisted in a charter outlining the general principles relative to the work organization that would take place in the future building. Each operational team was thus invited to plan to establish internal rules related to remote working, to its functioning in a flex desk environment, and so on. Furthermore, 60 ambassadors were designed among the employees to act as relays between the project teams and the operational teams. In addition, external coaches were recruited to provide each team manager with individualized support throughout the process. Finally, an interactive platform was set up, on which employees and managers could raise issues with their workspace, ask questions, or send requests. With the addition of all those mechanisms aimed at

[4] Source: Internal document from the company: "Behaviors Training Plan" (2014).

enrolling both employees and local managers in the transformation process, it can now be asserted that both sensegiving and enrolment practices at BIC have been numerous and carefully designed by top management.

The Emergence of NWW at BELTRANS

Created in 1954, BELTRANS employs around 7000 workers at the national level, including 700 employees in its head office, where the field research was conducted. In the early 2000s and under the influence of their CEO, BELTRANS committed to a change project in which the primary objective was to adopt the principles of "New Public Management" (see e.g. McLaughlin, Ferlie, & Osborne, 2005, 19–26). This process was designed to allow the company to better respond to the changing context of the new century and to offer a better service to customers. The project was followed a few years later by a decision to move the headquarters to a renovated building. This change was made possible by the combination of two factors: the poor state of the previous building and the wish to revitalize the company by giving it a more "modern" image, more able to attract qualified candidates and to respond to the customers' expectations in terms of efficiency.

At BELTRANS, the ambition was to design each floor of the new building with large open spaces and non-attributed desks, as well as to diversify the workspace with small meeting rooms (called "cocoons") and coffee corners. The new building, described by the project holders in the press as the "symbol of a new dynamic" and a "concrete evidence of the company's ambition", was designed as a hot-desking and an activity-based workplace. Because space was planned on the basis of a 0.8 ratio, implying eight workstations for ten workers, employees' mobility became a key objective of the project teams. The strategic management also aimed to lay the foundations of a new company culture towards more leadership and performance, as well as towards new organizational modalities such as participative management, increased employee autonomy, project-based activities, flexible working hours, and the systematic virtualization of documents. In accordance with the NWW discourses, hierarchical symbols were, for the most part, suppressed from the organizational space, with the exception of the CEO and the Deputy CEO who kept the privilege of having an attributed office.

Sensegiving and Enrolment Practices at BELTRANS

During the planning phase of the new headquarters, a project team was formed around a financial manager (who became the project leader), two managers from the HR department (including the director of human resources), a manager in charge of communication, and two engineers. This project team became the main vector of sensegiving within the company, and emphasized the necessity to embark the whole company into an NWW project:

> *We must make the most of this opportunity to initiate a significant change of corporate culture (…) We believe that the concept of hot-desking best suits the new values of BELTRANS: enthusiasm, responsibility, commitment, open-mindedness, transparency, and team spirit.* (Project leader)

Persuasive and top-down communication was plentiful and aimed to convince all BELTRANS employees of the benefits of the new workspace organization (such as "greater autonomy" or "flexibility"). Brochures were distributed to the employees with images and description of the new facilities, and internal emails kept everyone informed of the changes to come, with a particular emphasis on the "new philosophy" that the relocation would represent.

Enrolment practices, however, remained scarce. Although the change towards a flex-desk space setting had great implications in terms of working habits and culture change, workers were not consulted during the planning phase. A few information sessions were organized, but remained mostly unidirectional and driven by the upper management, with little room left for dialogue:

> *What bothered us is that we were not consulted. People decided everything on our behalf but they didn't know how we really worked. It could have been discussed with us preventively.* (BELTRANS employee)

Team managers were never officially given any specific role by the project team and were not enrolled as supports for the project. They were drawn into this process at the very end, just before the relocation, to deal with operational issues such as the number of seats and storage needed by their teams. While BELTRANS' case illustrates a diversity of sensegiving activities driven by the top management, those activities remained essentially unidirectional and were not aimed to gain the support of middle managers and employees. Enrolment practices, in sum, remained minimal and rare.

Comparing the Change Management Processes

Change processes at BIC and BELTRANS feature intriguing similarities as well as sharp differences, which are summarized in Table 12.1. First,

Table 12.1 A comparison between BIC and BELTRANS processes of NWW implementation (authors' own)

Case 1: BIC	Case 2: BELTRANS
Local discourses and ideal-type of space	
Relocation and space rationalization	Relocation and space rationalization
Workspace split into "zones"	Workspace split into "zones"
No one has his or her own office any longer	No one has his or her own office anymore (besides the CEO and the Deputy CEO)
Sensegiving practices	
Production and promotion of "guiding principles" (autonomy, responsibility, trust, results)	Production and promotion of "guiding principles" (autonomy, flexibility, proximity, transparency)
Intensive communication via brochures, intranet, and internal emails	Intensive communication via brochures, intranet, and internal emails
Enrolment practices	
"Bricks, Bytes, Behaviors" project teams	Multidisciplinary project team
Roadmap, team agreements, workshops and training sessions, ambassadors, coaches, interactive platform	Workers neither involved nor consulted
Middle managers were strongly involved	Middle managers were not given any role

strong parallels may be drawn between the conceived space at BELTRANS, the conceived space at BIC, and in the ideal-type built in the introduction of this chapter. Indeed, in both cases, there is an ambition to implement non-attributed workspaces (deterritorialization) which will replace traditional workstations with "modern" and "mixed" settings with diverse properties (differentiation). Discourses promoting flexibility, autonomy, and mobility are highly emphasized at BIC and at BELTRANS (fluidity), while hierarchical privileges in space are for the most part abolished (horizontalization). Both cases confirm the appropriateness of the ideal-type suggested for characterizing NWoW projects. Additionally, sensegiving practices are relatively similar. On either side, there is an explicit emphasis on a set of principles (autonomy, flexibility, etc.) that are supposed to become the leading principles of the change project, as well as intensive actions of communication undertaken by the project teams.

By contrast, the analysis reveals striking differences in the way to design and implement an NWW project. In the case of BIC, the project was mostly driven by the HR director of the company, while BELTRANS choose a financial manager to be the project leader. The insurance company enrolled around 40 actors who were split into several specific project teams, while the transportation company continued to work around a unique and centralized project team. At BIC, an impressive arsenal of enrolment devices was deployed, involving a roadmap for all departments of the company, multiple workshops, and training sessions, the development of a platform, and the recruitment of "ambassadors" and "coaches". None of the above was observed at BELTRANS, where workers and middle managers remained periodically informed but neither involved nor consulted.

In conclusion, according to our analysis of the change management process in both companies, we should expect the translation process of the four-dimensional ideal-type of workspace to be more successful at BIC than at BELTRANS. To the extent that enrolment practices were given much more attention in the first case, workers and middle managers should have better internalized and accepted the NWW ideal-type when the relocation occurred. In other words, we expect the gap between discursive space and lived space to be more important at BELTRANS, in which the change management process appeared flawed in comparison with change management standards, than at BIC, where workers and team managers were repeatedly exposed to the discourses surrounding the conceived space prior to the relocation. In the following section, we depart from each of the four dimensions of the NWW ideal-type of workspace successively and examine how they translated into the actual workspaces of both companies.

Findings: From Discursive Space to Lived Space: Comparing Space Appropriation Mechanisms

From Deterritorialization to Colonization

Once the relocation occurred, workers at BIC and BELTRANS suddenly became confronted with the "lived" space and able to make use of this space, as well as to divert from the usages promoted by the project teams to their own advantage. Concrete manifestations of individual interests and power games became visible as local forms of space appropriation began to develop. At BIC, those effects had been anticipated and planned for more than one year before the relocation. Fearing that employees would oppose the loss of their personal desk or office, the project teams had organized multiple information and training sessions. However, it quickly appeared that, although the new workspace was formally supposed to be unattributed and therefore devoid of any territorial marking, the actors managed to recreate invisible boundaries over time:

> *I would not really consider sitting on the right side of the floor. Well, you know, people working there are mostly from [department A]. And our department [B] usually sit on the left side. I already tried to go there, but you feel like a stranger.* (BIC employee, two months after the relocation)

Even if workstations were not individually attributed any longer, portions of the floors seemed to remain collectively owned by specific teams or departments. Language differences also contributed to recreate new territories:

> *French-speaking people go to a table, and Dutch-speaking people go to another one. Well, no one will throw rocks at you if you break that rule, but it seems like people gather like this naturally.* (BIC local manager, nine months after the relocation)

Similar effects were observed at BELTRANS, where, although the linguistic separation was not an issue, employees actively worked to recreate new, informal territories, mostly based on portions of the floor. Behaviors (such as frequently staying at the same place) and visual markers (such as a green plant on the corner of a desk) contributed to recreate divisions in a workspace that was thought and designed as freed of any territorial boundaries in the first place. Over time, workers both at BIC and BELTRANS managed to re-territorialize their workspace, by informally bypassing the formal rule of space non-attribution.

From Differentiation to Operational Constraints

In both companies, workspace design was driven by the ambition to diversify space settings through the creation of various zones—such as focus zones, "bubbles", collaboration zones, "coffee corners", or "dynamic rooms". Each of those zones was supposed to serve a specific purpose (facilitating discussion, allowing phone calls, holding a confidential meeting, and so on). Employees were expected to move from one zone to another according to the task at hand, hence participating in the development of an "activity-based" workplace, in which activity would become the primary factor taken into account for deciding which workstation to occupy. Our analysis of BIC's and BELTRANS' lived spaces, however, reveals that such an activity-based *modus operandi* remained far from achieved.

At BIC, the differentiation of the workspace did not make much sense for employees and middle managers. An overwhelming majority of the employees are insurance agents who were required to take (and make) phone calls at any time during their working day. Consequently, they at first refused to settle in focus zones (in which phone use was formally forbidden) and in collaboration zones, and massively stay in the standard work zones—named "semi-focus". Once those standard zones became overcrowded, some of them decided to move towards the focus zones, but began to use them as if the specific rules of focus zones did not apply: they spoke in a loud voice and did not hesitate to pick up their phone. A general consensus arose around the inevitability of receiving phone calls, and as a result, the project teams' ambition to create a diversified workplace was overshadowed by operational constraints:

> *If there is no more room in the semi-focus zones, you have no other choice but to come here and take your phone calls just like everyone does. We know that this is supposed to be a focus zone. But no one really cares if you give a phone call here. Well, with a few exceptions. But what I mean is, you have to be available for your customers, and everyone in the company is well aware of that.* (BIC's employees, two months after the relocation)

At BELTRANS, it is the work zones' attractiveness and comfort that prevailed over their intended use. Workers who had the opportunity to arrive early at work rushed to the workstations that were considered the best—close to the windows, and far from the internal corridors or from noise sources (such as elevators) in general. Settling in a specific zone quickly became not a conscious choice to perform a given activity according to the tasks at hand, but rather a default choice for the employees who were repeatedly forced to sit wherever room was available. The "race" for the workstations considered as being the most desirable quickly became a prevalent issue for most employees, which emphasized the primacy of comfort and general properties of the workspace (lightning, acoustics, temperature, etc.) over activity-based considerations.

From Fluidity to Inertia

One of the most interesting issues we witnessed as BIC teams relocated to the new building was the "double screen" debate. Most employees were used to work using two screens, one for consulting the customer request or complaint, another for inputting data in the system. However, while designing the new workspace, the project teams had deliberately omitted to install two screens at some places—such as in meeting rooms, collaboration zones, and parts of concentration zones—to promote a fluid and diversified conception of the material space. Frustration grew quickly among employees who argued that the lack of screens made their work extremely uncomfortable. Local managers backed up their claims, arguing that productivity would decrease as a result of those inadequate working conditions:

> *It was so stupid. We all need two screens to do our job, it has always been like that. Like, everyone in the company knows that but them [the project teams]!* (BIC's team manager, two months after the relocation)

Faced with such discontent, the project teams decided to give in and add extra screens. However, when reflecting on those events some weeks later, they did not appear to be convinced by their own decision:

> *If you ask me, well, I cannot believe that people really need two screens all the time. For reading your emails, you do not need two screens. So, maybe we overestimated the need of our employees to move around.* (Project member, two months after the relocation)

A similar issue occurred at BELTRANS. Because most workstations were only equipped with one screen, several workers sent requests to the Internal Prevention and Protection Service (IPPS) in order to request an additional screen. Those requests, however, were received by the IPPS employees as attempts to avoid the mobility and the fluidity enforced by the new workspace:

> *Some workers are asking for multiple screens, citing medical reasons such as eye comfort and the like. But over here, we all know that their real goal is to obtain a fixed, attributed desk.* (BELTRANS IPPS employee)

At BELTRANS, the ideal-type of a fluid workspace in which workers frequently move around and switch workstations according to their needs was strongly contested and appeared undesirable and unproductive in the eyes of most employees. An interesting illustration of silent opposition was found in the operating mode of one specific team, which decided to switch places on a daily basis and on a predefined order:

> *It is simple, we always sit together, but each day, we just move to the workstation on our right. By acting like that, we are not at the same place every day, so we respect the principles of the new building. And it also allows us to work together.* (BELTRANS employee)

Empirical illustrations from BIC and BELTRANS cases indicate that some employees are actively resisting the fluidity imperative of their new workplace. Simply stated, they appear to be reluctant to move around during their working day. Instead, employees require and recreate stability and inertia by asking specific arrangements of their workstations or by pretending to be mobile.

From Horizontalization to Stratification

As we mentioned already, the NWW projects at BIC and BELTRANS explicitly aimed to abolish distinctive signs of hierarchy, as no one in the company had a designated workspace in the new building any longer. However, in both cases, managers attempted to reclaim informal ownership over some places, which was not to all employees' liking. At BIC, once the relocation occurred, several managers gathered together in specific spaces in the collaboration zone, although they were obviously not collaborating at all. After a few days, the employees ironically referred to one of these zones as "the managers' table", while carefully avoiding to sit near to the same table. Some employees began to complain to the project teams that their superiors were not obeying the "rules" of the new workplace, and the project teams promptly reminded the managers that they had to move around and to sit elsewhere. While most local managers did comply over time, some directors were still resisting several months after the relocation:

> *Our director has its own place, and his two secretaries as well. You cannot sit there. No one does. And yes, it is against the NWW project, and yes, the project*

team is informed! But it is a director, so … When you see that your director can do whatever he wants to regarding NWW, you are reminded that hierarchy remains hierarchy. (Local manager, nine months after the relocation)

At BELTRANS, managers began to overuse the "bubbles"—the small rooms initially planned for hosting meetings between two or three people—by staying there all day long without being involved in any meeting. The managers argued that their responsibilities and the nature of their work justified spending more time in quiet and isolated areas. The recreation of the hierarchy in the workspace was even, to a certain extent, supported by employees:

In an organization like BELTRANS, I think it's natural for senior managers to have access to a private area of their own. (BELTRANS employee)

Those observable behaviors tend to indicate a process of "re-stratification" of the workspace, in which the hierarchical symbols and signs, which the project teams had attempted to banish from the organization, were recreated by the actors themselves. The ambition of the NWW project to flatten the factors related to hierarchical position only partly succeeded. Even deprived of their own offices, directors and managers could recreate specific privileges in their new workspace.

Discussion

Two major conclusions can be drawn from our empirical observations. First, the analysis of BIC's and BELTRANS' lived spaces concurs to illustrate the gap that exists between the normative aspects of the conceived space and the lived spaces resulting from organizational change projects. Confronting the NWW ideal-type of space with the actual practices of space appropriation by the actors reveals a striking contrast that is summarized in (Table 12.2). To a large extent, workers at BIC and BELTRANS have rejected the redefinition of their workspace that the project teams attempted to promote. By doing so, they have recreated their own lived

Table 12.2 From the ideal-typical space to the lived spaces of NWW (authors' own)

Ideal-type of space	Empirical illustrations of contestation	Lived space
Deterritorialized	Appropriation of floors Linguistic separations	Colonized
Differentiated	Misuse of zones Operational considerations	Constrained
Fluid	Double-screen event Unwilling operators	Inert
Horizontal	Visible symbols of status Systematic occupation of space	Stratified

space, of which the dimensions radically differ from what is usually encouraged and advertised by NWW promoters.

We suggest that the four dimensions of the ideal-type of space were renegotiated and contested by team managers and employees. Far from being deterritorialized, the new workspaces at BIC and BELTRANS are subject to efforts of colonization, through which specific teams and departments attempt to retake control of specific portions of the space. The uses made of the different zones that form the workspace appear to be determined not by the tasks at hand, but by operational constraints such as the arrival time at the office or the zones' availability. The ideal of fluidity and hyper-mobility has not come to fruition, since employees adopt stationary behaviors and are for a large part unwilling to move around during their working day. Finally, far from being devoid of all signs and symbols of hierarchical differentiation, the new workspaces are subject to opportunistic attempts of managers to recreate more or less visible forms of stratification.

These observations concur with pre-existing studies that have mentioned resistance behaviors and practices in recently implemented NWW workspaces (Brunia, De Been, & Van der Voordt, 2016; Gorgievski, van der Voordt, van Herpen, & van Akkeren, 2010; Kingma, 2018). However, the causes underlying those behaviors have remained either unexplored or largely attributed to missteps and blunders in the change management process (Brunia et al., 2016; Moll & Leede, 2017). For instance, Moll and De Leede argue that "reducing resistance and seeking support by relevant people" are crucial to "facilitate a successful implementation [of NWW projects]" (2017, 99). This study, while providing extensive information regarding the way the change process was handled, seems to suggest otherwise. Surprisingly, despite two very different ways of conducting the change in the two cases, we witnessed striking homogeneity in the employees' modes of space appropriation in the new working environment. Regardless of the sensegiving activities that had previously been performed, users tended to behave in a much less mobile and flexible way than what was initially expected by the project teams. Eventually, the lived space differed greatly from the conceived space, intended as deterritorialized, differentiated, fluid, and horizontal.

A second major conclusion to draw is therefore that the observable forms of space appropriation do not seem to be related to the sensegiving and enrolment practices deployed by the top management. This observation reminds us that space is essentially a "social product" (Lefebvre, 1991), shaped by the political and social forces at play. Instead of the change management process, what seems to matter the most are the behaviors and the rationalities of the actors living in the work environment, able to achieve strategies and political games while pursuing their interests. Social dynamics, whether horizontal (between employees) or vertical (between employees and managers), ultimately unfold in the lived space. Those results seem to suggest that, because of the unavoidable political restructuration of space, the ideal-type of space depicted in the literature promoting NWW is difficult to translate into actual working environments, and as such, remains essentially discursive and normative.

References

Bijl, D. W. (2011). *Journey towards the new way of working. Creating sustainable performance and joy at work*. Zeewolde, NL: Par CC.

Blok, M. M., Groenesteijn, L., Van den Berg, C., & Vink, P. (2011). New ways of working: A proposed framework and literature review. *Ergonomics and Health Aspects of Work with Computers*, 3–12.

Brunia, S., De Been, I., & Van der Voordt, T. (2016). Accommodating new ways of working: Lessons from best practices and worst cases. *Journal of Corporate Real Estate, 18*(1), 30–47.

Callon, M. (1986). Some elements of a sociology of translation: Domestication of the scallops and the fishermen of St Brieuc Bay. In J. Law (Ed.), *Power, action and belief. A new sociology of knowledge?* (pp. 126–229). London: Routledge & Kegan Paul.

Callon, M., & Law, J. (1982). On interests and their transformation: Enrolment and counter-enrolment. *Social Studies of Science, 12*(4), 615–625.

Creighton, J. (2014, September 28–October 1). *Managing a new way of working environment.* New Ways of Working Symposium, Paris.

Czarniawska, B., & Sevon, G. (2011). *Translating organizational change.* Berlin: Walter de Gruyter.

De Leede, J. (2017). *New ways of working practices: Antecedents and outcomes.* Bingley: Emerald Group Publishing Limited.

Flamend, J. (2011). *Le nouveau monde du travail: l'histoire de Getronics.* 73p. Retrieved from https://docplayer.fr/4518708-Le-nouveau-monde-du-travail-l-histoire-de-getronics.html

Gates, B., & Rasmus, D. (2005). *Digital workstyle: The new world of work.* White Paper. Redmond, WA: Microsoft.

Gioia, D., & Chittipeddi, K. (1991). Sensemaking and sensegiving in strategic change initiation. *Strategic Management Journal, 12*(6), 433–448.

Gorgievski, M., van der Voordt, T., van Herpen, S., & van Akkeren, S. (2010). After the fire: New ways of working in an academic setting. *Facilities, 28*(3/4), 206–224.

Hoendervanger, J., De Been, I., Van Yperen, N., Mobach, M., & Albers, J. (2016). Flexibility in use: Switching behaviour and satisfaction in activity-based work environments. *Journal of Corporate Real Estate, 18*(1), 30–47.

Kerber, K., & Bueno, A. F. (2005). Rethinking organizational change: Reframing the challenge of change management. *Organizational Development Journal, 23*(3), 23–38.

Kingma, S. (2018). New ways of working (NWW): Work space and cultural change in virtualizing organizations. *Culture and Organization, 25*(5), 1–24.

Lansdale, M., Parkin, J., Austin, S., & Baguey, T. (2011). Designing for interaction in research environments. A case study. *Journal of Environmental Psychology, 31*(4), 407–420.

Lefebvre, H. (1991). *The production of space.* Oxford: Blackwell.

Léon, E. (2010). Territorialité et bureaux virtuels: un oxymore. *Annales des Mines—Gérer et Comprendre, 99*, 32–41.

McLaughlin, K., Ferlie, E., & Osborne, S. (Eds.). (2005). *New public management: Current trends and future prospects.* London: Routledge.

Moll, F., & De Leede, J. (2017). Fostering innovation: The influence of new ways of working on innovative work behavior. In D. Leede (Ed.), *New ways of working: Antecedents and outcomes* (pp. 95–143). Bingley: Emerald Group Publishing Limited.

Pichault, F. (2013). *Change management: Towards a polyphonic management.* Paris: De Boeck Superieur.

Van Koetsveld, R., & Kamperman, L. (2011). How flexible workplace strategies can be made successful at the operational level. *Corporate Real Estate Journal, 1*(4), 303–319.

Vos, P., & van der Voordt, T. (2002). Tomorrow's office through today's eyes: Effects of innovation in the working environment. *Journal of Corporate Real Estate, 4*(1), 48–65.

Wyllie, T., Greene, M., Nagrath, R., & Town, A. (2012). *Activity based working.* Working Paper. Sydney: Jones Lang Lasalle. Retrieved from https://www.slideshare.net/MichelleMoore40/jllauactivitybasedworking2012-68352230

13

Transmateriality of Architectural Representation and Perception

Angela Bargenda

Introduction

This chapter aims to establish architecture as a symbolic mediator in organization scholarship. It addresses the complex problem of organizational representation by situating buildings in the arena of identity-giving artifacts. Embedded in specific cultural, social, political, and historical contexts, buildings are reflective of broader extra-organizational parameters. These extrinsic cultural and historical variables are fundamental in the transformation from purely economic to symbolic organizational identity. The contribution of collective social identity provides resources that connect physical materiality with signifying narratives and content.

Taking issue of the visual modalities of architecture to transcribe organizational identity, this chapter develops a research strand that remains "largely unexplored in organization and management research" (Meyer, Höllerer, Jancsary, & Van Leeuwen, 2013, 490). However, in practice,

A. Bargenda (✉)
ESCE International Business School/INSEEC U. Research Center, Paris, France
e-mail: angela.bargenda@esce.fr

N. Mitev et al. (eds.), *New Ways of Working*, Technology, Work and Globalization,
https://doi.org/10.1007/978-3-030-61687-8_13

organizations increasingly mobilize visuality to perpetuate elite power structures (Kerr & Robinson, 2016), project an idiosyncratic identity (Bargenda, 2013, 2014), and increase legitimacy claims (De Vaujany & Vaast, 2016). Artifacts and spatial design legitimize organizations by interrelating social and material spaces into sociomaterial dynamics (Berg & Kreiner, 1992; Yanow, 1995).

As a result of the materiality turn, the interpretability and intentionality of spatial artifacts have regained interest in organization studies. Countering the digitalization of social and organizational processes (Van Dijk, 2012), the renewed emphasis placed on material mediations is situated within the broader debate about the status of materiality. Mostly, the relationships between space and time, built spaces, objects and artifacts, infrastructures and superstructures have been discussed from an ontological perspective (Carlile, Nicolini, Langley, & Tsoukas, 2013; Dameron, Lê, & LeBaron, 2015; Robichaud & Cooren, 2013).

Based on Gagliardi's (1990) symbolic approach, the post-discursive expressions of artifacts generate meaning by means of a culturally coded discourse. Architectural materiality therefore is not discussed here as purely "brick and mortar" materiality, but as a semantic device within broader social relationships. The "generative building" actively contributes to an organization's capacities (Kornberger & Clegg, 2005), providing embodied, subjectified, and interpersonal space experience that occur in organizational space configurations. This "site ontology" (Schatzki, 2005), where the context (a site) and social life interact, performs a sociomaterial symbiosis between material arrangements and human practices. Architecture represents a nexus, which elicits responses from stakeholders at emotional, aesthetic, phenomenological, and cognitive levels.

This chapter thus endeavors to contribute to the understanding of architecture as a symbolic artifact in organizational environments. Architectural space is theorized as a lived experience of physical and social realities, given that we have always been intrinsically spatial beings and active participants in the social construction of our embracing spatialities (Soja, 1996, 1). In this sense, organizations are thought of as "material, spatial ensembles—not just cognitive abstractions" (Clegg, 2010, xvi).

Various methodological approaches will be outlined to provide interpretive grids for a sociomaterial analysis of architecture. To identify the complex processes by which architectural representation translates into ontological meaning for organizations, the inquiry draws on multidisciplinary resources from management and non-management scholarship. The literature review will therefore include references from aesthetics, sociology, architectural theory, and history. Next, bank buildings of classical architecture will be analyzed for their symbolic contents. Some concluding remarks will close this chapter.

Organizational Aesthetics

If aesthetic approaches have become conceptual references for a host of theoretical analyses in organization studies (Taylor & Hansen, 2005), they essentially adopt a post-rational stance, derived from the etymological meaning of *aisthetikos* ("sensitive, sentient"). They imply that aesthetic knowing is mostly different from intellectual realizations (Biehl-Missal, 2011). Centered on the emotionally perceiving subject, aesthetic approaches reject the "dominance of the semiotic in aesthetic theory" (Böhme, 1993, 115). Böhme (1993, 116) conceptualizes the "new aesthetics" as a general theory of aesthetic work, understood as the production of atmospheres. Atmospheres are conceptualized following the eighteenth-century definition of the term as something in the air, an emotional tinge of space, which communicates a feeling to participating subjects. Böhme views architectural atmospheres as totalities, as they imbue the entire space and induce a certain mood in the subject (Böhme, 2017, 2013a [2006]). Architectural atmospheres mediate between the material qualities of the environment and the bodily and sensory experience of space. Akin to theatrical scenographies, atmospheres set the stage that allows for a specific affective participation in the world. In the aesthetic economy of advanced capitalism, Böhme (2003) argues, the stage value dominates use value and economic value. By means of synaesthesiae, organizations potentially create a signature style through sensory artifacts, which affect our feelings and produce similar effects of emotional significance (Böhme, 2013b, 27).

The creation of atmospheres is a cornerstone of quality architecture, as we perceive spaces "through our emotional sensibility" (Zumthor, 2006,

13). For example, we instantly sense buildings upon entering them and immediately react to "complex environmental and social situations" (Pallasmaa, 2017, 66). This aesthetics of reception rely on holistic and integrated emotional intelligence in architectural perception. Conversely, production aesthetics provide organizations with multisensory qualities of physical materiality, a *genius loci*, that is spirit of the place (Norberg-Schulz, 1980), which can be purposely employed to express meaning and identity.

In this production-oriented perspective, the production of atmospheres serves to stage products and managers, motivate employees, and seduce clients. Biehl-Missal (2011) critically interrogates these managerial practices by means of a visual analysis of the trading floor of the Frankfurt Stock Exchange. She shows how atmospheric conditions are used as strategic tools that exert a behavioral, cognitive, and emotional influence on stakeholders (Biehl-Missal, 2013).

Organizational aesthetics explore organizational life as a non-rational, intuitive "form of human knowledge" (Strati, 1999, 2), problematizing "the rational and analytic" (Strati, 1999, 7). Arguing that aesthetics in organizational life provide a form of human knowledge through sensory faculties, Strati (1990, 1992, 1996, 1999, 2000) presents aesthetic resources as innovative heuristic tools in organization studies. Refuting purely cognitive methodologies that investigate organizational members as "pure thought" and rational entities stripped of corporeality (Strati, 1999, 3), he opens up a debate about the status of aesthetics. Strati points out that organizations draw on aesthetic artifacts to enhance their products and services, while creating an identity immediately communicable to customers, employees, and society at large (Strati, 1999, 4). Linstead and Höpfl (2000, 1) consider the aesthetic as an epistemic "Other" of modernity, as it offers an alternative mode of cognition.

Derived from Merleau-Ponty's phenomenological philosophy (1968, 2013), the visual mode has been conceptualized in organization studies as a form of knowledge resulting from the embodied involvement with surrounding space, where all sensory perceptions converge. In fact, it is not the eye, but the body that looks and generates meaning (Merleau-Ponty, 1993). The Cartesian dualism between body and mind is rejected in favor of the continuous bond between the perceptual engagement of the body with the object, included in the same dimension, because "he who sees is of it (flesh) and is in it" (Merleau-Ponty, 1968, 100). The understanding of the world by relating to it through the senses supplements rational and cognitive epistemologies of spatial interpretation that will be presented in the following sections.

Sociology of Space

In a sociological perspective, the conception and realization of organizational space are mostly viewed in the Bourdieuian tradition as a circuit of capital conversion. Dominant economic and financial elites transform built form into symbolic capital for legitimization and reputation purposes (Bourdieu, 1994). Bourdieu's central concept of the social field indicates a "kind of arena in which people play a game which has certain rules [...] which are different from those of the game that is played in the adjacent space" (Bourdieu, 1991, 215).

In their analysis of the architecture of the Royal Bank of Scotland's corporate campus, Kerr and Robinson (2016) show how architecture converts the bank's economic power into symbolic capital through the replication of asymmetrical power relations. Dovey (2014 [1999]) emphasizes Bourdieu's notion of "complicitous silence" (Bourdieu, 1977, 188), noting that corporate buildings are taken for granted and silently accepted as spatial realizations of social and economic domination. Within complex cultural systems, architectural representations receive ideological meaning through the cultural territories, historical perspectives, and societal developments in which they are embedded. Social agents acting in a particular field possess economic and cultural capital, which can be used to negotiate and consolidate power positions. As reified material objects, buildings endow the bearer to project a vision of the world and to impose it on others (Bourdieu, 2012). However, beyond materiality, architectural realizations also represent symbolic capital, insofar as they legitimate organizations through accrued prestige and honor (Bourdieu, 1994).

The dynamically interrelated framework of architectural materiality and symbolic power oscillates according to the cultural heritage of people and places. In culturally constituted systems, organizational settings and collective identities produce shared meanings that evolve synchronically with the *Zeitgeist*, given that "every building exists within a social and cultural context, and receives much of its meaning from it" (Goldberger, 2009, 174). Thus, organizations operate in a spatiotemporal paradigm, which receives ontological meaning with regard to specific spatial and temporal conditions. It is argued that a building's symbolic capital is not so much inherent in the building itself, but rather generated by the ideological context, as it is "moved around from one temporary landmark to another" (Dovey, 1999, 4), thereby situating organizational architecture in a larger societal context.

As a culturally determined conduit, architecture reflects our economy, culture, and society (McGoun, 2004, 1105). For instance, the capitalistic mode of production has generated an urban environment determined by prevailing economic and social conditions. In the Fordist model, space configurations were designed to maximize production output and profit in commodified and standardized organizational processes. However, in postmodern economies, the values of architectural narratives, creative layout, aesthetic and ergonomic space design, experiential and multisensory décor, environmentally friendly and sustainable buildings, and so on have become constitutive elements of architectural practice. In addition, ideological transformations have renewed interest in local and regional production and distribution systems. Similarly, the decline of the international modern style has favored architectural regionalism and locally oriented building techniques that promote the "enduring significance of symbols of place and location" (Lash & Urry, 1994, 284).

In postmodern urban systems, architectural production is characterized by stylistic variations and visual storytelling. Hence, organizational architecture has mutated from performance and efficiency-driven functionality to representational, ontological, and identity-projecting iconicity (Klingmann, 2007, 7). Therefore, architects and architecture assume a pivotal role in constructing meanings, social spaces, and organizations, as they articulate both material and interpretive forms (Dale & Burrell, 2007, 32).

To explore the social construction of space in organization theory, Henri Lefebvre's philosophy of space provides insightful perspectives

(Watkins, 2005). In his spatial triad (1991, 38–39), Lefebvre conceptualizes three interrelated types of space: representations of space (conceived space), spatial experiences (perceived space), and representational spaces (lived space). Representational spaces, he argues, are dominant in society as they build on symbols, codifications, and abstract representation. Architectural space represents the primary locus of our engagement with the world. Hence, spatial practices, embracing "production and reproduction, and the particular locations and spatial sets characteristic of each social formation" (Lefebvre, 1991, 33), demonstrate the dynamics of space experience. Spatial practices are being formed continually, according to evolving social encounters, conventions, and relational arrangements.

Concomitant with Lefebvre's conceptual framework, Martina Löw also rejects objectivist understandings of space as material and external realities. She posits space as meaningful horizon and atmosphere created by the subjective experience of materiality (Löw, 2016). Löw synthesizes the sociology of space and cultural sociology, thereby identifying a plurality of spatial articulations correlated with class, age, and ethnic constructions (Löw, 2016), as well as sexual identity and gender (Löw, 2006). Löw subscribes to the "consonance between the constitution of being and the forms of cognition" (Bourdieu, 1997, 159).

Sociological theory invariably conceptualizes space as a mutant and processual phenomenon, producing social meaning in a given context. But how exactly is meaning generated through architectural materializations? As will be argued in the following part, the materiality of contemporary social and organizational environments is increasingly symbolically coded. Architecture harbors interpretive cues through self-referentiality and reflexivity of surrounding social and cultural systems.

Organizational Symbolism

Henri Lefebvre considers architecture in terms of "archi-textures", stipulating that each building should be treated in its surroundings and context, the urban area and associated networks in which it is established as a particular form of space production (Lefebvre, 1991, 118). Architecture's dual role, both as material and social space, serves functional and aesthetic purposes, which convey signifying content to build form. A specific location, style of building, formal properties, or architectural repertoire hold semantic value in that they refer to canons of architecture and art history (Kornberger, Kreiner, & Clegg, 2011). In view of its multidimensionality, architecture translates the "real nature" of its period (Giedion, 1967, 19), whilst proclaiming "symbolic and metaphorical messages" (Conway & Roenisch, 2005, 20). Operating on the premise that architecture carries signifying properties and decodable regimes of meaning, architectural design is theorized as a narrative structure, which symbolically translates content.

> Architecture not only communicates, but also communicates rhetorically [...]. Architectural items not only tell us their meaning and function, but also influence our behavior. Architecture is rhetorical because it induces us to do what others would have us to do. Architecture [...] is a persuasive phenomenon, and therefore deserves to be studied by rhetorical critics. (Hattenhauer, 1984, 71)

Contrary to the predominant sensual mode of knowing propounded by aesthetic theory, which opposes intellectual and rational knowledge, architectural narratives are cognitively coded as a discursive form of expression. This process of semanticization transforms the material dimensions of objects (weight, color, volume, etc.) into meaningful substances, such as values, a symbolic universe, a lifestyle, and so on (Heilbrunn, 2015, 6–7).

Yanow (1995) notes that architectural styles tell stories in and of themselves that purposely generate meaning. In the sense of an "expressive system" (Bonta, 1979), architectural discourse offers an alternative route to the understanding of socially and culturally produced relations between organizations and their historical and economic environments. In his essay "Meaning and Building", Rykwert (1960) emphasizes the symbolic narratives of architecture as related to sociology, anthropology, psychology, and advertising.

Architectural expression offers symbolic resources for identification (Norberg-Schulz, 1963, 2000). When space is made tangible in concrete, qualitative terms, it symbolically carries meaningful content. Norberg-Schulz notes that "the purpose of symbolization is to free the meaning from the immediate situation, whereby it becomes a 'cultural object'" (Norberg-Schulz, 1996 [1976], 421). Architectural signs form a dialectic sign system, as buildings have a primarily utilitarian function, while, as signifying forms, they convey messages. Architecture is a multi-faceted construct open to multiple interpretations and meanings. In the following, the theoretical concepts will be applied to the classical architecture of bank buildings.

Financial Architecture

Financial architecture represents a particularly emblematic area of investigation, given that the finance sector is undergoing profound transformations. The accelerated de-materialization of money has disrupted the conventional circuits of monetary transactions and the traditional functional role of bank buildings. In fact, large storage facilities for cash money are no longer needed, as scriptural money makes up for most of the monetary mass in circulation today. With financial products representing merely an accounting unit, the architectural geography of bank buildings is rapidly shifting from purpose-built objects to eye-catching flagship venues. While non-descript branches are massively closed down, emblematic headquarters and main branches are stylishly redesigned as representative organizational icons. If buildings can be seen as "cultural artefact, sign, object of value and spatial system" (Goss, 1988, 392), they hold symbolic value and "enter the cultural sphere as real estate, as corporate image, *and* as architecture" (Martin, 2010, xvii, emphasis in original). Thus, bank architecture relies primarily on the symbolic aspects of buildings, which stand out as landmarks in their environment, and powerfully shape social aesthetics and communities.

From the beginning of banking in the Italian Renaissance, banks have used architecture to project identity and status. In today's environment, architecture counterbalances de-materialized digital money flows insofar as built form conveys a sense of permanence and solidity (Ittelson, Proshansky, Rivlin, & Winkel, 1974, 358). Beyond the fact that bank buildings generate rental assets (Leyshon & Thrift, 2007), they symbolically communicate "safety" and "security" (McGoun, 2004, 1104) and speak to the senses "in a way that the cerebral appeal of pure information cannot" (McGoun, 2004, 1085). Buildings articulate the ideological self-understanding of financial organizations, and perhaps even the financial system as a whole, as suggested by Davison (2009, 2013, 2014). Within the financial ecosystem, bank buildings project plutocratic ideologies congruent with the status of perennial power organizations.

> Created by private capital to serve pragmatic functions for its owners, bank architecture at the same time turns a public face to its community in a vigorous attempt to communicate, persuade, assure, impress, and convince [...]. Contemporary attitudes regarding money, respectability, security, and corporate aesthetics are reflected [...]. Bank architecture thus communicates the importance of banks as institutions, assuring us of their stability, prosperity, and permanence and inviting us inside to do business. (Nisbet, 1990, 8)

As a material embodiment of the "phenomenology of capital" (Martin, 2010, xvii), banks occupy both a geographic and cultural territory within space and time. Founded as lending institutions for local farmers in the Renaissance or as capital providers for fast-growing industrial firms in the nineteenth century, banks are intrinsically linked to the socio-economic environment in which they operate. For example, the predominant political and economic ideology of industrial capitalism was aesthetically expressed through the eclectic Beaux-Arts style in the mid-nineteenth century. Its allegorical and structural elements symbolically translate organizational identity within the surrounding urban development. Two examples of Beaux-Arts bank buildings will illustrate the symbolic resources conveyed by architectural narratives.

The Colonnades of Capital

The headquarters of UBS in Zurich's Bahnhofstrasse exemplify the expressive value of organizational architecture within the urban context. At the beginning of the twentieth century, the Bahnhofstrasse was planned to become a sectorial hub of the banking industry, thus creating the city's myth as a center of international finance. Since 1919, UBS has occupied its headquarters in the so-called *Münzhof*, an iconic building in the Beaux-Arts style.

The massive concentration of financial capital in the sector of Bahnhofstrasse and Paradeplatz produces a spatial conception along the space-time paradigm of a universal civilization (Giedion, 1967). The way buildings relate to their environment either by continuity or disjuncture allows for semantic readability. In the case of UBS, the classical formal structure of the building aligns with the predominantly classical order of the adjacent buildings. Classical architecture projects timeless and perennial values that are at the core of the banking activity:

> Banks [...] adopted classical architectural form for strategic reasons. Classicism expresses stability, strength, and security, and communicates timeless values. [...] A bank's appearance should convey an impression that reflects the institution's character by its air of stability, dignity and security. Thus, the less tangible attributes of a bank its image can be communicated through architectural form. (Schroeder, 2002, 92)

However, within this urban context, UBS's distinctive landmark stands out for the monumental proportions of its distinctly Greco-Roman frontispiece. By adopting the *genera* of the Doric order, the architectural repertory of style allows for a genderized interpretation. In fact, Vitruvius links the Doric order to the male body, in contrast with the symbolic inferences of the Ionic and Corinthian orders, allusive of the female body (Vitruvius, 1999). For Roger Scruton, the height of these Doric columns is indicative of the moral force of human posture (Scruton, 1979, 253). By means of its classical façade, connecting the building with its urban context through a propylaea, the bank positions itself in the aesthetic heritage of civic buildings and temples of classical Greece. Vitruvius indicates that the anthropomorphic nature of the Doric order serves as a vehicle for archetypal values of spatial organization, such as physical strength, virility, sobriety, and purity (Vitruvius, 1999). The impressive façade, orchestrated by this classical alignment, refers directly to secular paradigms of architecture: "the column, the arch, the pediment, represent by themselves a form of construction representative of the name of architecture" (De Portzamparc, 2006, 42). Prevailing classical attributes prime the aesthetic experience of the building, with the colossal volumetric elevation of the columns translating the financial and social power of the organization. The extremely narrow intercolumniation emphasizes the façade's longitudinal accent, thereby reinforcing the perception of verticality and hierarchy. Schroeder (2002, 99) notes that "closely spaced columns serve to signal strength and protection, slender columns can signal grace and beauty, massive columns connote power and dominance".

As the organization's architectural language derives directly from the vocabulary of the ancient world, it mobilizes classical genealogy to symbolize its ontological status. Placing an emphatic reference on the *classici*, the ruling class of Roman citizenry, the building symbolically confers an elite status to the organization.

The convergence of classical form places the institution in the lineage of Western civilization. From a functional point of view, the Greek columns are reminiscent of the rite of passage of the temple. As the new cathedral of capital, however, the place of worship is transformed into a sanctuary of financial power, where the capitalistic cult has replaced ancient myths.

Despite the formal references to the canon of classical architecture, the UBS building does not authentically replicate Vitruvian proportions. Classical axioms appear as stylizations and abstractions so as to carry the bank's organizational message more efficiently. For example, the imposing verticality of the front façade deviates from Vitruvian proportions to formulate the central authority of the organization more forcefully through its unusually high elevation.

As speaking compositions of stone, classical buildings articulate an expressive vitality, conveying symbolic and mythical power upon organizations. The preponderance of classical forms has dominated western architecture for 2000 years. Through the symmetrical features of its ordered and harmonious structure, the classical canon is a metaphorical vector of values in that it represents an ideal cosmic order. Thus, the sublimation of architectural form into a meaningful cosmogony significantly contributes to the articulation of organizational identity and legitimacy. Particular architectural narratives, conveyed through allegorical figures, further enhance the symbolic power of architecture.

On the UBS building, Hermes is represented as the most salient decorative motive, appearing on all lintels along the frontal colonnade.

In Greco-Roman mythology, Hermes, messenger of the gods, god of commerce and travel, is represented with a helmet, a caduceus, winged sandals, and a purse. The mascaron on UBS's central façade features several of these symbolic attributes. It is interesting to note, however, that Hermes's sculpted relief only partially reproduces the god's traditional iconography given that the purse is missing. At first glance, this omission raises questions in view of the organization's core financial business. A possible interpretation could consist in the purposeful reinforcement of symbolic value. Negatively signifying by its iconographic absence, the purse, as a metaphorical sign of material wealth, is provided to the customer by the bank. Thus, the bank places itself in the interstices of the incomplete iconography, filling the symbolic deficit by the eventual provision of capital once the customer has entered the building. Through its financial services, UBS supplements the omitted pieces of the architectural composition and restores the picture to its signifying totality.

Following Merleau-Ponty, Löw (2006, 120) points out that we not only perceive things, but also "interspaces between things", leading to the formation of syntheses. Likewise, in the interstitial perception of Hermes, viewers substitute the missing purse through their own interpretation. Furthermore, the iconographic insistence on the god's somniferous wand, flanking the bust on the right and on the left, could ironically symbolize narcotic influences and the transport of visitors to the underworld. Hence, the manipulative power of finance could be seen as foreshadowing calamitous financial crises. *In fine*, architecture opens up various layers of interpretation according to subjective and cultural contexts, but the narrative frame of Western cultural history remains an unchanging reference. As an open, yet closed system, classical architecture imbues organizations with cultural and symbolic capital, as it visually translates the original democratic principles of Athens:

> Classicism, like language, is precise but flexible. It can suggest commercial probity, as we see in the classical architecture of bank buildings and above all, the New York Stock Exchange. It can radiate culture, as in the neoclassical art museum in Philadelphia [...]. In the early nineteenth century the Greek temple form pledged allegiance to the democratic principles that Americans traced back to ancient Athens. (O'Gorman, 1998, 95)

By means of the preponderant citation of central classical motives, the UBS façade represents what Vitruvius (*De Architectura*, I, 16) calls the *logos opticos*, that is, an expressive link with the foundations of Western civilization. As the aesthetic vehicle of nineteenth-century bourgeois ideology, the neoclassical style optimally transcribes the financial and political aspirations of the emerging bourgeoisie. In his study on the classical orders, John Onians shows that the haptic quality of stone serves a reflective human experience, facilitating social contact and interaction, as much as it allows for introspection and meditation: "these forms were striking features of the buildings in which people in Western Europe formulated and developed their relationships to the gods, to each other, to themselves; and it was often through their use that these relationships were articulated" (Onians, 1988, 3). Thus, common aesthetic predilections for classical motives create inter-elite identities between the organization and stakeholders at the sociomaterial level.

The Wings of the Lion

The architectural creation of financial sanctuaries is also apparent in smaller bank branches, for example, the building of Société Générale in Dieppe, Normandy. The structural and formal architectural principles follow the same patterns as in the UBS building to signal the status of the organization. Built in 1880 by architect Louis Lorrain, the so-called *Maison Frosmont*, after its first owner, was erected in the Flemish style.

The original building was equipped with a bell tower that allowed the view over the sea and a fountain in front of the main entrance. However, subsequent structural adjustments to the building were made, including the construction of a central staircase. A barometer is placed on the curved pediment, framed by volutes, and the balcony on the first floor is supported by four colonnettes, small and thin columns, decorated with dolphins and acanthus leaves.

The building features several symbolic references to Venice, a major trading partner of Dieppe. The building is located next to the Venetian Villa, and, most importantly, two statues representing winged lions are placed on either side of the stairs, facing visitors and the city. Originally, these statues were placed right and left of the central fountain and facing each other. The changing gaze, from looking at each other to looking at the Other, is significant for the self-understanding of the organization. When the bank acquired the building in 1901, it turned its face to the outside world. The bank's spatial transformation with the central stairs flanked by the two-winged lions generates meaning at multiple levels. First, the stairs institute the central perspective through which the building is perceived by the eye. From the bottom of the stairs, the visitor looks at the building, which unfolds visually from an initial state of motionless. The gaze regime (Löw, 2006, 124) of the central perspective subsequently transforms into the haptic, empirical practice of space when walking up the stairs toward the main entrance. The field of vision, where the building is merely perceived as an object, becomes subjectified corporeality through the felt experience when climbing up the stairs toward the organization. Thus, approaching the inner sanctuary, the body experiences an elevation, phenomenologically and mentally, which inspires awe and a sense of worship, admirably described by Gill:

> Whether we approached a bank in order to deposit money or to borrow it, we were made to feel humbly grateful—indeed, that we were allowed to cross the threshold of the Arcanum at all was in itself a reason for congratulation. Passing between majestic stone pillars and even through mighty gilded bronze portals, we would find ourselves at last inside a lofty chamber, vaulted and domes, floored and wainscoted in marble, and ringed around with tiny altars, each of which was set within a cage of slender,

protective bars and presided over by a resident priest, usually male and wearing a habit of dark blue serge. (Gill, 1990, 4)

The staircase creates the stage set for the theatrical atmosphere that visitors experience when performing this rite of passage. Representing power on land and sea, the winged lions symbolically translate the status of an organization with historical pedigree. Moreover, the architectural narratives indicate the bank's involvement in the development of the city's international trading activities. At the level of phenomenological experience, the power and status of the organization are experienced by the interplay between subjective bodily perception and material arrangements. For instance, the architectural structure of the building with the central stairs symbolically represents the material and elevation of capital and social development.

Banks signal their vigor and solvency by the adoption of the classical morphology, intended to project values of stability and strength *sub specie aeternitatis*. "As Greece and Rome had come to be seen as the cultural sources of virtue, a return to classical architectural rules of proportionality, regularity, harmony, and decorum in the form of a neoclassical style would express this virtue in the form of a building" (McGoun, 2004, 13).

As the value of money itself is built on symbolic exchange value, the internal logic of financial circuits entirely depends on the public's perception of its stability, mediated by the Greek style: "Western banks were built to resemble classical temples, the severe Grecian style helped the often unstable institutions express security" (Pevsner, 1976, 202). Architectural historians Tzonis and Lefaivre (1986) point out the semantic potential of classical architecture, where built structure refers to perceptual themes that invariably signify perfection and harmony.

> These works have been adored through centuries and continents for their persistence of "balance" and "symmetry," "focus," and "finality," and "proportionality and hierarchy;" their divisibility through distinct, elementary, concise themes; and their unity through explicit, computable, standard, generative, combinatorial plans. [...] Indeed, what characterizes any work [...] put together according to the rules of composition that originated in classical poetics and rhetoric is its identity as something "complete and

whole," "perfect," whose particular order sets it off from its surroundings (Aristotle, *Poetics*, 2, 4). (Tzonis & Lefaivre, 1986, 4)

However, the classical architectural canon is severely questioned as the symbolic reference to existing power structures, as the following part will discuss.

Discussion

Architectural theorists argue that "classicism visually reinforces the power structure in any period, today and yesterday" (Conway & Roenisch, 2005 [1994], 16). Considered as the emblematic outgrowth of early capitalism, the historicist style of the Greco-Roman repertory has come to represent an obsolete political system at the end of the nineteenth century. Classical architecture was to be superseded by the more moral, transparent, and socially responsible aesthetics of modernism: "In Europe, during the 1890s, a demand for morality in architecture arose in many different countries. As van de Velde puts it, people saw that the reigning architecture was a 'lie', all posturing and no truth, and that greater purity of expression was needed" (Giedion, 1967, 25).

Thus, the practice of neoclassical *citationism* (Tzonis & Lefaivre, 1986, 179) mobilizes past architectural resources to generate meaning for contemporary audiences. However, it is not the result of a creative, innovative process, where architectural poetics are written *ex nihilo*. If classical architecture is reduced to pastiche and a simulacrum of past times, its semantic substance becomes irrelevant for contemporary audiences.

Architectural artifacts generate ontological meaning when material structure and human substance are synthesized in a sociomaterial perspective. In the economic environment of today, the social conduct of organizations therefore needs to correlate with the expectancies created by an organization's architectural paradigm. Without behavioral substance, the visual representation turns into insignificant formalism. Essential values, such as reciprocity, trust, credibility, legitimacy, transparency, satisfaction, and mutual comprehension, must fundamentally determine the governance of organizations (Grunig, 1993, 121–139).

Deficits in terms of governance could provoke dissonances and inadequacies between the dignified classical architecture and organizational practices, thus transforming iconicity into irony. For instance, the prominent display of Hermes on the UBS building could be satirically perceived as a symbol of the bank's kleptomaniac practices, as Hermes was also the god of thieves.

Conclusion

Architecture offers interpretive cues by means of the structuration of space and cultural symbols derived from site-specific historical canons. The classical architectural production represents an ideal cosmic order, where the scale of building elements is correlated with the proportions of the human body. These *regula e ordine* of proportion and harmony govern the metaphorical expression of immutable and perennial values. The material solutions of classical repertoires convey stability and endurance, given that "the posts, pillars, and columns which have assured people in many cultures [...] have been just as critical in resolving other uncertainties and anxieties" (Onians, 1988, 3).

However, the classical repertory is also a vector of political and social power structures. Sharoff (1997, 43) notes that "the whole language of classicism is very much associated with colonialism". For this reason, the classical style was rejected for the construction of the World Bank in Washington (Schroeder, 2002, 106).

The universally recognized symbolic values inherent in the classical canon represent an ideal means to establish organizational legitimacy, given that bank architecture "communicates the importance of banks as institutions, assuring us of their stability, prosperity, and permanence and inviting us inside to do business" (Nisbet, 1990, 8).

The culturally embedded materiality of buildings functions as a counterpoint to the ephemeral and volatile nature of financial markets and to the virtuality of electronic platforms. However, buildings carry meaning in a semantic sense only within specific social, historical, and political contexts. Symbolic spaces and atmospheres are produced as scenic functions to stage organizations in their environment. The disjuncture from the architectural canon often bears the risk of losing legitimacy in a given cultural context. For example, organizational architecture in the twentieth century was characterized by the aesthetic transition from Beaux-Arts classicism buildings to high-rise buildings. At first, the predominant structural elements of classical architecture were incorporated in the tall building to increase their acceptance. "Partly in response to the dominance of Beaux Arts classicism and perhaps mindful of the limited legitimacy that tall buildings had, the dominant model for early tall buildings was generally one that stressed horizontal banding, usually with a three-part base, column and capital decoration" (Parker, 2015, 224).

Architectural narratives are subject to interpretation, as it is impossible to feel, to speak, to think, and to act in a non-interpretive way (Abel, 1999). Thus, buildings represent a social locus, which receives meaning both through the representation of cultural heritage and the atmospheric potency experienced through bodily perception.

References

Abel, G. (1999). *Sprache, Zeichen, Interpretation*. Frankfurt/Main: Suhrkamp.

Bargenda, A. (2013). Corporate architecture as a branding tool. In R. Gambetti & S. Quigley (Eds.), *Managing corporate communication: A cross-cultural approach* (pp. 337–357). London: Palgrave Macmillan.

Bargenda, A. (2014). *Communication visuelle dans le secteur bancaire européen. L'Esthétique de la Finance*. Paris: L'Harmattan.

Berg, P. O., & Kreiner, K. (1992). Corporate architecture. Turning physical settings into symbolic resources. In P. Gagliardi (Ed.), *Symbols and Artifacts* (pp. 41–67). New York: de Gruyter.

Biehl-Missal, B. (2011). *Wirtschaftsästhetik. Wie Unternehmen die Kunst als Inspiration und Werkzeug nutzen*. Wiesbaden: Gabler.

Biehl-Missal, B. (2013). The atmosphere of the image: An aesthetic concept for visual analysis. *Consumption Markets and Culture, 16*(4), 356–367.

Böhme, G. (1993). Atmosphere as the fundamental concept of a new aesthetics. *Thesis Eleven, 36*(1), 113–126.

Böhme, G. (2003). Contribution to the critique of the aesthetic economy. *Thesis Eleven, 73*(1), 71–82.

Böhme, G. (2013a [2006]). *Architektur und Atmosphäre*. Munich: Wilhelm Fink.

Böhme, G. (2013b). Synaesthesiae within the scope of a phenomenology of perception. *Wolkenkuckucksheim—Cloud-Cuckoo-Land, 31*, 23–33. Retrieved February 13, 2017, from http://cloud-cuckoo.net/fileadmin/issues_en/issue_31/artikel_boehme.pdf

Böhme, G. (2017). *The aesthetics of atmospheres*. London & New York: Routledge.

Bonta, J. (1979). *Expressive Systems in Architecture and Design*. London: Lund Humphries.

Bourdieu, P. (1977). *Outline of a theory of practice* (Vol. 16). Cambridge: Cambridge University Press.

Bourdieu, P. (1991). *Language and symbolic power*. Cambridge: Polity Press.

Bourdieu, P. (1994). Rethinking the state: Genesis of structure of the bureaucratic field. *Sociological Theory, 12*(1), 1–18.

Bourdieu, P. (1997). Die männliche herrschaft. In I. Döllingand & B. Krais (Eds.), *Ein Aalltägliches Spiel. Geschlechterkonstruktion in der Sozialen Praxis* (pp. 153–217). Frankfurt am Main: Suhrkamp.

Bourdieu, P. (2012). *Sur l'état*. Paris: Raisons d'agir/Seuil.

Carlile, P. R., Nicolini, D., Langley, A., & Tsoukas, H. (Eds.). (2013). *How matter matters: Objects, Artifacts, and materiality in organization studies*. Oxford: Oxford University Press.

Clegg, S. (2010). *SAGE directions in organization studies*. London: Sage.

Conway, H., & Roenisch, R. (2005[1994]). *Understanding architecture: An introduction to architecture and architectural history*. Hove: Psychology Press.

Dale, K., & Burrell, G. (2007). *The spaces of organisation and the organisation of space: Power, identity and materiality at work*. Basingstoke: Palgrave Macmillan.

Dameron, S., Lê, J. K., & LeBaron, C. (2015). Materializing strategy and strategizing material: Why matter matters. *British Journal of Management, 26*, S1), S1–S1),S12.

Davison, J. (2009). Icon, iconography, iconology: Visual branding, banking and the case of the bowler hat. *Accounting, Auditing & Accountability Journal, 22*(6), 883–906.

Davison, J. (2013). The visual organization: Barthesian perspectives. In E. Bell, S. Warren, & J. E. Schroeder (Eds.), *The Routledge companion to visual organization* (pp. 33–44). London: Routledge.

Davison, J. (2014). Visual rhetoric and the case of intellectual capital. *Accounting, Organizations and Society, 39*(1), 20–37.

De Portzamparc, C. (2006). *Architecture: figures du monde, figures du temps*. Paris: Collège de France/Fayard.

De Vaujany, F. X., & Vaast, E. (2016). Matters of visuality in legitimation practices: Dual iconographies in a meeting room. *Organization, 23*(5), 763–790.

Dovey, K. (2014[1999]). *Framing places: Mediating power in built form*. London: Routledge.

Gagliardi, P. (1990). *Artefacts and symbols: Views of the corporate landscape*. Berlin: de Gruyter.

Giedion, S. (1967). *Space, time and architecture: The growth of a new tradition*. Cambridge: Harvard University Press.

Gill, B. (Ed.). (1990). *Money matters: A critical look at Bank architecture*. New York: McGraw-Hill.

Goldberger, P. (2009). *Why architecture matters*. London & New Haven: Yale University Press.

Goss, J. (1988). The built environment and social theory: Towards an architectural geography. *The Professional Geographer, 40*(4), 392–403.

Grunig, J. (1993). Image and substance: From symbolic to behavioral relationships. *Public Relations Review, 19*(2), 121–139.

Hattenhauer, D. (1984). The rhetoric of architecture: A semiotic approach. *Communication Quarterly, 32*(1), 71–77.

Heilbrunn, B. (2015). *Market mediations: Semiotic investigations on consumers, objects and brands*. Basingstoke: Palgrave Macmillan.

Ittelson, W. H., Proshansky, H. M., Rivlin, L. G., & Winkel, G. (1974). *An introduction to environmental psychology*. New York: Holt, Rinehart & Winston.

Kerr, R., & Robinson, S. (2016). Architecture, symbolic capital and elite mobilisations: The case of the Royal Bank of Scotland corporate campus. *Organization, 23*(5), 699–721.

Klingmann, A. (2007). *Brandscapes: Architecture in the experience economy*. Cambridge, MA: The MIT Press.

Kornberger, M., & Clegg, S. (2005). Bringing space back in: Organizing the generative building. *Organization Studies, 25*(7), 1095–1114.

Kornberger, M., Kreiner, K., & Clegg, S. (2011). The value of style in architectural practice. *Culture and Organization, 17*(2), 139–153.

Lash, S. M., & Urry, J. (1994). *Economies of signs and space*. London: Sage.

Lefebvre, H. (1991). *The production of space*. Oxford: Blackwell.

Leyshon, A., & Thrift, N. (2007). The capitalization of almost everything: The future of finance and capitalism. *Theory, Culture and Society, 24*(7–8), 97–115.

Linstead, S., & Höpfl, H. J. (2000). Introduction. In S. Linstead & H. Höpfl (Eds.), *The aesthetics of organization* (pp. 1–11). London: Sage.

Löw, M. (2006). The social construction of space and gender. *European Journal of Women's Studies, 13*(2), 119–133.
Löw, M. (2016). *The sociology of space: Materiality, social structures, and action.* New York: Springer.
Martin, R. (2010). *Utopia's ghost. Architecture and postmodernism, again.* Minneapolis, MN: University of Minnesota Press.
McGoun, E. G. (2004). Form, function, and finance: Architecture and finance theory. *Critical Perspectives on Accounting, 15*(8), 1085–1107.
Merleau-Ponty, M. (1968). *The visible and the invisible: Followed by working notes.* Evanston, IL: Northwestern University Press.
Merleau-Ponty, M. (1993). Eye and mind. In G. A. Johnson (Ed.), *The Merleau-Ponty aesthetics reader: Philosophy and painting* (pp. 121–149). Evanston, IL: Northwestern University Press.
Merleau-Ponty, M. (2013). *Phenomenology of perception.* London: Routledge.
Meyer, R. E., Höllerer, M. A., Jancsary, D., & Van Leeuwen, T. (2013). The visual dimension in organizing, organization, and organization research: Core ideas, current developments, and promising avenues. *Academy of Management Annals, 7*(1), 489–555.
Nisbet, R. (1990). Men and money: Reflections by a sociologist. In B. Gill (Ed.), *Money matters: A critical look at Bank architecture* (pp. 7–13). New York: McGraw-Hill.
Norberg-Schultz, C. (2000). *Principles of modern architecture.* London: Andreas Papadakis.
Norberg-Schulz, C. (1963). *Intentions in architecture.* Oslo: Universitetsforlaget.
Norberg-Schulz, C. (1980). *Genius loci: Towards a phenomenology of architecture.* New York: Rizzoli.
Norberg-Schulz, C. (1996 [1976]). The phenomenon of place. In K. Nesbitt (Ed.), *Theorizing a new agenda for architecture: An anthology of architectural theory* (pp. 412–428). New York: Princeton Architectural Press.
O'Gorman, J. F. (1998). *ABC of architecture.* Philadelphia: University of Pennsylvania Press.
Onians, J. (1988). *Bearers of meaning: The classical orders in antiquity, the middle ages, and the renaissance.* Princeton, NJ: Princeton University Press.
Pallasmaa, J. (2017). Embodied and existential wisdom in architecture: The thinking hand. *Body and Society, 23*(1), 96–111.
Parker, M. (2015). Vertical capitalism: Skyscrapers and organization. *Culture and Organization, 21*(3), 217–234.

Pevsner, N. (1976). *A history of building types*. Princeton, NJ: Princeton University Press.

Robichaud, D., & Cooren, F. (Eds.). (2013). *Organization and organizing: Materiality, agency, and discourse*. London: Routledge.

Rykwert, J. (1960). Meaning and building. *Zodiac 6: International Magazine of Contemporary Architecture*, 193–196.

Schatzki, T. R. (2005). Peripheral vision: The sites of organizations. *Organization Studies, 26*(3), 465–484.

Schroeder, J. E. (2002). *Visual consumption*. London and New York: Routledge.

Scruton, R. (1979). *The aesthetics of architecture*. Princeton, NJ: Princeton University Press.

Sharoff, R. (1997, March 6) World bank: Architecture as diplomacy. *New York Times*, p. 43.

Soja, E. (1996). *Thirdspace: Journeys to Los Angeles and other real-and-imagined places*. Oxford: Basil Blackwell.

Strati, A. (1990). Aesthetics and organizational skill. In B. A. Turner (Ed.), *Organizational symbolism* (pp. 208–222). Berlin, New York: Walter de Gruyter.

Strati, A. (1992). Aesthetic understanding of organizational life. *Academy of Management Review, 17*(3), 568–581.

Strati, A. (1996). Organizations viewed through the lens of aesthetics. *Organization, 3*(2), 209–218.

Strati, A. (1999). *Organization and aesthetics*. London: Sage.

Strati, A. (2000). The aesthetic approach in organization studies. In S. Linstead & H. J. Höpfl (Eds.), *The Aesthetics of organization* (pp. 13–34). London: Sage.

Taylor, S. S., & Hansen, H. (2005). Finding form: Looking at the field of organizational aesthetics. *Journal of Management Studies, 42*(6), 1211–1231.

Tzonis, A., & Lefaivre, L. (1986). *Classical architecture: The poetics of order*. Cambridge, MA: MIT Press.

Van Dijk, J. (2012). *The network society. Social aspects of new media*. Thousand Oaks, CA: Sage Publications.

Vitruvius. (1999). *Ten books on architecture*. Cambridge: Cambridge University Press.

Watkins, C. (2005). Representations of space, spatial practices and spaces of representation: An application of Lefebvre's spatial triad. *Culture and Organization, 11*(3), 209–220.

Yanow, D. (1995). Built space as story. *Policy Studies Journal, 23*(3), 407–422.

Zumthor, P. (2006). *Atmosphere: Architectural environments—Surrounding objects*. Basel, Boston & Berlin: Birkhäuser Verlag.

14

Technology and the Simultaneous Collapsing and Expanding of Organizational Space: A COVID-19 Experience

Anouk Mukherjee

Introduction

A curious thing happened to me during the complete lockdown in France between 17 March and 11 May due to the coronavirus pandemic of 2020. Having close family abroad—specifically in Canada and India—I felt compelled to keep closer contact with them than usual. I would organize daily *Skype* calls with those in Canada and daily phone calls to those in India. Some in my family being elderly, and in one case isolated, this daily contact felt like an obligation. I was worried, like many, that my family may go through the terrible experience of others where members get taken to hospital and die in solitude without ever having any contact with family. This daily contact made me feel closer to those I love and even gave me the time to get to know them better. Although lockdown conditions have

A. Mukherjee (✉)
Université Paris-Est Créteil, Créteil, France
e-mail: anouk.mukherjee@u-pec.fr

N. Mitev et al. (eds.), *New Ways of Working*, Technology, Work and Globalization,
https://doi.org/10.1007/978-3-030-61687-8_14

eased since 11 May in France, I have maintained this daily contact and have organized my routine to include these precious moments. These pleasant breaks somewhat rhythm my day, especially since I need to take into account the various time-zones and time differences. So far, nothing surprising or original about my experience—I have many friends who seemed to share similar experiences, even those who had relatives in the same country. What is interesting is that this specific family experience was very spatial and could be contrasted with my other online experiences, especially those involving my work as a university lecturer.

How could my spatial experience be any different during these calls with family far away when compared to when I was performing other tasks, such as reading a book or just composing emails? After all, I was in the same room the whole time. But over a period of several weeks, and with repetition on a daily basis, I was able to notice specific patterns in my experience—specifically regarding my perception of space. What would happen is that I would feel somewhat transported to my parents' home in Canada or my uncle's rooftop terrace in India (he would almost always take calls there in the evenings). Although my parents' webcam was fixed in one of the rooms, I could perceive the whole flat from my position thousands of kilometers away. I could hear the footsteps of my father approaching the computer from the hallway, the television in the living room, the phone ringing occasionally. I could see movement in the room, get a sense of the atmosphere, and also a feeling of the time of day and weather conditions with the ambient light coming in from the window. Similarly, when I would call my uncle in India, he would describe to me current weather conditions, pollution levels, and how starry the night sky was on the particular evening (the lower levels of air pollution due to the significantly lower levels of traffic made stars visible for the first time in years in big cities in India). Being in a tropical climate, my uncle would occasionally describe the various fragrances emanating from the evening blooms. In both cases, I was there! Yet, at the same time I wasn't! The experience of space very much peculiar, especially when compared to my experiences while doing virtual classes with my students, or virtual meetings with my colleagues.

When doing virtual classes or online meetings, the perception of space was very different. Absent was the impression of being 'somewhere', not even in my immediate physical environment. There was an underlying desperation of trying to get clues as to where my interlocutors were located—an impression of their environment. Were they in their kitchen? Basement? With others around them? Why does the person keep on peering over the screen of their laptop? What is distracting them? A cat? Another screen? These were the sorts of signals I felt my perceptive tentacles reaching out to capture. And these were instances where a webcam was used. In other instances, where a webcam wasn't used, it would be even more frustrating since the presence of the various individuals on the call was never certain—had they stepped away from their computer? (always a suspicion when the microphone would be muted). This impression would be accentuated during virtual classes with the larger number of persons connected, along with the fact that most would never say a word during a three-hour long session. This leads to the widespread suspicion that most students were slackers during the period of institutions being closed and would only connect to appear as 'present' without much involvement in online interaction (I don't necessarily believe this to be true for the vast majority of students). The problem here is that there were few signals to go with in order to perceive the spaces occupied by the others involved, let alone their presence. I was unable to project myself into the homes of my colleagues or students. Not having any sort of representation of the remote spaces, the experience was diminished and reduced to an abstraction of common presence. Unless one looks at the list of those connected, one cannot be aware of whether one is in the company of a handful of students, or 50 of them. What was helpful with students was that I had met them in person during regular class sessions. It was therefore useful to imagine their persona during interactions with them.

Confronting these two experiences has been a fascinating exercise. Why in instances where I would be interacting with my family over long distances, my experience of space was richer and made it seem like my space was augmented, whereas little or no such perception was in evidence during my interactions with colleagues and students? Of course, ICT-mediated interactions with one or two persons at a single site are certainly less complex and demanding than those involving many persons scattered over several physical sites. It is easier to project spatially onto a single site over a *Skype* or telephone call than onto several sites.

However, it seems to me to be more complex than this dimension. The reason perhaps why I felt I could project easily onto sites that were familiar to me is that I could imagine myself there. Having never been in my colleagues' homes, I am unfamiliar with their surroundings, and therefore confused and disorientated about what I see on the screen. It seems the more familiar I am with an environment, the easier it is to 'be there' while on a call (with a camera or not). This was particularly evident from the active role I took in organizing grocery deliveries for my parents remotely. Grocery stores found their IT infrastructure overwhelmed overnight with increased online shopping and a surge in delivery service demand. This meant that for my parents' usual grocer, orders needed to be placed in the night of Sunday to Monday so as to obtain a delivery slot within the next week. Otherwise, orders would be delayed for up to three weeks. Given the time difference between France and Canada, I would have the advantage of being able to place the order on Monday morning well before all of the available slots would be taken. I carefully coordinated delivery slots such that they would be convenient and fit into my parents' routine. It was as if I was there, imagining the space in which they lived, where and how the groceries would be delivered, even the doormen who would be present to help my parents take the delivery. Again, I was 'there'.

The COVID-19 crisis has been a running experiment on how we organize ourselves in space. These are rare occasions when previously invisible assumptions about how we live and work are exposed. For example, we have seen that many office workers are able to perform many tasks from their home and switching university programs entirely online is possible overnight. Of course, the process has been painful, and much economic activity has been stopped in its tracks—factories, small shops, cafés, and restaurants have all fallen silent in many jurisdictions during the lockdown. However, the demonstration wouldn't have been possible without such a crisis. This demonstration that it is indeed possible to organize society differently in terms of space will likely have lasting impact on organizational space. As we can see from my personal experience of space during the COVID-19 crisis, it is important to understand how new practices influence the manner in which our perceptions are altered while interacting with others via ICT. The radical shift in attitudes and practices necessary for us to cope with the situation where much of our interaction is done online means that a detailed understanding of how our perceptions and experiences are shaped by our spatial practices is required.

In this chapter, I will argue that recent advances in the field of neurosciences have provided added support to the thesis that organizational space is both simultaneously collapsed and expanded thanks to ICT as far as our experience is concerned. I will first present the findings of my research on the experience of space by academics before showing how neuroscientists have provided—perhaps unwittingly—support for the phenomenology of perception of Maurice Merleau-Ponty. Support for specific key concepts of Merleau-Ponty will be focused on before showing how the concept of the Bayesian brain helps explain the experience of organizational space, both proximate and remote.

The Spatial Experience of Academics—Findings of My Thesis Research

Overall Findings

At the time I started my doctoral thesis project in 2012, I was as struck in a similar way about how my experience of space would vary according to my engagement with screens. I, like most other academics, would spend hours in front of a computer screen. I realized that during certain long periods of work in front of the screen, my state of mind would have peculiar characteristics which would be contrasted with other periods when I would not be in front of the screen. This realization made me wonder about how organizational space was affected by ICT, especially for those of us who worked most of our time in front of a computer screen. I specifically wanted to understand how ICT-supported practices helped shape organizational space. I ended up studying the work practices of academics in business schools (Mukherjee, 2017)—specifically two business schools in a comparative case study. After some exploratory work, my research question ended up being: How is technology shaping the experience of organizational space more broadly? By studying how ICT was involved in the day-to-day organization of various tasks, it emerged that the experience of space was significantly shaped by ICT and in unexpected ways.

The findings show how academics' experience of space, while engaged in a practice, shapes their bodily movements, and how this in turn shifts their experience. The experience of space is the result of phenomenological engagement of the body in the world, this engagement being directed at a certain physical environment. The study proposes a theoretical perspective based on the phenomenology of perception of Merleau-Ponty (1945). This perspective suggests that, based on the experience of academics, technology simultaneously collapses and expands space. ICT acts as a point of singularity where proximate and remote spaces converge to produce a singular sphere of experience. This study further develops Merleau-Ponty's concepts of intentionality, body schema, habitus, knowing body, and habitual body in the context of the spatial practices of academics. As a matter of experience, space is not rendered irrelevant with technology, but rather it is both collapsed and expanded simultaneously. The combination of proximate and remote spaces for a given practice expands the space in the sense that the individual has at-hand more space (remote), yet it is collapsed because it is condensed into his experience as being at-hand at the same level as proximate space.

It can be argued the experience of the academic in a business school is similar in nature to those of other knowledge workers from the perspective of spatial practices. Like freelancers or consultants, academics are freer to choose when and where they work when compared to other categories of workers. Their technology-mediated experience of space is therefore more likely to shape their daily work practices. Understanding the relationship between the daily spatial practices of workers and technology is of paramount importance given the increasing amount of time spent staring at screens (Introna & Ilharco, 2006; Twenge, 2017). Such is our absorption into our screens, the city of Honolulu has started handing out fines to pedestrians crossing the street while distracted on their mobile devices (Mohn, 2017). The risk to life and limb is taken even more seriously for those using their mobile phones while behind the wheel in

France where one in ten road accident deaths is due to distraction from a mobile device (Richebois, 2017).

Theoretical Framework Based on Merleau-Ponty

The theoretical framework developed from this study of the spatial practices of academics was primarily based on Merleau-Ponty's work on the phenomenology of perception (1945). Phenomenology is the study of experience which, by definition, removes the epistemological limits of the subject-object dichotomy. Experience is unitary and doesn't distinguish the subject from the object. Both are the same when it comes to experience in phenomenological terms. From the perspective of space, by definition, experience is spatial. Therefore, spatial practices are the basis of all experiences. Without motion, our world as we know it is inconceivable. In fact, it is for this reason we have developed brains with evolution—in order to be able to move in space. Perception is what allows humans to survive when moving within the environment. Our brains have also evolved to perceive the environment with the primary goal of survival—feeding, reproducing, evading danger, and so on. These hardwired circuits are the basic building blocks of how we experience the world and can explain our most natural gestures and engagement with our environment. However, as conscious beings with large brains, we experience the world and this very experience shapes our future experiences through memory. Basing his phenomenology of perception on evidence collected from psychology and neurological studies of his time, Merleau-Ponty was able to provide a theoretical framework for understanding how our conscious minds experience the world and the naïve contact with this very same world that is perception. It is based on the concepts of intentionality, body schema, habitus, and knowing body. Each of these concepts will now be defined.

Intentionality

In Merleau-Ponty's phenomenology of perception, the body and mind are not separate entities. For him, the body (and mind) is as much a part of the world we experience as the environment. There is no distinction or boundary. For example, he describes how the hand grasps a fork or a hammer just as much as the hammer 'grasps' the hand itself. It is as if the hammer is one with the hand and body, forming a unified whole with one intended action—to strike a nail. This is the operational intentionality, or what Husserl refers to as *fungierende Intentionalität*: that which unites our being and the world in a natural and antepredicative manner. Intentionality is what gears our body to encounter the world with a certain posture, a certain predisposition. For example, when playing football, our bodies are geared toward following the motion of the ball and preparing for reception of the ball should it ever come our way. When composing emails, one is absorbed by the text on the screen and our bodies are postured over the keyboard for typing without requiring any conscious effort. Intentionality determines the manner in which the body engages in the world and calls upon a certain body schema.

Body Schema

The body schema is a pre-conscious awareness of available bodily movements and spatial relationships. It is a repertoire of kinetic possibilities in the world that our body projects unto the world. For example, the body schema will project 'grasping' when engaged in hammering a nail into a piece of wood or of 'catching' when playing baseball. This 'grasping' or 'catching' doesn't depend on conscious effort or calculations—they are already available and activated at a pre-conscious level by intentionality. Our hand seems to grab the hammer or reach out to catch a ball in flight without the mobilization of concepts such as ballistics or the calculation of force and distance. Our hand just reaches out for the hammer or the ball, even with the ball in full flight. 'Grasping' or 'catching' is part of the body schema associated with hammering a nail in wood and playing baseball. In the case of an academic in front of a screen—be it his smartphone or his desktop—'grabbing' the mouse is part of the body schema for 'doing emails'. These body schemata are composed of possibilities for bodily engagement in the world and these possibilities are drawn from habitus.

Habitus

According to Merleau-Ponty's phenomenology of perception, habitus is the full range of possibilities for bodily engagement in the world. These are either hardwired in our brains through evolution or can be acquired with experience. In terms of experience, we do not distinguish these two sorts of habitus. As beings with large brains and culture, our habitus is mainly acquired through experience. Habitus is a general repository of renewable action that can be drawn upon to generate specific body schemata serving a particular intentionality. For example, 'grabbing' and 'catching' are renewable actions which can be just as useful when engaging in hammering a nail in wood than when reaching for a mug of coffee while reading an email on the desktop screen. 'Grabbing' is a renewable action drawn from habitus which is then added to the repertoire of available bodily movements for 'doing emails'.

Knowing Body

The knowing body is a body already in contact with the world before the machinery of judgement kicks. The body takes for granted its relationship with the world—the face on the other side of the head, the room behind the closed door, the hand at the end of the arm, or the phonograph in the next room. Merleau-Ponty studied amputees and their enduring perception of having continued use of the limb which has been severed. Their body had memory of the possibilities for action provided by the arm and the hand at the end of the arm. These actions were readily available to the amputee, even if this was not in reality possible. Likewise, when hearing music originating from a phonograph located in another room through a wall, the body continues to be aware of the presence of the phonograph without ever having to see it. The body knows it is there.

Loose Ends

Although Merleau-Ponty based his phenomenology of perception on empirical data, through interviews and observations of amputees, access to the most important source of data—the brain—was inaccessible at the time. Since more than a decade, the field of neurosciences has been actively researching the phenomenology of perception using the most advanced understanding to date on how the human brain functions.

Neuroscience and Perception

The so-called cognitive revolution initiated by Noam Chomsky in the middle of the twentieth century has broadly eclipsed behaviorism as the dominant paradigm in understanding human perception (Miller, 2003). More recently, advances in neuroscience research have provided the most compelling evidence against the behaviorist model, as we will see in this section. It is in fact very easy to demonstrate the significant limits of the behaviorist model of perception that conceptualizes the human being as a passive receiver of stimuli to which there is a predetermined brain response. For most behaviorists, the human perceives the world as it is through all the available senses and that which is received from the 'outside' is sufficient to generate a corresponding response. Some of the most advanced neuroscience research to date shows that what we perceive to be the world is as much generated by external stimuli as by our own brains.

Proof of Behaviorist Limits

Electromagnetic Spectrum

Perhaps the most fundamental limitation of the behaviorist model of perception is the fact that our senses are from the start limited. For example, our sense of hearing is limited to a certain range of audible frequencies (and this range diminishes with age). We also know that a very small fraction of the electromagnetic spectrum is 'visible' to our eyes. The electromagnetic spectrum is composed of wavelengths of 1 picometer (Gamma rays) to thousands of kilometers (extremely low frequency). Humans can only see those frequencies between 400 (ultraviolet) and 700 (infrared) nanometers, making us practically oblivious to much of the electromagnetic radiation bathing our universe from the gamma rays emitted by solar flares to the various man-made radio waves generated by terrestrial broadcasters or all of our connected devices using Wi-Fi and Bluetooth technologies. As far as the electromagnetic spectrum is concerned, we are mostly blind.

What is more interesting, as far as perception is concerned, is we believe that colors are received by our visual system exactly as we perceive them. In fact, the receptive capacity of our sensory organs (eyes) is more limited than most of us imagine, and much of what we perceive as color is in reality generated by our brains. This is explained by the mechanism of trichromatic color vision where our visual system combines signals from three types of cones in the retina to produce the rich set of colors we perceive (Rowe, 2018). In short, the retina in our eyes is able to respond to an even smaller set of wavelengths than that of the fraction of the full electromagnetic spectrum represented by the visible light. What we perceive to be the full visual spectra is in fact produced by our brains using the mechanism of trichromatism sensing an even smaller subset of wavelengths from our environment. Perception is therefore happening in large part in the brain.

Lilac Chaser

The construction of our visual experience is not limited to trichromatism. Our brains will, depending on our visual focus, exclude certain elements in the field of vision from perception. There are usually several mechanisms at work at once, and all are likely to have evolved to help us survive in environments full of motion and danger. Although the explanations are complex and beyond the scope of this chapter, an empirical demonstration can be made with Jeremy Hinton's Lilac chaser experiment.

It consists of a set of blurred magenta colored discs arranged in a circular fashion on a gray background. This image is animated in that each disc disappears for a fraction of a second in a circular, clockwise motion. The illusion occurs when one stares at cross placed at the center of the circle for longer than five seconds: The magenta discs disappear and instead we see a green disc moving around in a clockwise motion. This green disc appears at the location in the circle where the briefly disappearing magenta disc is located. This experiment accessible to anyone demonstrates how our visual experience is constructed. We can observe as we stare at the cross our peripheral vision fading for all static objects yet maintaining a perception of movement. Although the discs have no edges, our brains infer movement. The appearance of green discs where the magenta discs disappear to leave the gray background is called the afterimage effect. Although we don't yet understand why our visual systems perceive in this manner, we can imagine these mechanisms had evolved when humans needed to maintain an awareness of movement in the environment.

Adelson's Checkerboard

Adelson's checkerboard (Fig. 14.1) is another optical illusion demonstrating how our visual systems construct experience. In this experiment, a green cylindrical object is positioned on one corner of a checkerboard with its shadow cast upon the rest of the checkerboard. We perceive the squares 'A' and 'B' as being of different shades of gray, 'A' being darker

Fig. 14.1 Illusion (Adelson, 1995) (no copyright, checkershadow images may be reproduced and distributed freely). See http://persci.mit.edu/gallery/checkershadow

Fig. 14.2 Illusion revealed (Adelson, 1995) (no copyright, checkershadow images may be reproduced and distributed freely). See http://persci.mit.edu/gallery/checkershadow

than 'B'. However, 'A' and 'B' are exactly the same shade, and this is shown in Fig. 14.2. This illusion can be explained by the brain compensating the perception of dark objects in shadow by making them appear lighter in contrast to other objects outside of the shadow.

Undecipherable Image in Black and White

Other visual experiments demonstrate another manner in which our brains construct our visual experience. One of these experiments demonstrates how our visual experience can be shaped by previous visual experiences and our memory of it. In one such experiment, a black and white image is shown with undecipherable shapes depicted (see Shores, 2019). One is unable to make out the objects in the image. This is followed by a high-definition photo revealing the objects in the first image of which only some of the outlines were visible. Once this high-definition photo is seen, upon looking at the first image, we recognize the objects which were undecipherable at first glance. Nothing has changed in terms of sensory input when looking at the first image after having seen the photograph. All that has changed is previous visual experience which has provided your perception with a template or a filter assisting this perception and helping you make out the objects in the first image. Once this process is complete, the first image is no longer mysterious, and one is unable to reproduce the same visual experience at the first glance.

Audible Experience

The equivalent phenomenon can be observed with the perception of sound and the making out of voice recordings. Anil Seth, neuroscientist at the Sackler Centre for Consciousness Science at the University of Sussex, performed an experiment during his famous TED Talk in 2017 where he played back a recording of someone speaking for a few seconds. Speech was undecipherable, yet upon hearing the recording, one could make out a human voice speaking. Immediately after, Anil Seth played the original recording and we can clearly perceive his voice and him saying, "I think Brexit is a terrible idea". The first version of the recording was doctored to render speech undecipherable, in much the same way that it can be when a vinyl record is played at the wrong speed. Once one has heard the original recording, the doctored version is decipherable when it is played back. The brain fills in the blanks with its previous audible experience.

Modeling the Brain as a Bayesian Inference Machine

What neuroscience has found is that our visual cortex—along with other sensory systems—constructs our experience. It is a combination of brains, bodies, and histories which construct our experience, as demonstrated by the experiments just reviewed. Neuroscientists such as Anil Seth describe our brains as prediction machines. They provide us with the best guess of what is happening in the world by combining sensory inputs with memories of prior experience. This theory, also known as Bayesian brain (Seth, 2014), posits that perception is the result of the brain inferring the most likely causes of sensory input by confronting these inputs with expectations of signals based on predictive models formed over time with experience. The gap between that which is predicted, and sensory input is called prediction error, and this error 'corrects' perception by updating predictive models. Perception is therefore the product of prior 'belief' and sense data, or an estimate 'best guess' of reality (Fig. 14.3).

Prediction Error

Prediction error is a concept which has been developed for some time in neuroscience (Friston, 2009; Seth, 2013) and is based on the theory that

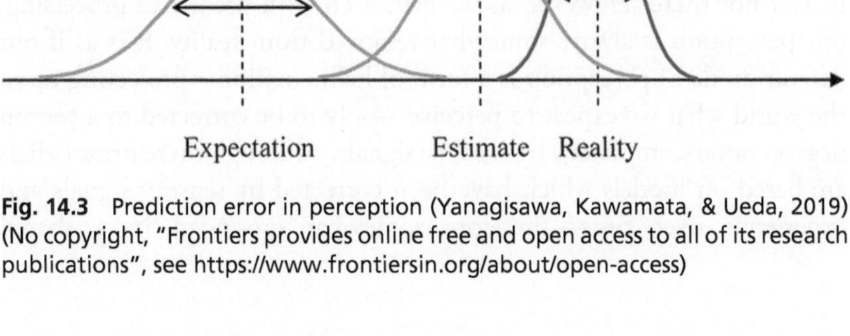

Fig. 14.3 Prediction error in perception (Yanagisawa, Kawamata, & Ueda, 2019) (No copyright, "Frontiers provides online free and open access to all of its research publications", see https://www.frontiersin.org/about/open-access)

the brain continuously sends predictions out to the world in order to confront this with sensory data. There being a difference between this expectation and the sensory input is a perfectly normal situation since perception is a continuous process of calibration that explains away prediction errors to refine approximate inferences about the world. Our perception is therefore in large part generated by the brain and not purely based on sensory input as behaviorists believed. It is as if we start with what we believe to expect from the world in a given situation and see how sensory input matches that expectation. Our brains then adjust these predictions to better fit the sensory input. Much of our perception therefore depends on our prior 'beliefs' about the world and what we have learned over time with experience.

Pareidolia

An interesting illustration of how expectations are a dominant part of perception is the phenomenon of pareidolia—when we perceive an object as being something that in reality it is not. The most common occurrence of this phenomenon is seeing faces in clouds or in food (often deities on toast). According to predictive processing, this phenomenon can be explained by our predictions overwhelming sensory data such that we 'see' objects that are in fact not really there, yet patterns in sensory data are unable to correct for this error.

Controlled Versus Uncontrolled Hallucination

Pareidolia can be likened to a form of hallucination, seeing things that are in fact not there. However, as we have seen with predictive processing, our perception is always somewhat removed from reality. It is as if our default mode of perception is a form of hallucination—projecting upon the world what we expect to perceive—only to be corrected to a certain degree, never completely, by sensory signals. Although these prior beliefs are based on models which have been corrected by sensory signals and experience over time—therefore somewhat grounded in a shared reality—it would not be completely unreasonable to say that we are in fact subject to a continuous form of controlled hallucination while conscious. This can be contrasted with uncontrolled hallucinations such as dreams, where sensory input is limited and therefore perception is no longer grounded in reality. Being able to fly or be in two places at once is therefore never perceived as unusual since there is no correction. Some hallucinogenic agents are known to alter perception to the point of disrupting predictive error correction and allowing beliefs to be projected on our world without any form of grounding in reality through sensory signals. In fact, in some cases, these very same signals can reinforce errors and accentuate departures from reality.

The Beholders Share

Gombrich (1961, 181) in *Art and Illusion* says, "It is the power of expectation rather than the power of conceptual knowledge that molds what we see in life no less than in art". This expectation is what he calls the beholders share. What our bodies and our minds anticipate in the world determines how we perceive it. Conceptual knowledge only intervenes as an after-thought, only once we've engaged with the world. This expectation can be likened to Merleau-Ponty's concept of intentionality, in that one adopts a certain posture—or expectation—when engaging in the world with a certain state of mind or focus. Doing emails or catching a ball for example.

How Objecthood is Manifest in Our Experience

An experiment combining virtual reality and augmented reality technologies to understand how everyday objecthood is manifest in our experience (Suzuki, Schwartzman, Augusto, & Seth, 2019) supports theories of perception emphasizing the influence of sensorimotor contingencies on visual experience. Coupling physical objects with virtual ones, the experiment sought to understand how our brains would predict the kinetic movement of handheld objects in response to certain manipulations. The experiment found that, as our daily experience would suggest, we perceive certain physical attributes of objects which may not be accessible through sensory input (vison or touch). That is to say, just as we perceive the room behind the door, our brains project attributes upon everyday objects in order to be able to predict how they would react to some form of manipulation. We perceive a box as having six sides and would react in a certain way when one side is pushed. These kinetic expectations are what the body schema would integrate with respect to certain types of objects and intentionality.

How Neuroscience Supports Merleau-Ponty's Phenomenology of Perception

In his days, Merleau-Ponty was unable to benefit from the most recent advances in neuroscience and our understanding of the brain and of perception. Although his theories were based on a certain number of empirical findings, it is remarkable that his phenomenology of perception appears to be supported by recent experiments and theories in neuroscience. Each of the concepts of intentionality, body schema, and habitus seem to emerge out of the field of neuroscience without the explicit aim of testing them against new sets of findings. It seems clear that modeling the brain as a Bayesian inference machine, where the body projects upon the world its perception of it as much as the world provides stimuli, aligns perfectly with Merleau-Ponty's theories of the phenomenal body. The sorts of predictions a brain projects unto the world are determined by a certain state depending on the activity engaged in by the body. These sets of predictions are dependent upon intentionality, or the posture one takes vis-à-vis the world. Predictions will not be the same when we are sitting in front of a keyboard and screen as when we are playing baseball. Furthermore, predictions are based on models which are mainly constructed based on prior experience, or what Merleau-Ponty calls habitus. With prediction errors, these models are refined, and thus habitus renewed. Accordingly, the repertoire of actions available to the body will depend on these predictive models, and thus a certain body schema will be composed to catch the baseball or grab a hammer.

In terms of our experience of space, and more specifically that of organizational space, neuroscience lends more support to the pursuit of phenomenological and experiential approaches to understanding the consequences of ICT on organizational space. With our brains as Bayesian inference machines, we can better understand how we experience space as being both proximate and distant at the same time when engaging intensely with ICT on a daily basis. Just like we have predictive models of how proximate objects will react to manipulation, we also have predictive models of how remote objects will react and behave to certain actions. Objects need not be physical, as the experiments by Suzuki et al. (2019) demonstrate, and the brain will complete our perception of full objects such that they can be useful and at-hand for manipulation. This means that virtual or digital objects are just as accessible to manipulation as are physical objects to the phenomenal body, albeit calling for a completely different body schema and sets of predictive models. Manipulating a paper folder with as content a set of A4 papers will call upon a certain set of predictive models, whereas the manipulation of a virtual folder with spreadsheets will call upon another set of predictive models. Each will be animated by a different kind of intentionality. Likewise, our experience during videoconferencing calls will be determined by a certain set of expectations of how remote objects (or bodies) will move along with their spatial relationships. When in a videoconferencing call—or even a telephone call—our bodies adopt a certain stance and our body schema projects expectations about our experience of space, whether proximate or remote. Remote space, as far as experience is concerned, is in fact proximate, even though this space is not experienced in the same way as proximate space. Predictive models for what happens in the home office of a coworker with whom one is doing a visioconference call will be different from the predictive models of what happens with the space in our immediate vicinity. Furthermore, the more experience we have of the remote spaces we encounter in our day-to-day routines through ICT, either from direct physical contact or indirectly through videoconferencing calls, our predictive models will be enhanced and produce a more unified experience of space. Over time and with the cumulation of experience, the experience of space—remote and proximate—will merge into a unified, singular phenomenon. With ICT, organizational space is therefore simultaneously collapsed and expanded.

Conclusion

A phenomenological approach to understanding our experience of space in our digital age, supported by advances in the field of neuroscience, supports the thesis that organizational space is both simultaneously collapsed and expanded. The Bayesian brain, based on predictive models, allows one to experience space as a singular sphere of experience, whether remote or proximate. A richer habitus based on prior experience will enhance this singular experience of space. Merleau-Ponty's concepts of intentionality and body schema are also supported as they determine which predictive models will be called upon depending on the posture taken vis-à-vis the world. The resulting body schema, or adapted repertoire of action, will project a certain form of objecthood upon objects in the world and make predictions about how they will react to manipulation—whether digital or physical. In the end, as a matter of experience, the digital and the physical are indistinguishable.

With the better understanding afforded by recent advances in the field of neurosciences, I feel better able to explain the differences in my experience of space during the COVID-19 lockdown and the intensive use of technology to engage with the world. When on the phone with my uncle on his terrace in India or in a videoconferencing calls with my parents in Canada, I was 'there' because my predictive models were well developed on the basis of prior experience of actual physical presence in these specific locations with these same individuals. This experience of being 'there' would break down somewhat when dealing with a large number of individuals with whom I had less direct experience engaging in those spaces from which they were connected. This meant that my experience was less unified and more fragmented, resulting in a sense of absence (on the part of my interlocutors) and in turn a decreased feeling of engagement on my part. Having a richer habitus, or an enhanced set of experiences of those remote places where my interlocutors are located, would likely produce a less fragmented experience of organizational space.

Studying organizational space from the perspective of the phenomenology of perception, supported by findings from the field of neurosciences, will help better understand how individuals and organizations can deal with the challenges of our increasingly 'virtual' working and personal lives. Simplistic approaches treating organizational space as having been fragmented by ICT and regarding 'remoteness' as inferior to proximity in terms of human interactions will lead us to an impasse and poor decisions. The experience of 'remoteness', while not equivalent to proximity, has the potential to be rich and satisfying. A better understanding of our experiences of space is required for this point to be driven home in management practice. With the help of neuroscientists and phenomenologists, a path to this goal is thankfully within reach.

References

Adelson, E. H. (1995). *Checkershadow illusion*. Retrieved from http://persci.mit.edu/gallery/checkershadow

Friston, K. (2009). The free-energy principle: A rough guide to the brain? *Trends in Cognitive Sciences, 13*(7), 293–301.

Gombrich, E. H. (1961). *Art and illusion*. New York: Pantheon Books.

Introna, L. D., & Ilharco, F. M. (2006). On the meaning of screens: Towards a phenomenological account of screenness. *Human Studies, 29*(1), 57–76.

Merleau-Ponty, M. (1945). *Phénoménologie de la perception*. Paris: Bibliothèque des idées, Editions Gallimard.

Miller, G. A. (2003). The cognitive revolution: A historical perspective. *Trends in Cognitive Sciences, 7*(3), 141–144.

Mohn, T. (2017, October 23). Reading this while walking. Honolulu, it could cost you. *The New York Times*.

Mukherjee, A. (2017). *Organizational space collapsed, organizational space expanded: Experiencing space with ICT, affordance and the body*. Doctoral dissertation, Université Paris-Dauphine, Paris.

Richebois, V. (2017, October 28). Le portable au volant, la mort au tournant. *Les Échos*.

Rowe, M. H. (2018). Trichromatic color vision in primates. *Physiology, 17*, 93–98.

Seth, A. K. (2013). Interoceptive inference, emotion, and the embodied self. *Trends in Cognitive Sciences, 17*(11), 565–573.

Seth, A. K. (2014). The cybernetic Bayesian brain. From interoceptive inference to sensorimotor contingencies. In T. Metzinger & J. M. Windt (Eds.), *Open MIND*: 35(T). Frankfurt am Main: MIND Group.

Shores, G. (2019, September 3). Our inner universes: The neuroscience of reality. *Better Questions Than Answers Blog*. Retrieved from https://better-questions-than-answers.blog/2019/09/03/the-neuroscience-of-reality/

Suzuki, K., Schwartzman, D. J., Augusto, R., & Seth, A. K. (2019). Sensorimotor contingency modulates breakthrough of virtual 3D objects during a breaking continuous flash suppression paradigm. *Cognition, 187*, 95–107.

Twenge, J. M. (2017, September). Have smartphones destroyed a generation. *The Atlantic, 9*.

Yanagisawa, H., Kawamata, O., & Ueda, K. (2019). Modeling emotions associated with novelty at variable uncertainty levels: A Bayesian approach. *Frontiers in Computational Neuroscience, 13*(2), 10p.

Part V

Organizational Aspects of New Ways of Working

15

From Innovations at Work to Innovative Ways of Conceptualizing Organization: A Brief History of Organization Studies

Lise Arena and Anthony Hussenot

Introduction

While organizational scholars have recently investigated varied organizational phenomena, such as social movements, artistic activities, non-profit organizations or informal collectives of people, mainstream organization research has historically carried out empirical work in companies, factories or networks of firms,[1] mainly because of the dominance

[1] This proximity with business has led to a confusion between organization studies, management research (George 1968; Wren 1972) and the theory of the firm. Management research is interested in improving the economic performance of companies and organizations; the theory of the firm concentrates on the economic dimensions of firms. In this chapter, we suggest to highlight the distinction between organization studies, management research and the theory of the firm.

L. Arena (✉) • A. Hussenot
Université Côte d'Azur, Nice, France
e-mail: lise.arena@univ-cotedazur.fr; Anthony.hussenot@univ-cotedazur.fr

N. Mitev et al. (eds.), *New Ways of Working*, Technology, Work and Globalization,
https://doi.org/10.1007/978-3-030-61687-8_15

of the industrial context after the Second World War. As such, organization studies are rooted in social sciences (such as economics, sociology and philosophy), and have mainly but not only focused on the evolution of work and management practices. As most of social sciences, organization studies have evolved in line with society, and more specifically, business, managerial and work innovations. Consequently, the relation between innovations at work and the theoretical developments has led to different understandings of the matter of organization over time. If an organization was initially conceptualized as a social and/or economic entity evolving into an environment, this view has since been challenged by scholars. Recent organization theories have suggested to understand organization as an open phenomenon, always in a state of becoming. An organization is not conceptualized as an entity but as an elusive movement ongoing re/defined in practices. The initial essentialist view of organization was forged in a context of industrialization and mass production, dominated by Fordist practices, while the current elusive view of organization has emerged in the context of 'liquid modernity' (Bauman 2000) and the 'projectification' of work (Jensen et al. 2016).

In this chapter, we suggest studying the relation between work innovations and the evolution of organization theories. We emphasize the relation between management and work innovations and new ways of conceptualizing the matter of organization over time. The aim is to show how innovations at work have influenced the way scholars have conceptualized organizational phenomena over time.

We describe and analyze this relation from the 1950s to the 2010s. We study this relation through four periods covering the mass production-based organization of the 1950s to the projectification of work of the 2010s. Of course, these periods are used for analytical purposes as each new period partly overlaps with the previous ones.

Period 1: The Development of Industrial Innovations—Theorizing Organization as a Centralized Managerial Hierarchy

The period following the Second World War was marked by an unprecedented economic expansion in Western countries that depended on the significant rise of consumption and national modes of capitalism (Arena 2011). Rising working-class prosperity led to mass consumption and Fordist mass production replaced manual work with machines leading to increased labor division and repetitive tasks. Social and technological changes that shaped the second half of the twentieth century built on the first industrial revolution in the nineteenth century; the second industrial revolution was based on the development of organic chemistry, electricity and nuclear physics in the first half of the twentieth century and molecular biology since the 1950s. Post-Second World War advances in engineering, computer science and electronics also paved the way towards the third 'electronic' industrial revolution characterized by a smaller number of firms than the ones that shaped the second industrial revolution. These successive waves of inventions shaped industries all over the world, with Europe catching-up the US. The US developed innovations and gained competitive advantage in the computer (e.g. IBM) and car (e.g. General Motors) industries. In the same period, Europe gradually caught up particularly in the chemical (e.g. Haber-Bosch) and car (e.g. Volkswagen) industries in Germany and the transport industry in France (e.g. SNCF). The UK differed slightly as industrial policy was limited and most innovations appeared in the service industry (e.g. financial sector). Organizational forms shaped by industrial innovations in this period resulted from national characteristics: managerial capitalism in the US, state-led nationalized enterprises in France, cooperative capitalism with cartelization in Germany and proprietary capitalism with family-owned businesses in the UK.

Centralized Managerial Hierarchies and the Rise of Professional Management

To a large extent, the main characteristics of organizational forms in the post-Second World War period appeared as a continuity of inter-war managerial innovations. Business historian Alfred Chandler claimed that the structures of companies and the role of management played a significant part in the evolution of capitalism (Chandler 1990). Hence, US capitalism success could be explained by the ability of American managers to develop multidivisional enterprises, characterized by centralized hierarchies, administrative coordination and the rise of managerial services. By contrast, British managerial backwardness was due to the predominance of small firms (mostly family-owned businesses) and a small number of 'white collars'.[2] Innovations were supported by "the new forms of transportation and communication [which] permitted the rise of modern mass production. […] Thus, came into being a new economic institution, the managerial business enterprise and a new subspecies of economic man, the salaried manager" (Chandler 1990, 1). These organizations appeared as an alternative to decentralized market mechanisms and they routinized transactions among units, lowering their costs. Organizational models were based on administrative coordination and task specialization that allowed product specifications and market services to be adjusted more rapidly to customer needs. At the management level, salaried middle and top managers supervised and controlled the different units. As a result, management became a profession with a direct interest in organization (and innovation), in contrast to shareholders who were still generally driven by short-term profit interest.

Based on this vertical integration model inherited from Frederick Taylor's "Principles of Scientific Management" (first published in 1911) and labor division popularized by Henri Ford, managers and workers of the 1950s took part in a large transformation of work practices. On the one hand, control was placed at the center of managerial corporations, as

[2] Based on historical case studies (monographs) of the 200 largest US, UK and German firms, Chandler's study showed the rise of professional managers and 'organization men' as a new category of businessmen (Chandler 1990).

managers of multidivisional units were the guardians of standardized methods. The professionalization of management and the emergence of salaried managers justified the development of management education in the US and in Europe which soon became an urgent need to train this new category of businessmen (Arena 2011). Yet, over the 1960s, the top-down understanding of control gradually faded away to allow more room to a consensual view of the employment contract in which workers could develop further adaptability and gain welfare.

On the other hand, the inheritance of Taylor's methods stimulated labor movements which later encouraged the consideration of employees' working conditions and the creation of research committees in America and in Britain to address the 'labor problem'. During the inter-war period, 'labor problems' were due to high turnover, high absenteeism and low workers' motivation and drove employers in large businesses to think about the relationship between workers' welfare and productivity. It was in this context that a number of American firms—such as Proctor & Gamble, General Electric, Eastman Kodak and U.S. Steel—began to develop a range of new initiatives about work welfare that took the form of financial and non-financial measures.[3]

Pioneer Organization Theories: The Tavistock Institute, the Aston Group and the Carnegie School

Pre-1945 ideas about management and organization developed by engineers such as Henri Fayol, Henri Ford and Frederick Taylor equipped enterprises with new forms of labor specialization that were disseminated beyond America, as the most efficient mode of organization in industrial factories. Although Europe never witnessed a 'scientific management' movement like its American equivalent, Taylorism and Fordism still received a fair amount of attention, mainly positive, by British, French

[3] This included measures to improve basic working conditions (e.g. provision of shower rooms, cafeterias and drinking fountains), to enhance workers' sense of being part of a factory team (e.g. publication of company magazines, organization of educational lectures and athletic clubs), to recognize seniority in employment status (e.g. bonuses, pension plans, medical assistance and company housing) and to provide training opportunities (e.g. vocational schools and apprenticeship programs) (Moriguchi 2000, 13–14).

and German engineers (Chevalier 1937; Whilston 1997). Moreover, the theoretical analysis of bureaucracy by sociologist Max Weber (1922), translated and expanded upon by Talcott Parsons (1942, 1947) and Robert Merton (1949/1968), played an important role in the development of early organization theories (Shenhav 2003). This is exemplified by the publication of the first academic articles about organization such as the work of sociologist Philipp Selznick who published *An Approach to a Theory of Bureaucracy* in 1943 and *Foundations of the Theory of Organization* in 1948. In the same period, Herbert Simon published in 1947 *American Behavior: A Study of Decision-Making Processes in Administrative Organization*. As a result, new modes of organization in industrial factories and pioneer publications in the field led to the emergence of three major schools of thought: The Tavistock Institute (London, UK), the Aston Group (Birmingham, UK) and the Carnegie School (Pittsburgh, US).

The Tavistock Institute: The Working Group as a Sociotechnical System

The first wave of reactions to the scientific method of organizing enterprises comes from the 'human relations' movement. This movement was exemplified by the Hawthorne studies—some of the best known and most influential investigations in the history of organizational research—that took place at the Western Electric Company (US) between 1927 and 1932. In the same period, the French industrial engineer Henri Fayol (1916/1949) put a greater (than Taylor) emphasis on the management level (and less on the workers) and discussed the aim of the managerial function.[4] Management anticipates actions (planning), aims at structuring the organization (organizing), disseminates orders (commanding), guarantees the coherence of actions (coordinating) and checks results (controlling).

[4] Fayol was the managing director of the French *Commentry-Fourchambault et Decazeville* Company (a large mining and steel firm) for 30 years (1888–1918). Fayol's initial contribution (*Administration Industrielle et Générale,* published in French in 1916) was translated into English in 1930 by J. A. Coubrough, and then by J. Storrs in 1949 with the title *General and Industrial Management.*

Social psychology of work and early studies on groups as organizations went one step further and significantly rose in the UK in the 1960s. In particular, Eric Trist, with a number of colleagues in the Tavistock Institute (such as Emery, Rice and Miller), conducted a series of investigations into groups and organizational functioning. Their main contribution to the emergence of organization studies led to a 'system approach' to organizational behavior. In particular, they showed that working groups were neither a social system nor a technical system but an interdependent sociotechnical system. In their view, the traditional technocratic bureaucracy is limited when organizations have to face turbulent and innovative environments. Control systems could be seen as cumbersome and costly even if, thanks to this control, an unskilled worker in a narrow job is inexpensive to replace and takes little time to train. As early as the 1960s, these authors suggested alternative organizational designs for turbulent environments in which "individuals and units have wide repertories of activities to cope with change", and an improved quality of working life "by keeping the technological determinants of worker behavior to a minimum to satisfy social and psychological needs by the involvement of all" (Hickson and Pugh 2007/1964, 153).

The Aston Group: The Structure of Organizations

The structuralist view was deeply anchored in Max Weber's contribution to sociology and its translation in English by Talcott Parsons. A small interdisciplinary (social psychology, sociology, anthropology, political science and economics) group of researchers (1961–1970) at the University of Birmingham in the UK echoed this initial trend and sought to understand variables influencing organizational structures (such as technology, size, environment and culture).[5] Aiming to make a contribution to the interdisciplinary study of management behavior, the Aston group tested the idea that organization structure fits its operational context (Greenwood and Devine 1997, 202). Based on a statistical analysis, the group, whose principal investigators were Derek Pugh and David Hickson, collected

[5] Further details about the history of organization and management studies at Birmingham can be found in Minkes (2011).

firms' data that enabled them to build organizational taxonomies. In this sense, the Aston Group's contribution to organization theory also has to be assessed at a methodological level since it was seen as "somewhere in between the tracing of processes over time […] and the postulating of causal explanations informed by wider sampling" (Pugh and Hickson 1972, 273). Their willingness to develop from a descriptive to an analytical discipline led the Aston research team to initiate 'strategic contingencies theories' in a research cooperation with the University of Alberta in Canada.

The Carnegie School: Decision-Making Processes in Organizations

In the last chapter of his book *The Functions of the Executive* published in 1938, Chester I. Barnard, President of the New Jersey Bell Telephone Company at the time, observed that there was a need for "a science of organization" (Barnard 1968/1938, 290).[6] The publication of Herbert Simon's *Administrative Behavior* in 1947 explicitly relied on Barnard's effort to develop a science of organization. Simon's initial ambition was to formalize Barnard's contribution from a conceptual perspective. He sought to "describe, in words, exactly how an administrative organization looks and exactly how it works" (Simon 1947). Simon's concept of 'bounded rationality' directly contributes to the development of organizational theory, as organizations are seen as useful instruments "for the achievement of human purpose".[7] Organizations are therefore seen as a way to economize on cognitive resources, seen as scarce in a context of bounded rationality. Simon discussed innovation in relation with a

[6] Barnard identified this gap in social sciences: "there is no science of organization or of cooperative systems; and the development of the sciences called social has clearly lagged far behind those called physical and mathematical. One reason for this appears to be a false emphasis upon intellectual and mental processes both as factors in human relations and as matters of study" (Barnard 1968/1938, 290).

[7] Herbert A. Simon challenged the well-established concept of 'perfect rationality' used at the time in economics. For him, human cognitive capabilities are limited in information and knowledge and cannot formulate a 'rational' choice resulting from an optimization process. Humans simplify their choice process and can do so when replacing the goal of 'maximizing' with the goal of 'satisficing'.

problem-solving framework. Innovation (technical or organizational) is seen as a significant process in the expansion of firms. As innovation and creativity are a type of complex problem-solving, he argued that it could be captured in terms of simple heuristics and satisficing criteria (by contrast with optimization which was the predominant paradigm in economics at the time). Simon's contribution to 'design science' paved the way towards new models of innovations mainly based on knowledge transfers and information-based approaches.

To a large extent, the publication of Simon and March's book on *Organizations* in 1958, and Cyert and March's book in 1963, imported innovation issues in organization theories. In particular, Cyert and March argued that their general theory was "of considerable relevance to the prediction of innovations" (1963, 278). They focused on the notion of failure and argued that firms innovate both when successful and unsuccessful. In the case of successful firms, the existence of organizational slack allows resources to be channeled towards innovative activities. In the same vein, they showed that, in service organizations, managers "prefer to copy the ideas of others or to search for ready-made solutions instead of seeking innovation" (Nutt 1984, 445). They linked innovations with the concept of 'organizational learning', as firms revise their search procedures on the basis of experience (Cyert and March 1963, 124).

This first period (1950–1980) constituted the rise of management as a profession with "concepts, research methods, and specialized techniques of practice that could be studied, taught, communicated and improved by the acquisition of scientific information" (Scott 1992, 25). Organizations were seen as administrative entities and closed systems in which innovation was attributed to the visionary capacities of top managers. As rightly stated by Slappendel (1996, 110), in this perspective, "the actions of individuals are not seen to be constrained by external factors, instead individuals are perceived to be self-directing agents who are guided by the goals that they set".

Period 2: Immaterial Innovations and the Knowledge-Based Economy—Theorizing Organization as a Learning Institution

The second period of analysis is concerned with the development of the 'electronic' century (Cortada 2011), also characterized as the second wave of the Information Technologies (IT) revolution enabled by the advent of the personal computer during the 1980s and the Internet during the 1990s (Porter and Heppelman 2014). Innovations are essentially immaterial and developed within the context of a global knowledge economy, with distributed supply chains easing coordination and integration across activities. From the 1980s onwards, large managerial corporations turned into innovative enterprises characterized by coordinated business organizations that adopted technologies and learned to adapt in a context of high uncertainty and turbulence. In the US, the *Management in the 1990s Research Program*, a close collaboration between academic researchers at the MIT Sloan School of Management and representatives of major corporations, represents the organizational archetype of the 1990s and their organizational, work and technological innovations. The final report of the program strongly emphasized the role of information in the evolution of 1990s firms (Scott Morton 1991). Information was considered, for the first time, as a fourth factor of production: "as an 'information engine', it can do for business what the steam engine did in the days of the Industrial Revolution" (Scott Morton 1991, 8). The diffusion of IT implied potential organizational change, as it offered the opportunity for organizations to react constructively to environmental turbulence. In the 1980s, most technological innovations were concerned with hardware, software, networks, workstations robotics and smart chips. These information-based technological innovations gave firms the opportunity to lower their operating costs while improving their efficiencies (Cortada 2011; Porter and Heppelman 2014). For example, in the 1990s, the emergence of supply-chain enhanced the coordination of work and the management of flows of goods, supplies, processes and expenses within the organization.

The Knowledge-Based Economy and Horizontal Informational Structures of Companies

While the US economy had a significant competitive advantage with a well-established IT industry composed of large corporations such as IBM and Microsoft, the Japanese computer industry arose in the 1980s, from capabilities developed in long-established firms making electrical and telecommunications equipment, such as Fujitsu Limited or Toshiba Corporation. This has to be understood in relation with the evolution of Japanese capitalism based on financial business and conglomerates. The Japanese industrial success of the 1980s was mainly explained by national specificities such as stable shareholding, permanent employment and main-bank lending (Lazonick 2010). In his comparison of two archetypal firms (the American and the Japanese models), the economist Masahiko Aoki observed the rise of the Japanese economy in the 1980s and explained it through a shift from primary and secondary activities (agriculture and manufacturing) to information-based production (telecommunications and computers[8]). The Japanese organizational model paved the way towards a knowledge-based economy[9] characterized by flexible specialization, mass customization and lean manufacturing. The shift from a vertically integrated organization to a more flexible way of organization is largely rooted in the archetype of 1980s Japanese firms.

The development of horizontally coordinated organizations led to various changes in the nature of work. This period constituted a breaking point with the Fordist era. "The heightened expectations of people in Western Europe and North America are giving rise to pressures to improve

[8] This phenomenon was also observed in the US to a lesser extent at the time under the term "Post-Fordism".

[9] While embryonic approaches of information and knowledge-based organizational theories originated in the 1960s, they only became popular 30 years later. One example of this theoretical trend is probably the dissemination of resource-based approaches to the firm as a result of Edith Penrose's early contribution to organizational theory. In her 1959 book, entitled *The Theory of the Growth of the Firm*, Penrose views firms not like standard economists of her time as price (and output) takers whose access to extra-profits is limited to situations of high degrees of market power (imperfect competition). Instead, she emphasizes that the firm is a device for innovation, problem-solving and cumulative learning through production. She underlines the idea of an endless knowledge-creating process and argues that "the very processes of operation and of expansion are intimately associated with the process by which knowledge is increased" (Penrose 1959, 125).

the quality of working life and the quality of the environment. This is resulting in a changing concept of what constitutes value" (Scott Morton 1991, 3). In addition, cooperative work enabled by IT tended to alter most tasks in organizations, as the primary objective of organizations moved to coordinate the delivery of goods and services to customers. As a result, traditional roles of managers changed, as employees had "more access to data, they will take over many of the functions associated with supervisors" (Osterman 1991, 236). Managers had to learn to share their knowledge of the production process and of technologies with less qualified workers. As teams became a more common organizational form within firms, workers also had to learn new roles and skills. Jobs were no longer specified in detail and workers had to rotate among various jobs, and the development of skills and tacit knowledge became key to firms' strategies.

New challenges faced by organizations involved a need to train high skilled workers and to develop a 'learning organization'. Therefore, knowledge gradually became one of the most important assets in the development of firms' competitive advantage. The practice of knowledge management was introduced as "the identification, optimization, and active management of explicit or tangible informational assets (such as data physically stored in a computer or on a piece of paper) and tacit knowledge (information and insights residing largely in people's heads)" (Cortada 2011, 24). In line with this knowledge-view of the organization, communities of practice emerged as triggers to collective 'learning-by-doing' and started attracting scholars' attention (Lave and Wenger 1991). New forms of learning organizations rely on the growth of communities of practice with people who share a concern or a passion for something they do and learn how to do it better as they interact regularly.

Reinforcing the Mainstream or Being Against? Neo-Institutionalism, Postmodernism and the Critical Perspective in Organization Studies

These managerial innovations and generally speaking the social and intellectual contexts of the 1960s and 1970s inspired organization scholars during the 1980s and 1990s to either reinforce the mainstream perspective in organization studies or disrupt it by introducing alternative ways of defining and studying organization. To exemplify this tension in the field, the following section introduces the neo-institutionalism, the post-modernism and the critical management studies.

Neo-institutionalism: Isomorphism and Legitimacy

From the 1950s, the notion of 'organizational behavior' has been dominant in organization studies. The premise of organizational behavior studies is that an organization is an entity that can (almost) behave on its own. However, others have argued that society and institutions influence this behavior. During the late 1970s, a new form of institutionalism, called 'neo-institutionalism', emerged to understand how organizational behavior is situated and influenced by other organizations and wider social forces (Lounsbury and Zhao 2014). For these scholars, any organization evolves in communities of organizations that interact with each other (DiMaggio and Powell 1983). These interactions create an 'institutional logic', that is symbolic and material elements tied together and providing order and meaning (Friedland and Alford 1991). According to the neo-institutionalist view, organizations conform to institutional prescriptions to gain legitimacy with key audiences (Meyer and Rowan 1977). Legitimacy is understood as immaterial capital enhancing status, reputation and survival chances (Rao 1994). Organizations implement innovations as a way to conform with institutional logics, and not necessarily because of requirements of technical, human or financial efficiency. These institutional pressures lead to 'isomorphism' among organizations, that is organizations imitate each other by adopting common structures, practices and technologies (Meyer and Rowan 1977). Unlike organization theories developed in the first period, the focus of neo-institutional theory is not the relation between the organization and its environment, but rather networks of organizations, such as innovation systems.

Postmodernism: The Role of Language in the Emergence of Organizational Phenomena

As much as neo-institutionalism can be understood as expanding mainstream organization studies, the postmodern perspective was developed by some scholars in organization studies during the 1980s and the 1990s and initiated a radical change in the way organization has been studied since. However, the notion of postmodernism covers at least two different meanings: postmodernism (without a hyphen) as a way of studying organizational phenomena (Cooper and Burrell 1988; Burrell 1994; Cooper 1989; Chia 1995, 2003; Parker 1992); and the post-modern organization (with a hyphen) as a during the 1980s and the 1990s (Clegg 1990).

Postmodernism is rooted in European philosophy of the 1970s and 1980s, in particular the French theories of Jacques Derrida, Michel Foucault and Jean-François Lyotard, among others. The postmodern view insists on the role of language in constituting organizational phenomena. In such a view, there is no ultimate truth about organization and management but only forms of discourses. Postmodernism is thus based on a critique of positive and normative science seeking laws for good practices, which is the foundation of modernist organization studies and management. Instead, postmodern scholars urge scholars to study the situatedness of organizational phenomena and how they are performed through discourses.

Conversely, the post-modern perspective characterizes a new form of organization as flexible and niche-marketed and based on a multi-skilled workforce held together by IT networks and outsourcing (Clegg 1990, 181). These new organizational forms are claimed to be innovation-oriented, and flexible with no clear center of power or spatial location. Japanese innovative working methods illustrate the post-modern organization. Japanese engineers designing products followed the product from the lab to the manufacturing facility (Aoki 1990). Workers had to become capable of coping with unexpected emergencies as managers increasingly delegated their decision-making power. Knowledge had to be shared and the new challenge was the codification and transmission of tacit knowledge from expert to non-expert workers, and the organization had to develop learning and adaptation capabilities, rather than concentrate on minimizing transaction costs. This organizational form follows a just-in-time production process which begins when customers order a product and in which each worker has skills to adapt to this new type of production.

Critical Management Studies: The Deconstruction of Hidden Assumptions in Management

Partly based on the postmodern turn, some scholars have started to question the assumptions of management both as an academic discipline and as a practice. This has led to the emergence of critical management studies (CMS), first initiated by Alvesson and Wilmott (1992). According to critical management thinkers, modern management is mainly instrumental and only serves the profit of companies (Adler et al. 2008). Innovations at work such as improvement of working conditions, self-development and self-determination are only adopted by companies if they help to improve business performance. This raises ethical and political questions regarding the value of such ends, and consequently, the responsibility of scholars reinforcing such practices through normative research and teaching. "CMS aims to show how such beliefs and practices are nurtured by, and serve to sustain, divisive and destructive patterns and structures; and also, how their reproduction is contingent and changeable, neither necessary nor unavoidable" (Adler et al. 2008, 3). CMS aim at denunciating the instrumentalism, patriarchism, racism, imperialism, productivism (etc.) that are inherent in modern management.

Period 3: Liquid Modernity—Theorizing Organization as a Movement

In 2000, sociologist Zygmunt Bauman published a book called *Liquid Modernity*. This book marked a turning point in social sciences as his key idea is that we have been entering a society in which the core institutions are diluting. The expression 'liquid modernity' was a way to express one of the main trends of our society: the liquefaction of social institutions. For Bauman (2000), this liquid modernity means that individuals can rely only on themselves as their relations with others are uncertain, evolving and temporary. Jobs, family, friendships are becoming more and more uncertain. There are many explanations for this liquefaction of society and some of them can be found in the counter-cultures of the 1960s and 1970s, when people started to free themselves from rigid social orders (religion, patriarchism, patriotism, etc.). However, in the 2000s, the world became more globalized than ever, with large-scale exchanges between people. With the end of the Soviet Union at the beginning of the 1990s and market deregulation all over the world, cultures and economies became more globalized and a reality that people could experience in their daily life. This globalization generated a period of economic growth and social development for many countries, but at the same time, an intensification of competition between companies. Outsourcing, offshoring, mergers and acquisitions were the main consequences of this fierce global competition.

Innovation as the Main Driver in Management

To face these threats, companies had to innovate constantly, again and again. This has become a motto in many sectors. Of course, innovation had been a key activity for companies for decades, but the novelty became the intensity of innovation. Instead of waiting for the end of their products' life cycle before launching a new one, companies started to constantly launch new products on the market as a way to beat competitors. This period of development coincided with the second wave of IT-driven transformation, characterized by the rise of the Internet with its cheap and ubiquitous connectivity (Porter and Heppelman 2014). This led to enhanced coordination between suppliers and customers across space and time.

This innovation intensity is not only the result of increased competition, it is also the sociological consequence of the liquefaction of society. As people's identity was no longer based on belonging to institutions (company, religion, state, etc.), mass consumption became a way to define oneself (Bauman 2000). Consumption is motivated by the desire to become someone and belong to groups sharing the same consumption. As innovation became the only way to make business, management and work practices became more knowledge-oriented in order to generate more ideas. This is referred to as the knowledge-based economy, an economy in which knowledge is considered as the core asset and provides competitive advantage for companies. The 2000s was the age of knowledge management, competencies management, communities of practices, learning organizations. All of these notions and managerial practices have aimed at ensuring constant learning, sharing, storing and creation of knowledge for the sake of innovation. Technologies also played an important role in this evolution, as the fast development of the Internet during the 1990s and 2000s and the constant improvement of computers and infrastructures have enabled people to work together and access large amounts of information. These technological developments also participated in the innovation race. Information systems management became another crucial area for companies, as information systems were considered a key element to compete in this knowledge-based economy.

Towards 'Organizational Mindsets': The Process View, Practice-Based View and Sociomateriality

Facing this globalized world in which companies were constantly evolving, merging with each other, diversifying their activities, competing and partnering on a global level, organizational scholars could not rely on the essentialist view of organization any longer—the organization as an economic or social entity. Inspired by postmodernism in organization studies (Parker 1992; Chia 1995, 2003), but also by feminists such as Judith Butler and Karen Barad and posthumanists such as Andrew Pickering and Bruno Latour, organizational scholars shifted from a quest to develop ultimate explanations about the organization to developing organizational 'mindsets' (Cabantous and Sergi 2018), that is a way to provide plausible accounts about how organizational phenomena are produced and maintained on a daily basis by actors. An organization is no longer a company but a constant process of defining outputs and inputs of activities. Chia (1997, 1999) expanded on this idea arguing that organization is a process of world-making. In such a view, an organizational phenomenon is an ontological activity that consists in defining the world, a situated definition of the world in order to act. By distinguishing the notions of organization as an ontological activity from company as a legal object, the study of organizational phenomena belonging to this globalized world became possible.

These mindsets are based on two core premises. The first is the primacy given to action, what people do. Organizational phenomena emerge and are maintained only through action. This moves away from the essentialist view that gave primacy to the structure. The second premise is based on relational ontology (Slife 2004; Cooper 2005). Relational ontology means that everything exists only in relationship to other things. 'Things' have not inherent properties and their singularity emerges from their interrelatedness. Interrelatedness is not passive and imposed on 'things'. According to the principle of action, it is in action that technologies, rules, roles, statuses and so on are mutually defined. Many 'mindsets' have been developed based on these two premises: performativity (Gond et al. 2016), the narrative approach (Rantakari and Vaara 2017), the communication constitutive organization (Cooren et al. 2011), the process view (Langley and Tsoukas 2010), the practice-based view (Gherardi 2012), sociomateriality (Orlikowski and Scott 2008) and so on. They all put action first, but have suggested different foci, such as language, social practice or technologies. As a way to exemplify this stream of research, we outline below three key 'organizational mindsets': the process view, the practice-based view and sociomateriality.

The Process View: Understanding Organization as a Movement

The process view is anchored in postmodernism and process philosophy which draws on various philosophers from the pre-Socratic Greek philosophy of Heraclitus to the metaphysics of Alfred North Whitehead, the American pragmatism, German phenomenology, Henri Bergson, Gilles Deleuze and so on (Rescher 1996, 2001; Helin et al. 2014). Their key assumption is that reality is constantly flowing and we cannot really grasp it, but only create images as a way to make it tangible and actionable (Bergson 2009/1907). Cooper (1976, 2005, 2007, 2014) and Chia (1995, 1997, 1999, 2003) defined key principles of the process view. Action and relational ontology are two of them, but the originality has been to add the principle of immanence (Chia 1999). Immanence means that everything exists in the current moment. The past, the present and the anticipated future are not a series of separate events, but are co-defined and co-redefined in the current moment. In other words, past events can always be reinterpreted according to the evolution of action, while anticipated events can always be redefined. It means that current action always brings the past, present and anticipated events. Key challenges of process organization scholars are to understand constant change (Tsoukas and Chia 2002) and how 'things' occur and are maintained in a constantly flowing world.

The Practice-Based View: Understanding Organization from Practices

The practice-based view is the second main mindset that has influenced organization studies since the 2000s. Practice-based studies are rooted in the work of various sociologists and philosophers such as Bourdieu (1972, 1980), Lyotard (1979), Foucault (1980), Taylor (1995) and Giddens (1979, 1984). Pierre Bourdieu and Anthony Giddens can be considered as the key inspirations for the practice-based view. For Bourdieu (Bourdieu 1980), the world is made objective through practices, while Giddens (1984) insists on the role of social practices in the making of social structures. The main assumption of the practice-based view is that organizational phenomena are not given but emerge and are maintained through practices (Schatzki 1996, 2001; Corradi et al. 2010). For these authors, the practice-based view is thus a "way of seeing", with the aim of understanding "the situatedness of practical reasoning and the contingent nature of organizational rationality" (Corradi et al. 2010, 268). However, the concept of practice is difficult to define as practice can be anything participating in the shaping of the social world. Generally speaking, practice is simply what actors do with rules, words or things. The practice-based view is about understanding how everyday activities produce, reproduce or transform social structures "that are at the heart of collective action" (De Vaujany et al. 2016a, 25). Consequently, the unit of analysis becomes what actors do, or make visible through their actions.

Sociomateriality: The Relation Between the Social and the Material

During the 2000s the matter of materiality regained popularity among organizational scholars, partly due to the ubiquity of technologies at work. A stream of research called sociomateriality (with or without a hyphen) emerged as a way to study the entanglement of the social and the material. Mainly anchored in agential realism (Barad 2003, 2007), post-humanism (Pickering 1995), actor-network theory (Latour 2005) and the practice-based approach in organization studies (Orlikowski 2000), studies focused on how the social and the material gain status and roles through their intertwining in practice (Orlikowski and Scott 2008; Introna 2013; Jones 2013; Shotter 2013). Here again, primacy is given to action and the relational ontology. Entities "have a shared being and a mutual constitution" (Slife 2004, 811). From this entanglement perspective, any separation is merely analytical (Orlikowski and Scott 2008), as what we call the technical, the social and the organizational are mutually constitutive, only existing as doing (Shotter 2013) in their radical otherness (Introna 2013). The core question of this research stream has been how 'matter matters', and more importantly how entities matter in practices, how forms and their relations appear (Jones 2013, 223).

These mindsets can be considered as renewing ontological debates about organization. However, they have been confronted to their own contradictions about the ontology of organizational phenomena. Contradictions have come from the way scholars have dealt with relational ontology. In most of these mindsets, scholars' work can be divided into two groups: advocates of a weak relational ontology versus advocates of a strong relational ontology (Slife 2004). In the weak relational ontology, 'things', such as actors, technologies, roles, statuses, have their own existence. Despite their interaction and imbrication, 'things' remain distinct, interdependent phenomena. Strong relational ontology states that 'things' do not exist on their own but are entangled and intertwined; 'things' gain status only through their interpenetration and intra-action (Barad 2003). A more managerialist view of these mindsets has also emerged. Anchored into weak relational ontology, it has attempted to provide managerial contributions as a way to help companies face economic challenges. This can be found in various research streams in between management research and organization studies, such as strategy-as-practice, community-of-practice, socio-materiality (with a hyphen) and the weak process view dedicated to the understanding of the innovation process.

Period 4: Working and Collaborating Without a Company—Current Developments in Organization Studies

In 2008, the financial crisis revealed an ugly truth to the world. The banking system had played dangerously with people's money leading to a dramatic economic crisis, seizure of properties, bankruptcies, unemployment and so on. The consequences were dreadful and governments all over the world tried desperately to contain the crisis. This crisis made more visible social challenges such as wealth inequality and unemployment. This led to an unprecedented crisis of faith that has since nurtured various social movements and political extremism. At the same time, environmental challenges have become more urgent. Climate change, scarcity of resources, pollution, loss of biodiversity, deforestation have started to question the industrial and mass-consumption model. The risk of a global collapse is considered a serious scenario by numerous scientists. In such a context, a rather young, educated, globalized and progressist elite—often ironically called hipsters—has been experimenting with alternative lifestyles and New Ways of Working, living and consuming. Living and gentrifying neighborhoods of big cities, such as East London, they have developed a new economy called the 'flat-white economy' by

McWilliams (2015), based on alternative ways of manufacturing and consuming. Veganism, eco-friendly products, the sharing economy, personal development have become some of the key trends; while the development of new digital and mobile technologies such as social media, smartphones and high-speed mobile networks enable them to develop their business from anywhere.

Against the 9 to 5 Office Job: The Lifestyle Entrepreneurship

These people are the tangible manifestation of many changes in society, especially at work. They tend to reject the traditional employment culture, that is 9 to 5 office hours, the hierarchy, job titles and the perks among others, and embrace 'lifestyle entrepreneurship, that is a strong belief in self-empowerment through entrepreneurship. Many terms have been proposed to name these new workers: mumpreneurs, makers, digital nomads, creative freelancers, influencers, coworkers, solopreneurs and so on. Most of the time they are independent workers, working collaboratively with other independent workers or companies. They reinvent ways of collaborating by relying on online platforms or social media or joining a shared working space such as a coworking space or a makerspace. Hypothetically they can work where and when they want, on the projects they want to, with whom they want and with no subordinate relation with anyone (Hussenot and Sergi 2018). This 'lifestyle entrepreneurship' also means that work and life are not separate activities any longer, and the entrepreneurial activity serves a lifestyle. The notion of 'workation' is a good example of this renewed relationship between work and life as it expresses the idea that work and vacation could be experienced at the same time. However, this idealistic scenario (as it has often been depicted on social media, blogs and press articles) has been tarnished by the so-called gig economy—short-term tasks-based activity carried out by independent workers—which has brought uncertainty and financial insecurity to many workers (Acquier et al. 2017). Car drivers and riders delivering food are two of the most common examples of this gig economy in which workers are paid per task.

Theorizing Organization Without a Company: Towards New Challenges and Frameworks in Organization Studies

In such a fast changing and interrelated world, theories and mindsets developed during the 2000s have served as a core background for organizational scholars. Critical management studies, the process view, practice-based theory and the performative-based view are still playing an important role in the intellectual debate. Awareness of this changing global context has encouraged organizational scholars to research new topics such as social movements (Haug 2013; Yousfi 2013), bikers' collectives (Wilhoit and Kisselburgh 2015) or terrorist networks (Schoeneborn and Scherer 2012; Stohl and Stohl 2011). Traditional topics such as management and work are explored through the lens of these global trends; changing work practices are happening outside of big companies and often deal with social, economic and environmental challenges. For instance, freelancers, makers and coworkers question our assumptions about working space, working time, but also collaboration, leadership, collective identity, power relations and so on and traditional dualisms such as work versus life, social concerns versus economic ones, companies versus their environment and so on. These dualisms seem to disappear in our interrelated world. Social, environmental and economic challenges have been at the heart of debates for the last decade and the study of companies has become less of a priority. This has been called the 'societal turn in organization theories' (De Vaujany et al. 2016b). Recent themes addressed at the European Group for Organization Studies conferences (the main European research association in organization studies) speak for themselves: 'Bridging continents, cultures and worldviews' (2013), 'Reimagining, rethinking, reshaping: Organizational scholarship in unsettled times' (2014), 'Organization and the examined life: Reason, reflexivity and responsibility' (2015), 'The good organization: Aspiration, interventions, struggle' (2017), 'Enlightening the future: Challenge for organization' (2019) and 'Organizing for a sustainable future: Responsibility, renewal and resistance' (2020).

Theoretically speaking, the current challenge is to envisage organizational phenomena not only as open but also fluid (Schreyögg and Sydow 2010), where activities and relationships are constantly evolving, members are not clearly identified and boundaries are open or permeable (Blagoev et al. 2019; Dobusch and Schoeneborn 2015). In such organizational phenomena, work can be done not only anywhere and at any time, but in multiple spatialities and temporalities. Another challenge is to conceptualize organizational phenomena with no separation between work and life. This is, for example, the case with influencers who have built their business based on their private life (Duffy 2016), or digital nomads who have decided to travel the world, while their professional activity is carried out exclusively remotely (Nash et al. 2018). As a way to understand these open and fluid organizational phenomena, new theoretical concepts have been suggested recently. For instance, the concept of 'organizationality' (Dobusch and Schoeneborn 2015; Schoeneborn et al. 2019; Blagoev et al. 2019) and the events-based approach (Hernes 2014a, b; Hussenot and Missonier 2016; Hussenot 2019; Hussenot et al. 2020).

Organizationality: Understanding Organization as an Adverb

In 2015, Dobusch and Schoeneborn introduced the notion of organizationality to understand how organizational dynamics manifest themselves in fluid organizational phenomena. They suggest to understand organization as an adverb (Schoeneborn et al. 2019). The organization is what characterizes the organizing process (in the same way that the adverb is what characterizes the verb). The organization is what qualifies the activities. An organization is not an entity but the very definition of the activity (goal, purpose, roles, actors, coordination modes, etc.). The authors invite us to rethink dynamics such as collective identity, actorhood and the interconnected instances of decision-making in fluid organizations (Dobusch and Schoeneborn 2015). This approach recognizes the existence of organizational dynamics in fluid organizational phenomena, but emphasizes their emergent, openness and situated nature. These authors propose an interesting approach, as understanding organization as an adverb is a stimulating way to study how organizational dynamics are produced and reproduced by actors, whichever their activities and their interrelatedness with all aspects of actors' life. This approach offers an alternative way to analyze organizational identity, actorhood and decision-making without necessarily ascribing mechanisms to actors.

Events-Based Approach: Understanding Organization as a Temporality

As an attempt to offer an alternative way of thinking and studying organization, Hernes (2014a, b) has suggested to focus on events and temporality. Based on this, Hussenot and Missonier (2016), Hussenot (2019), Hussenot et al. (2020) have developed the events-based approach. It suggests that organizational phenomena are temporal, emerge and are maintained through the ongoing configuration and co-definition of past, present and future events that define both the current moment and the continuity of the activity. The events-based approach suggests to shift from an essentialist view of organization—that is a view reducing organization to an entity delimited in space and time—to a view in which the organization is a shared history, past, present and future, that enables actors to act collectively. In such a view, 'things' such as rules, technologies, actors and so on gain a meaning, a role and a status through this enacted temporality. Any 'thing' is understood as a temporal phenomenon. Conversely, these 'things' also participate in the co-definition and configuration of the past, present and future events (Hussenot 2019) and organization is defined as a structure of events (Hernes 2014b). By reframing the ontological category (events and not things) and the ontological dimension (situated temporality and not time and space) of organizational phenomena, the events-based approach offers an alternative to understand phenomena in which there is no given space, boundaries, members and so on; but a continuous movement of defining activities in which various actors, technologies, goals, histories and so on are delineated through a shared temporality. The events-based approach is an attempt to study these liquefied, nomadic and rhizomic contemporary organizational phenomena.

Conclusion

Based on a historical perspective, the aim of this chapter was to enquire about the way innovations at work have influenced organization theories over time. By focusing on the interrelations between technological innovations, the evolution of organizational phenomena and evolutions of ways of working, we have argued that organization theories have evolved along with innovations at work. This historical attempt opens new avenues of research in both organization studies and organizational history which could provide a better understanding of current work practices as being part of a more 'longue durée' phenomenon in line with the evolution of capitalism. For example, longitudinal studies and monographs on the evolution of work practices in companies could provide further material to think about current and future work practices as evolutions anchored into past transformations.

References

Acquier, A., Daudigeos, T., & Pinkse, J. (2017). Promises and paradoxes of the sharing economy: An organizing framework. *Technological Forecasting and Social Change, 125*, 1–10.

Adler, P., Forbes, L. C., & Willmott, H. (2008). Critical management studies. *The Academy of Management Annals, 1*(1), 119–180.

Alvesson, M., & Wilmott, H. (1992). *Critical management studies*. London: Sage.

Aoki, M. (1990). Toward an economic model of the Japanese firm. *Journal of Economic Literature, 28*(1), 1–27.

Arena, L. (2011). Les modèles nationaux d'enseignement de la gestion d'entreprise: Formes de capitalisme et modes d'organisation. *Entreprises et Histoire, 65*(4), 6–10.

Barad, K. (2003). Posthumanist performativity: Toward an understanding of how matter comes to matter. *Signs—Journal of Women in Culture and Society, 28*(3), 801–831.

Barad, K. (2007). *Meeting the universe halfway: Quantum physics and the entanglement of matter and meaning*. Durham, NC: Duke University Press.

Barnard, C. I. (1968/1938). *The functions of the executive*. Cambridge, MA: Harvard University Press.

Bauman, Z. (2000). *Liquid modernity*. Cambridge, UK: Polity Press.

Bergson, H. (2009/1907). *L'évolution créative*. Paris: Presses Universitaires de France.

Blagoev, B., Costas, J., & Kärreman, D. (2019). We are all 'herd animals': Community and organizationality in coworking spaces. *Organization, 26*(6), 894–916.

Bourdieu, P. (1972). *Esquisse d'une théorie de la pratique*. Paris: Le point.

Bourdieu, P. (1980). *Le sens pratique*. Paris: Les Éditions de Minuit.

Burrell, G. (1994). Modernism, post modernism, and organizational analysis: The contribution of Jürgen Habermas. *Organization Studies, 15*(1), 1–19.

Cabantous, L., & Sergi, V. (2018). Seeing the potentialities at the intersection: A reflection on performativity and processuality mindsets. *M@n@gement, 21*(4), 1229–1243.

Chandler, A. D. (1990). *Strategy and structure: Chapters in the history of the industrial enterprise*. Cambridge: MIT Press.

Chevalier, J. (1937). *La technique de l'organisation des entreprises—Livre 1: Le gouvernement de l'entreprise*. Paris: Dunod.

Chia, R. (1995). From modern to postmodern organizational analysis. *Organization Studies, 16*(4), 579–604.

Chia, R. (1997). Essai—Thirty years on: From organizational structures to the organization of thought. *Organization Studies, 18*(4), 684–707.

Chia, R. (1999). A 'rhizomic' model of organizational change and transformation: Perspective from a metaphysics of change. *British Journal of Management, 10*(3), 209–227.

Chia, R. (2003). Organization theory as postmodern science. In H. Tsoukas & C. Knudsen (Eds.), *The Oxford handbook of organization theory* (pp. 113–142). Oxford: Oxford University Press.

Clegg, S. R. (1990). *Modern organizations: Organization studies in the postmodern world*. London: Sage.

Cooper, R. (1976). The open field. *Human Relations, 29*(11), 999–1017.

Cooper, R. (1989). Modernism, post modernism and organizational analysis: The contribution of Jacques Derrida. *Organization Studies, 10*(4), 479–502.

Cooper, R. (2005). Relationality. *Organization Studies, 26*(11), 1689–1710.

Cooper, R. (2007). Organs of process: Rethinking human organization. *Organization Studies, 28*(10), 1547–1573.

Cooper, R. (2014). Process and reality. In J. Helin, T. Hernes, D. Hjort, & R. Holt (Eds.), *Process philosophy and organization studies* (pp. 585–604). Oxford: Oxford University Press.

Cooper, R., & Burrell, G. (1988). Modernism, postmodernism and organizational analysis: An introduction. *Organization Studies, 9*(1), 91–112.

Cooren, F., Kuhn, T., Cornelissen, J. P., & Clark, T. (2011). Communication, organizing and organization: An overview and introduction to the Special Issue. *Organization Studies, 32*(9), 1149–1117.

Corradi, G., Gherardi, S., & Verzelloni, L. (2010). Through the practice-lens: Where is the bandwagon of practice-based studies heading? *Management Learning, 41*(3), 265–283.

Cortada, J. (2011). *Information and the modern corporation*. Cambridge, MA: MIT Press.

Cyert, R., & March, J. (1963). *A behavioral theory of the firm*. Englewood Cliffs, NJ: Prentice Hall.

De Vaujany, F. X., Dameron, S., & Rouleau, L. (2016a). Introduction au tournant pratique. In F. X. De Vaujany, A. Hussenot, & J.-F. Chanlat (Eds.), *Théories des organisations: nouveaux tournants* (pp. 25–42). Paris: Economica.

De Vaujany, F. X., Hussenot, A., & Chanlat, J. F. (Eds.). (2016b). *Théories des organisations: nouveaux tournants*. Paris: Economica.

DiMaggio, P. J., & Powell, W. W. (1983). The iron cage revisited: Institutional isomorphism and collective rationality in organizational fields. *American Sociological Review, 48*(2), 147–160.

Dobusch, L., & Schoeneborn, D. (2015). Fluidity, identity, and organizationality: The communicative constitution of anonymous. *Journal of Management Studies, 52*(8), 1005–1035.

Duffy, B. E. (2016). The romance of work: Gender and aspirational labour in the digital culture industries. *International Journal of Cultural Studies, 19*(4), 441–457.

Fayol, H. (1916/1949). *General and industrial management* (translated from *Administration industrielle et générale*). London: Pitman & Sons.

Foucault, M. (1980). *Power/knowledge: Selected interviews and other writings 1972–1977*. London: Harvester.

Friedland, R., & Alford, R. R. (1991). Bringing society back in: Symbols, practices, and institutional contradictions. In W. W. Powell & P. J. DiMaggio (Eds.), *The new institutionalism in organizational analysis* (pp. 232–263). Chicago, IL: University of Chicago Press.

George, C. S. (1968). *The history of management thought*. Prentice Hall, Englewood Cliffs.

Gherardi, S. (2012). *How to conduct a practice-based study: Problems and methods*. Cheltenham, UK: Edward Elgar Publishing.

Giddens, A. (1979). *Central problems in social theory*. Berkeley, CA: University of California Press.

Giddens, A. (1984). *The constitution of society*. Berkeley, CA: University of California Press.

Gond, J.-P., Cabantous, L., Harding, N., & Learmonth, M. (2016). What do we mean by performativity in organizational and management theory? The uses and abuses of performativity. *International Journal of Management Reviews, 18*(4), 440–463.

Greenwood, R., & Devine, K. (1997). Inside Aston: A conversation with Derek Pugh. *Journal of Management Inquiry, 6*(3), 200–208.

Haug, C. (2013). Organizing spaces: Meeting arenas as a social movement infrastructure between organization, network, and institution. *Organization Studies, 34*(5–6), 705–732.

Helin, J., Hernes, T., Hjorth, D., & Holt, R. (Eds.). (2014). *Oxford handbook of process philosophy and organization studies*. Oxford: Oxford University Press.

Hernes, T. (2014a). *A process theory of organization*. Oxford: Oxford University Press.

Hernes, T. (2014b). Alfred North Whitehead. In J. Helin, T. Hernes, D. Hjorth, & R. Holt (Eds.), *Oxford handbook of process philosophy and organization studies* (pp. 255–271). Oxford: Oxford University Press.

Hickson, D. J., & Pugh, D. S. (2007/1964). *Writers on organizations* (6th ed.). London: Penguin Business.

Hussenot, A. (2019). *L'organisation à l'épreuve des makers. Propositions pour une approche par les événements*. Laval, Québec: Presses Universitaires de Laval.

Hussenot, A., & Missonier, S. (2016). Encompassing stability and novelty in organization studies: An events-based approach. *Organization Studies, 37*(4), 523–546.

Hussenot, A., & Sergi, V. (2018). Collaborating without formal organization. In C. Cézanne & L. Saglietto (Eds.), *Human capital-intensive firms* (pp. 53–72). Hershey, PA: IGI Global Publications.

Hussenot, A., Hernes, T., & Bouty, I. (2020). Studying organization from the perspective of the ontology of temporality: Introducing the events-based approach. In J. Reinecke, R. Suddaby, A. Langley, & H. Tsoukas (Eds.), *About time: Temporality and history in organization studies*. Oxford: Oxford University Press.

Introna, L. D. (2013). Otherness and the letting-be of becoming: Or, ethics beyond bifurcation. In P. R. Carlile, D. Nicolini, A. Langley, & H. Tsoukas

(Eds.), *How matter matters: Objects, artifacts, and materiality in organization studies* (pp. 260–288). Oxford: Oxford University Press.

Jensen, A., Thuesen, C., & Geraldi, J. (2016). The projectification of everything: Projects as a human condition. *Project Management Journal, 47*(3), 21–34.

Jones, M. (2013). Untangling materiality. In P. R. Carlile, D. Nicolini, A. Langley, & H. Tsoukas (Eds.), *How matter matters: Objects, artifacts, and materiality in organization studies* (pp. 197–226). Oxford: Oxford University Press.

Langley, A., & Tsoukas, H. (2010). Introducing perspectives on process organization studies. In T. Hernes & S. Maitlis (Eds.), *Process, sensemaking and organizing* (pp. 1–26). Oxford: Oxford University Press.

Latour, B. (2005). Reassembling the social. In *An introduction to actor-network-theory*. Oxford: Oxford University Press.

Lave, J., & Wenger, E. (1991). *Situated learning: Legitimate peripheral participation*. Cambridge: Cambridge University Press.

Lazonick, W. (2010). Innovative business models and varieties of capitalism: Financialization of the U.S. Corporation. *Business History Review, 84*(4), 675–702.

Lounsbury, M., & Zhao, Y. E. (2014). *Neo-institutional theory (Management Oxford bibliographies)*. Oxford: Oxford University Press.

Lyotard, J. F. (1979). *La Condition postmoderne*. Paris: Les Éditions de Minuit.

March, J. & Simon H. A. (1958). *Organizations*. Wiley: Blackwell Business.

McWilliams, D. (2015). *Flat white economy: How the digital economy is transforming London & other cities of the future*. New York: Harry N. Abrams.

Merton, R. (1949/1968). *Social theory and social structure*. New York: Free Press.

Meyer, J. W., & Rowan, B. (1977). Institutionalized organizations: Formal structure as myth and ceremony. *American Journal of Sociology, 83*(2), 340–363.

Minkes, L. (2011). Early years in University development in management education: Reflections and reminiscences on the University of Birmingham (1950s–1970s). *Entreprises et Histoire, 65*(4), 83–95.

Moriguchi, C. (2000). *The evolution of employment relations in U.S. and Japanese manufacturing firms, 1900–1960: A comparative historical and institutional analysis*, Working Paper Series, WP 7939. Cambridge, MA: National Bureau of Economic Research.

Nash, C., Jarrahi, M. H., Sutherland, W., & Phillips, G. (2018). Digital nomads beyond the buzzword: Defining digital nomadic work and use of digital technologies. In G. Chowdhury, J. McLeod, V. Gillet, & P. Willett (Eds.),

Transforming digital worlds. iConference 2018 (Lecture notes in computer science, vol. 10766). Cham, Switzerland: Springer.

Nutt, P. C. (1984). Types of organizational decision processes. *Administrative Science Quarterly, 29*(3), 414–450.

Orlikowski, W. J. (2000). Using technology and constituting structures: A practice lens for studying technology in organizations. *Organization Science, 11*(4), 404–428.

Orlikowski, W. J., & Scott, S. V. (2008). Sociomateriality: Challenging the separation of technology, work, and organization. *The Academy of Management Annals, 2*(1), 433–474.

Osterman, P. (1991). Impact of IT on jobs and skills. In M. S. Scott Morton (Ed.), *The Corporation of the 1990s—Information technology and organizational transformation* (pp. 220–243). Oxford: Oxford University Press.

Parker, M. (1992). Post-modern organizations or postmodern organization theory. *Organization Studies, 13*(1), 1–17.

Parsons, T. (1942). Max Weber and the contemporary political crisis. *The Review of Politics, 4*(2), 155–172.

Parsons, T. (1947). Introduction. In A. M. Henderson & T. Parsons (Eds.), *Max Weber: The theory of social and economic organization* (pp. 1–11). New York: Free Press.

Penrose, E. (1959). *The theory of the growth of the firm*. Oxford: Oxford University Press.

Pickering, A. (1995). *The mangle of practice: Time, agency, and science*. Chicago, IL: The University of Chicago Press.

Porter, M. E., & Heppelman, J. E. (2014). How smart and connected objects are transforming competition. *Harvard Business Review, 92*(11), 64–88.

Pugh, D. S., & Hickson, D. J. (1972). Causal inference and the Aston studies. *Administrative Science Quarterly, 17*(2), 273–276.

Rantakari, A., & Vaara, E. (2017). Narratives and processuality. In A. Langley & H. Tsoukas (Eds.), *The Sage handbook of process organization studies* (pp. 271–285). London: Sage.

Rao, H. (1994). The social construction of reputation: Certification contests, legitimation, and the survival of organizations in the American automobile industry; 1895–1912. *Strategic Management Journal, 15*(1), 29–44.

Rescher, N. (1996). *Process metaphysics: An introduction to process philosophy*. Albany, NY: State University of New York Press.

Rescher, N. (2001). *Process philosophy: A survey of basic issues*. Pittsburgh, CA: University of Pittsburgh Press.

Schatzki, T. R. (1996). *Social practices: A Wittgensteinian approach to human activity and the social.* Cambridge, UK: Cambridge University Press.

Schatzki, T. R. (2001). Introduction. Practice theory. In T. R. Schatzki, K. Knorr-Cetina, & E. von Savigny (Eds.), *The practice turn in contemporary theory* (pp. 1–14). London: Routledge.

Schoeneborn, D., & Scherer, A. G. (2012). Clandestine organizations, al Qaeda, and the paradox of (in)visibility: A response to Stohl and Stohl. *Organization Studies, 33*(7), 963–971.

Schoeneborn, D., Kuhn, T. R., & Kärreman, D. (2019). The communicative constitution of organization, organizing, and organizationality. *Organization Studies, 40*(4), 475–496.

Schreyögg, G., & Sydow, J. (2010). Organizing for fluidity? Dilemmas of new organizational forms. *Organization Science, 21*(10), 1251–1262.

Scott, W. G. (1992). *Chester I. Barnard and the guardians of the managerial state.* Lawrence, KS: Kansas University Press.

Scott Morton, M. S. (Ed.). (1991). *The corporation of the 1990s: Information technology and organizational transformation.* Oxford: Oxford University Press.

Selznick, P. (1943). An approach to a theory of bureaucracy. *American Sociological Review, 8*(1), 47–54.

Selznick, P. (1948). Foundations of the theory of organization. *American Sociological Review, 13*(1), 25–35.

Shenhav, Y. (2003). The historical and epistemological foundations of organization theory: Fusing sociological theory with engineering discourse. In H. Tsoukas & C. Knudsen (Eds.), *The Oxford handbook of organization theory* (pp. 183–209). Oxford: Oxford University Press.

Shotter, J. (2013). Reflections on sociomateriality and dialogicality in organization studies: From 'inter-' to 'intra-thinking'… in performing practices. In P. R. Carlile, D. Nicolini, A. Langley, & H. Tsoukas (Eds.), *How matter matters: Objects, artifacts, and materiality in organization studies* (pp. 32–57). Oxford: Oxford University Press.

Simon, H. (1947). *Administrative behavior: A study of decision-making processes in administrative organization.* New York: Macmillan.

Slappendel, C. (1996). Perspectives on innovation in organizations. *Organization Studies, 17*(1), 107–129.

Slife, B. D. (2004). Taking practice seriously: Toward a relational ontology. *Journal of Theoretical and Philosophical Psychology, 24*(2), 158–178.

Stohl, C., & Stohl, M. (2011). Secret agencies: The communicative constitution of a clandestine organization. *Organization Studies, 32*(9), 1197–1215.

Taylor, F. W. (1911). *Principles of scientific management*. New York & London: Harper & Brothers Publishers.

Taylor, C. (1995). *Philosophical arguments*. Cambridge, MA: Harvard University Press.

Tsoukas, H., & Chia, R. (2002). On organizational becoming: Rethinking organizational change. *Organization Science, 13*(5), 567–582.

Weber, M. (1922 [1978]). *Economy and society*. Berkeley, CA: University of California Press.

Whilston, K. (1997). The reception of scientific management by British engineers: 1890–1914. *Business History Review, 71*(2), 207–229.

Wilhoit, E. D., & Kisselburgh, L. G. (2015). Collective action without organization: The material constitution of bike commuters as collective. *Organization Studies, 36*(5), 573–592.

Wren, D. A. (1972). *The evolution of management thought*. Ronald Press Company.

Yousfi, H. (2013). Rethinking hybridity in postcolonial contexts: What changes and what persists? The Tunisian case of Poulina's managers. *Organization Studies, 35*(3), 393–421.

16

Community Management Practices in Coworking Spaces: Being the 'Catalyst'

Aurore Dandoy

My nearest coworker complains about how noisy it has been for a week. A start-up is making a permaculture furniture in the open space, with a circular saw. I think of telling them to stop because we are not a fablab but then, I wonder: coworking spaces are not libraries. Why should it be quiet?
—23/11/2016, autoethnographic notebook

Introduction

Coworking spaces are new work configurations, that intent playing the role of facilitators for collaboration and innovation (Fabbri & Charue-Duboc, 2013) through the creation of workers' community. Nonetheless, it is not easy to define what those communities are, as Spinuzzi (2012, 418) shows that actors of coworking "provided definitions that were far from unanimous". Indeed, 'community' is very polysemic because of the numerous uses made in common language and in different research

A. Dandoy (✉)
PSL-Université Paris Dauphine, Paris, France

N. Mitev et al. (eds.), *New Ways of Working*, Technology, Work and Globalization,
https://doi.org/10.1007/978-3-030-61687-8_16

disciplines (Hirschhorn, 2010). Also, community self-described by coworkers through their individual experiences is part of a performative discourse—"how the participants perceive the object of coworking affects how they coconstruct it" (Spinuzzi, 2012, 418). That means they co-construct the community altogether which leads to the rise of the 'community feeling'—named by Garrett, Spreitzer, and Bacevice (2017, 1) the 'sense of community'.

However, in the coworking literature, this community feeling seems to emerge from proximity (Parrino, 2015; Capdevila, 2015; Merkel, 2018), from collaborative activity between coworkers (Butcher, 2013; Spinuzzi, 2012; Waters-Lynch & Potts, 2017) and from amenities (Bilandzic, Schroeter, & Foth, 2013; Fabbri & Charue-Duboc, 2013). A few articles (Garrett et al., 2017; Merkel, 2015; Rus & Orel, 2015) evoke the role of the community manager as a 'wheelwork' of the community emergence process and only one article mentions it as coming from inside the community (de Vaujany, Dandoy, Grandazzi, & Faure, 2018).

Through a critical autoethnographic design (Doloriert & Sambrook, 2012; Holt, 2003; Madison, 2011), I took advantage of my position as a part-time community manager and as a researcher in two coworking spaces to understand this role and to tease out invisible activities carried out by community managers to make the community. Thus, this research leads to question larger aspects of community management, which I do using the activity theory framework (Engeström, 2009). Accordingly, my research question tries to address what it is to be a community manager of coworking spaces in the French context, based primarily on my autoethnographical approach, and why this position needs to be better investigated and acknowledged. According to my own experience and to interviews I conducted with twenty-four other community managers, being a community manager implies considering the job itself but also several levels of analysis from job tasks to personality and history of the individual, to the economic environment and political context. Those are the first elements we will explore, then I rely on my experience to suggest a model of analysis of my own experience that allows me to propose to envisage the community manager as a 'catalyst' (Brafman & Beckstrom, 2006).

Critical Overview of the Economic and Political Context of Coworking

A contextual overview is mandatory to understand the community manager's activity; in activity theory there is one activity and several actions and tasks. The context impacts on business trends, community management and economic survival based on the community key success factors (Bouncken, Aslam, & Reuschl, 2018). Coworking spaces emerged more than ten years ago on the international, technological, entrepreneurial and innovative stages. They were aiming to address the issue of loneliness experienced by non-waged employees (i.e. freelancers, entrepreneurs) by creating a community. Defined as "spaces and places whose facilities, aesthetics codes, temporalities, enacted values, atmospheres, and spatial configurations are aimed at fostering horizontal collaborations" (de Vaujany, Dandoy, et al., 2018, 4), coworking spaces appear to be the most business-oriented (Gandini, 2015; Spinuzzi, 2012) of all kinds of collaborative spaces—for example, hackerspaces, makerspaces, third-places and so on. This means they are both ideological (within the collaborative ideology and economy) and commodified (industrialization of coworking developed more recently with numerous so-called big actors such as the American coworking space company WeWork).

This phenomenon now concerns millions of people worldwide (Uda, 2013; Fuzi, 2015; Waters-Lynch & Potts, 2017)—from start-uppers to teleworkers to even researchers. It is now part of the public debate and has caused, for instance, universities to open their own coworking spaces (Bouncken, 2018; Fasshauer, Meyer, & Bourret, 2015). National public institutions want to understand this phenomenon to better control public funding (see Vignette 16.1). For example, in France, a national report was published in October 2018 after public consultation (Levy-Waitz, 2018) since public funding is one of the first funding strategies for collaborative space projects; after the report, more than €100 million will be mobilized by the French government to open 300 collaborative spaces by 2021.

Vignette 16.1 Local Public Policies Discovering Coworking (Extract of My Interview with the Mission Manager of a Parisian District, 2015)

The department has a laboratory of 'public ideas'... which is managed by a general secretary and which aims to test some concepts that emerge from public debate. To see if there is sufficient consent on the subject, to see if this is a topic that can be deployed in large-scale public policies. (...) So, there are topics like the collaborative economy and third-places where we found had strong support from actors, enough for us to continue in this direction. So, it's not a service within the department, you see. It is really a person who brings these reflections to the department. And there's a lot of experimentation going on, including on the collaborative economy, and budgets dedicated to the social and solidarity economy. I tell you that because it has guided, quite a bit, the vision we have today of third-places. It remains very strong in the understanding that we have today.

However, from a more critical perspective, the growth of the coworking market is also anchored in a global context of socio-economic crises and a loss of meaning at work (Graeber, 2018; Alter, 2013; De Gaulejac, 2005, 2011). The managerial discourse called "managerial newspeak" by Vandevelde-Rougale (2017)—in a strong reference to the novel *1984* (Orwell, 1954)—refers to how the traditional ways of working in large companies have been under attack. This managerial newspeak is a discourse underpinned by the US idealistic start-up culture, of individuals instantly becoming billionaire web geniuses and so on. Entrepreneurship, in this context, is presented by many business, social and political actors as the solution to re-empower one's working life. It has become a status symbol to not work at the company office every day, leading to the growth of teleworking, digital nomadism, home offices, mobile offices and coworking spaces (de Vaujany, Bohas, Carton, Fabbri, & Leclercq-Vandelannoitte, 2018).

Nonetheless, as pointed out by Bouncken, Aslam, and Reuschl (2018, 135), coworking spaces can also lead to personal, interpersonal and/or social issues: "the professional and social dynamics in coworking spaces bear the risk of stress, exploitation, conflicts and distrust, which negatively affect entrepreneurial self-efficacy and passion, undermining the advantages of coworking spaces and leading to withdrawal of entrepreneurs". Indeed, those social dynamics are not exclusive to large hierarchical companies. Social dynamics are associated to social structures of power (Follett, 1919) and trigger strong emotions such as fear and passion. Moreover, becoming a coworker means taking a psychological risk, an engagement in a new and 'other' environment, which can raise interpersonal issues (see Vignette 16.2).

Vignette 16.2 Interpersonal Issues (Extract of My Autoethnographic Notebook, 2017)

Apparently Lucie has caused a new scandal: Vanessa accused her of leaving the heater all night but Lucie said it was not her fault... she yelled in the open space where she rents a private office. So, Vanessa spoke with the Board recently and she is considering evicting her, since this is the third time Lucie has caused a problem.

Vanessa is also a bit angry with the group formed by Lucie, Geneviève and Patrick because they have a negative influence on the community, especially the newcomers, and because they criticize everything she does. It is true that they are constantly critical. They no longer use the digital networking platform she launched six months ago to facilitate professional synergy, they even uninstalled the application, but they still complain about a lack of synergy...

Fortunately, the presence of Sarah [the fourth member sharing a shared private office with the three above] *helps. She invited international colleagues this week in the co-working space. I think it proves that she is more and more proud of our space because she had never invited them before.*

To investigate further interpersonal issues, it is important to mention authors such as Menet and Zimmer (2018) who warn about the 'bullshitization' (Graeber, 2018) of the start-up dream. They call contemporary start-uppers the 'new digital proletarians' (Menet & Zimmer, 2018, 48). In her book, Ramadier (2017) writes about how she "survived the coolness of start-ups". Her description of the managerial and entrepreneurial newspeak mixed with the feeling of being in the 'new generation of proletarians' increases for her the feeling of a dream becoming a nightmare even before it really started. As shown in Vignette 16.3, sometimes people work for start-ups while still being unemployed and are not paid for what they do and/or the time they spend on projects.

Vignette 16.3 Digital Proletarians (Extract of My Autoethnographic Notebook, 2016)

A student who worked with one of the start-ups has just arrived and settled with us [I always seat in the open space]. *He told us that he is completing the development of a platform before leaving the project. I asked why but he did not really want to answer that. I think it is related to our former discussion about his issues with the Unemployment Office.*

Theoretical Framework

The autoethnographic approach I used in my research allows for such a critical insight in depicting a coworking community from an insider perspective and helps make visible the complexity of being a community manager in such spaces, not often present in the literature.

To analyze this further, I use Spinuzzi's (2012) framework that takes into account the multiple spatiotemporal dimensions of coworking spaces and is based on the fourth generation of cultural-historical activity theory 4G-CHAT (Engeström, 2009).

Theoretically speaking, activity theory, and in particular the third and fourth generations of activity theory (Engeström, 1999, 2000, 2008, 2009, 2015), is a complex model of nodes and networks of different dimensions impacting an object, with a common finality. The model studies several dimensions: subjects, rules, tools, community, objects, division of work. They impact each other, can have different characteristics (material, immaterial, human, non-human), can be multi-dimensional (a community chart can be part of three dimensions: rules, tools and objects) and take place in different space and times, at different levels (micro, meso, macro) (see Fig. 16.1).

These interconnections take place at different moments, sometimes simultaneously. As Engeström (2000, 309) points out, "processes become simultaneous, multidirectional, and often reciprocal. The density and crisscrossing of processes make the distinction between processes and structure somewhat obsolete".

Spinuzzi (2012, 404) emphasizes the importance of the fourth-generation activity theory to study the phenomenon of coworking:

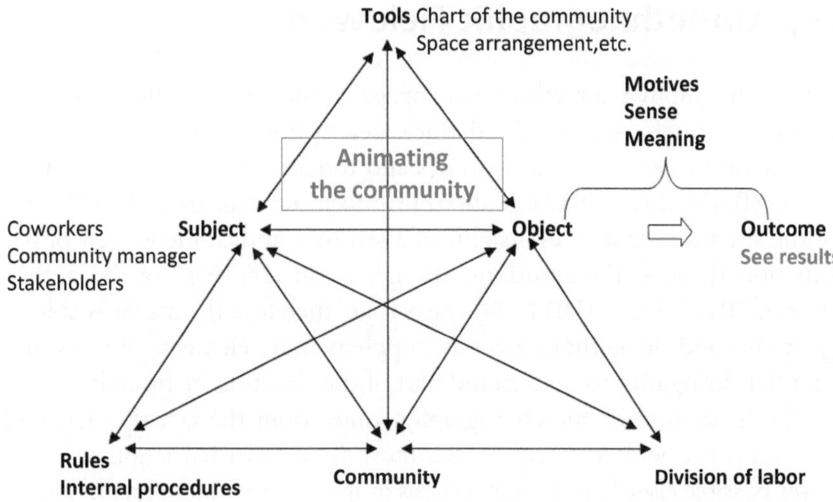

Fig. 16.1 Activity theory model applied to the activity 'animating the community' (adapted by the author from Engeström, 2009)

"4G-CHAT understands internetworked activities by examining the interorganizational collaborations to which they contribute". Exploring the emergence of a community such as constantly evolving coworking space needs a model that takes into account spatial, temporal and multiple other aspects (e.g. rules and artifacts). It is an activity system sharing collaborative objects that are "bounded hubs of concentrated coordination efforts" (Engeström, 2009, 310) with "collaborations and engagements with a shared object in and for relationships of interaction between multiple activity systems" (Yamazumi, 2009, 13).

I use the 4G-CHAT approach to analyze internetworked activities in a coworking space community by examining the interorganizational collaborations to which they contribute. This approach examines "peer production in textured activities" (Engeström, 2009), objects shared by activity networks (Yamazumi, 2009) and multi-activity interagency (Edwards, 2009), and is based on a phenomenological understanding of 'being in the world' (Engeström, 1989).

My Autoethnographic Fieldwork

Autoethnography is a method that engages authors to take the reader on a journey through contextualized thick descriptions of actions, contexts, temporalities, personalities, attitudes and tones in non-verbal communication (Bazin, 2011, 2013). It also transmits more than an analytical sense of the situation, as it gives insights of a sensitive and aesthetic view of the situation through the emotions, thoughts and reflexivity of the author (Bazin, 2011). Bazin (2011, 94) states that "therefore the reader is able to grasp, beyond the author's analysis, supplementary elements of the situation that bring him to understand part of the situation by himself".

The frustration of autoethnography comes from the fact that I would need an entire book to describe the context of each situated action, which is never possible elsewhere than in a thesis or in a research monograph. Here I first describe the two coworking spaces in which I worked as a community manager and then give a glimpse of my 'daily life' through vignettes.

Moreover, following Ybema, Yanow, Wels, and Kamsteeg (2009), I study an organizational topic in an environment, a culture, a language and a context (France, entrepreneurship, universities, Paris suburbs, labor markets, etc.) I am familiar with. As Ybema et al. (2009, 4) write, "rather than trying to grasp the entire gestalt of the organization 'village', organizational ethnographers seem increasingly oriented toward following (…) a specific organizational practice (…) or an object or 'fact'". I investigate my own organizational practice from the inside and I expose below the key elements I will include as parts of the explanations of the findings I present later on.

My fieldwork took place in two coworking spaces, Uni-Lab and Sub Smart, summarized in Table 16.1.

Uni-Lab

Uni-Lab is a coworking space for 'student-entrepreneurs', a specific status for students who want to launch their business during or just after graduation.[1] In September 2015 when I met Céline, the project manager,

[1] French government legislation about the specific status of 'student-entrepreneur' is available at http://www.enseignementsup-recherche.gouv.fr/cid79926/statut-national-etudiant-entrepreneur.html.

Table 16.1 Overview of my two field sites (author's own)

	Uni-Lab	Sub Smart
Governance	A meta-organization of several French universities, with a pyramid hierarchical structure	Association with a board and annual general meetings
Ecosystem	University entrepreneurship all over France and multiple stakeholders	Situated in a local neighborhood, with several other coworking spaces and communities elsewhere, multiple stakeholders
Public	Student-entrepreneurs	General public (e.g. freelancers, teleworkers, students and entrepreneurs)
Location	Center of Paris	Paris residential suburb
Funding for research	Partly from responding to a call from a local public institution for a citizen participatory budget program and partly from public university funding	Partly from personal funding, partly from crowdfunding, partly from partnerships and entrepreneurial public contributions
First entrance on the field	1 month before opening	<6 months after opening
Space budgeting basis	Annually every school year, renewable (the business model has evolved since then)	Depends on coworkers' contributions (19% ended their contract between 2015 and 2017)
Rental flexibility	None for the students Seasonal for their trainees	Ultra-flexible (from hourly to monthly rental contracts)

Uni-Lab was just starting. Céline and I co-organized the opening and the launch with the Mayor of Paris (see Vignette 16.4). While she managed external relations (management of studentships and university contacts), I participated in the daily management of the Uni-Lab coworking community during its first year of existence.

For example, my first day consisted of taking chairs out of their packaging in the empty open space that was still a work in progress—where carpenters were installing fitted furniture. Indeed, Uni-Lab has adopted a fixed immovable design with customized furniture and tables around the building's electrical shaft columns. I had many discussions and sometimes arguments with the architect about the design, especially the need for wall space for a whiteboard (see Vignette 16.4).

Vignette 16.4 Uni-Lab (Extract of One of My Conference Papers, 2017)

As mentioned above, I came into the field before the opening of Uni-Lab. With the project manager, I helped with the design and the choice of furniture, and I organized the launch event, I had many discussions with the architect about the design so was part of the creation of the space and, through its materiality and uses, the sense of community which emerged later.

For example, I asked for a whiteboard because it was obvious to me that a coworking space needed one, that coworkers could use for their internal meetings and we could use for events. It took two weeks to persuade the institution, but in exchange we had to accept that the whiteboard would be hidden behind a wood structure. For more than a year, this wood structure has been left opened due to constant use.

We organized the launch official photo in front of the whiteboard, to implicitly legitimate my fight for it. It was symbolic for the project manager and I, even if we knew that nobody except us and the architect knew about it. Legitimation is not always visible, but after this small victory over the whiteboard, I felt sufficiently supported by the coworkers to then change other things set up before my arrival. I felt legitimate as a 'catalyst' of the space.

During my second week, we set up rules, from good conduct to explicit procedures. Some of my suggestions, such as an automatic coffee machine and monthly payment of rents, were taken up after my departure when they hired a full-time community manager. I carried on fieldwork there which enabled me to compare the two practices within the same space and made me reflect on what I had done, what I could have done differently and what I would have liked to have thought of during my year as community manager there.

Sub Smart

Sub Smart is located in the heart of a Parisian suburban city. It opened in June 2015 and I discovered it in November 2015, when I interviewed Véronique (the founder) for my thesis. The space has six private offices, a large meeting room, an open space for twenty coworkers that can be transformed into an event space, a face-to-face meeting room and a kitchen. Sub Smart is the first coworking space in this town. It is a local municipality building with low rent, due to a national policy on local and regional economic development. The local and regional councils are very active in attracting entrepreneurs, like Véronique. A former marketing director in a multinational company, Véronique decided to follow an opportunity and become an entrepreneur. She set up Sub Smart according to her values and professional interests: well-being at work, collaboration and education. Sub Smart works closely with the local university, many of the coworkers are well-being consultants, and many events are co-created and based on collaboration.

My participation in Sub Smart was both as a coworker, a member of the community, a participant to many events, and as I was supposed to become an employee (but that did not happen for administrative reasons), I was recognized as a member of the management team (Vignette 16.5). For example, I looked after the space during Véronique's holidays and she introduced me to the collective of community managers in the Paris area; so, I was considered as one of them or at least accepted by them in their meetings.

Vignette 16.5 My Job Interview at Sub Smart with Véronique (Extract, 2015)

We have defined the role of a person in charge of this space... well it does not mean it's fixed, that it cannot evolve. We have decided what the best way of functioning and the number of employees should be (...) The role of site manager has three aspects or 'resources': animator, connector, facilitator. It's my job every day. A resource is defined as a half-time activity, that is to say that if I am supposed to do something else, here or elsewhere, it's up to me. (...)

The idea is to have a co-host (...) That's why we are interested in your application. In the original role of co-host we had planned, it was not such a rich profile. Indeed, I looked at your profile on LinkedIn, you already have a great experience. What interests me is the fact that you already have experience, that you research this specific subject, and that you know human resources because I try to give a HR color to this place. So, it can bring interesting and relevant things. And the fact that you also work with students, because it is a place that wants to be for students. And you as a teacher. These synergies make your profile super interesting. And the role we had planned was a simple co-host, for me it could be much more... (...) We can be a double act, as co-facilitator, co-connector and co-animator.

The Community Manager in Coworking Spaces

Investigating the Role

In the coworking literature, the community manager is barely studied although it is at the intersection of several dimensions of coworking spaces. Defining this role is difficult (Bohas, Faure, & de Vaujany, 2017; de Vaujany, Bohas, et al., 2018) in terms of the range of tasks and different spaces. Some examples of tasks are welcoming newcomers, dealing with accounts, replacing soap in restrooms or organizing events for coworkers. Further, when the host is both the founder-entrepreneur behind the project and the community manager, daily activities are even more diverse although always centered on coworkers, which may not be the case when hosts are low-paid employees.

Because of the heterogeneity of this role (Bohas et al., 2017), I will generally refer to them as 'community managers'. In my research, the community managers were the owner and/or founder of the coworking space, or me (see above). I also combine here managing the community and managing the space which is a situation often encountered in independent French coworking spaces and also at Uni-Lab (although not independent). Moreover, the French coworking market has grown with large actors, such as the American WeWork, and networks of coworking spaces (Hub, NextDoor, Startway, Betahaus, Stopandwork, etc.) whose entrepreneurial dynamics are different. My focus is on Parisian independent coworking collaborative spaces and Fig. 16.2 positions them within the French market. Their community managers may be alone or in a team for a single coworking space and can be part- or full-time jobs. I also include Uni-Lab, even if it is a university-based coworking space, because I managed it for its first year and it is an independent project with minimal public funding, therefore with interesting do-it-yourself bricolage practices.

Community managers of coworking spaces can be related to community managers of online communities; building and maintaining online communities are often tasks carried out by coworking spaces community managers who commonly use online tools and online social networks.

In most offline and online communities, community management includes behavioral evenhandedness, conflict resolution, personal interactions, professional support, informal coaching and network building.

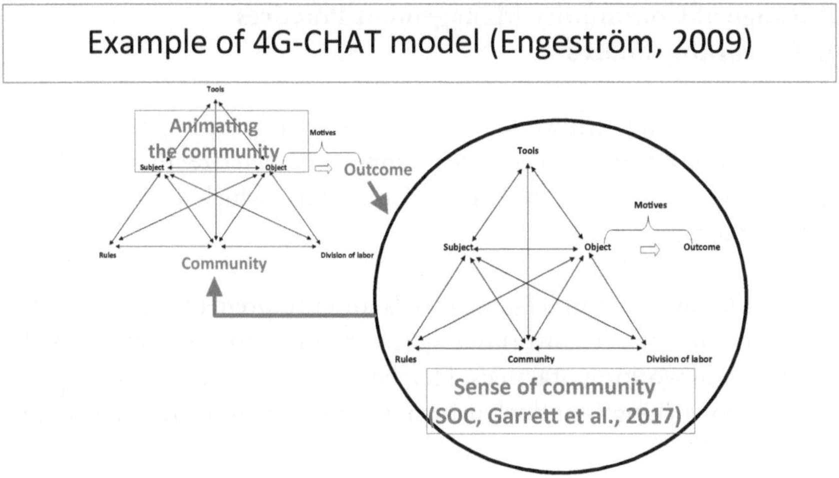

Fig. 16.2 Research focus on independent coworking spaces (author's own)

These competencies and tasks require many social qualities among which are social and emotional intelligence, a lot of empathy and a sense of caring (see Vignette 16.6).

Vignette 16.6 Conflicts and Community Managers (Extract of My Auto-ethnographic Notebook, Uni-Lab, 2016)

When I arrived today, Céline [the community manager] *showed me an email conversation with Pierre* [a start-upper who was one of the first community members, and a pillar of the community]. *The university owning the coworking space wants him and his co-founders to pay one year for an office for their trainees. I agree they have too many trainees, sometimes three for two months. Except that... initially it had been agreed that they would pay only on a pro rata basis. I was there, I remember. Since then, the number of trainees recruited by other start-ups has increased. But the university department is not acting properly! Pierre was there this afternoon. I tried to reduce the tension but there is still strong resentment.*

After that, Martine told me she is convinced this is my role in the community. I quite agree, especially since Julien, the new community manager, has been recruited. He is not really interested in conflict resolution and empathy. He is not even working in the open space with the coworkers.

A Range of Community Management Practices in Coworking Spaces

According to my fieldwork, community management practices keep reconfiguring themselves and we cannot characterize them dichotomously. Figure 16.3 represents a continuum, which covers my two autoethnographical experiences.

From left to right:

(1) The owner-founder-manager is an entrepreneur who takes the initiative to open a coworking space in order to participate in the evolution of working practices. He/she has an idea or a preconception of what coworking is and what it should provide to his/her customers (Vignette 16.7).

Vignette 16.7 Owner-Founder's Views (Extract of My Interview with a Co-founder Community Manager in a Cooperative Coworking Space, 2016)

I would like to write an article at the moment... I wanted to take tomorrow to write it but... still too many things to deal with... to basically say that co-working is dead... And explain how unhappy I am with current trends, the collaborative economy is dead, I want to say the same thing for coworking. And all the harmful dynamics, repetitions of buzzwords, semantics, etc., all the original values being put aside. And also, to try to recreate this collective dynamic, even if occasionally it has taken place. But there is still little awareness by the general public of the true uniqueness and potential of the movement, rather than... It could be a purely alternative and independent movement, a little risky but there is no awareness yet that there is a real value for public policies to support us. And support us not on the idea of a single package offer but of diversity and territorial dynamics that bring added value. And so that's very difficult to understand and we have seen it recently... But institutional dynamics are becoming very complicated and do not support small spaces. Spaces that start from needs, spaces that start from collectives of entrepreneurs and citizens... It is becoming very packaged, very big structures that build their thing. So here it is. I am a little afraid of this industrialization of the market, because we lose the original values.

Fig. 16.3 Continuum of community management in coworking spaces (author's own)

These thoughts reflect discussions I have had about how much coworking should not be a market; even the word 'customer' could become a non-sense or even a betrayal for such community managers. I remember a training session I ran for future community managers. When I talked about their 'customers', they stopped me by telling me they felt uncomfortable with this word. It was really surprising to me to discover that they identify themselves more as members of their own communities with more responsibilities than as entrepreneurs who had chosen a service-oriented business.

(2) Being a member of a community management team is the other extreme of this continuum. Community managers are trainees or employees in non-traditional structures with a traditional working contract. They can also be associated as co-founders or members of a cooperative, or members of an association, or former coworkers needing a part-time activity and so on. I met some but not directly interviewed many, apart from a pair of co-founders who opened a cooperative coworking space (one of which features in Vignette 16.7). Their community management team was composed of both the co-founders and two other persons at a time, employed under a French short-term contract, and intended to help them gain experience before launching their own collaborative space. Because I knew the co-founders well, I met five of these people over three years and I often go to the coworking space opened later by one of them. Employing future entrepreneurs in this way is an example of social learning through experiencing; and the community management team is seen positively by coworkers in the space, who feel that it is composed of people like them.

Difficulties Encountered by Community Managers

Paradoxically, the community manager is not only a person who cares for others and deals daily with their issues, he/she can also be an entrepreneur. But after launching his/her space, the community manager does not always get acknowledged by other entrepreneurs (aka coworkers) in the coworking space—because of the business contract between them, coworkers are customers and he/she is the provider. Which is interesting when remembering some community managers do not want to call them customers. This situation can lead to emotional distress and work difficulties, encountered in many service jobs (cashiers, receptionists, housekeepers, caretakers, nurses, etc.) studied extensively in organizational studies.

Community managers do not all face the same issues or feel the same way; however, this distress risk is a tacit issue almost never taken into consideration. In human resources and entrepreneurship practices and theories, psychosocial risks and burnouts are well-known but they are rarely addressed for those who are both caring for coworkers in a coworking space and being an entrepreneur. Individuals buy into the myths that caring for others should make one happy at work, or that working in a new work configuration (such as coworking spaces) automatically brings meaning and serenity forever (Vignette 16.8).

Vignette 16.8 Community Managers' Burnouts (Extract from My Autoethnographic Notebook, 2017)

Last week, Céline told me she was leaving. She wants to have a healthier work environment. And tonight, Jessica explained to me that, together with three other people, they are thinking of writing an article to tell their daily experience. I think it is an excellent idea. It is true that there is a real need to talk, to exchange, to discuss conflicts, distress and burnouts openly.

Indeed, there are many facilities for entrepreneurs and start-uppers in coworking spaces, from training sessions to informal social learning (Bilandzic & Foth, 2013; Merkel, 2018; Parrino, 2015; Rus & Orel, 2015), and many social events, to overcome loneliness, despair and feelings of failure (common in entrepreneurs). But strangely, those who organize all those facilities and events are the last to benefit from them. In other words, the enthusiasm for improving the work conditions of entrepreneurs and teleworkers contrasts with the tough working conditions of community managers.

More than a Community Manager, It Is About Being a Catalyst

Souls of the Coworking Space

At first, I took advantage of being in those spaces to experiment with a new way of working. I had worked as a human resources (HR) manager for a few years. I chose to go back to school to try to understand what I thought was a disturbing phenomenon: people (including me) are not happy at work. I was the one who was recruited to hire and develop careers but in reality, I fired people and refused days-off when a child was sick. That is why I entered coworking spaces enthusiastically: I needed to believe that another way of working was possible. I entered coworking spaces not as a worker but as a (community) manager and I found it had similarities with the HR role I was familiar with. Additionally, having experienced several spaces provided me with an 'insider-outsider' perspective, which allowed me to both belong to these communities and take a step back when I needed to be a researcher.

After six months in the field I came to realize that 'community manager' was insufficient to describe what I was doing with Céline and Véronique. I started developing a conceptual framework to study this role (see Fig. 16.4). I needed to understand what made each coworking space I worked with or visited different and found it was mostly about the uniqueness of each community manager (Vignette 16.9).

Vignette 16.9 The Uniqueness of Community Manager Is Key (Extract from My Autoethnographic Notebook, 2015)

I visited Sub Smart today and it was a pleasure. I really like the atmosphere, which owes everything to Véronique and Lola, the designer. (...) Lola, for her part, is very surprising. She is an artist, who lives her role and her art. She has created a 'cocoon' atmosphere within Véronique's well-being coworking project. Their two qualities make it a unique space.

The uniqueness is due to a combination of the community manager's personality, an understanding of his/her former professional activities, his/her coworking experience and sense of belonging, even his/her motivation in life and experience of the world. In a phenomenological perspective, this inner self and experience is felt in the coworking space community he/she manages. It also resonates with my HR manager experiences. I suggest the concept of 'phenomenology of activity' (Fig. 16.4), adapted from activity theory and based on a phenomenological understanding of being in the world in one's professional practice.

As an example drawn from my own experience as community manager at Uni-Lab, I remember a discussion with the architect while exploring the space just before the opening. He was explaining why he created two panels in one of the large immovable, one intended for official communications and locked with a key.

I tried to explain to him that this was not adequate but I had already fought for my whiteboard (Vignette 16.4) so I could not start a new

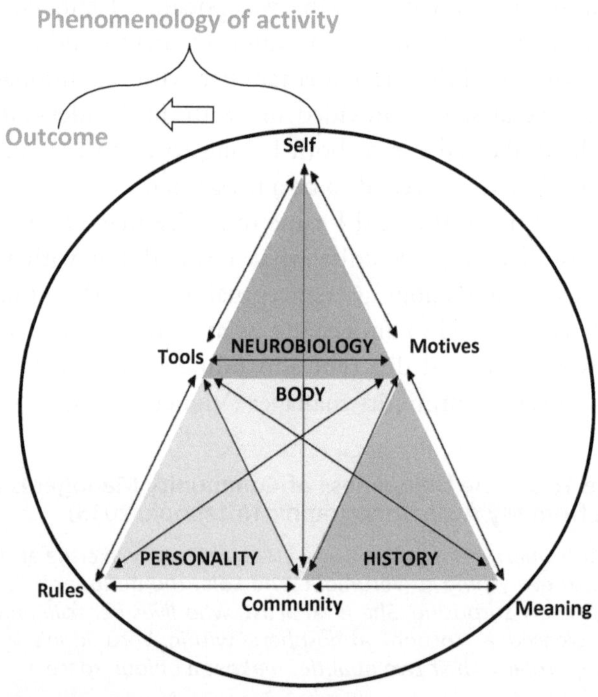

Fig. 16.4 Phenomenology of activity (author's own)

battle. He said that he was totally against 'sellotape decorations' and 'pictures of kittens', which he obviously thought was what students would do, entrepreneurs or not. I decided that I would consider them as entrepreneurs and that I would trust them to be professional. I decided not to use the key and told them to appropriate the space and do exactly what they wanted. For me, community management was all about trust.

I also noticed a marked difference between coworking spaces with and without a host to welcome in or to deal with daily issues and it is harder to gain a 'community feeling' when no one introduces you to the collective social norms.

Understanding the Community Feeling with 'Phenomenology of Activity'

The 4G-CHAT framework can be used to study intertwined organizational contexts through time and space and multiple levels of organizing. The community dimension of the activity theory model (see Fig. 16.1) is interesting to focus on when community is also the outcome studied. Having tried to understand community management through what I called the 'phenomenology of activity' (see Fig. 16.4), I wanted to understand community feeling through the phenomenology of activity and how to improve this feeling as a community manager.

Figure 16.5 suggests that there are two retrospective loops. In the first one, community feeling is an outcome of the coworking space through the community manager's daily work of animating the community. The person holding the role of community manager has an impact over time on the community, on the space, on community feeling and so on. Decisions he/she takes (e.g., space design and location, hours, rules, pricing, events, etc.) influence how coworkers understand and experience coworking and all dimensions of the coworking animation activity.

This creates a second retrospective loop. Community feeling is co-constructed by coworkers and the community manager who, reciprocally, is also influenced by this community feeling. Rules and meanings interact with values and perceptions of interpersonal issues and social norms. This loop integrates psychological, physical and biological dimensions in the emotional process of decision-taking (Cyrulnik et al., 2012; Damasio, 2012; Morin & Cyrulnik, 2011) according to the phenomenological perspective.

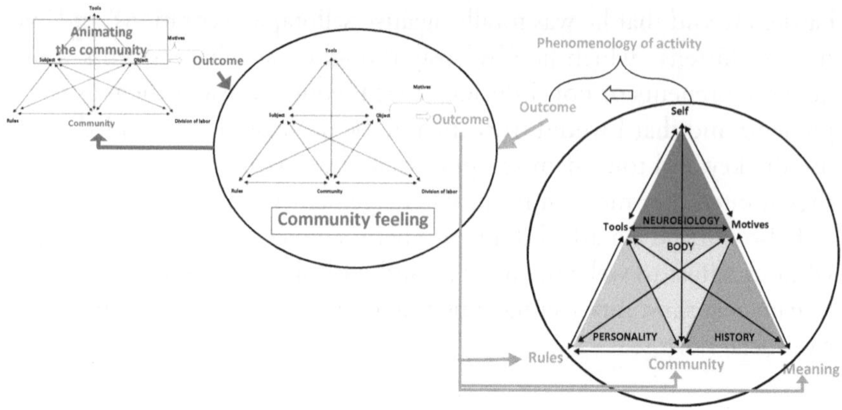

Fig. 16.5 Two retrospective loops of the sense of community co-constructed by the community manager (author's own)

Other factors have an impact on the perception of the space by coworkers. For example, they may prefer some locations because they are close to certain amenities (e.g. nurseries), suggesting that other activities (e.g. parenting) also influence coworking. As mentioned earlier, the political and economic environment affects coworking, and also community management. Coworking seems not to be a single activity, and participants' perceptions of coworking relate to how it intersects with their network of activities. These interconnections continually pull participants' perceptions of coworking in different directions. As cities and infrastructure change, we expect coworking will continue to evolve.

Community feeling is both influencing and influenced by its members. Members are the community manager, the coworkers and the stakeholders and partners of the entrepreneurial space project. The sense of community constantly emerges (Mead, 1934): it is more than the sum of its components and less than the complexity of each. This sense of community is part of how the rules are enacted in the coworking space.

It corresponds to the community dimension of the activity theory model. Members constitute this community so its feeling is an outcome of their activities. But it also plays an important role in imparting meaning to members in their professional and personal identities (for instance, in terms of personal views and beliefs, see Vignette 16.7). Figure 16.6 illustrates how community feeling emerges from those two retrospective loops:

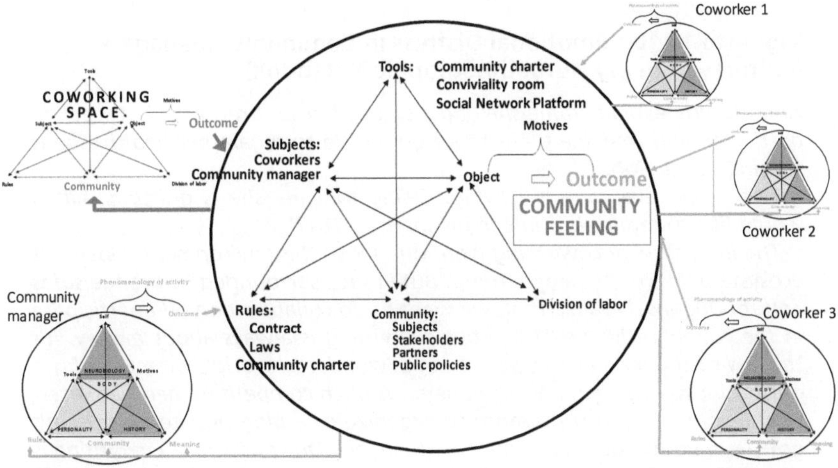

Fig. 16.6 How community feeling emerges in coworking spaces, adapted from 4G-CHAT (Spinuzzi, 2012; Engeström, 2009) and my concept of 'phenomenology of activity' (author's own)

1. The community, as a promise of the coworking space, emerges from it. It means that without the physical space, there would be no community. It is possible to create a coworking community without walls. Véronique, for example, opened the community before the space by bringing volunteers around the entrepreneurial project itself which had an immaterial and symbolic value, but it eventually needs to be materialized.
2. The community feeling is both resulting from the actions of the community manager and of the coworkers, and participating in (1) the sense of producing tacit and explicit rules, and shared meanings, and (2) the sense of belonging which drives the members to act as and for the community.

Finally, through being a community manager in the field, realizing the implications of the construction of community feeling, and carrying out research interviews with other community managers, I became aware of a broader issue: how coworkers feel disregarded by 'mainstream' professionals.

My own experience can illustrate this. When I opened Uni-Lab, I became very frustrated as one of the funders said to me "You are a volunteer? That's good!"; this meant to me that it was good I had worked for free, as a member of this 'new proletariat' (Vignette 16.10).

Vignette 16.10 Emotional Distress in Community Managers (Extracts from My Autoethnographic Notebook)

And Clotilde explained me she had a sort of burnout recently, last week in particular, and that she plans to let go a little to regain her health. She is turning to religion.

This week, everyone is leaving: Céline told me she is quitting, Alban would like to reduce his time in his space… (2017)

The little stars of coworking went out. I love this environment, I love this ecosystem, I love the people there. But in fact, surrounded by orange sofas and toboggans, I realize that, we want to do collaboration and participate in the collaborative economy, but everything is always about money. It's the law of the market. We are not in a 'wonderful world', we must all run our business. (…) Even I need money… A pitch competition here, an after-work event there, a conference to organize or a blog post to write? Let's go! Get paid for lectures? Do a part-time job? Do consulting? Everything is good! The irony is that money is the problem of coworking but we work for free when it's needed! (2016)

Furthermore, I met many people who understood community management as managing online communities. I struggled with this comparison as I now see coworking community management as much more than what I did as an online community manager in previous jobs. Dealing with a coworking space community is a demanding activity, including running events, providing psychological support, supporting networking and so on. I understand how being seen as animators in the sense of entertainers for adults is hurtful.

As illustrated by Sandra (Vignette 16.11), the difficulty is not only in describing the job for ourselves (as community managers), for coworkers or for stakeholders or, idealistically, gaining credit for its complexity. It is also about helping entrepreneurs to make it understandable for the layman of the professional world, for instance in their curriculum resumes, let alone the general public.

Vignette 16.11 What Is Your Job Title? (Extract of My Interview with Sandra, 2017)

My job title was supposed to be fun at first but I found it a little difficult to sell elsewhere, in case it does not go well here. So, I became 'responsible of animation'. And now I am 'responsible for development'. Which does not mean much either, but in fact, I think I do so much, it's a bit complicated to have a title. To bring in an anecdote which is revealing, when I left my previous job, to explain to a woman who runs a coworking space in Neuilly, I said: "I also launched my coworking space." She said to me "Ah, you too will become a mother?" And I think of what she told me very often.

Having explored the literature, the most appropriate concept I could find which describes our community manager's role is 'catalyst' (Brafman & Beckstrom, 2006) which they use in the context of 'leaderless' decentralized online organizations such as *Skype*, *eMule* or *Craigslist*. Catalysis is a chemical phenomenon which initiates a reaction without melting into it. In organization studies, a catalyst is "the person who initiates a circle [in contrast to a hierarchical pyramid] and then fades away into the background" (Brafman & Beckstrom, 2006, 92). The authors compare catalysts to traditional leaders and CEOs and argue that the main differences are that catalysts transfer responsibility, do not own the circle (the community in coworking spaces) and have an 'ephemeral' position. Their concept of 'catalyst' appears to me closer to my experience in coworking spaces than any other management concepts or leadership theories, and more integrative than 'community manager'. The French national report on coworking and third-places (Levy-Waitz, 2018, 4) identifies "three challenges to make third places local catalysts" implying that places are catalysts. I would argue that people are catalysts, I was a catalyst.

Conclusion

The concept of 'catalyst' could help acknowledge professionals who manage coworking space communities. My autoethnographic narrative provides insights into the human aspects of this role which is key to the future of work and New Ways of Working. Empirical work in other coworking spaces would help further the understanding of the uniqueness and complexity of coworking community managers.

Drawing on activity theory corresponded to my practice-oriented autoethnographic field approach. Nevertheless, a human resource-based study could bring further insights, for instance, on employee turnover in coworking spaces or on the well-being and burnout experiences in coworkers and community managers. Empirical research in non-independent spaces and in workspaces in traditional companies could reveal different patterns and configurations.

Developing methodologies to capture data on phenomenological ethnographies and autoethnographies, such as a partnership with a psychological research laboratory, could compare participants' neuronal activity and physical health indicators to their expressed emotion.

The concept of 'phenomenology of activity' could also be applied to other contexts, for instance, with independent workers working on their own or in distributed, interorganizational, collaborative knowledge work.

Finally, bearing in mind the emotional distress I discovered during my fieldwork, it would be valuable to think through the issues of proletarization in the collaborative economy.

References

Alter, N. (2013). Les trois piliers de l'innovation. *Paris Tech Review, 1*, 10–20.

Bazin, Y. (2011). *L'institutionnalisation des pratiques organisationnelles: le cas du diagnostic en psychiatrie*. Thèse de doctorat en sciences de gestion. Conservatoire National des Arts et Métiers, Paris.

Bazin, Y. (2013). Understanding organisational gestures: Technique, aesthetics and embodiment. *Scandinavian Journal of Management, 29*(4), 377–393.

Bilandzic, M., & Foth, M. (2013). Libraries as co-working spaces: Understanding user motivations and perceived barriers to social learning. *Library Hi Tech, 31*(2), 254–273.

Bilandzic, M., Schroeter, R., & Foth, M. (2013). Gelatine: Making co-working places gel for better collaboration and social learning. In *Proceedings of the 25th Australian Computer-Human Interaction Conference on augmentation, application, innovation, collaboration—OzCHI '13* (pp. 427–436). Adelaide, Australia: ACM Press.

Bohas, A., Faure, S., & de Vaujany, F.-X. (2017). *Tiers-lieux & espaces collaboratifs: laboratoires et révélateurs des nouvelles pratiques de travail* (Research Report). Paris: Paris-Dauphine University, Research Group on Collaborative Spaces (RGCS).

Bouncken, R. B. (2018). University co-working-spaces: Mechanisms, examples, and suggestions for entrepreneurial universities. *International Journal of Technology Management, 77*(1–3), 38–56.

Bouncken, R. B., Aslam, M. M., & Reuschl, A. J. (2018). The dark side of entrepreneurship in coworking spaces, in Tur Porcar, A., Ribeiro Soriano, D. (Eds.), *Inside the mind of the entrepreneur: Cognition, personality traits, intention, and gender behavior* (pp. 135–147). Cham, Switzerland: Springer International Publishing,

Brafman, O., & Beckstrom, R. A. (2006). *The starfish and the spider: The unstoppable power of leaderless organizations.* New York: Penguin.

Butcher, T. (2013). Co-working: Locating community at work. In *Proceedings of the 27th Annual Australia New Zealand Academy of Management (ANZAM) Conference* (pp. 1–13), 4–6 December, Hobart, Tasmania.

Capdevila, I. (2015). Co-working spaces and the localised dynamics of innovation in Barcelona. *International Journal of Innovation Management, 19*(3), 1540004.

Cyrulnik, B., Bustany, P., Oughourlian, J.-M., André, C., Janssen, T., & Van Eersel, P. (2012). *Votre cerveau n'a pas fini de vous étonner*. Paris: Albin Michel.

Damasio, A. (2012). *Self comes to mind: Constructing the conscious brain.* New York: Vintage.

De Gaulejac, V. (2005). *La société malade de la gestion*. Paris: Seuil.

De Gaulejac, V. (2011). L'injonction d'être sujet dans la société hypermoderne: la psychanalyse et l'idéologie de la réalisation de soi-même. *Revue française de psychanalyse, 75*(4), 995–1006.

De Vaujany, F.-X., Bohas, A., Carton, S., Fabbri, J., & Leclercq-Vandelannoitte, A. (2018). *Le futur du travail en 2030: quatre atmosphères?* (No. 3, p. 35). Paris: Paris-Dauphine University, Research Group on Collaborative Spaces (RGCS).

De Vaujany, F.-X., Dandoy, A., Grandazzi, A., & Faure, S. (2018). Experiencing a new place as an atmosphere: A focus on tours of collaborative spaces. *Scandinavian Journal of Management, 35*(2), 101030.

Doloriert, C., & Sambrook, S. (2012). Organisational auto-ethnography. *Journal of Organizational Ethnography, 1*(1), 83–95.

Edwards, A. (2009). From the systemic to the relational: Relational theory and activity theory. In A. Sannino, H. Daniels, & K. D. Gutierrez (Eds.),

Learning and expanding with activity theory (pp. 197–211). New York, NY: Cambridge.

Engeström, Y. (1989). *Developing thinking at the changing workplace: Toward a redefinition of expertise*. San Diego, CA: Center for Human Information Processing, University of California.

Engeström, Y. (1999). Activity theory and individual and social transformation. *Perspectives on Activity Theory, 19*(38), 19–30.

Engeström, Y. (2000). Activity theory and the social construction of knowledge: A story of four umpires. *Organization, 7*(2), 301–310.

Engeström, Y. (2008). *From teams to knots: Activity-theoretical studies of collaboration and learning at work*. Cambridge University Press.

Engeström, Y. (2009). The future of activity theory: A rough draft. In A. Sannino, H. Daniels, & K. D. Gutierrez (Eds.), *Learning and expanding with activity theory* (pp. 303–328). Cambridge, UK: Cambridge University Press.

Engeström, Y. (2015). *Learning by expanding*. Cambridge University Press.

Fabbri, J., & Charue-Duboc, F. (2013). The role of physical space in collaborative workplaces hosting entrepreneurs: The case of the "beehive" in Paris. In F.-X. de Vaujany & N. Mitev (Eds.), *Materiality and space. Organizations, artefacts and practices* (pp. 117–134). Basingstoke, UK: Palgrave Macmillan.

Fasshauer, I., Meyer, C., & Bourret, C. (2015). De la participation à la coopération entre enseignants et étudiants dans le cadre d'un espace de co-working à l'université. In *Biennale Internationale de l'Education, de la Formation et des Pratiques Professionnelles*, 30 June–3 July, Paris, Conservatoire National des Arts et Métiers.

Follett, M. P. (1919). Community is a process. *The Philosophical Review, 28*(6), 576–588.

Fuzi, A. (2015). Co-working spaces for promoting entrepreneurship in sparse regions: The case of South Wales. *Regional Studies, Regional Science, 2*(1), 462–469.

Gandini, A. (2015). The rise of co-working spaces: A literature review. *Ephemera, 15*(1), 193.

Garrett, L. E., Spreitzer, G. M., & Bacevice, P. A. (2017). Co-constructing a sense of community at work: The emergence of community in co-working spaces. *Organization Studies, 38*(6), 821–842.

Graeber, D. (2018). *Bullshit jobs*. Paris: Éditions Les Liens qui libèrent.

Hirschhorn, M. (2010). La communauté: du concept à l'idée directrice. In I. Sainsaulieu, L. Amiotte-Suchet, & M. Salzbrunn (Eds.), *Faire communauté en societé. Dynamique des appartenances collectives* (pp. 9–13). Rennes, France: Presses Universitaires de Rennes.

Holt, N. L. (2003). Representation, legitimation, and auto-ethnography: An auto-ethnographic writing story. *International Journal of Qualitative Methods, 2*(1), 18–28.

Levy-Waitz, P. (2018). *Rapport mission co-working—Faire ensemble pour mieux vivre ensemble*. Paris: Ministère de la cohésion des territoires, 264p.

Madison, D. S. (2011). *Critical ethnography: Method, ethics, and performance*. Thousand Oaks, CA: Sage Publications.

Mead, G. H. (1934). *Mind, self and society* (Vol. 111). Chicago: University of Chicago Press.

Menet, N., & Zimmer, B. (2018). *Start-up, arrêtons la mascarade: Contribuer vraiment à l'économie de demain*. Malakoff, France: Dunod.

Merkel, J. (2015). Co-working in the city. *Ephemera, 15*(1), 121–139.

Merkel, J. (2018). 'Freelance isn't free.' Co-working as a critical urban practice to cope with informality in creative labour markets. *Urban Studies, 56*(3), 526–547.

Morin, E., & Cyrulnik, B. (2011). *Dialogue sur la nature humaine*. Paris: Seuil.

Orwell, G. (1954). *Nineteen eighty-four*. New York: Signet Classic.

Parrino, L. (2015). Co-working: Assessing the role of proximity in knowledge exchange. *Knowledge Management Research & Practice, 13*(3), 261–271.

Ramadier, M. (2017). *Bienvenue dans le nouveau monde*. Paris: Premier Parallèle.

Rus, A., & Orel, M. (2015). Co-working: A community of work. *Teorija in Praksa, 52*(6), 1017–1038.

Spinuzzi, C. (2012). Working alone together: Co-working as emergent collaborative activity. *Journal of Business and Technical Communication, 26*(4), 399–441.

Uda, T. (2013). *What is co-working? A theoretical study on the concept of co-working*. Discussion Paper, Series A, 265, 1–15. Sapporo, Japan: Hokkaido University. Graduate School of Economics & Business Administration. Available at SSRN: https://ssrn.com/abstract=2937194

Vandevelde-Rougale, A. (2017). *La novlangue managériale: emprise et résistance*. Toulouse: Editions érès.

Waters-Lynch, J., & Potts, J. (2017). The social economy of co-working spaces: A focal point model of coordination. *Review of Social Economy, 75*(4), 417–433.

Yamazumi, K. (2009). Expansive agency in multi-activity collaboration. In A. Sannino, H. Daniels, & K. D. Gutierrez (Eds.), *Learning and expanding with activity theory* (pp. 212–227). New York, NY: Cambridge University Press.

Ybema, S., Yanow, D., Wels, H., & Kamsteeg, F. H. (2009). *Organizational ethnography: Studying the complexity of everyday life*. London: Sage.

17

Rise and Fall of a New Way of Working: A Testament of an Organizational Identity Mimicry

Marie Antoine

Introduction

For the past three decades and with the help of information and communications technologies (ICTs), numerous organizations have enrolled in the 'new world of work', also referred to as NWOW. Under this umbrella label lies a diversity of practices, often summed up as "bricks, bytes and behaviors" (de Kok, Koops, & Helms, 2014). These New Ways of Working are about practices of spatial-temporal flexibility, such as flexible working hours, working from home, clean-desk policies, mobile teleworking, and tele-centers, among other arrangements (Ajzen, Donis, & Taskin, 2015).

While research on New Ways of Working, and especially the spatial dimension of organizations, is not new, the meaning of a transition toward the new world of work is understudied. We know little about the side effects of new office arrangements and how they influence organizational life. In this chapter, based on my doctoral dissertation at the

M. Antoine (✉)
Université Catholique de Louvain, Louvain-la-Neuve, Belgium

N. Mitev et al. (eds.), *New Ways of Working*, Technology, Work and Globalization,
https://doi.org/10.1007/978-3-030-61687-8_17

Université Catholique de Louvain (Antoine, 2018), I address what the transition toward the new world of work might mean for an organization's identity. In particular, I focus on the spatial component of an NWOW project, that is to say, the transition toward an activity-based work environment.

This chapter is structured as follows. First and based on the literature, I present the new world of work, its principles and promises, but also its materiality, that is to say, the physical and spatial component at heart. Second, I mobilize the work of Henri Lefebvre to show that space is a social construct, but that it is also likely to influence social constructions. Third, I briefly review how identity is closely related to space and, in particular, the identity issues in line with the organizational space and its alterations. In line with previous research, I argue that organizational identity might also be intrinsically related to organizational space, especially when this latter is prone to changes. Fourth, since the present chapter rests upon empirical research, the methodological design of this research is presented, as well as a description of the case study, the company *ORES* where I conducted this research. Fifth, empirical findings are presented. In the discussion section, I use the empirical findings to show how *ORES* decision to embrace the new world of work and the difficulties the company meets in this process reflect a broader attempt to mimic a corporate ideology, in line with a 'modernity' ideal, cleansed of all the remainders of a bygone working era. This chapter concludes with theoretical and practical implications.

The New World of Work: Rhetoric and Materiality

Since the 1980s and following the emergence of teleworking, organizations have been increasingly investing in NWOW. Whether it refers to New Ways of Working or—more ambitiously—the new world of work, it seems that there is no company which does not know what NWOW means, nor that it should be considered as a 'movement' worthy of consideration and potential investment. Indeed, the temptation to follow the move is strong, so numerous are the promises of this new world of work. New ways of working are argued to stimulate communication, collaboration, and creativity; to develop workers' autonomy; to reduce real estate cost; to diminish an organization's carbon footprint; to improve workers' work/life balance and well-being, ultimately leading to increased performance and productivity (Brunia, De Been, & Van Der Voordt, 2016; Gavroglou, Ford, Totterdill, Savage, & Sacquepee, 2001).

According to a systematic review of the literature realized by Ajzen et al. (2015), New Ways of Working refer to three broad categories of practices: (1) practices of spatial and temporal flexibility, (2) collaborative work organization methods, and (3) practices of participative management. Moreover, these practices are enabled by information and communication technologies and require organization to align with a particular vision about democracy, collaboration, and sustainable governance (Taskin, 2012). Agreeing with this characterization, numerous authors summarize New Ways of Working as being about "bricks, bytes, and behaviors", respectively referring to the workspace design, the technological infrastructure, and expected behavioral changes (de Kok et al., 2014; Jemine, 2016). Even though it is rather difficult to dissociate these three components, this chapter focuses primarily on the bricks dimension, which is the physical work environment.

Although changes in the work environment are not new (Haigh, 2012; van Meel, 2011), flexibilization has grown since the 1980s. While workspace flexibility used to refer to the opportunity for a worker to practice home-based or mobile teleworking, more recently workspace flexibility has also been related to internal flexibility, that is the possibility for a worker to choose his/her work environment within the organization. Following the open-space (originally *bürolandschaft*) which appeared in the 1960s, the activity-based workspace appears as one of the last office trends that seem to have emerged since the 1980s. The activity-based workspace, also called 'non-territorial office', 'hot desking', or 'clean-desk', is an open-space "where employees are not assigned dedicated desks but work from any that happen to be vacant" (Millward, Haslam, & Postmes, 2007, 547). Allen and Gerstberger (1973) explain that activity-based workspaces provide a diversity of workstations such as meeting rooms, rooms dedicated to highly focused work, enabling each worker to choose a work environment suiting his/her work activities throughout the working day. This office is 'non-territorial' in the sense that workers are provided a personal locker in which to put their belongings.

In terms of contextualization of this trend, it is interesting to observe that this type of work environment emerged in the 1980s, an era characterized by the global rise of the so-called knowledge-based economy in which knowledge and digital capacities were defined as core ingredients of economic success (Godin, 2006; Huws, 2014; Sum & Jessop, 2013). Degryse (2016, 13) explained this digital economy "necessitates erasure of silo-based organization methods in favor of a horizontal and open form of organization within which the flows of information will circulate". This is somewhat reminiscent of the activity-based workspace. Therefore, it is likely that the increasing appearance of the activity-based workspace since the 1980s is not unconnected with the current economy and what it seems to promote as an ideal organizational model.

This brief review of the literature on the new world of work indicates that the activity-based workspace trend comes with rhetoric of modernity, adaptability, and innovation, but it also comes with spatial materiality. Yet, this spatial component of the new world of work does not limit itself to providing a workspace, but it takes place in the social world and influences it.

The Office as a Social Construct

Until the 1970s, space was generally considered a neutral architectural feature and was rather unquestioned regarding its effects (Marrewijk & Yanow, 2010). It is only since the 1970s and the 1980s that researchers became interested in studying how space influenced organizations. Applied to the organizational milieu, this consideration for space led to what some scholars have named the "spatial turn", that is the acknowledgment of the spatial dimension as a "key dynamic in understanding management and organizations" (Taylor & Spicer, 2007, 341). This spatial turn is mainly studied with two approaches: a behavioral approach, for example, questioning the effects of workspace conditions on behaviors and attitudes (Edenius & Yakhlef, 2007; Zhong & House, 2012); and a subjective approach, for example, studying how space embodies symbols and meanings (Dale & Burrell, 2008a; Halford, 2004; Tyler & Cohen, 2010).

When it comes to considering space in the symbols, meanings, and interpretations it embodies, most scholars relate to Henri Lefebvre's work (1991). In *The Production of Space* (1991), the sociologist argues that "(social) space is a (social) product" (Lefebvre, 1991, 26) and proposes a triad that identifies how space underlies different aspects and shows how these aspects interact with each other. The three components of this triad are (1) representations of space, (2) spatial practice, and (3) representational spaces. Representations of space refer to how space is conceived, that is "the space of scientists, planners, urbanists, technocratic sub dividers and social engineers" (Lefebvre, 1991, 38). Spatial practice is about how space is perceived, which encompasses the spatial competence and performance each society member acquires through experience. Representational spaces correspond to the lived space, which is "the space of 'inhabitants' and 'users'" (Lefebvre, 1991, 39). These three components of Lefebvre's spatial triad interact with each other in a dynamic process, which means that they produce the social as well as they are produced by it. Drawing on this concept, organizations are specific social milieus and organizational space is a manifestation of the social relations and the anthropology of an organization. When it comes to organizational space and the meanings that are ascribed to it, many authors have shown that organizational space—whether it is about architecture, decoration, or office design—embodies meanings in terms of power and hierarchy, gendered relations, and identity issues (Dale & Burrell, 2008b; Shortt & Warren, 2012; Tyler & Cohen, 2010; Warren, 2006; Zhang & Spicer, 2014). Since this chapter is specifically about organizational identity, I will develop the identity issue related to organizational space further.

At the Heart of the Space: An (Organizational) Identity Issue

Among the authors subscribing to a perspective considering identity as fluid, dynamic, and socially constructed, only a few have examined how space influences identity. They argued that spatial contexts are a key feature that influences the construction and affirmation of one's identity (Elsbach, 2003; Petriglieri & Petriglieri, 2010). When it comes to the organizational environment, the idea that one's identity might be connected to his or her work environment is easily covered by the 'workplace identity' concept which refers to "the distinctiveness and status self-categorizations used by an individual to signal his or her identity in a specific workplace" (Elsbach, 2003, 623). This concept echoes research in human geography and sociology explaining how individuals develop territorial behaviors in order to control their living space and showing their belonging to this space (Brown, Lawrence, & Robinson, 2005; Byron & Laurence, 2015; Inalhan, 2009). Among the researchers that have embraced the spatial turn in organization studies, only a few have examined identity in new workspace arrangements. For instance, Wapshott and Mallett (2012) showed how home-working challenged workers' ability to set boundaries between their professional and their private life because working from home operated as a spatial domination of work into the domestic area. Baldry and Barnes (2012) showed how an open-plan work environment for academics challenged their professional identity by degrading their physical working conditions and eroding their professional status. In a more critical approach, a few researchers in organizational studies highlighted how workspace redesigns mold individuals' identities so that they fit the "post-bureaucratic model worker" (Hancock & Spicer, 2011; Minchella, 2015). These few pieces of research are enough to argue that whether it is the product of an intentional identity regulation practice or not, organizational space is much likely to take part in one's identity, either at the individual or at the professional level and either by threatening it or by intervening in its continuous development.

Even though researchers identified that workspaces influence organizational identity, research on how identity is constructed is rather scarce. Much of the literature focuses on identity issues at the individual, micro level, neglecting how identity at a meso level is constructed. While the literature on organizational identity is prone to theoretical debates, from a constructivist perspective it is defined as the whole of organizational members' shared interpretations about the characteristics which compose their organization and distinguish it in its social context (Gomes Da Silva, 2010, 200). In other words, according to a constructivist approach, an organization's identity is not defined a priori nor transmitted in a top-down process, but resides in an organization's members' beliefs. Organizational identity then is a collective shared vision about what the organization is. Therefore, an organization's identity entails how organizational members perceive their organization, such as its ethos and purpose, its characteristics, and how work is accomplished. From this perspective, organizational identity is considered as a continuously constructed sense, prone to evolutions depending on organizational members' changing perceptions of their organization (Alvesson & Empson, 2008; Gombault, 2003; Humphreys & Brown, 2002).

A corporate decision to reconfigure the organization's work environment in a way that embraces NWOW might lead employees to redefine their understanding of the organization and its identity. Research on organizational aesthetics supports this assumption as it showed how renovations act "as a media of meaning construction for both employees and clients" (Chugh & Hancock, 2009, 464). With a social constructionist view of identity and an aesthetic approach to organizational space, I ask the following questions. How does an organization's spatial redesign influence an organization's identity? What does such change tell about an organization's identity?

Methodology

In order to address these research questions, I conducted qualitative empirical research. This research was based on a single-case study (Yin, 2014). I chose this research method because case studies allow researchers to understand and study a phenomenon in depth within its context, enabling the production of knowledge about social situations that cannot be grasped if not studied from the inside.

I chose to study *ORES Wallonia-Picardy*, one of the sites of the seven areas of operations of the Belgian company *ORES*. For the sake of simplicity, I will use the shortened name *ORES WaPi* from now on. This case was chosen because, at the time of the study, workers of *ORES WaPi* had recently moved from a previous building, located in Tournai, to a new one designed in accordance with 'new world of work' principles, and located in Leuze-en-Hainaut.[1] This site was the pilot project for the new headquarters of *ORES*. This means the project was substantial enough to base my research on and had happened in a time frame not exceeding two years (in order to prevent memory biases, excessive turnover, etc.).

ORES is a distribution system operator for electricity and natural gas in Wallonia,[2] one of the three regions of Belgium. The company is in charge of distributing medium to low-voltage electricity and natural gas to residential and private customers and is responsible for public lightning in Wallonia municipalities. *ORES* provides 75% of the Walloon municipalities, putting the company in a quasi-monopoly situation (ORES, 2017). Moreover, *ORES* is an inter-municipal association wherein at least two municipalities conjointly manage municipal interests (Portail des Pouvoirs Locaux, 2015). In Belgium, municipalities are responsible for satisfying citizens' primary needs, electricity and gas distribution, thus often times gather together in order to provide common services. *ORES* is a fusion of 197 municipalities that decided to come together in 2013 and create *ORES Assets*.[3] The period of activity of *ORES Assets* is agreed upon until 2045 (Statuts coordonnés ORES, 2017). At the time of research, *ORES* employed around 2300 workers (ORES, 2016b).

Since *ORES* is in charge of the whole Walloon Region (except a few autonomous municipalities), the region is separated into seven areas of operations. Support services operate in the head office, but each area has at least one head office that is in charge of the operational management of the area. *ORES WaPi* is one of these seven areas of operations, managed primarily from Leuze-en-Hainaut. An area director manages this site, and it is composed of three main services, each managed by an executive. At the time of the research, 164 persons worked on this site: 140 employees, 20 managers, and 4 executives (including the director).

As previously explained, the company chose *ORES WaPi* as a pilot project for a broader NWOW project of *ORES*, called the *DOMO*

[1] Workers moved in July 2016, and data were collected between March and November 2017.

[2] Wallonia accounts for 55% of Belgium and a third of the Belgian population.

[3] *ORES Assets* is a legal entity; *ORES* is the subsidiary in charge of managing operational activities of distribution. Both these structures result from the energy market liberalization dating back to 2007 in the European Union.

project. In July 2017, workers from this site moved from their previous building located in Tournai to a new one located in Leuze-en-Hainaut. In the next section dedicated to the results, I will describe more extensively this new work environment.

For this research, I used different data collection methods to offer data triangulation. Data triangulation offers a rich depiction of the case, provides multiple sources of evidence, and develops "converging lines of inquiry" (Yin, 2014, 119–120) (Demers, 2003; Gombault, 2006; Myers, 2013; Yin, 2014). Specifically, I conducted semi-structured interviews, participant observation, and engaged in documentary analysis. Between March and November 2017, I conducted 81 semi-structured interviews with 74 employees, 4 top managers, a consultant in charge of accompanying the NWOW project, the HR director, and the CEO. These informants had different professional profiles. Some were administrative workers, and others had a more technical background. Broadly speaking, I will refer to these workers as administrative workers and technical workers. Among the 81 interviews, I recorded 79 with the interviewees' agreement and 65 of them were fully transcribed. The interviews lasted on average 75 minutes. All the names in this chapter are pseudonyms to ensure interviewees' anonymity. I based my interviews on an interview guide with several open questions. This guide was reviewed and adapted twice, reflecting new issues coming from previous interviews, in an inductive process (Demers, 2003; Myers, 2013). I conducted interviews until data saturation (Eisenhardt, 1989; Yin, 2014).

While the semi-structured interviews provided most of the data collected for this research, I also collected data through observation and documentary analysis. I conducted observations for a three-month period when I integrated *ORES WaPi*, and employees were aware of my presence and its purpose (Junker, cited by Groleau, 2003; Peretz, 2004). Through this type of observation, I had the opportunity to observe and experience the work environment, workers' daily practices, take part in their discussions and to hear anecdotes about work, management, and the building among other things. This type is unique to observation and thus supplemented my interviews. Finally, through internal documents, corporate presentation supports, and official reports, documentary analysis allowed me to gather additional information about the company, the project, the corporate strategy, and so on.

I followed Paillé and Mucchielli's (2012) method of analysis and, through multiple readings of the data, conducted two types of coding: a thematic analysis and an analysis by categories of concepts. I used NVivo qualitative data analysis software to assist me in the coding process.

Empirical Findings

The Goals of the DOMO Project

As previously explained, in the company *ORES*, the NWOW project titled DOMO refers to the Latin word meaning "the house". The corporate strategic plan 2015–2020 (internal document) articulates and explains the goals of the project:

> *The DOMO program consists in implementing in ORES what is called [...] the "New World of Work" which concerns several dimensions: teleworking and adapted work schedules, unified communication, adaptation of the equipment and workspaces for more relationships, conviviality, flexibility and mobility...*
>
> *Through the implementation of this new way of working, the DOMO program inspires* ***a new corporate culture of collaboration, innovation, agility, wellbeing at work****. It is based on a* ***trust-based management that is results-oriented, giving autonomy and aiming at the responsibility*** *of everyone, managers and collaborators.* [Strategic plan 2015–2020. State of progress in December 2016, p. 23; emphasis added]

As the aforementioned quotation illustrates, the DOMO project is a cultural change project, which is one of the three challenges identified by the board in its strategic plan (ORES, 2016a). Figure 17.1 illustrates the cultural change that is pursued by the company in terms of management and behaviors.

What internal documents do not explain about this project is the final purpose of this cultural change. As one of the persons in charge of the project explains, the ultimate goal is to boost the company's productivity, as illustrated by Mathias who explains, "*We are a private company. So, behind everything we do, the goal is to improve customer service and be more*

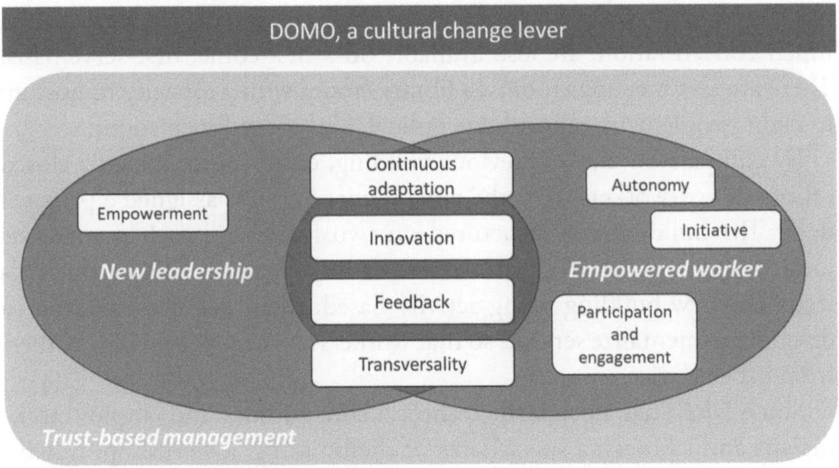

Fig. 17.1 Illustration of the DOMO project and its purpose. (Source: Adapted from internal PowerPoint about the DOMO project at ORES)

productive. [...] The company that says it does not do that to be more productive, it's lying. Every company wants to be more productive."

According to the strategic report, the cultural change rests upon four working lines: (1) IT tools to enable collaboration and mobility, (2) document management (i.e. digitalization of paper-format documents), (3) change in terms of behaviors and attitudes that should meet the corporate values, and (4) architecture adapted to tasks and prone to interactions (ORES, 2016a). The last line—architecture—seems to be the context enabling to change behaviors and attitudes of workers.

The Materialization of the DOMO Project

As previously explained, in July 2016 *ORES Wallonia-Picardy* workforce moved from their previous building to a new one, built in accordance with the new world of work philosophy. In terms of interior design, the new building is completely open with a clean-desk policy for all the workers, regardless of their position. Each employee is assigned a locker and they can choose a desk in a space for a single worker or for two to six workers. Small rooms, called "bubbles", and dedicated to tasks requiring much concentration, are also available on a first-come, first-serve basis. There are also meetings rooms, a library (room with a capacity to host up to eight people, with a no-phone policy), and a vast lunch room.

By comparison, in the previous building, each worker shared a closed office with co-workers from the same service and was assigned a personal desk. The building was structured on two floors and each service was located in a specific area. Thus, services were spatially compartmentalized. The new building being activity-based, there was the intention to de-compartmentalize services so that workers can mingle with co-workers from other services.

Since *ORES* has a primarily technical core business and employs technicians and laborers, a special area of the building, a workshop, is dedicated to these workers. In this area, laborers working on a technical site have cloakrooms, a technical supplies storage, and a few meeting rooms.

Workers' Perceptions and Adoption of the New Way of Working

After having explained the purpose underlying the DOMO project, and having illustrated and described the new building, in this section, I address workers' reactions toward this NWOW project.

Working in an Activity-Based Workspace

In many NWOW architectural projects, the activity-based workspace aims at promoting mobility within the building in order to encourage communication across people working in different services. However, echoing previous research, in *ORES WaPi* quite the reverse is true. After a few weeks spent in this building, I observed that the majority of the workers were located on a daily basis at the same desk with co-workers of the same service, leading to a re-compartmentalization of the pre-existing services. As the worker in the following excerpt explains quite aggressively, this inertia is explained by the fact that workers do not have that much of activities diversity that requires them to work according to an activity-based principle.

Always in the same place, like everyone else. Because the thing from [the Flemish architect], she said something like "Every workspace for every job". Well, stupid bitch, didn't you understand that we always do the same thing in here? [Raphaël]

Beyond his critique of the architect's assumption that employees have diverse activities, other informants suggest that workers' low mobility stems from wanting their documents and cabinets near them. Gaspard explains:

We still have cabinets with plans, with files about the [electric and gas] cabins, lots of things so the technical aspect. The cabinets [of the operations service] are there, the [cabinets] of the [technical solutions service] there, those of construction there, those of gas there. Without consulting each other, the [technical solutions service] agents sat there, near their documents.

Another aspect by which some workers justify their noncompliance with the activity-based working concerns technical issues. For instance, employees in charge of emergency phone lines require a fixed desk, and thus they are unable to move throughout the building. These employees are an exception since they are the only ones who do not have the technical possibility to be mobile. However, broadly speaking, the majority of workers do not use the activity-based workspace as initially conceived. Moreover, through numerous excerpts, workers explain how this inertia reinforces itself since, for instance, some workers wishing to move do not dare to do so, by fear of being the black sheep, as illustrated below:

Everything is grouped. It becomes like in Tournai while, initially, it was not that. So we, if we change places, well we are a little badly seen. There are places where you don't want to be. So it started from a good intention, but in the end, it fell through. [Edouard]

Beyond the potential non-usefulness of the activity-based workspace in a company such as *ORES*, another failure explanation might be found in the digitalization process the organization went through in order to promote this activity-based workspace, and the limits they met with this process.

The Limits of Digitalization in *ORES*

As previously explained, one of the four lines of the DOMO project is about document management and, in particular, the digitalization of the majority of paper-format documents. As explained by one of the executives below, this whole project of digitalization changes the way workers perceive their daily routines and their job, making it look more interesting, smarter, and more professional:

> *In all that is DOMO, there is also the IT. […] It feels good; people have the impression of having a much smarter, more interesting, more professional work. Finally, it's the impression that it leaves. You don't come in the morning with your little notebook "What am I going to do this morning?" and do your routine. No, it's really enthralling.* [Jean]

However, for several reasons, this digitalization is potentially jeopardized. Two reasons dominate: (1) the technical core business of the company and (2) the legal obligations related to this core business, which is managing gas and electricity issues.

While a few clerical positions, such as customer advisors, had the ability to work in an entirely digitalized manner after most of their documents were digitalized, there remained a wide range of employees who explained how complicated working without paper was for their work. This is especially the case of workers dealing with technical issues, which require big plans only available in a paper format. Jeanne highlights the complexity of digitalizing large and complex plans and technical documents. She explains, "*In some departments, they still have great plans like the tables here and they still have things that they are still obliged to do with the paper. So they have no choice, there are still things they have to do with paper.*" Similarly, Gaspard asserts, "*You always need a minimum of paper supports. Explaining a job to a technician without a plan, to tell him: 'You go from there to there,' it is not possible.*"

Moreover, the inability to be fully digitalized is not only explained by the core business requiring paper-format documents but also by the legal obligations circumscribing *ORES*' activity. Indeed, since the company deals with gas and electricity, it is subjected to much regulation mainly for security reasons. Therefore, even if the company found solutions making digital work doable for all workers, it would not be in its legal right to do so. As explained by the worker below, *ORES* has the legal obligation to keep paper-format documents related to pipes, installations, and so on in case of emergency and in case of a computer bug.

> *Researcher: "Is the paperless difficult for your position?"*
>
> *I cannot, I have legal documents regarding law that are defined by the royal lands, for the evidence, etc. So no paper, no. [...]. Downstairs, we have cabinets with all our plans for the watch job because it's mandatory, once again regarding the legislation, to have paper documents in case of a computer bug. If we have an intervention, we cannot afford to let a gas leak for three days until the program recovers.* [Karl]

This means that the whole digitalization process at the heart of the New Ways of Working project in *ORES* is intrinsically connected to the core business of the company itself. Yet, as the literature about NWOW and as numerous corporate experiences about this NWOW show, digitalization is a key pillar in any NWOW project. The fact that the DOMO project has been thought about without considering the strong limitations—that might have been avoided if took into account—related to the core business of the company tells a lot about *ORES* and its identity.

A Project Denying *ORES* Organizational Identity

Beyond the digital issue, numerous workers, all with varied occupations, addressed that the new world of work, its spatial materialization, and the labor organization it promotes are not aligned with *ORES*' specific core business, but that it rather reflects companies that are active in non-industry—related services, such as IT, insurance, or banking industry. Aurélie illustrates this, stating:

> *Well, most of the time, when one talks about the new world of work, etc., one imagines Google or the banking world. Here, they are technicians, we work with big plans, well we always need to have room, to have paper, to have lots of things and it is true that it is not always easy to live this every day.*

As this excerpt shows, workers were concerned about what one of them called "*too much DOMOTIZATION*", meaning that the company might have gone too far in the new world of work, disregarding the company and what it does, that is what is part of its core identity. Moreover, workers regret that the building, even though it has been designed by an architect consultant specialized in NWOW work environments, looks like a vulgar copy of any type of NWOW building this consultant had already designed in the past. As Edouard expresses below, this work environment does not fit *ORES*; it is common and not adapted to the company:

> *It's an ordinary building we'll say, for everyone. This is not a building specific to ORES, for me. Any company could settle here. [...] Anyway, the one who made the decoration and all that, she did exactly... She showed us videos, we saw a building, it was exactly the same building that here almost, and inside it was the same thing. In fact, she took the same... she makes copy-pasted [projects].*

This new work environment, and its lack of fit with the company's business, led a few workers expressing doubts about the future of the company since the strategy seemed to set aside the technical aspects related to the company. As Antoine expresses, the NWOW project gave the impression that *ORES* wanted to invest more in the administrative work to the detriment of the technical work, which remains the company's main feature. She explains:

> *We have the impression that we are going more towards the administrative than the technical, which is the basis of our work. We really have this impression because [it's the only thing that matters] and the technique has no more value.*

Most employees rejected the 'New Ways of Working' environment. They expressed an inadequacy between their work environment, their needs, and the core business of the company. *ORES WaPi* employees expressed their surprise that such a building has been thought for a company like *ORES* since it seems so irrelevant and so distant from their daily practices.

The degree to which this project did not meet its expectations and how the work environment seemed inadequate prompts the question, why did *ORES* decide to go for this project, and why was the project not implemented more carefully in order to preserve what is core in its business and workers' daily routines and needs? Arthur, the top executive, alludes to the answer. He explains:

> *We will never be loved by people. I am not Google. I am not an iPhone. That, you're in pampering in front. We love it. TV, all that, it's fun, it's entertainment, it's glitter. I'd be Netflix, I'd be Canal+, even Proximus [author's note: a Belgian telecom company], I would like to be loved. I would like customers to love me and say "Thanks to them, we had a great time on Saturday. Thanks to them, we had a nice time". I don't bring pleasure, let's be very clear. [...] We are just the guys who put the pipes. It's only hassle, it's opening the sidewalk, it's not being on time, it's only hassle. So we are condemned to not being loved.*

Through this excerpt, the executive expresses the sadness of being "*nothing but a technical company*" and a wish to aspire to be something else. As he says himself, customers will not love *ORES* due to the nature of the services it provides. In addition, he argues *ORES* does not create much enthusiasm unlike companies like Google and Apple, among other technical firms, which embody modernity and NWOW. Between the lines, Arthur expresses a desired organizational identity and alludes to the idea that the DOMO project was a means to pursue this modern identity, far from paper plans. However, this project was doomed to failure because the concretization of the NWOW, especially when it is only thought of as a standardized model that can be applied to any organization, disregarding the company's initial identity. Through this project, *ORES* did attempt to mimic other companies' identities, which led to the denial of its own.

Discussion

Throughout the previous pages, I have highlighted empirical results showing how a NWOW project might differ in its results from the initial expectations and what this failure might tell about an organization and its identity. In the case of *ORES* and especially of *ORES WaPi*, results show how workers did not understand this new work environment and these new working practices. While previous research illustrated that no corporate change appears without troubles, what is interesting in this case is that the failure is explained not only by workers' resistance to change but rather by the nature of the work conducted in the organization.

Whether it is officially written in the corporate strategy or confessed during an interview, it seems that this 'New Ways of Working' project carries the hope of becoming all of a sudden a digital and modern company and to mimic supposed successful companies. However, since the project appears as completely disconnected from the corporate reality, the intrinsic core business and what it requires, the project is doomed to failure, since it embodies the wish to be something the company cannot be. This misfit between the project such as conceived and the company—between the ideal and the real—explains the impression of mimicry some workers evoke when they say that *ORES* tries to be "*like Google*".

Beyond the case of *ORES*, this failure tells a lot about the new world of work and its popularity among companies. Indeed, even though it seems that activity-based work environment (and probably NWOW projects, as well) are not dominant (yet) (Actineo & CSA, 2014, 2015), their implementation in a range of industries suggests companies merely strive to be new, become more modern, leading to a de-legitimization of previous structures and organizations of work. However, this ideal of 'modernity' is superficial. Becoming 'modern' is never fully described and is positioned as an end in itself, rather than as a means; it appears rather unquestioned, not challenged by companies and business consultants, testifying to the obviousness of the quest for modernity and the emergency to change accordingly. This modernity is most of the time unexplained; it leads to an excessive standardization of the work environments, work practices, expected behaviors, and skills, disregarding the company's real needs.

Does it mean that the new world of work is a privilege that only already modern companies can afford? Certainly not. And the illustration in this chapter leads to several practical contributions and precautions companies can take in future 'new world of work' transitions. First, despite the thrilling promises within the new world of work, companies wishing to change toward NWOW should first think about the end they want to reach, and second about the means they adopt in order to reach such end.

New ways of working are only but means at the service of an end, and not the other way around. The second recommendation relates to the work environment. Most NWOW projects share a key pillar, which is about changing the work environment, making it activity-based or more opened at the very least. While the temptation to standardize the workspace is strong, it is essential that executives in charge of the project think about the work environment as a tool enabling employees to do their work in an effective manner. The work environment should support work, not undermine it. In line with this second recommendation, this research emphasizes that it is important to involve workers when initiating major changes that will affect workers. When it comes to the work environment, the main suggestion is to consult workers from different departments and occupations about their needs so that architects can design the work environment in a way that accords with their daily use. Eventually, and in a more critical perspective, one might invite executives and companies to caution when confronted with what Abrahamson (1996) called "managerial fashion" and their gurus.

Conclusion

In this chapter, I showed why an NWOW project resulted in failure and how this failure is rooted in the organization's identity. The empirical research conducted at *ORES Wallonia-Picardy* recounts the goals and the expectations underlying the DOMO project. In particular, this chapter has focused on the material dimension of this new world of work, that is to say in this case the installation of an activity-based workspace. As we have seen, this new work environment came with new work practices, especially in terms of digitalization of work. However, results show how this work environment and its digitalization might conflict with employees' real work and the company's core business. This led to discussing the embodied meaning of the DOMO project, its failure, and what the case teaches about the organization, its identity, and its desired identity.

In the discussion, I took a broader perspective and attempted to debunk the myth according to which 'the new world of work' is the new corporate must and the key to becoming a company at the forefront of modernity and innovation. It underlines how mimicry might damage an organization and might undermine its core identity. The discussion also offers a series of practical contributions for organizations wishing to embrace the new world of work and to change their work environment.

While this chapter is critical toward the new world of work, its actors, and the new work environment it promotes, its purpose is not to discourage companies to implement change, but rather to take a step to examine their organizational identity. They can do this by articulating what the organization's identity entails, identifying what its actors do, determining how the organization can achieve its strategy, and embracing these meanings rather than deny them.

References

Abrahamson, E. (1996). Management fashion. *The Academy of Management Review, 21*(1), 254–285.

Actineo, & CSA. (2014). *Qualité de vie au bureau: qu'en est-il en Europe? Résultats d'une étude inédite ACTINEO.* Paris: ACTINEO Observatoire de la Qualité de Vie au Travail & CSA Research.

Actineo, & CSA. (2015). *Quelle vie au bureau en 2015?* Paris: Baromètre ACTINEO/CSA. Retrieved from http://www.actineo.fr/sites/default/files/presentation_barometre_actineo_2015_vdef.pdf

Ajzen, M., Donis, C., & Taskin, L. (2015). Kaléidoscope des nouvelles formes d'organisation du travail: L'instrumentalisation stupide d'un idéal collaboratif et démocratique. *Gestion 2000, 31*(3), 125–148.

Allen, T. J., & Gerstberger, P. G. (1973). A field experiment to improve communications in a product engineering department: The nonterritorial office. *Human Factors: The Journal of the Human Factors and Ergonomics Society, 15*(5), 487–498.

Alvesson, M., & Empson, L. (2008). The construction of organizational identity: Comparative case studies of consulting firms. *Scandinavian Journal of Management, 24*(1), 1–16.

Antoine, M. (2018). *Unveiling the organisational identity: A spatial approach based on the office. The case of ORES Picardy Wallonia transition towards an activity-based workspace.* Doctoral dissertation, Louvain School of Management, Université Catholique de Louvain, Louvain, Belgium. Retrieved from http://hdl.handle.net/2078.1/207031

Baldry, C., & Barnes, A. (2012). The open-plan academy: Space, control and the undermining of professional identity. *Work, Employment & Society, 26*(2), 228–245.

Brown, G., Lawrence, T. B., & Robinson, S. L. (2005). Territoriality in organizations. *Academy of Management Review, 30*(3), 577–594.

Brunia, S., De Been, I., & Van Der Voordt, T. J. M. (2016). Accommodating new ways of working: Lessons from best practices and worst cases. *Journal of Corporate Real Estate, 18*(1), 30–47.

Byron, K., & Laurence, G. A. (2015). Diplomas, photos, and tchotchkes as symbolic self-representations: Understanding employees' individual use of symbols. *Academy of Management Journal, 58*(1), 298–323.

Chugh, S., & Hancock, P. (2009). Networks of aestheticization: The architecture, artefacts and embodiment of hairdressing salons. *Work, Employment & Society, 23*(3), 460–476.

Dale, K., & Burrell, G. (2008a). *Identity in organizations. Building theory through conversation*. Basingstoke, UK: Palgrave Macmillan.

Dale, K., & Burrell, G. (2008b). Building people: Identities and spaces. In K. Dale & G. Burrell (Eds.), *Identity in organizations. Building theory through conversation* (pp. 99–133). Basingstoke, UK: Palgrave Macmillan.

de Kok, A., Koops, J., & Helms, R. (2014). Assessing the new way of working: Bricks, bytes and behaviour. In *PACIS Pacific Asia Conference on Information Systems 2014* (Vol. 7, pp. 9–40), 24–28 June, Chengdu, China.

Degryse, C. (2016). *Digitalisation of the economy and its impact on labour markets*. Research Paper-Working Paper 2016-02. Brussels, Belgium: European Trade Union Institute.

Demers, C. (2003). L'entretien. In Y. Giordano (Ed.), *Conduire un projet de recherche. Une perspective qualitative* (pp. 173–210). Paris: Editions EMS.

Edenius, M., & Yakhlef, A. (2007). Space, vision and organizational learning: The interplay of incorporating and inscribing practices. *Management Learning, 38*(2), 193–210.

Eisenhardt, K. M. (1989). Building theories from case study research. *The Academy of Management Review, 14*(4), 532–550.

Elsbach, K. D. (2003). Relating physical environment to self-categorizations: Identity threat and affirmation in a non-territorial office space. *Administrative Science Quarterly, 48*(4), 622–654.

Gavroglou, S. P., Ford, C., Totterdill, P., Savage, P., & Sacquepee, S. (2001). *New forms of work organisation: The benefits and impact on performance.*

Thematic paper presented to Direction Générale Employment & Social Affairs. Brussels, Belgium: The European Work Organization Network (EWON).

Godin, B. (2006). The knowledge-based economy: Conceptual framework or buzzword? *The Journal of Technology Transfer, 31*(1), 17–30.

Gombault, A. (2003). La nouvelle identité organisationnelle des musées. Le cas du Louvre. *Revue Française de Gestion, 29*(142), 189–204.

Gombault, A. (2006). La méthode des cas. In P. Roussel & F. Wacheux (Eds.), *Management des ressources humaines. Méthodes de recherche en sciences humaines et sociales* (pp. 31–64). Paris: De Boeck Supérieur.

Gomes Da Silva, J. R. (2010). La dynamique identitaire entre organisations et individus. Le cas de cinq organisations brésiliennes [The identity dunamics between organizations and individuals. The case of five Brazilian organizations]. *Revue Française de Gestion, 4*, 185–204.

Groleau, C. (2003). L'observation. In Y. Giordano (Ed.), *Conduire un projet de recherche. Une perspective qualitative* (pp. 211–244). Paris: Editions EMS.

Haigh, G. (2012). *The office: A hardworking history*. Melbourne: Melbourne University Publishing.

Halford, S. (2004). Towards a sociology of organizational space. *Sociological Research Online, 9*(1), 13–28.

Hancock, P., & Spicer, A. (2011). Academic architecture and the constitution of the new model worker. *Culture and Organization, 17*(2), 91–105.

Humphreys, M., & Brown, A. D. (2002). Narratives of organizational identity and identification: A case study of hegemony and resistance. *Organization Studies, 23*(3), 421–447.

Huws, U. (2014). Introduction. In U. Huws (Ed.), *Labor in the global digital economy: The cybertariat comes of age* (pp. 7–26). New York: Monthly Review Press.

Inalhan, G. (2009). Attachments. *Journal of Corporate Real Estate, 11*(1), 17–37.

Jemine, G. (2016). Le new way of working. Discours, dispositifs et pratiques d'un processus de changement organisationnel. *Sociologies Pratiques, 32*(2), 107.

Lefebvre, H. (1991). *The production of space*. Oxford: Blackwell.

Marrewijk, A. Van, & Yanow, D. (2010). Introduction: The spatial turn in organizational studies. In A. Van Marrewijk & D. Yanow (Eds.), *Organizational spaces: Rematerializing the workaday world* (pp. 1–16). Northampton, MA: Edward Elgar Publishing.

Millward, L. J., Haslam, S. A., & Postmes, T. (2007). Putting employees in their place: The impact of hot desking on organizational and team identification. *Organization Science, 18*(4), 547–559.

Minchella, D. (2015). *Le rôle de la spatialité dans la mise en place du New Model Worker: Du projet Valmy aux tours de La Défense de la Société Générale.* Doctoral dissertation, Dauphine Recherche en Management. Paris: Université Paris-Dauphine.

Myers, M. D. (2013). *Qualitative research in business & management* (2nd ed.). London, UK: Sage Publications Ltd.

ORES. (2016a). *Plan stratégique 2015–2020.* Wallonia, Belgium.

ORES. (2016b). *Rapport d'activités 2016—Bilan & perspectives.* Wallonia, Belgium.

ORES. (2017). *Qui sommes-nous?* Wallonia, Belgium: Retrieved October 31, 2017, from https://www.ores.be/qui-sommes-nous

Paillé, P., & Mucchielli, A. (2012). *L'analyse qualitative en sciences humaines et sociales.* Paris: Armand Colin.

Peretz, H. (2004). *Les méthodes en sociologie. L'observation.* Paris: La Découverte.

Petriglieri, G., & Petriglieri, J. L. (2010). Identity workspaces: The case of business schools. *Academy of Management Learning & Education, 9*(1), 44–60.

Portail des Pouvoirs Locaux. (2015). *L'intercommunale* [The intermunicipal association]. Wallonia, Belgium. Retrieved October 31, 2017, from https://pouvoirslocaux.wallonie.be/jahia/Jahia/site/dgpl/accueil/pid/956

Shortt, H., & Warren, S. (2012). Fringe benefits: Valuing the visual in narratives of hairdressers' identities at work. *Visual Studies, 27*(1), 18–34.

Statuts coordonnés ORES. (2017). *Assets au 22 juin 2017.* Wallonia, Belgium. Retrieved from https://netoresorchardcms.blob.core.windows.net/media/Default/Informations_Financieres/Divers/Statuts coordonnés ORES Assets au 22 juin 2017.pdf

Sum, N.-L., & Jessop, B. (2013). Competitiveness, the knowledge-based economy and higher education. *Journal of the Knowledge Economy, 4*(1), 24–44.

Taskin, L. (2012). *Déspatialisation: Enjeux organisationnels et managériaux. Perspectivre critique et études de cas sur la transformation du contrôle dans le cadre du télétravail à domicile.* Saarbrücken, Germany: Éditions u.

Taylor, S., & Spicer, A. (2007). Time for space: A narrative review of research on organizational spaces. *International Journal of Management Reviews, 9*(4), 325–346.

Tyler, M., & Cohen, L. (2010). Spaces that matter: Gender performativity and organizational space. *Organization Studies, 31*(2), 175–198.

van Meel, J. (2011). The origins of new ways of working. *Facilities, 29*(9/10), 357–367.

Wapshott, R., & Mallett, O. (2012). The spatial implications of homeworking: A Lefebvrian approach to the rewards and challenges of home-based work. *Organization, 19*(1), 63–79.

Warren, S. (2006). Hot-nesting: A visual exploration of the personalization of work space in a hot-desking environment. In P. Case, S. Lilley, & T. Owen (Eds.), *The speed of organization* (pp. 119–146). Copenhagen: Liber & Copenhagen Business School Press.

Yin, R. (2014). *Case study research: Design and methods* (5th ed.). Thousand Oaks, CA: Sage Publications, Inc.

Zhang, Z., & Spicer, A. (2014). "Leader, you first": The everyday production of hierarchical space in a Chinese bureaucracy. *Human Relations, 67*(6), 739–762.

Zhong, C.-B., & House, J. (2012). Hawthorne revisited: Organizational implications of the physical work environment. *Research in Organizational Behavior, 32*, 3–22.

18

Deconstructing New Ways of Working: A Five-Dimensional Conceptualization Proposal

Grégory Jemine

Introduction

As many large companies have recently committed to major overhauls of their workspaces and work practices, the topic of "New Way(s) of Working" (NWW) has begun to gain increased scholarly attention. Yet, the academic literature remains divided and uncertain on the status to confer to NWW and has been unable to unite researchers around a common consensus on what NWW is. Our argument is that most authors have invested their energy into defining what NWW entails or should entail, thus competing with the fashion setters themselves, rather than attempting to clarify what NWW is. Through an in-depth and critical literature review, the present chapter aims to clarify the current debates by introducing a five-dimensional conceptualization of NWW.

G. Jemine (✉)
Université de Liège, Liège, Belgium
e-mail: gjemine@uliege.be

N. Mitev et al. (eds.), *New Ways of Working*, Technology, Work and Globalization,
https://doi.org/10.1007/978-3-030-61687-8_18

The Origins of a Fashion: From *Het Nieuwe Werken* to New Ways of Working

In the last two decades, a strong interest has grown among many managers and consultants for a set of specific practices, discourses, and devices clustered under the term "New Ways of Working". Both the Netherlands and Belgium have witnessed a surge of third-sector companies developing and deploying change projects and claiming to implement NWW. An abundant managerial literature on the topic has progressively bloomed with the successive books of Veldhoen (2005), Baane et al. (2010), Bijl (2011), and Broere (2016) among others. Attempts to retrace the origins of what is now called "New Ways of Working" most often lead to two trails, the first one being the Dutch consultant Erik Veldhoen and the second one being the famous company Microsoft (Netherlands). In both cases, NWW seems to originate from the Netherlands. The term itself is a late English translation of the Dutch *Het Nieuwe Werken*, which was already used in the 1990s by Dutch consultants, among which Erik Veldhoen, one of the earliest promoters of the fashion.

The first company to ever explicitly implement a project based on *Het Nieuwe Werken* is recognized by many authors to be the Dutch insurance company Interpolis in 1996 (Baane et al. 2010; De Jonge and Rutte 1999; Kingma 2018; Lamers 2013). To understand the roots of *Het Nieuwe Werken*, it is interesting to engage in a more detailed description of the project undertaken at Interpolis. The project consisted in relocating eight separate sites (or approximately 2500 employees) to a single building located at Tilburg (Netherlands). Workplace utilization surveys were carried out in all sites, and revealed strikingly different modes of using space: for instance, the Public Relations staff occupied the workspace for an average of 10% of their working day (Mawson 2006). The decision was taken to reduce the total amount of desks on the basis of a "sharing ratio" of 0.8—which means that ten people would have to share eight desks. Practices of shared desks, remote working, and paperless working became promoted and generalized (Mawson 2006).

What is particularly interesting to note is that the consultant Erik Veldhoen was commissioned by Interpolis Board to support the transition from the separated sites to the consolidated one. He apparently played a major role in "persuading the Board that [a flexible workspace] was a good idea" despite the Board being initially "not in favor of a flexible workplace" (Mawson 2006, 6). Erik Veldhoen was already "known for his ideas on flexible working" (Mawson 2006, 2) and had recently published a book entitled *Kantoren Bestaan Niet Meer* ("Offices Do Not Exist Anymore"), in which he predicted the demise of the traditional office and the development of new, more flexible forms of workspaces, which would form *Het Nieuwe Werken* (Veldhoen 1995). However, we could hardly speak of a managerial trend before Veldhoen published another book, *The Art of Working*, in 2005. Veldhoen's new book was based on the idea that "innovative offices" would rely on the development of "a new culture of flexibility" and on the expansion of information and communication technologies at work (Veldhoen 2005). It offered a "practical classification" around three pillars constitutive of space: the physical, the virtual, and the mental (Kingma 2018, 7). Also written in Dutch, the book was massively distributed and became increasingly popular in the Netherlands (Kingma 2018).

Meanwhile, in a white paper from the same year (Gates and Rasmus 2005), Microsoft leaders stated that current organizations were not properly equipped to face the rise of information technologies and that new ways of managing people in the digital age had to be found (Gates and Rasmus 2005). Their paper describes rising trends affecting the "world"—the "New World of Work"—which would supposedly generate major challenges for all organizations and in all economic sectors. In their perspective, the "New World of Work" goes beyond organizational boundaries, as it describes a "connected" world deeply transformed by a series of technological innovations developing at an increasing pace (Gates and Rasmus 2005). At the heart of Gates and Rasmus's whitepaper lies the idea of a gap that never closes between organizations and their ever-changing environment, the first ones always being late to adapt to the second. The tone of Gates and Rasmus's whitepaper is definitely normative as they urge companies to establish ways to address those emerging technological challenges.

Following a relocation project of their headquarters, research reports of Microsoft Netherlands revealed a progressive semantic shift from

"New World of Work" to "New Way of Working". In 2008, Microsoft opened a new building in Schiphol (Netherlands) and saved more than $640,000 per year in location costs by reducing the available office space and implementing "flexible desks" and remote working policies (Meerbeek et al. 2009). Due to the scale of their project as well as the advertising they generated around it, Microsoft Netherlands was described as being a trendsetter company when it came to New Way of Working (Ajzen et al. 2015) and a significant contributor to the dissemination of the NWW acronym. Although the initial conception of a New Way of Working by Microsoft was mostly based on the rise of new computing technologies and the growing role of information at work (Gates and Rasmus 2005), subsequent publications on the matter also began to emphasize the importance of "empowering people" (Lamers 2013). Rabobank Nederland, another forerunner company of New Way of Working, argued that in order to provide the best possible service to the customer, flexibility and people empowerment had to become the primary strategic objectives of the organization (Van Egmond and Lokin 2006; Lamers 2013).

The term "New Way of Working" was then found again many times in the managerial literature, for example, in Bijl's work, who called for "rethinking office design" and "implementing contemporary management theories" in service businesses (Bijl 2011, 7). Bijl, who is also a consultant, adopts a more radical tone while denunciating the supposed limits of bureaucracy:

> The New Way of Working believes in the strength of people and wants to tap into their rich potential (…) NWW (…) creates a work environment in which people are enticed and equipped to give their best in their work (…) The post-industrial society is choking and we're not capitalizing on the opportunities that are out there (…) We are clinging frenetically to the machine bureaucracy with its hierarchic top-down organizational model, the command and control management with work bound to time and place. Employees demand greater freedom, vision, empowerment, flexibility, intuition, diversity, trust, responsibility, and accountability (…) The New Way of Working's proposition is as follows: organizations are more effective and more efficient if they give the staff the following: trust,

> freedom, responsibility and a sense of connection (...) NWW places the worker center-stage and then looks at what that worker requires to do his work well, or better. (Bijl 2011, 17–31)

Through such discourses, the bases of the New Way of Working fashion are set: organizations are assumed to be "old-fashioned" and inadequately equipped to face an ever-changing world; as a result, they need to change. Up until this point, there is generally a shared consensus between all the actors (consultants, academics, and local managers) that are interested in New Way(s) of Working: the fashion is about changing the organization. What is unclear, however, is the content of the change, and what it entails or should entail. Should it, as suggested by Veldhoen (2005), articulate the physical, virtual, and mental spaces? Or rather, as implied by the Interpolis and Microsoft experiments, should it focus on a reduction of the workspace and on non-attributed space allocation? Does it depart from technological considerations, in line with Gates and Rasmus's proposal (Gates and Rasmus 2005), or from the acknowledgment that the current way of organizing work is unsatisfying, as Bijl suggests (2011)? Can a New Way of Working change project include all these questionings simultaneously? Do local actors in organizations even care about them, or do they borrow the label "New Way of Working" without further reflecting on what it may entail? As management books and consultancy firms do not provide definitive answers to these questions, we might want to turn our attention toward the academic literature on New Way(s) of Working.

The Academic Treatment of New Ways of Working

Several academics interested in workspace transformations have investigated what has been broadly framed as being "new forms of organizing" (Ajzen et al. 2015). These contributions share the view that many companies are now prompted to move toward more flexible ways of organizing themselves due to a series of major changes in their environment, such as the emergence of new technologies (Demerouti et al. 2014;

Engelen et al. 2019), global mobility issues (Sewell and Taskin 2015), or the evolution of work practices toward knowledge-intensive tasks (Ruostela et al. 2015). Recent case studies illustrate the managerial transformations undertaken by companies as an answer to those evolutions and usually label those transformations as "NWW" (Blok et al. 2012; De Leede 2017; Kingma 2018) or "NWoW" (De Kok et al. 2015; Vink et al. 2012), which, in line with the managerial literature presented in the previous section, commonly refers to "New Way(s) of Working".

In its current state, existing scientific literature on New Ways of Working is relatively limited and can be framed into three categories. Relying on both qualitative and quantitative methods, the first set of contributions mainly aims to explore the effects or outcomes of New Ways of Working on organizations, groups, and individuals. A common research focus consists in questioning whether NWW projects actually make organizations more efficient and innovative (De Spiegelaere et al. 2015), help them to better pursue their objectives (Blok et al. 2012), or increase performance and productivity (Laihonen et al. 2012; Ruostela et al. 2015). Researchers investigate the effects of NWW projects on organizational teams with a focus on specific variables such as knowledge sharing (De Kok et al. 2015) or managerial control (Sewell and Taskin 2015). On the individual level, scholars have attempted to better understand the effects of NWW projects on workers' conditions, well-being, performance, health, and autonomy (Ten Brummelhuis et al. 2012; Demerouti et al. 2014; Nijp et al. 2016). The second research perspective consists in describing the change process and the practical issues surrounding the implementation of NWW in organizations (Gorgievski et al. 2010; Taskin et al. 2017), or even proposing frameworks to facilitate its deployment (De Kok et al. 2014). Finally, some authors have been more concerned with definitional stakes and with pinpointing the constitutive elements and the boundaries of New Ways of Working (Blok et al. 2011; De Leede 2017; ten Brummelhuis et al. 2012; Taskin et al. 2017).

Academics usually concur on the fact that defining NWW is not an easy task (De Kok et al. 2014; De Leede 2017). However, they seem to give little importance to this observation that looks, to us, critical. Indeed, we argue that NWW definition and delineation are two major issues that remain unsolved by the academic literature at the time of writing. Let us begin with the definitional issue: authors do not agree on what NWW is. For some, it is a "phenomenon" (De Kok et al. 2014; Eskola and Neuvonen 2016; Gerards et al. 2018); for others, it is a "set of measures" (Blok et al. 2011), a "concept" (De Leede 2017; Kingma 2018; Ruostela et al. 2015), a "type of work organization" (Nijp et al. 2016), a "philosophy" (Blok et al. 2016), a "tool" (Ruostela et al. 2015), a "set of facets" (Gerards et al. 2018), or a "mix of practices" (Peeters 2014; Taskin et al. 2017). These terms are sometimes used interchangeably by authors: De Leede (2017) simultaneously speak of NWW as being a "big word", a "concept", a "management fashion", and a "discourse"; De Spiegelaere et al. (2015) describe NWW as a "conception", a "set of principles", a "concept", a "popular topic", and a "context". The academic literature has so far been, to say the least, divided and uncertain on the status to confer to NWW and has been unable to unite researchers around a common consensus on what NWW is.

However, this has not prevented researchers to attempt to delineate the perimeters of their research object. For unclear reasons, when conducting studies of NWW-labeled projects undertaken by organizations, most researchers found it necessary to build their own definitions of NWW beforehand. As a consequence, a plurality of pseudo-conceptualizations of NWW began to flourish. For instance, Demerouti et al. (2014) identified three dimensions constitutive of NWW: work-time flexibility, spatial flexibility, and new media technologies supporting remote working. Ajzen et al. (2015) also build on three dimensions of NWW, although not the same ones: flexible spatiotemporal practices, collaborative work practices, and participative management. For their part, Gerards et al. (2018) used five dimensions: time and location independent work, output-based management, knowledge accessibility, flexible working relations, and accessible, open workplace. As Table 18.1 illustrates, the chosen definitions are often divergent from one author to another.

Table 18.1 features five proposals of NWW "conceptualization". The reader might quickly realize that none of them perfectly matches the others. As such, we might have expected the authors to comment on the differences between their dimensions and those of the existing literature; such discussions, however, remain scarce. An unexpected consequence of

Table 18.1 Some dimensions of NWW according to the academic literature

Baane et al. (2010)	1. Time and place independent work 2. Self-management 3. Flexible employment relations
Blok et al. (2012)	1. Changes in the physical workplace 2. Technological changes 3. Changes in the organization and management 4. Changes in the work culture
Demerouti et al. (2014) Ten Brummelhuis et al. (2012)	1. Work-time flexibility 2. Spatial flexibility 3. New media technologies as a support
Ajzen et al. (2015)	1. Flexible spatiotemporal practices 2. Collaborative work practices 3. Participative management
Gerards et al. (2018)	1. Time and location independent work 2. Output-based management 3. Knowledge accessibility 4. Flexible working relations 5. Open workplace

Author's own

the academic appropriation of NWW is that it resulted in additional and unnecessary complexity. The consultancy and managerial construct of NWW, as many authors underlined, was already difficult to apprehend, because of the diversity of the empirical situations to be observed. The project that was carried out at Microsoft, for instance, was to some extent different from what was done at Interpolis or at Rabobank; yet all of those companies formally claimed to implement NWW. The academic literature added a further layer of complexity around the acronym NWW by creating additional definitions based on their necessarily limited empirical findings. Moreover, NWW began to be used by academics as a construct of their own. Organizational change projects that would embed non-attributed desking, remote working, and a desire to implement a new managerial culture would be labeled by researchers as being NWW even though the field actors themselves were unaware of what the term meant. For example, Assarlind et al. (2013) compared NWW adoption among 12 small companies, while it remains unclear whether all of them were effectively using the term NWW in the first place.

What is really depicted by those definitions and dimensions? Our argument is that instead of contributing to the understanding of NWW, the academic literature has added considerable complexity around the term itself and what it entails (or should entail) by creating multiple versions of NWW. The abundant generation of so-called NWW definitions is of little help for the researchers willing to study NWW-labeled transformation projects. How to deal with a case study that does not match any of the five definitions to be found in Table 18.1 and yet features actors who constantly speak of their transformation project as being a New Ways of Working one (e.g. Jemine et al. 2020)? The ensuing question is, who is legitimate to qualify various projects as being NWW or as being something else? Should we refer to the managerial construct of NWW? Should we dismiss it because academics have claimed that NWW was not what the consultants said it was? Should we turn NWW into a so-called scientific label that we can stick on change projects displaying a set of common characteristics, hence bypassing the interpretations of the field actors themselves?

We argue that the difficulty to define and delineate NWW is illustrative of three larger and crucial issues that have been unnoticed so far in contributions interested in NWW: (1) the practical impossibility of framing NWW in terms of contents, (2) the underestimation of the defining task, and (3) the centrality of the defining work.

Producing a unique definition of NWW that simultaneously and faithfully accounts for all managerial and academic conceptions, as well as for all empirical situations, seems almost impossible, especially in presence of conflicting or contradicting empirical evidence. For instance, if an NWW project in a firm A involves remote working practices, but if a firm B also claims to implement NWW without deploying such practices, how should we build a content-based definition of NWW? Does NWW include remote working practices or not? Two solutions may appear. First, one may impose a definition in which they decide what "dimensions" or factors should prevail over others. Defining NWW, then, inevitably becomes an act of normative nature, as NWW is turned into a pseudo-theoretical ideal to which organizations comply to a certain extent or with a variable degree of success. Hence, it becomes possible to distinguish between "best practices" and "worst cases", between "success" and "failure" (Brunia et al. 2016). However, such normative approaches to NWW are *in fine* rather close to the ones developed by consulting companies and disguise the complexity of empirical realities behind a set of selected "performance" indicators.

A second solution, quite popular among scholars while being just as unsatisfying as the first one, would consist in framing empirical realities into what is NWW and what is not. For instance, one might view workplace transformations as a part of NWW but might consider remote working practices as a marginal change that it is beyond the perimeter of NWW. Such framing strategies certainly grant to the researchers much more comfort in their research process, as they become free to decide what they want or do not want to include in their definition of NWW, the rest of the empirical evidence becoming mere contextual factors or "local variables" (Nijp et al. 2016). This is to forget that framing induces simplification and reduction and that it produces an "artificial result" that results from a "violent effort to extricate the agents (…) and push them onto a clearly demarcated 'stage' which has been specially prepared and fitted out" (Callon 1998, 251–252). In other words, we do not caution the process that consists in producing a definition of NWW by framing it either rather arbitrarily or, worse, outside empirical evidence. We plead for an empirically grounded approach of NWW in which the field actors play a determining role in framing what NWW mean or do not mean for them.

A second argument that explains our suspicion toward existing definitions of NWW in the academic literature is the underestimation by researchers of the task consisting in defining it. On the basis of all the concerns that have been expressed, we have developed the certainty that formulating a proper definition of NWW is a complex and delicate task. Yet, definitions of NWW continue to flourish on very thin theoretical and/or empirical bases. Authors who have proposed or adopted definitions of NWW often seem to have taken the task quite lightly. It seems to bother no one to speak indiscriminately of a "fashion", a "concept", a "philosophy", or a "mix of practices". The act of defining NWW, in other terms, has been neglected, or at least has not been paid enough attention, in most existing works.

Finally, and somewhat paradoxically, we might wonder whether creating definitions is what researchers should do. Obviously, researchers are not the sole producers of definitions of NWW; as we just saw, several consultancy firms and various authors have published books or, more modestly, written articles and web pages, in which they have asserted what NWW is. Nowadays, many companies claiming to implement such projects come up with their own definition and vision of what it should mean and entail. Researchers have no monopoly on the production of NWW definitions. From the moment that they produce research outputs similar to the ones in Table 18.1, they inevitably compete with consultants and managers who share the same goal—imposing one and unique definition of NWW. Where does, therefore, lie the added value of defining NWW for research? Should research really invest so many resources into a definitional work that seems, at first sight, questionable to say the least?

Our argument is that most authors who have studied NWW projects have invested energy into substantialist definitions of NWW, expressed in terms of contents (what NWW entails or should entail), thus competing with the fashion setters themselves. Any content-based approach of NWW would necessarily conclude from the literature that NWW is an "umbrella term" (Giroux 2006) for designating a (very) wide range of managerial considerations—workplace design, IT tools, management style, employees' well-being and performance, company branding, and customer orientation—as well as the concrete arrangements deriving from those considerations—remote work, flexible work, paperless work processes, objective-based control, and new managerial practices (Ajzen et al. 2015). Although defining NWW as a "mix" is a common approach in the existing literature (Taskin et al. 2017), we believe that such a statement is of little value for research and that further effort should be put into the understanding of what NWW is, rather than into what NWW is about or ought to be about.

To sum up, we argue that NWW has been, in our opinion, insufficiently problematized in most existing works, which often build on incomplete and unconvincing definitions of what NWW is. Naturally, some of these works have been crucial for understanding the effects of New Ways of Working projects on, for instance, distantiation and territorialization (Sewell and Taskin 2015) or spatiotemporal interactions (Kingma 2018). The rather critical tone of our literature review should not wipe out the contributions that have been produced by researchers who have studied NWW. However, it certainly questions the interest of conducting further research by building on a body of literature that appears to be fragmented, emergent, and controversial at the same time. In the following section, we attempt to overcome this issue by providing a reconceptualization of NWW around five key dimensions.

Toward a Five-Dimensional Conceptualization Proposal

In this section, we plead for developing a non-substantialist definition of NWW. As shown by the literature review, most actual definitions of NWW describe it as a mere "mix" of practices or measures. By doing so, they contribute to reify NWW and to turn it into a set of abstract principles of limited generalizability and empirical validity. We argue that most contributions have been interested in defining what NWW does or entails, rather than what it is. The suggestion developed in this chapter is that NWW is first and foremost (1) a management fashion, (2) locally translated into discourses by strategic actors, (3) turned into projects of organizational change, (4) that, through material transformations to the workplace, (5) aim to promote new forms of work practices.

New Ways of Working as a Management Fashion

We suggest that management fashions are a first manner to conceptualize NWW. A management fashion designates a transitory and collective belief that some management practices and techniques constitute the most adequate path for a company to follow (Abrahamson 1996). Central to the diffusion of those fashions are the fashion setters, such as consulting firms, who develop convincing narratives around the fashions that they are trying to promote (Abrahamson 1996). As illustrated at the beginning of the chapter, NWW discourses as conveyed by consultants indeed bear a strong narrative rhetoric telling business leaders how they should act (Benders and van Veen 2001). All managerial declinations of NWW share at least the common characteristic of calling for "modernizing" organizations and offer a strong criticism of "old" ways of organizing work, which are said to be imperfect, dysfunctional, or even "nightmarish" (Bijl 2011). Popular discourses on NWW usually prompt the organizations to change (or to "evolve") by building upon a critical and oversimplified view of existing organizations, which are supposedly old-fashioned, inadequate, and ill equipped to face an ever-changing world (see Bijl 2011). Such outdated organizations become the "strawman" (Friedberg 2000) of NWW promoters, who urge them to change as a result of their alarming observations. To the extent that pleas for New Ways of Working indeed convey their share of promises and threats, they might be considered as a "management fashion" (Abrahamson 1996; Benders and van Veen 2001).

In this perspective, NWW is viewed as something that has its own existence outside of organizations. It is an external element to organizations that develops through books, conferences, websites, and networks. The central question in this perspective is to understand how, and to what extent, companies draw on those external sources, and/or how such a fashion may spread, through the investigation of processes of diffusion and mimicry (Di Maggio and Powell 1983). NWW becomes a series of discourses and myths which, under pressures of all sorts (Di Maggio and Powell 1983), and as the result of the "purposive action" of "competent" and "vigilant" actors within organizations (Lawrence and Suddaby 2006; Perkmann and Spicer 2008), is "adopted" by these organizations.

This conceptualization of NWW is certainly not the most common one to be found in the literature. At best, some authors have merely hinted that NWW might be viewed as a management fashion in the sense of Abrahamson (1996; De Leede 2017). Defining NWW as such involves taking seriously the corpora of texts and ideas that constitute the fashion, as well as studying the networks through which these corpora are diffused and transmitted. In this perspective, researchers should account for the networks and the actors that constitute the field, or the ecosystem, supporting the fashion. Revealing the diffusion mechanisms and the adoption logic of NWW becomes the main objective of the researcher, which implies an empirical investigation that exceeds organizational boundaries. The fact that an overwhelming majority of the literature on NWW is based on case studies, in which one or several organization(s) are the prime unit(s) of analysis, may explain why NWW has rarely been conceptualized as a management fashion. As a result, our knowledge of the genesis and the spread of NWW among all kinds of organizations and structures remain relatively limited. Field-level studies may be needed to develop a better understanding of NWW as a management fashion, involving in-depth documentary research as well as targeted interviews with pivotal members of the managerial NWW ecosystem(s).

New Ways of Working as a Set of Discourses

As Giroux (2006) underlined, the integration of management fashions into the organization depends on the conscious efforts of various coalitions of actors to make the fashion appear consistent with the interests of the organization. Many management fashions only pass through without being adopted by organizations; at the organizational level, the fashion requires "purposeful action" to be transformed into "an accepted element of organizational life" (Perkmann and Spicer 2008, 813). Such purposeful action often takes a discursive form. Building legitimacy around a management fashion requires designing convincing accounts and diffusing normative justifications within and beyond the organization, a task for which discourse is a powerful tool, as it enables specific ways of thinking and acting while rejecting others (Phillips and Lawrence 2004). Greenwood et al. (2002) have argued that discursive actions of theorization were central in the adoption of new practices, as they turned management fashions into "institutional imperatives" (p. 60) and strengthened moral legitimacy (Suchman 1995). Narration and storytelling (Vendelo 1998), production of texts (Phillips and Lawrence 2004), education (Lawrence and Suddaby 2006), and advocacy (Perkmann and Spicer 2008) are further illustrations of the discursive strategies deployed by the actors to legitimate management fashions such as NWW.

A second way to conceptualize NWW, then, is to consider that it consists of performative discourses and narratives advocated by specific actors within organizations at a given point of time. This view focuses on the storytelling strategies of the top managers and other actors who introduce NWW within organizations. The main questions raised by this approach are related to the legitimacy of ideas: why is NWW adopted in an organization, and how is it progressively recognized as something desirable in the eyes of its members (Greenwood et al. 2002)? In this view, the problems, the interests, and the strategies of local actors are primordial. The local construction of NWW may turn out to be a relatively faithful application of the fashion if the organizational actors are relatively inclined to mimic existing projects or consultancy discourses. However, if the fashion itself is strongly contested by the actors, then what will be labeled NWW locally might have only a few remaining connections with the NWW fashion. The word local is paramount here, as it allows to differentiate between the management fashion and their appropriation (which is necessarily an operation of translation) by specific firms and organizations. Maintaining a clear separation between both conceptions allows to distinguish between the fashion and the local discourses and to view those discourses as the result of a local construction process through which actors may borrow elements from the fashion, but mostly design their own problems and solutions.

Few studies actually tackle the question of NWW adoption in detail, which may be attributed to two main methodological difficulties. A first, obvious one, is primarily a question of field access: to grasp the managerial intents and discourses, researchers need to secure interviews with project leaders and top managers of the organizations that they wish to study. In many existing cases, we know little about the managerial intents behind the introduction of NWW in organizations, or those intents are summarized in a nutshell and in a way that seems unproblematized, for instance, by merely stating that NWW was introduced for "financial reasons". A second difficulty with an empirical study of NWW as a set of discourses is that any ex post reconstitution of those discourses is a perilous exercise. Of course, strategic discourses may be partially reconstructed through post-occupancy types of interviews conducted with any member of the organization, but the risk is that most members are likely to have limited knowledge of the construction process of those discourses. As we illustrated somewhere else (Jemine et al. 2019), the initial discourses legitimizing NWW projects in organizations are rapidly turned into black boxes, which made it possible for the project to grow, but difficult for the researcher to retrace the discursive work performed by the actors in all its complexity. In order to develop a better understanding of the discursive strategies that make it possible for NWW projects to be approved and hence deployed, one needs to discover how specific meanings and narratives slowly become taken for granted in organizations, by investigating the motivations of their project leaders and decision-makers.

New Ways of Working as Projects of Organizational Change

Over the years, NWW became more than a sum of discourses and narratives. In the wake of Interpolis in 1998, several organizations decided to commit to transformation projects and claimed to implement New Ways of Working. Project teams and taskforces were set up, actors were enrolled and mobilized, budgets were allocated, meetings were held, and work environments were designed. In these organizations, a machinery of actors was deployed in order to carry out change projects based on the ideas of NWW. While the two former approaches were primarily based on discourses, we argue that, in this third conceptualization of NWW, actors and problems should receive all the researcher's attention. We draw heavily on several theoretical approaches to legitimate this conceptualization of NWW, mainly on the sociology of power (Crozier and Friedberg 1980) and on the sociology of translation (Callon 1986). In both perspectives, discourses (on NWW) are relegated to a lower analytical priority. Instead, what matters to the observer are the interactions taking place, the interests of the actors participating in these interactions, and the formulation of problems and compromises. A crucial implication of this posture is that NWW and NWW projects are, in fact, two very different research objects: NWW projects are much more about actors, problems, negotiation, design, compromises, coalitions, and conflicts than about the constitutive elements of the NWW management fashion itself (Jemine et al. 2020).

Curiously, few authors have been interested in studying NWW as projects of organizational change and are usually quick to jump from a description of the managerial intents to commit to an NWW project to the actual deployment of NWW environments. In most existing accounts of NWW projects, the design process itself is often concealed, although it has been repeatedly acknowledged that design is an inherently political process, involving contestation, power games, and compromises (Larkin 2013). However, when scholars describe NWW experiments in organizations, they focus on a visible and stabilized result of the negotiation process at a given time. We know very little about the actors who were involved in the design process, about the controversies that arose, about the trade-offs that were found: in a word, there are at the present time very few political studies of NWW able to explain how strategic decisions to initiate NWW projects are being translated and organized.

Such an approach requires a radical theoretical turn as well as a strong methodological investment. Theoretically, studying NWW as a change project means that the researcher's focus should be on actors and power games taking place between them (Crozier and Friedberg 1980) or on problems and their translation through time (Callon 1986). A direct implication of this posture is that the researcher should refrain from dictating his own definition of NWW beforehand: rather, what NWW entails should be empirically determined by the field actors themselves in the course of the negotiation process which is the object of study. On the methodological level, such an approach implies to gather extensive data on the change process itself, meaning that longitudinal methods, including regular observations of the meetings through which the project takes shape, have to prevail. The fact that most NWW projects are being developed on a fairly long timescale might explain why accounting empirically for NWW as a project of organizational change has remained difficult until today.

New Ways of Working as Material Workspaces

To the extent that NWW discourses are ultimately translated into material devices that bear particular scripts prescribing desired actions (Akrich

2006), NWW may further be conceptualized as being a specific kind of material workspace. An NWW project always seems to result in visible and concrete changes to the workplace and to the physical infrastructures of the organizations, which has brought some authors to explore the materiality of NWW (e.g. Kingma 2018). An NWW workspace is characterized by openness and flexibility, is devoid of hierarchical symbols, and is inhabited by mobile users (Dufresne et al. 2018).

Such a description probably sounds very familiar to whoever has studied or observed NWW workspaces. Despite slight local variations in their implementation, the material and spatial arrangements of NWW remain relatively similar and almost always include open plans, non-attributed desks, and a workspace made of heterogeneous zones. This observation has even led some authors to view those spatial settings as the core of NWW and to equate New Ways of Working with shared activity-based workplace (e.g. Brunia et al. 2016). As the reader might have guessed by now, we rather believe that viewing NWW as a specific set of material devices is only one possible way to study and conceptualize NWW. We hold that NWW as a workplace is the visible and tangible embedment, at a given point of time, of elements borrowed from the NWW fashion, of discourses and narratives deployed by the top management, and of twists occurring during the course of the change project.

We suggest that a fourth conception of NWW consists in viewing in NWW a label to designate specific spatial arrangements of the workspace. This argument has already been explored by several authors who have often equated NWW with visible changes in the physical infrastructures of the organization, hence developing a quasi-architectural conceptualization of NWW (De Bruyne et al. 2014; Van Meel 2011). A first, relatively common way to investigate those material arrangements is to observe their concrete impacts on users and teams (Hoendervanger et al. 2016; Keeling et al. 2015). However, it is also possible to study NWW workspaces as being the material translations and the visible outcome of strategic decisions and of a bargaining process themselves. In that sense, we rely on a processual study that aims to explore the change process through which discourses are progressively turned into material infrastructures intended to last over the long term (Bowker et al. 2010). In both cases, the data collection process implies rigorous and detailed observations of the interactions between users and the workspace or, if the design process is still ongoing, of the way discourses are translated into material devices (such as plans, maps, pictures, or visual representations of the workspace to design).

New Ways of Working as a Set of Practices

Finally, New Ways of Working may be viewed as a set of emergent work practices. Faced with a new workspace, as well as with discursive prescriptions and expectations (for instance, regarding how management style is supposed to evolve toward more trust- and objective-based practices), users will deploy a series of observable behaviors that will either converge toward the ideal-typical depiction of how workers should behave according to managerial NWW discourses or, conversely, diverge from this ideal-type (hence resulting in what is somewhat quickly portrayed as "resistance" behavior). Organization studies acknowledge that actors always maintain a margin of freedom in the way they deal with innovations and organizational change (Crozier and Friedberg 1980). With this observation in mind, one may wonder how employees and managers effectively behave once they are directly confronted by NWW environments. The new workspace and the managerial prescriptions that come with it offer new opportunities to the actors who might inscribe them differently in their daily work practices (Akrich 2006). A study of the actors' concrete practices may reveal gaps between their actual behaviors and the managerial discourses of the project leaders. Common controversies involving work practices in NWW environments include, for instance, the unwillingness of employees to use all the working zones at their disposal (Blok et al. 2012; Dufresne et al. 2018) or the reluctance of managers to monitor increasingly virtualized teams (Kingma 2018).

At first glance, it appears to be one of the most prevalent approaches in the existing literature: multiple contributions examine the effects of NWW environments on employees' productivity (De Leede 2017; Laihonen et al. 2012), performance (Engelen et al. 2019; Palvalin et al. 2015; Ruostela et al. 2015), work engagement (Gerards et al. 2018; Ten Brummelhuis et al. 2012), work-family balance (Demerouti et al. 2014), and teamwork behavior (De Leede 2017). All these studies share a similar interest in the study of the actual effects of NWW environments on employees and managers and refer to NWW as being a set of observable work practices. On the methodological level, conducting such studies requires having access to an already existing and established NWW workspace.

Discussion

We hold that the five ways to conceptualize NWW developed above have their own theoretical questionings and methodological implications, of which Table 18.2 offers a summary view. As we stated, the study of the NWW fashion involves serious consideration of the organizational fields and of the actors who are part of this field, and questions the diffusion and mimicry mechanisms of NWW through those fields. At the organizational level, the focus is set on storytelling, sense giving, or other discursive strategies aimed at legitimizing NWW within organizations. When projects of organizational change are initiated, a longitudinal approach of the decisional work through which actors translate and make sense of strategic decisions becomes necessary. Those projects, in turn, aim to produce new kinds of workspaces (or new infrastructures), of which the properties and/or the design process may be investigated. Finally, researchers may question the practices adopted by the actors in those "new" working environments.

The complexity of exploring and articulating the five levels of analysis together, as well as the plurality of methods needed to simultaneously account for these five dimensions, probably explains why most contributions to the literature have so far opted for adopting a single, specific conceptualization of NWW. While we do not claim that these five conceptualizations are exhaustive, we argue that Table 18.2 provides a more accurate and non-substantialist conceptualization proposal of NWW that could be useful to position and situate further research on NWW and NWW projects. As it has been pointed out earlier, NWW has, in the academic literature, been hastily described by a myriad of inaccurate and

Table 18.2 Five theoretical and methodological perspectives on New Ways of Working

Conceptualization of NWW	Primary unit of study	Theoretical questioning	Actors	Methodological implications
Management fashion	Texts and networks	Diffusion mechanisms	Organizational field	Documentary research and targeted interviews
Set of discourses	Narratives and rhetoric	Legitimacy	Strategic management	In-depth interviews
Organizational change	Change project	Decisional work	Project teams, decisional entrepreneurs	Longitudinal observations
Workspace	Material devices	Infrastructural work	Project teams, users	Field observations
Set of work practices	Behaviors	Practices' rationality	Users	Interviews and/or surveys

Author's own

unfounded qualifiers. We suggest reviewing some of those qualifiers, as well as their potential validity with regard to our findings, in the following paragraphs.

Perhaps the most common way to describe NWW is to view it as a "concept" (De Kok et al. 2014; De Leede 2017; Kingma 2018; Ruostela et al. 2015; Taskin et al. 2017). While NWW may be depicted in many ways, we disagree with this assertion and are inclined to think that it may potentially have dangerous implications for research. Turning NWW into a "concept" does indeed essentialize and reify a definition of NWW in terms of contents and nature. The dangers of turning NWW into a "concept" are multiple. As we have shown elsewhere (Jemine et al. 2020), it leads to the negation of the actual empirical realities of the actors being studied and conceals the power games taking place between them. Because the researcher believes that NWW is a "concept" with defined boundaries, he or she accounts for his or her fieldwork through the lenses of what his or her precarious definition of this supposed concept indicates. Moreover, such a definition of NWW lacks critical distance toward the object being studied. At best, we might argue that it is in the interest of some of the field actors to convince others that NWW is a concept that should be trusted. There is, in fact, no empirical evidence that NWW is actually a concept. While some researchers have attempted, for unclear reasons, to create a construct of their own that they have labeled NWW, as shown in Table 18.1 (Ajzen et al. 2015; Baane et al. 2010; Blok et al. 2012; Gerards et al. 2018), these constructs have a limited validity and applicability to other cases—which is not the case of the conceptualization proposal introduced in this chapter.

Another common way to describe NWW is to speak of it as being as a "mix" or a "set" of "practices" and "measures" (Blok et al. 2011; Gerards et al. 2018; Peeters 2014; Taskin et al. 2017). This perspective may at first glance appear relatively close to the fifth conceptualization that we just developed. However, the status of those "practices" and "measures" is often left unclear; are they (as we argue) the empirically verified practices adopted by the actors? Or are they attempts by researchers to bundle the empirical realities that they have observed together? "Practice" is often used in a very generalist way, to designate, for instance, "teleworking" (De Leede 2017), "transformational leadership" (Gerards et al. 2018), or even "flexible working practices" (Demerouti et al. 2014). To state that NWW can be viewed as a set of practices deployed by rational actors in a new workspace and to state that a given set of clearly identified practices are constitutive of NWW are two very different things. To infer a substantialist and essentialist definition of NWW on the basis of the (limited) observation of some practices in NWW environments is, in our view, of limited use for research.

Other efforts to define NWW could be discussed in the same way. For instance, speaking of a "phenomenon" (De Kok et al. 2014; Eskola and Neuvonen 2016) is of little conceptual value and does not really provide further insight about how NWW should be approached or dealt with. Claiming that NWW is a "philosophy" (Blok et al. 2016) is, according to us, another attempt to designate the NWW management fashion—the consultancy books, networks, and promoters that contribute to its growth and dissemination. The outright assertion that NWW is a distinctive "type of work organization" (Nijp et al. 2016) sounds relatively bold in comparison to the empirical material at our disposal. We argue that all those varied but inaccurate denominations indicate a difficulty to conceptualize NWW and legitimate our attempt to offer an alternative conceptualization proposal, which we hope will be of use for further research on NWW and NWW projects.

It should be noted that the existing literature massively continues to be interested in NWW as a workplace and as a set of work practices, hence viewing NWW as a given product rather than an ongoing process. The questions of adoption, design, and deployment of NWW projects remain gray areas in the literature. Studies recognize the development of a management fashion and have been able to pinpoint its foundational books and texts on the one hand and have offered insights on the effects and consequences of NWW environments on employees, managers, and organizations on the other hand. What happens in between, however, remains vastly underexplored. These gray areas include the strategic decision to adopt NWW, which in most studies is taken for granted; the setting up of project teams and the designation of groups of actors in charge of managing the change project; and, crucially, the translation process of the strategic decision itself, up to the point of the creation of a new workspace. The absence of research on these questions is ever more surprising as NWW projects usually extend over several years, which leaves room for many changes and unexpected twists to occur.

Conclusion

The present chapter aimed to clarify common misconceptions in the literature about an increasingly popular managerial object, New Way(s) of Working. We showed that scholars have so far referred to NWW imprecisely and indiscriminately as a "philosophy", a "phenomenon", a "concept", a "mix of practices", or a "type of work organization". Instead, the present chapter suggests five theoretically supported and empirically grounded ways to conceptualize New Ways of Working and explores their theoretical and methodological implications for future research. We argue that continuing to merely speak of NWW in organization studies is confusing and misleading, as one might simultaneously designate a managerial fashion, a set of discourses and ideas, a project of organizational change, a material workspace, or a set of work practices, and/or several of those elements at once. Even if these five dimensions may partially overlap, they refer to different units of study (ideas, discourses, relations, infrastructures, and practices), bear specific methodological and theoretical implications, and imply five distinct ways to study NWW. Consequently, deconstructing NWW appears to be a necessary preliminary exercise for any further academic research on the matter.

References

Abrahamson, E. (1996). Management fashion. *The Academy of Management Review, 21*(1), 254–285.

Ajzen, M., Donis, C., & Taskin, L. (2015). Kaléidoscope des nouvelles formes d'organisation du travail : L'instrumentalisation stupide d'un idéal collaboratif et démocratique. *Gestion, 2000*(3), 125–148.

Akrich, M. (2006). Les utilisateurs, acteurs de l'innovation. In M. Akrich, M. Callon, & B. Latour (Eds.), *Sociologie de la traduction. Textes fondateurs* (pp. 253–265). Paris: Presses des Mines.

Assarlind, M., Eriksson, H., Gremyr, I., & Jakobsson, T. (2013). Adopting new ways of working in small and medium-sized enterprises: Findings from interventions in 12 European companies. *Total Quality Management and Business Excellence, 24*(8), 945–958.

Baane, R., Houtkamp, P., & Knotter, M. (2010). *Het Nieuwe Werken Ontrafeld. Over Bricks, Bytes and Behavior*. Assen, The Netherlands: Koninklijke Van Gorcum.

Benders, J., & van Veen, K. (2001). What's in a fashion? Interpretative viability and management fashions. *Organization, 8*(1), 33–53.

Bijl, D. W. (2011). *journey towards the new way of working. Creating sustainable performance and joy at work*. Zeewolde, The Netherlands: Par CC.

Blok, M., Groenesteijn, L., van den Berg, C., & Vink, P. (2011). New ways of working: A proposed framework and literature review. In M. M. Robertson (Ed.), *Ergonomics and health aspects of work with computers*. Lecture Notes in Computer Science, vol. 6779. International Conference on Ergonomics and Health Aspects of Work with Computers EHAWC 2011 (pp. 3–12). Berlin: Heidelberg Springer.

Blok, M., Groenesteijn, L., Schelvis, R., & Vink, P. (2012). New ways of working: Does flexibility in time and location of work change work behavior and affect business outcomes? *Work, 41*, 2605–2610.

Blok, M., van der Meulen, F., Dhondt, S. (2016). A comparison between new ways of working and sociotechnical systems. *Advanced Series in Management, 16*, 145–162.

Bowker, G. C., Baker, K., Millerand, F., & Ribes, D. (2010). Toward information infrastructure studies: Ways of knowing in a networked environment. In J. Hunsinger, L. Klastrup, & M. Allen (Eds.), *International handbook of internet research* (pp. 97–117). Berlin: Springer.

Broere, A. (2016). *Het Nieuwe Werken. Hoe Werk je Effectiever en Productiever*. Houten-Antwerp, Belgium, The Netherlands: Spectrum.

Brunia, S., De Been, I., & Van der Voordt, T. (2016). Accommodating new ways of working: Lessons from best practices and worst cases. *Journal of Corporate Real Estate, 18*(1), 30–47.

Callon, M. (1986). Some elements of a sociology of translation: Domestication of the scallops and the fishermen of St Brieuc Bay. In J. Law (Ed.), *Power, action and belief: A new sociology of knowledge?* (pp. 196–229). London: Routledge and Kegan Paul.

Callon, M. (1998). An essay on framing and overflowing: Economics externalities revised by sociology. *The Sociological Review, 46*, 244–269.

Crozier, M., & Friedberg, E. (1980). *Actors and systems. The politics of collective action*. Chicago, IL: University of Chicago Press.

De Bruyne, E., Beijer, M., Brunia, S., & Gosselink, A. (2014). PACT: Calculating NWoW accommodation that suits the organisations' work processes. *European Real Estate Society 21st Annual Conference*, Bucharest, 25–28 June 2014.

De Jonge, J., & Rutte, C. G. (1999). Een quasi-experimenteel veldonderzoek naar de psychologische effecten van een flexibel kantoorconcept. *Gedrag en Organisatie, 12*(6), 427–444.

De Kok, A., Koops, J., & Helms, R. (2014). The new way of working: Bricks, bytes, and behavior. *18th Pacific Asia Conference on Information Systems 2014*, 24–26 June, Chengdu, China.

De Kok, A., Esten, R., & Helms, R. (2015). Knowledge sharing in the new world of work: Effects of the new way of working. *Journal of Information Technology Services, 14*(2), 315–335.

De Leede, J. (2017). *New ways of working practices: Antecedents and outcomes*. Bingley, UK: Emerald Group Publishing Limited.

De Spiegelaere, S., Van Gyes, G., Benders, J., & Van Hootegem, G. (2015). The new world of work and innovative employee behaviour: A quantitative analysis. *Travail-Emploi-Formation, 13*, 141–156.

Demerouti, E., Derks, D., Ten Brummelhuis, L., & Bakker, A. (2014). New ways of working: Impact on working conditions, work-family balance, and well-being. In Korunka, C. & Hoonakker, P. (Eds.) The impact of ICT on quality of working life (pp. 123141). Dordrecht, Germany: Springer.

Di Maggio, P., & Powell, W. (1983). The iron cage revisited: Institutional isomorphism and collective rationality in organizational fields. *American Sociological Review, 48*(2), 147–160.

Dufresne, S., Jemine, G., Rondeaux, G., & Pichault, F. (2018). Beyond flexibility: Confronting normative and lived spaces of new ways of working. In *New ways of working: Rematerializing organizations in the digital age*, 8th Organizations, Artifacts & Practices Workshop, 20–22 June 2018, Vrije Universiteit Amsterdam.

Engelen, L., Chau, J., Young, S., Mackey, M., Jeyapalan, D., & Bauman, A. (2019). Is activity-based working impacting health, work performance and perceptions? A systematic review. *Building Research and Information, 47*(4), 468–479.

Eskola, A., & Neuvonen, H. (2016). A Conceptual Framework for Understanding the Phenomenon of new Ways of Work. *11th European Conference on Innovation and Entrepreneurship Proceedings*, 183–186.

Friedberg, E. (2000). Going beyond the either/or. *Journal of Management and Governance, 4*, 35–52.

Gates, B., & Rasmus, D. (2005). *Digital workstyle: The new world of work*. White Paper, Microsoft Corporation.

Gerards, R., Grip, A., & Baudewijns, C. (2018). Do new ways of working increase work engagement? *Personnel Review, 47*(2), 1–33.

Giroux, H. (2006). 'It was such a handy term': Management fashions and pragmatic ambiguity. *Journal of Management Studies, 43*(6), 1227–1260.

Gorgievski, M., van der Voordt, T., van Herpen, S., & van Akkeren, S. (2010). After the fire: New ways of working in an academic setting. *Facilities, 28*(3/4), 206–224.

Greenwood, R., Suddaby, R., & Hinings, C. (2002). Theorizing change: The role of professional associations in the transformation of institutionalized fields. *The Academy of Management Journal, 45*(1), 58–80.

Hoendervanger, J., De Been, I., Van Yperen, N., Mobach, M., & Albers, C. (2016). Flexibility in use: Switching behaviour and satisfaction in activity-based work environments. *Journal of Corporate Real Estate, 18*(1), 30–47.

Jemine, G., Dubois, C., & Pichault, F. (2019). From a new workplace to a new way of working: legitimizing organizational change. *Qualitative Research in Organizations and Management*, vol. ahead-of-print.

Jemine, G., Dubois, C., & Pichault, F. (2020). When the Gallic village strikes back: The politics behind 'new ways of working' projects. *Journal of Change Management, 20*(2), 1–25.

Keeling, T., Clements-Croome, D., & Roesch, E. (2015). The effect of agile workspace and remote working on experiences of privacy, crowding and satisfaction. *Buildings, 5*(3), 880–898.

Kingma, S. (2018). New ways of working (NWW): Work space and cultural change in virtualizing organizations. *Culture and Organization, 25*(5), 1–24.

Laihonen, H., Jääskeläinen, A., Lönnqvist, A., & Ruostela, J. (2012). Measuring the productivity impacts of new ways of working. *Journal of Facilities Management, 10*(2), 102–113.

Lamers, J. (2013). *Work organisation and innovation. Case study: Rabobank Netherlands*. Dublin: European Foundation for the Improvement of Living and Working Conditions.

Larkin, B. (2013). The politics and poetics of infrastructure. *Annual Review of Anthropology, 42*, 327–343.

Lawrence, T., & Suddaby, R. (2006). Institutions and institutional work. In S. Clegg, C. Hardy, T. Lawrence, & W. Nord (Eds.), *Handbook of organization studies* (pp. 215–254). London: Sage.

Mawson, A. (2006). *ICT and offices; Practiced realities and their business benefits? Interpolis head office*. London: British Council for Offices.

Meerbeek, M., Randolph, K., Rasmus, D., Wilgenburgh, J., Meer, H., Witkamp, J., et al. (2009). A new way of working. In *The 7 factors for success, based on Microsoft Netherlands experience*. Microsoft: Corporation.

Nijp, H., Beckers, D., Van de Voorde, K., Geurts, S., & Kompier, M. (2016). Effects of new ways of working on work hours and work location, health and job-related outcomes. *Chronobiology International, 33*(6), 1–15.

Palvalin, M., Vuolle, M., Jääskeläinen, A., Laihonen, H., & Lönnqvist, A. (2015). SmartWoW—Constructing a tool for knowledge work performance analysis. *International Journal of Productivity and Performance Management, 64*(4), 479–498.

Peeters, P. (2014). Enjoying new ways to work: An HRM-process approach to study flow. *Human Resource Management, 53*(2), 271–290.

Perkmann, M., & Spicer, A. (2008). How are management fashions institutionalized? The role of institutional work. *Human Relations, 61*(6), 811–844.

Phillips, N., & Lawrence, T. (2004). Discourse and institutions. *The Academy of Management Review, 29*(4), 635–652.

Ruostela, J., Lönnqvist, A., Palvalin, M., Vuolle, M., Patjas, M., & Raij, A. (2015). 'New ways of working' as a tool for improving the performance of a knowledge-intensive company. *Knowledge Management Research & Practice, 13*(4), 382–390.

Sewell, G., & Taskin, L. (2015). Out of sight, out of mind in a new world of work? Autonomy, control, and spatiotemporal scaling in telework. *Organization Studies, 36*(11), 1507–1529.

Suchman, M. (1995). Managing legitimacy: Strategic and institutional approaches. *The Academy of Management Review, 20*(3), 571–610.

Taskin, L., Ajzen, M., & Donis, C. (2017). New ways of working: From smart to shared power. In V. Muhlbauer & W. Harry (Eds.), *Redefining management* (pp. 65–79). Cham, Switzerland: Springer.

Ten Brummelhuis, L., Bakker, A., Hetland, J., & Keulemans, L. (2012). Do new ways of working foster work engagement? *Psicothema, 24*(1), 113–120.

Van Egmond, H., & Lokin, V. (2006). *Rabo Unplugged.* Utrecht, The Netherlands: Rabobank.

Van Meel, J. (2011). The origins of new ways of working: Office concepts in the 1970s. *Facilities, 29*(9), 357–367.

Veldhoen, E. (1995). *Kantoren Bestaan Niet Meer. Uitgeverij 010.* Rotterdam, The Netherlands: Uitgeverij 010 Publishers.

Veldhoen, E. (2005). *The art of working.* The Hague, The Netherlands: Academic Service.

Vendelo, M. (1998). Narrating corporate reputation. *International Studies of Management & Organization, 28*(3), 120–137.

Vink, P., Blok, M., Formanoy, M., de Korte, E., & Groenesteijn, L. (2012). The effects of new ways of work in the Netherlands: National data and a case study. *Work, 41*, 5081–5085.

Afterword

Leo McCann

This volume was finalized by the authors, editors, publishers and production staff during the coronavirus pandemic of 2019–2020. The year 2020 has a peculiar ring to it. No doubt, large organizations had in prior years laid out grandiose plans for their 2020 leadership 'visions', involving turnarounds, step-changes, transformations and breakthroughs, perhaps premised on harnessing radical new technologies that are reshaping the world of work. Instead, the year has been calamitous. A new and poorly understood virus swept across the world causing illness, death, panic, isolation and extreme disruption. It was carried on the sails of globalization (international supply chains, airports, cruise ships, business conferences, mega entertainment events) and it multiplied in mundane domestic environments (care homes, hospitals, apartment blocks, abattoirs, buses). Governments, business and citizens reacted with a peculiar mixture of paralysis and denial alongside drastic, blanket mitigation policies.

Weeks of travel bans and lockdowns turned to months. Government bailouts and support packages were extended well beyond their budget envelope. Mega-events were canceled. Construction sites fell silent. Service industries and small businesses collapsed. Giant companies

N. Mitev et al. (eds.), *New Ways of Working*, Technology, Work and Globalization,
https://doi.org/10.1007/978-3-030-61687-8

furloughed staff, requested financial support and initiated bankruptcy procedures. This wasn't the 2020 we were promised.

Rather than calculating, managing and predicting commercial activity such as sales revenue, logistical operations and brand value, supercomputers and semi-autonomous algorithms collated and plotted curves of infection and generated real-time dashboards comparing international death rates, recoveries, new infections and hospital bed occupancy. Fragmentary factoids and disputed data points fed into risk calculi that would inform the raising or lowering of color-coded 'threat level assessments'. Government ministers and their appointed experts would try to indicate that the virus and the population are behaving according to expectations set via pre-planned, project-managed stages. A procession of supposedly 'game-changing' drugs, vaccines, test kits and tracing apps were boasted about, launched, found not to work and then quietly abandoned.

Menaced by a globalizing threat from a seemingly alien source, much of the media took on a nationalist, conspiratorial and "paranoid" style (Hofstadter 1964). Healthcare professionals, care workers, supermarket staff and truck drivers became 'local heroes'. The French president "declared war" on the virus.[1] The president of Brazil insisted the virus was a "media trick".[2] Conspiracy theories swirled in digital sewers of mistrust and abuse. The owners of social media platforms grappled with the ethics and praxis of removing, editing or attaching warnings and provisos to offensive and potentially dangerous misinformation, including certain posts by the U.S. president.

The emergence of the virus known as SARS-CoV-2 accelerated the existing trend whereby internationalism and globalization, for so long praised as inevitable, welcome and progressive (Giddens 1999; Friedman 2007), have become increasingly unpopular and feared (King 2017; McCann 2018, 109–127). Everywhere there was mistrust and blame,

[1] "Macron declares France 'at war' with virus, as E.U. proposes 30-day travel ban", *New York Times*, 16 March 2020.

[2] "Brazil's Jair Bolsonaro says coronavirus is a media trick", *The Guardian*, 23 March 2020.

building on the data-driven paranoia so beautifully and disturbingly captured in Nick Drnaso's graphic novel *Sabrina* (Drnaso 2018; see also Citron 2020). New informational, logistical, commercial and legal systems—ever-growing in their sophistication and interconnectivity—were supposed to bring the world together in a harmonious and logical fashion, increasing opportunities, stimulating innovations and reducing poverty. Instead, they were often regarded as vectors for an unwanted set of malicious forces. Internet scammers seized on vulnerable IT systems.[3] Paranoid internet ramblings built up into rapidly shared conspiracy theories that lockdowns are a 'Deep State' assault on commercial and civil liberties or that the virus didn't exist—instead it was a government cover story to mask the pernicious health effects of fifth-generation cellular networks. Vandals set light to 5G network towers. These flaming torches became a perfect symbol for a resurgence of fear and loathing around technological globalization.

There was no choice but to 'adapt and survive'. Facilities were made 'COVID-secure' as they eventually re-opened. Workers muddled through, learning how to use personal protective equipment while gingerly trawling their smartphones for estimates of how far a sneeze can propel virus-infected droplets and how long the novel coronavirus can survive on different surfaces. White-collar professionals, long since keyed in to remote and digitized work arrangements, hunkered down in their home offices or at their kitchen tables. Round-the-clock homeworking further fueled a hyper-dependence on broadband internet, cloud storage and powerful microprocessors. Co-working platforms continued their dizzy proliferation: Zoom, Google Hangouts, Skype, Microsoft Office Teams, Slack, Freedcamp, Asana and Podio among others. People got by.

But the work experiences would be far than ideal, the transfer far from seamless. Video meetings would be strangely more alienating and exhausting than usual. A new etiquette emerged of muting microphones and raising hands to request to speak. For all the promise that 'tech' provides flattened hierarchies, process disruption and workplace democracy, somehow video calls make it harder to get one's point across and tend to

[3] "How hackers extorted $1.14 m from University of California, San Francisco", *BBC News*, 29 June 2020.

empower the meeting's host rather than its participants. Frustrated workers the world over would log off from their Zoom meetings, feeling that the hours burnt through were even more tiring and wasteful than those of pre-COVID times.

As the chapters in this book reveal, the brave new world of work—van life, living labs, hackathons—was supposed to be about creativity, independent, freedom and innovation (Pink 2016). These new concepts and ways of operating do exist in some form. And yet, like the efforts put in to write, edit and produce this book itself, work always features important facets of social and historical continuity. For all the new developments associated with algorithms, big data, the gig economy and fintech, we will always have the human factors of stress, ambition, disappointment, ego, hubris, confusion, jealousy and exhaustion. Work and organization will always rely heavily on such intangible and often unmeasurable human inputs as skill, effort, mood, emotion, intuition, inspiration and guesswork. Much-vaunted systems of big data, machine learning, platform economies and key performance indicators will claim, like the HAL 9000 computer from Stanley Kubrick's *2001: Space Odyssey*, to be "foolproof and incapable of error" (Raymond et al. 2018). But, knowing what we know about the vast complexity and messy realities of human-to-human and human-to-system interaction, it would be foolish to accept such claims at face value.

The book documents our simultaneous attraction and revulsion toward new technologies and 'systems'. This has been a staple theme of science fiction, from Mary Shelley's *Frankenstein* (2003/1818), to the 1960s counterculture, and well beyond. HAL's confident reassurances in 1968 that "[n]o 9000 computer has ever made a mistake or distorted information", symbolized the moral emptiness of a technocratic elite responsible for the Vietnam War and Watergate. Alarming and elusive as it is, the promises associated with the replacement of human emotion with technological rationality remains seductive. A 562-page coffee table collectors' edition of *2001* artwork and conceptual drawings retails at £900 (Bizony 2015). Look at those computer workstations—so smooth and glossy. And the spacesuits—streamlined and colorful, much more appealing than NASA's bulky white hulks. Trust the private sector to come up with something more stylish than the government. Kubrick's spacesuits look a little like those worn by the crew of Elon Musk's SpaceX Falcon 9, with *The New York Times* suggesting that their image as "a tuxedo in space", might even fuel a resurgence of interest in "wearable tech"[4] which has disappointed its promoters with persistently low user take-up.

As the contributions to this book all note in their separate and combined ways, the world of work is always a site of contradiction. New technologies, innovations and 'disruptions' are attractive yet fearsome. 'New' workplaces continue to be fractured by distinctly old formations of class, gender, sexuality, ethnicity, disability and religion. Whatever 'intelligent' and 'flexible' systems they attempt to adopt, workplaces, in all their forms, will always rely heavily on distinctly human inputs and traits. The continuity of work efforts amid the terrible disruption of COVID-19 has shown this across an array of sectors. People get up, go to work and try to do their best. Even while enduring heavy workloads, insecurity, inequality and uncertainty, and while swimming against a backwash of digital detritus, human actors daily achieve at least some of what they set out to do.

References

Bizony, P. (2015). *The making of Stanley Kubrick's '2001: A space Odyssey'.* Cologne: Taschen.

Citron, D. K. (2020). Cyber mobs, disinformation, and death videos: The Internet as it is (and as it should be). *Michigan Law Review, 118*(6), 1073–1094.

Drnaso, N. (2018). *Sabrina*. Montreal: Drawn & Quarterly.

Friedman, T. (2007). *The world is flat: The globalized world in the twenty-first century*. London: Penguin.

Giddens, A. (1999). *Runaway world: How globalisation is reshaping our lives.* London: Profile.

Hofstadter, R. (1964). *The paranoid style in American politics*, Harper's, November.

King, S. D. (2017). *Grave new world: The end of globalization, the return of history*. New Haven, CT: Yale University Press.

[4]"Elon Musk's SpaceX suit is like a tuxedo for the starship Enterprise", *New York Times,* 27 May 2020.

McCann, L. (2018). *A very short, fairly interesting and reasonably cheap book about globalization*. London: Sage.

Pink, D. (2016). *Free agent nation: How America's new independent workers are transforming the way we live*. New York: Grand Central Publishing.

Raymond, A. H., Young, E. A. S., & Shackleford, S. J. (2018). Building a better HAL 9000: Algorithms, the market, and the need to prevent the engraining of bias. *Northwestern Journal of Technology and Intellectual Property, 15*(3), 215–254.

Shelley, M. (2003/1818). *Frankenstein: Or, the modern Prometheus*. London: Penguin Classics.

Index

N. Mitev et al. (eds.), *New Ways of Working*, Technology, Work and Globalization,
https://doi.org/10.1007/978-3-030-61687-8

T

U

V

W